FROM THE MOST TRUSTED NAME IN TRAVEL

Frommer's®
EASYGUIDE
TO
ALASKAN CRUISES
AND PORTS OF CALL
2nd Edition

**Quick to Read   Easy to Carry   For Expert Advice
In All Price Ranges**

Fran Golden and Sherri Eisenberg

FROMMER'S STAR RATINGS SYSTEM

Every hotel, restaurant, and attraction listed in this guide has been ranked for quality and value. Here's what the stars mean:

★ Recommended
★★ Highly Recommended
★★★ A must♦Don't miss!

AN IMPORTANT NOTE

The world is a dynamic place. Hotels change ownership, restaurants hike their prices, museums alter their opening hours, and buses and trains change their routings. And all of this can occur in the several months after our authors have visited, inspected, and written about these hotels, restaurants, museums, and transportation services. Though we have made valiant efforts to keep all our information fresh and up-to-date, some few changes can inevitably occur in the periods before a revised edition of this guidebook is published. So please bear with us if a tiny number of the details in this book have changed. Please also note that we have no responsibility or liability for any inaccuracy or errors or omissions, or for inconvenience, loss, damage, or expenses suffered by anyone as a result of assertions in this guide.

Kayaking on Chilkoot Lake in Lutak.

CONTENTS

A grizzly bear in Alaskan waters.

DISCARDED

A LOOK AT CRUISING ALASKA

Towers of blue ice, snow-capped peaks, and grizzly bears roaming flower-dotted meadows: Alaska will put a spell on you. It's little wonder that the 49th state is one of the world's great cruising destinations. Ships big and small can transport you to magical places where roads do not go. Whether your ride is pampered comfort, active adventure, or frills-free, get ready for scenic beauty of breathtaking scope. Get ready, too, for the chance to spot Alaska's bountiful wildlife in its native habitat: the likes of humpback whales, caribou, bears, sea lions, and bald eagles. You can soak it all up from your front-row seat aboard ship, or dive into a thrilling shore excursion, from kayaking glacial waterways to dog-sledding. You'll get a real immersion in Alaska's frontier spirit and Native cultures in the charming ports and small towns along the way.

Lindblad Expeditions' *National Geographic Sea Bird* among icebergs in remote Endicott Arm.

THE SHIPS

Kayaking Alaska's glassy seas is one of many activities offered by UnCruise Adventures (p. 168).

The outdoor pool deck on Royal Caribbean's *Radiance of the Seas* has two whirlpools, a bandstand, and a giant movie screen (p. 126).

Guests aboard Windstar's *Star Legend* do some high-flying ziplining on an active shore excursion (p. 146).

The expansive decks of Alaska Marine Highway ferries (here the solarium deck on the *Columbia*) are popular social hubs offering sublime scenic viewpoints (p. 179).

Drive your own dog sled on Oceania Cruises' dog-sledding shore excursions on Mendenhall Glacier, led by teams of frisky huskies like these (p. 107).

The spacious staterooms aboard American Cruise Lines ships come with private balconies (p. 159).

This full-service sushi bar is one of the numerous specialty restaurants on Norwegian Cruise Line's *Norwegian Pearl* (p. 99).

The elegant main dining room aboard Crystal Cruises' *Crystal Serenity* features crystal chandeliers and Villeroy & Boch porcelain (p. 79).

Guests from the Lindblad Expeditions ship *National Geographic Sea Bird* get up close to icebergs during Zodiac raft rides in Tracy Arm, Southeast Alaska (p. 163).

Cruising kids enjoy a demonstration of totem-pole carving in the atrium of Princess Cruises' *Ruby Princess* (p. 115).

Silversea's *Silver Shadow*, one of the line's Millennium-class luxury ships, in its evening berth (p. 137).

WILD ALASKA

Alaska's impressive glaciers are a big draw for cruise passengers, here in a skiff tour launched from Alaskan Dream's *Admiralty Dream* (p. 152).

Passenger peering through a keyhole of blue ice atop Mendenhall Glacier on a Carnival cruise. Although the ice is not really blue, glacier ice is so dense that it absorbs every other color of the spectrum except blue.

Even at a young age, Alaska's grizzly bears are expert salmon hunters, deftly snagging fish as they swim upstream to spawn.

The Northern Lights shimmer above Alaska's Brooks Range during a Carnival cruise (p. 66).

Guests aboard Lindblad Expeditions' *National Geographic Sea Lion* explore calved icebergs from Zodiac rafts in the Sawyer Glacier in the Tracy Arm Wilderness Area.

Stellar sea lions, which can grow to be 1,500 pounds, like to hang out in large groups and sun on rock outcroppings, like this perch in Glacier Bay.

Walking on ice: Guests aboard Holland America Line's *Zaandam* take a guided glacier hike on the Hole-in-the-Wall Glacier during a Juneau helicopter excursion (p. 89).

Humpback whales spend summers feeding in Alaskan waters and can be seen in places like Icy Strait, Frederick Sound (near Petersburg), Sitka Sound, and Kenai Fjords National Park (near Seward).

America's majestic national symbol, bald eagles are a common sight in Southeast Alaska, like this one in Sitka on Baranof Island. Look for bald eagles swarming the docks in Ketchikan and other fishing towns, on the hunt for freebies.

Alaska's caribou and Europe's reindeer are genetically identical, and both male and female caribou have antlers, which they shed annually. Look for caribou traveling in small groups in Denali National Park (p. 297).

A harbor seal (*Phoca vitulina*) rests on a sliver of ice calved from the South Sawyer Glacier in the Tracy Arm-Fords Terror Wilderness area.

PORTS, TOWNS & LOCAL CULTURE

Alaska's Russian heritage lives on in sites like the 17,500-square-foot St. Innocent Russian Orthodox Cathedral in Anchorage, which boasts 12 distinctive cupolas.

Alaska's 19th-century gold rush brought a quarter-of-a-million miners here to seek their fortune, many living in cabins in what is now Independence Mine State Historical Park, in Hatcher Pass in the Talkeetna Mountains.

An example of the traditional art of Northwest Coast Native craftspeople, this intricately carved and painted wooden totem pole is one of nine in Vancouver's Stanley Park (p. 205). Ketchikan alone has more than 70 standing totem poles, plus a museum dedicated to the oldest poles collected from abandoned Tlingit villages.

Dine on fish tacos, salmon chowder, and Dungeness crabs at the cannery-style Alaska Fish House restaurant in the historic fishing village of Ketchikan (p. 245).

Camp Skagway No. 1 of the Arctic Brotherhood, with its driftwood facade, was established in Skagway in 1899 for gold speculators arriving by steamers from Seattle.

Rustic wood buildings line Ketchikan's colorful Creek Street, a raised boardwalk tracing the Ketchikan Creek and site of the town's infamous former red-light district (p. 237).

The glittering port of Alaska's capital city, Juneau, at dusk (p. 221).

The skyline of the state's largest city, Anchorage, is backed by the snow-capped Chugach Mountains and fronted by the icy waters of Bootleggers Cove (p. 185).

Dating from 1896, the Cathedral of the Holy Ascension of Christ is the oldest cruciform-style Orthodox church in North America and sits alongside Iliuliuk Bay in the village of Unalaska, in Alaska's Aleutian Islands.

The Red Onion Saloon, built as a bordello in gold-rush Skagway in 1897, is now a restaurant, bar, and "brothel museum," with guided walking tours of the town's historic streets (p. 295).

One of four concrete sculptures by artist Rachelle Dowdy representing Alaskans' symbiotic relationship with wildlife, part of the public art at the Anchorage Museum, which exhibits art from Alaska and the big North (p. 188).

THE BEST OF ALASKAN CRUISING

Alaska is one of the top cruise destinations in the world, and when you're sailing through the calm waters of the Inside Passage or across the Gulf of Alaska, it's easy to see why: The jaw-dropping scenery is simply breathtaking.

Much of the coastline is wilderness, with snowcapped mountain peaks, immense glaciers that create a thunderous noise as chunks break off into the sea (a process known as calving), emerald rainforests, fjords, icebergs, soaring eagles, lumbering bears, and majestic whales—all easily visible from the comfort of your ship.

Visit the towns and you'll find people who retain the spirit of frontier independence that brought them here in the first place. Add Alaska's colorful history and heritage, with its European influences, its spirit of discovery, and its rich Native cultures, and you have a destination that is utterly, endlessly fascinating. Even thinking about it, we get chills, of the good kind.

The state celebrated its 55th anniversary of statehood in 2014. It was in January 1959 that the Union accepted what had once been a territory as a full-fledged state—the 49th. Every city, town, and hamlet seemed to hold celebrations in honor of the event, showing their Alaskan spirit. No doubt the 60th anniversary in 2019 will lead to similar enthusiasm.

The cruise industry in Alaska has also had reason to celebrate. In 2017, the number of cruise passengers in the state was expected to surpass the 1 million mark for the first time in several years. Officials of the Cruise Lines International Association (CLIA) tabulated the numbers at 33 ships making 498 calls to ports in Alaska, those ships carrying 1,060,000 cruise visitors. That's a whole lot of people. And more are coming, with 2018 expected to be another banner year (Princess Cruises, for one, will have its largest deployment ever in Alaska that year).

A downside is that in summer, some towns turn into virtual tourist malls. We're talking seasonal vendors, including jewelry stores geared toward the cruise crowd and shelves filled with imported souvenirs. However, the port towns you'll visit—from Juneau, the most remote state capital in the country, to Sitka, with its proud reminders of Native and Russian cultures—still manage to retain much of their rustic charm and historical allure. Sure, you may have to jostle for a seat in Juneau's popular Red Dog Saloon (the oldest tourist attraction in the state) or ask other visitors to step out of the way as you try to snap a picture of Skagway's historic gold-rush buildings or Ketchikan's picturesque Creek Street, but these are minor hassles for cruise-ship passengers.

We highly recommend you also consider getting out of the popular tourist towns, away from the crowds and into the vast and mesmerizing wilderness, whether on an organized shore excursion, touring on your own, or booking a small-ship cruise that goes to more remote parts. By signing up for the cruise lines' pre- or post-cruise land-tour packages (known as "cruisetours" or land + sea adventures) or renting a car on your own, you can also visit less-populated and in some cases ethereal inland destinations such as Denali National Park, Fairbanks, the Kenai Peninsula, the Yukon Territory, or the Canadian Rockies.

Even before you cruise, we can predict you'll want to visit again. This is a place that puts a spell on you. Fran first visited in the late 1990s and found her view of the world was forever changed. She quickly put the state at the top of her list of cruise destinations; numerous visits since have just confirmed her initial impression. She even traveled here in winter a few years ago to attend the Fur Rendezvous (Fur Rondy) in Anchorage, discovering a whole new side to Alaska (where they know how to have fun even in the cold). Sherri also visited for the first time in the '90s, with her father in tow. They agree it was the best trip they ever took together, and reminisce fondly about the salmon leaping out of the river over their kayak, and the fishing trip that resulted in freezers full of salmon for months.

Whether you're looking for pampering and resort amenities or a "you and the sea" adventure experience, you'll find it all on cruise ships in Alaska. Here are some of our favorites, along with our picks of the best ports, shore excursions, and sights.

THE best OF ALASKA'S SHIPS

o **The Best Ships for Luxury:** Luxury in Alaska in 2018 is defined by **Crystal Cruises, Regent Seven Seas, Silversea,** and most recently **Seabourn,** which has returned to the state with luxury expedition itineraries after a 15-year absence. All four lines offer a slick luxury experience with all the perks: suites (all, or at least some, with butler service), excellent food, and fine linens. The luxury players also include fine wine and booze and gratuities in their cruise fares, and Regent also includes airfare and shore excursions.

o **The Best of the Mainstream Ships: Celebrity**'s *Celebrity Solstice* is a contemporary stunner, with a half-acre of real grass on its top deck, a beautifully dramatic main dining room, an extensive modern-art collection, cushy public rooms, and an expanded spa area (and the line's older *Celebrity Millennium* and *Celebrity Infinity* are none too shabby either). You can't go wrong with the ships of **Princess Cruises** and **Holland America Line,** both lines that specialize in the region and do it well. And, in 2018, **Norwegian Cruise Line** introduces its brand new Alaskan-centric *Norwegian Bliss*, an exciting addition to the roster. For a step up in price, we're big fans of **Viking Ocean Cruises,** a newcomer to the market in 2019.

o **The Best of the Small Ships:** For a luxury Alaskan experience in a small-ship setting, check out the four "Luxury Adventures" vessels of **UnCruise Adventures,** where soft adventure comes with upscale accoutrements. There's just something special about cruising on a ship with only two or three dozen fellow passengers. That said, if it's new and shiny you want, **Lindblad Expeditions'** 100-passenger *National Geographic Quest* debuted in August 2017 (some cabins even come with balconies).

o **The Best Ships for Kids/Families:** All the major lines have well-established kids' programs, with **Carnival, Royal Caribbean,** and **Norwegian** leading the pack in terms of facilities and activities (*Norwegian Bliss* even has a go-kart track!). **Princess** and **Holland America Line** get a nod for their National Park Service Junior Ranger program, designed to teach kids about glaciers and Alaskan wildlife. Princess brings sled-dog puppies on board for a meet-and-greet "Puppies in the Piazza" event. But for kid appeal, no one can beat **Disney Cruise Line,** returning for its eighth year in Alaska in 2018 and cruising from Seattle with the *Disney Wonder*. Disney's schedule is chock-a-block with more activities than your kids could get to, from a coronation ceremony hosted by *Frozen*'s Elsa and Anna to a ship-wide scavenger hunt.

o **The Best Ships for Pampering:** Luxury line **Regent Seven Seas,** of course, pampers all around. Ditto for the very posh **Silversea, Crystal,** and **Seabourn.** The **Celebrity** ships have wonderful AquaSpas, complete with thalassotherapy (sea-water therapy) pools. We are also big fans of the thermal suite (complete with a hydrotherapy pool) in the Greenhouse Spas on **Holland America** ships. The spa on **Viking**'s *Viking Spirit* isn't just gorgeous; the thermal area, complete with a cold "snow" grotto, is complimentary for all guests, not just those booking spa treatments.

o **The Best Shipboard Cuisine:** **Crystal** ships, with their onboard Nobu-helmed sushi bars, have long been a culinary leader, and **Seabourn** also wows guests, particularly with their flawlessly executed Thomas Keller chophouse. We're also big fans of the specialty restaurants on **Viking,** from the Norwegian-style waffles with brown cheese or split-pea soup with brown bread in Mamsen's to the house-made pasta at Manfredi's.

o **The Best Ships for Grown-Up Onboard Activities:** The big ship lines—including **Carnival, Norwegian, Princess,** and **Royal Caribbean**—have rosters teeming with onboard activities that range from the sublime (such as lectures) to the ridiculous (such as contests designed to get passengers to do outrageous things). Princess's ScholarShip@Sea program is a winner for adults, with exciting classes in such diverse subjects as photography, computers, and even ceramics, plus the aforementioned "Puppies in the Piazza" program. **Holland America** has particularly impressive culinary classes

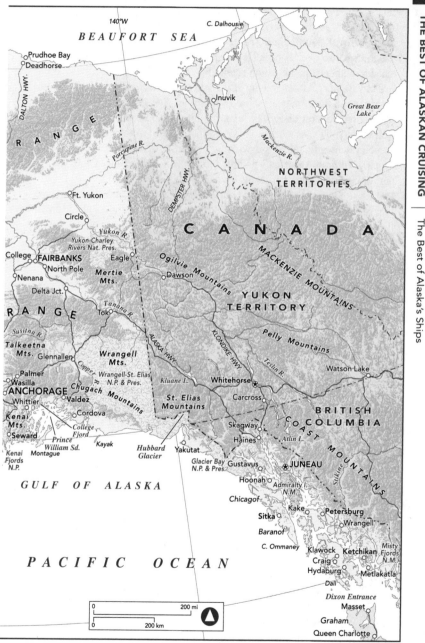

BEAUFORT SEA

140°W

C. Dalhousie

Prudhoe Bay
Deadhorse

Inuvik

Great Bear
Lake

DALTON HWY.

R A N G E

Porcupine R.

Mackenzie R.

NORTHWEST
TERRITORIES

CANADA

Ft. Yukon

Circle

Yukon R.

Yukon-Charley
Rivers Nat. Pres.

DEMPSTER HWY.

College
FAIRBANKS
North Pole

Eagle

Ogilvie Mountains

MACKENZIE MOUNTAINS

Nenana
Mertie
Mts.
Dawson

YUKON
TERRITORY

Delta Jct.

Tanana R.

R A N G E
Tok

ALASKA HWY.

Pelly Mountains

Susitna R.

KLONDIKE HWY.

Testlin R.

Talkeetna
Mts. Glennallen

Wrangell
Mts.

Watson Lake

Palmer
Wasilla
ANCHORAGE

Copper R.

Wrangell-St. Elias
N.P. & Pres.

Kluane L.

Whitehorse

Carcross

BRITISH
COLUMBIA

Whittier
Chugach Mountains

Valdez

St. Elias
Mountains

Kenai
Mts.
Cordova

College
Fjord

Skagway

Atlin L.

COAST MOUNTAINS

Seward

Prince
William Sd.
Kayak

Haines

Kenai
Fjords
N.P.
Montague

Hubbard
Glacier
Yakutat

Glacier Bay
N.P. & Pres.
Gustavus

Stikine R.

JUNEAU

GULF OF ALASKA

Hoonah

Chicagof

Admiralty I.
N.M.

Kake

Petersburg

Sitka

Wrangell

Baranof

C. Ommaney

Klawock
Ketchikan

PACIFIC OCEAN

Craig
Hydaburg

Misty
Fjords
N.M.

Metlakatla

Dall

Dixon Entrance

Masset

0   200 mi

Graham

0   200 km

Queen Charlotte

designed in partnership with America's Test Kitchen, and **Viking Ocean**'s cooking classes let you follow a chef to the market before cooking up your catch.

o **The Best Ships for Entertainment:** Look to the big ships here, too. **Disney, Carnival, Norwegian, Princess,** and **Royal Caribbean** are tops when it comes to an overall package of shows, nightclub acts, lounge performances, audience-participation entertainment, and show productions—even Broadway hits. On *Norwegian Bliss*, for example, you can see the Tony Award–winning Broadway show *Jersey Boys*. And on *Disney Wonder*, the stage-show version of *Frozen* is an icy hit. Princess presents particularly well-done shows, especially on ships that feature productions created by Stephen Schwartz, the award-winning composer of *Wicked*, *Godspell*, and *Pippin*. **Holland America** gets props for its B.B. King Blues Club, featuring rocking Memphis musicians.

o **The Best Ships for Whale-Watching:** If the whales come close enough, you can see them from any ship in Alaska—Fran spotted a couple of orcas from her balcony cabin on a **Holland America** ship. But smaller ships—such as those operated by **Lindblad, UnCruise Adventures,** and **Alaskan Dream Cruises**—might actually change course to follow a whale. Have your cameras and binoculars ready!

o **The Best Ships for Cruisetours:** With their own fleets of deluxe motorcoaches and railcars, **Princess** and **Holland America** are the market leaders in getting you into the Interior of Alaska, either before or after your cruise.

THE best PORTS

Juneau and Sitka are our favorite of the more mainstream ports. **Juneau** is one of the most visually pleasing small cities anywhere and certainly the prettiest capital city in America (once you get beyond all the tourist shops near the pier). It is fronted by the Gastineau Channel and backed by Mount Juneau and Mount Roberts, lies near the very accessible Mendenhall Glacier, and is otherwise surrounded by wilderness—and it's a really fun city to visit, too. **Sitka**'s Russian architecture, the totem-pole park, and the Raptor Rehabilitation Center are all top-flight attractions—and what we like most about Sitka is that it hasn't been overrun with stuff for tourists; it still feels like a community.

No town in Alaska is more historically significant than **Skagway,** and the old buildings are so perfect you might think you've stepped into a Disney version of what a gold-rush town should look like. But you must first get over the presence of more than a dozen upscale jewelry shops that have followed cruise passengers from the Caribbean, and all the other tourist shops and attractions. In short, Skagway has become very touristy. For a more low-key Alaskan experience, take the ferry from Skagway to **Haines,** which reminds us of the folksy, frontier Alaska depicted on the TV show *Northern Exposure* and is a great place to spot eagles and other wildlife. Some ships also stop at

Haines as a port of call, usually for a few hours after Skagway, and we're pleased to report this is one town that has not been changed by the advent of cruise-ship visitors. If you're on a small ship, the small communities of **Wrangell** and **Petersburg** will no doubt make an impression, both for the hearty, welcoming locals and the astonishing wilderness they call home (get your cameras ready!). Either is the kind of place real travelers (as opposed to tourists) will adore.

THE best SHORE EXCURSIONS

Flightseeing by **floatplane** or **helicopter** is an unforgettable way to check out the Alaskan scenery—if you can afford it. Airborne tours tend to be pretty pricey, from about $229 to more than $650 per head. However, a helicopter trip to a dog-sled camp at the top of a glacier (usually among the priciest of the offerings) affords both incredibly pretty views and a chance to try your hand at the truly Alaskan sport of dog-sledding, and it's a great way to earn bragging rights with the folks back home.

For a less extravagant excursion, nothing beats a ride on a clear day on the **White Pass & Yukon Route Railway** out of Skagway to the Canadian border or beyond. The steep train route is the same one followed by the gold stampeders of 1898. While you're riding the rails, try to imagine what it was like for those gold seekers crossing the same path on foot! We also like to get active with **kayak** and **mountain-biking** excursions offered by most cruise lines at most ports. In addition to affording a chance to work off those shipboard calories, these excursions typically provide optimum opportunities for spotting eagles, bears, seals, and other wildlife. (D.I.Y. types might consider renting bikes or kayaks and exploring on your own.) **Ziplining** is just plain fun for those who want to try soaring on a wire above the treetops—the adrenaline rush can be addictive. Fran has also gotten into snorkeling in Alaska (less cold than you think!).

Another popular (and less hectic) excursion is **whale-watching.** On one evening excursion out of Juneau in May, passengers on a small whale-watching boat got the thrill of seeing an entire pod of orcas, more than a dozen of the giant creatures, frolicking before their eyes.

CHOOSING YOUR IDEAL CRUISE

2

Just like clothes, cars, and gourmet coffee, Alaskan cruises come in all different styles to suit all different tastes. The first step in ensuring that you have the best possible vacation is to match your expectations to the appropriate itinerary and ship.

In this chapter, we explore the advantages of the two main Alaskan itineraries, examine the differences between big-ship cruising and small-ship cruising, pose some questions you should ask yourself to determine which cruise is right for you, and give you the skinny on cruisetours, which combine a cruise with a land tour that gets you into the Alaska Interior.

THE ALASKAN CRUISE SEASON

Alaska is very much a seasonal, as opposed to year-round, cruise destination; the season generally runs from May through September, although a few ships get an early jump, starting up in late April. May and September are considered the shoulder seasons, when lower brochure rates and more aggressive discounts are offered. We particularly like cruising in May, before the crowds arrive, when we've generally found locals to be friendlier than they are later in the season, at which point they're pretty much ready to see the tourists go home.

Also, at the Inside Passage ports, May is one of the driest months in the season. Although we have done late-May cruises where temperatures were in the 70s, perfect weather for hiking and biking, Alaskan weather is unpredictable (some years, there may be snow in May). September also offers the advantage of fewer fellow cruise passengers clogging the ports. The warmest temperatures are in late June, July, and August, when it's likely to be 50°F to 80°F during the day and cooler at night. Some years the temperature has soared higher—Juneau has been known to hit the 90s. When this happens, you'll hear much local speculation about global warming. As for clothing, the trick in coping with Alaskan weather is to dress in layers, with a lightweight waterproof jacket on top and a sweater and T-shirt underneath. You won't need a parka (if you do an excursion that has you outdoors on a chilly glacier, jackets are likely to be provided), but you will need to bring along outerwear and rain gear. Pack T-shirts, too. June tends to be drier than July and August. (We have experienced trips in July during which it rained nearly every day.) If you are considering traveling in a shoulder month, keep in mind that some shops and a few attractions don't open until Memorial Day, and the visitor season is generally considered over on Labor Day (although cruise lines operate well into Sept).

THE INSIDE PASSAGE OR THE GULF OF ALASKA?

For the purposes of cruising, Alaska can be divided into two separate and distinct areas, known generically as "the Inside Passage" and "the Gulf."

The Inside Passage

The Inside Passage runs through the area of Alaska known as Southeast (which the locals also call "the Panhandle"). It's the narrow strip of the state—islands, mainland coastal communities, and mountains—that runs from the Canadian border in the south to the start of the Gulf in the north, just above the Juneau/Haines/Skagway area. The islands on the western edge of the area give cruise ships a welcome degree of protection from the sea and its attendant rough waters (hence the name "Inside Passage"). Because of that shelter, such ports as Ketchikan, Wrangell, Petersburg, and others are reached with less rocking and rolling and thus less risk of seasickness. Sitka is not on the Inside Passage (it's on the Pacific Ocean side of Baranof Island), but is included in a fair number

---

SHORE excursions: THE WHAT, WHEN & WHY

Shore excursions offered by the cruise lines provide a chance for you to get off the ship and explore the sights up close. You'll take in the history, nature, and culture of the region, from strolling gold-rush-era streets to experiencing Native Alaskan traditions such as totem carving.

Some excursions are of the walking-tour or bus-tour variety, but many others are activity-oriented—among them, sea kayaking, mountain biking, horseback riding, salmon fishing, ziplining, ATV tours, and even rock climbing. You can see the sights by seaplane or helicopter—and maybe even land on a glacier and go for a walk or a dog-sled ride. You'll find quirky excursions, such as visits with local

artists in their studios. There's even snorkeling (highly recommended!).

With some lines, including Regent Seven Seas and the small ships of UnCruise Adventures, Alaskan Dream Cruises, American Cruise Lines, and Lindblad Expeditions, shore excursions are included in the cruise fare (when Viking Ocean Cruises debuts in the market in 2019, it will also include daily excursions). But with most lines they are an added (though sometimes very worthwhile) expense. See chapters 7 and 8 for information on the excursions available at the various ports. For details, see "Cruisetours: The Best of Land & Sea," later in this chapter, and chapter 9.

of Inside Passage cruise itineraries because it's a beautiful little port, with architecture and historical sites strongly reflective of Alaska's Russian past.

Southeast encompasses the capital city, **Juneau,** and townships influenced by the former Russian presence in the state (**Sitka,** for instance), the Tlingit and Haida Native cultures (**Ketchikan**), and the great gold rush of 1898 (**Skagway**). It is a land of rainforests, mountains, inlets, and glaciers (including Margerie, Johns Hopkins, Muir, and the others contained within the boundaries of **Glacier Bay National Park**). The region is rich in wildlife, especially of the marine variety. It is a scenic delight. But then, what part of Alaska isn't?

The Gulf of Alaska

The other major cruising area is the **Southcentral** region's Gulf of Alaska, usually referred to by the cruise lines as the "Glacier Discovery Route" or the "Voyage of the Glaciers," or some such catchy title. "Gulf of Alaska," after all, sounds pretty bland.

The coastline of the Gulf is that arc of land from just north of Glacier Bay to the Kenai Peninsula. Southcentral also takes in **Prince William Sound;** the **Cook Inlet,** on the northern side of the peninsula; **Anchorage,** Alaska's biggest city; the year-round **Alyeska Resort** at Girdwood, 40 miles from Anchorage; the **Matanuska** and **Susitna** valleys (the "Mat-Su"), a fertile agricultural region renowned for the record size of some of its garden produce; and part of the Alaska Mountain Range.

The principal Southcentral terminus ports are **Seward** or **Whittier** for Anchorage. Rarely do ships actually head for Anchorage proper, because that adds another full day to the route; instead, they carry passengers from Seward or Whittier to Anchorage by bus or train. (In 2010, Holland America made news by becoming the first big ship to visit Anchorage in 25 years, and in 2018 the cruise line will make a full-day call at Anchorage on its 14-night itinerary on the *Zaandam* out of Seattle.)

Let us stress that going on a Gulf cruise does not mean that you don't visit any of the Inside Passage. The big difference is that, whereas the more popular Inside Passage cruise itineraries run 7 nights round-trip to and from Seattle or Vancouver, BC, the Gulf routing is one-way—either northbound or southbound—between Vancouver and Seward or Vancouver and Whittier. A typical Gulf itinerary still visits such Inside Passage ports as **Ketchikan, Juneau,** and **Skagway.**

The Gulf's glaciers are quite dazzling and every bit as spectacular as their counterparts to the south. **College Fjord,** for instance, is lined with glaciers—16 of them, each one grander than the last. On one cruise, Fran saw incredible calving at **Harvard Glacier,** with chunks of 400- and 500-year-old ice falling off and crashing into the water to thunderous sounds every few minutes. (Concerns about global warming aside, it was spectacular.) Another favorite part of a Gulf cruise is the visit to the gigantic **Hubbard Glacier**—at 76 miles long, Alaska's longest—at the head of Yakutat Bay. It's also one of the fastest advancing glaciers, and the chunks in the water may remind you of ice in a giant punchbowl. Nothing beats a sunny day watching the glacier—hyperactive, popping and cracking, and shedding tons of ice into the bay. We should mention that on one visit to Hubbard Glacier we couldn't even get into the bay because another ship was blocking our path (and hogging the optimum views). Our fear is that, with so many new ships in Alaska, glacier viewing could become a blood sport.

And then there's the fact that, sadly, what you're really seeing is Alaska's glaciers in retreat, some receding quite rapidly.

Which Itinerary Is Better?

It's really a matter of personal taste. Some people don't like open-jaw flights (flying into one city and out of another)—which can add to the air ticket price—and prefer the round-trip Inside Passage route. Some specifically have Glacier Bay on the mind, a visit to the national park high on their bucket list. Others don't mind splitting up the air travel because they want to enjoy the additional glacier visits on the Gulf itineraries.

At one time there were practically no Gulf crossings. Then Princess decided to accelerate the development of its land components (lodges, railcars, motorcoaches, and so on), particularly in the Kenai Peninsula and Denali National Park areas, for which Anchorage is a logical springboard. To feed these land services with cruisetour passengers, Princess beefed up its number of Gulf sailings. In 2018, the line is doing its largest deployment ever in Alaska, with four ships in the Gulf—as well as a formidable Inside Passage capacity (including cruises out of San Francisco and LA). The other Alaska cruise giant, Holland America Line (HAL), has most of its seven-ship Alaska fleet doing the Inside Passage (out of Vancouver and Seattle), with two ships cruising across the Gulf (out of Vancouver and Seward). HAL tends to go more heavily into the Inside Passage than Princess because it is arguably stronger in Yukon Territory land services, which are more accessible from Juneau or Skagway.

BIG SHIP OR SMALL SHIP?

Picking the right ship is the most important factor in ensuring that you get the vacation you're looking for. Cruise ships in Alaska range from **small, adventure-type vessels** to **really big, resortlike megaships,** with the cruise experience varying widely depending on the type of ship you select. There are casual cruises and luxury cruises; there are educational cruises, where you attend lectures, and entertainment-focused cruises, where you attend musical revues; there are adventure-oriented cruises, where hiking, kayaking, and exploring remote areas are the main activities; and resortlike cruises, where aquatherapy and mud baths are the order of the day.

Besides the availability (or nonavailability) of the programs, the spas, the activities, and the like, there is another question you have to answer before deciding on a ship. Do you want, or do you need, to be with people, and if so, in an intimate daily setting or only on an occasional basis? On a small ship, there's no escape. The people you meet on a 22-passenger or even a

100-passenger vessel are the ones you're going to be seeing every day of the cruise. And woe betide you if they turn out to be boring, or bombastic, or slow-witted, or in some other way not to your taste. Some people may think that the megaships are too big, but they do have at least one saving grace: On a 2,000-, 3,000-, or 4,000-passenger ship, there's plenty of room to steer clear of people who turn you off. And because all these big, newer ships have lots of alternative restaurants, it's even easier to avoid those types at mealtimes, which is not so easy on a smaller ship. Finding like-minded people to hang out with plays a big part in the success or failure of any cruise experience—especially a small-ship cruise experience.

You'll need to decide what overall cruise experience you want. Itinerary and type of cruise are even more important than price. After all, what kind of bargain is a party cruise if you're looking for a quiet time? Or an adventure-oriented cruise if you're not physically in the best of shape? Your fantasy vacation may be someone else's nightmare, and vice versa.

Unlike the Caribbean, which generally attracts people looking to relax in the sun or possibly party 'til the cows come home, Alaska attracts visitors with a different goal: They want to experience Alaska's glaciers, forests, wildlife, and other natural wonders. All the cruise lines recognize this, so almost any cruise you choose will give you opportunities to see what you've come for. The main question, then, is how you want to see those sights. Do you want to be down at the waterline, viewing them from the deck of an adventure vessel, or do you want to spot them from a warm lounge or your own private veranda?

The hotel director on a Holland America ship once noted, "If you want to stay out until 4am, gamble wildly, and pass out in a lounge, you don't come on Holland America." And he's right. Picking the ship that's right for you is the key to a successful Alaskan cruise experience.

In this section, we'll run through the pros and cons of the big ships and the small and alternative ships. (See chapters 5 and 6 for detailed descriptions of the ships cruising in Alaska.)

The Big Ships

Big ships operating in Alaska vary in size, amenities, and activities, and include really big and really new megaships (most notably the Alaska-centric, 4,004-passenger *Norwegian Bliss*, debuting in 2018). All the big ships provide a comfortable experience, with virtual armies of service employees overseeing your well-being and ship stabilizers ensuring smooth sailing.

The size of the current crop of ships may keep Alaska's wildlife at a distance (you may need binoculars to see the whales), but they have plenty of deck space and comfy lounge chairs for relaxing as you take in the gorgeous mountain and glacier views, and sip a cup of coffee or cocoa (and, on Holland America, the famous Dutch pea soup). Because of their deeper drafts (the amount of ship below the waterline), the big ships can't get as close to the sights as the smaller ships, and they can't visit the more pristine fjords, inlets, and narrows. However, the more powerful engines on these ships do allow them to visit more ports during each trip—generally, popular ports where your ship may be one of several and where shopping for souvenirs is a main attraction. Some of the less massive ships in this category also visit alternative ports, away from the cruise crowds (the 458-passenger *Seabourn Sojourn* is one example).

It should be noted, too, that the bigger ships being built nowadays are equipped with some pretty powerful stabilizers—something to think about if you have the occasional bout with seasickness.

The big-ship cruise lines put a lot of emphasis on **shore excursions,** which often take you beyond the port city to explore different aspects of Alaska—nature, Native culture, and so on. (See the shore excursion listings in chapters 7 and 8 for more information.) Dispersing passengers to different locales on these shore trips is a must. When more than 10,000 passengers from several visiting ships converge on a small Alaskan town, much of the ambience goes out the window. On particularly busy days, there are more cruise passengers in some ports than locals. Take Skagway, for instance: In midsummer, even counting the influx of seasonal tourist-services-related employees, its population is well under 3,000. One large cruise ship will deposit that many people onto the streets—and on busy days, there may be as many as *four* ships in port!

The larger ships in the Alaska market fall into two categories: what we are terming midsize and megaships. **Midsize ships** in Alaska for 2018 are the luxurious Silversea's *Silver Shadow* and Regent Seven Seas' *Mariner,* Oceania Cruises' upscale *Regatta*, Seabourn's *Seabourn Sojourn*, and the modern midsize *Volendam*, *Amsterdam*, and *Zaandam* of Holland America Line. While Windstar's *Star Legend* carries only 212 passengers, it looks and acts like a small version of a midsize ship. In general, the size of these ships is less significant than the general onboard atmosphere. Holland America's midsize ships, for example, all have a similar calm, adult-oriented feel; Oceania's *Regatta* has an ambience akin to a floating country hotel.

Carrying as many as 4,004 passengers, the **megaships** look and feel like floating resorts. Big on glitz, they offer loads of activities, attract many families and seniors, have many public rooms (including fancy casinos and fully equipped gyms and spas), and provide a wide variety of meal and entertainment options. Although they may feature a couple of formal nights per trip, the ambience is generally casual. The Alaska vessels of the Carnival, Celebrity, Norwegian, Princess, and Royal Caribbean fleets all fit into this category, as do Holland America's *Eurodam*, *Nieuw Amsterdam*, *Noordam*, and *Westerdam*, and Disney's *Wonder. Word of caution:* Due to the number of people on board, debarkation from the biggest ships can be a lengthy process.

Both the midsize ships and the megaships have a great range of **facilities** for passengers, including swimming pools, health clubs, spas, nightclubs, movie theaters, shops, casinos, bars, and kids' playrooms. In some cases, especially on the megaships, you'll also find sports decks, virtual golf, computer rooms, and cigar clubs, as well as quiet spaces where you can get away from it all. There are so many public rooms that you more than likely won't feel claustrophobic. **Cabins** range from cubbyholes to large suites, depending on the ship and the type of accommodations you book. Cabins provide TVs and telephones, and some have minibars, picture windows, and private verandas.

Smaller ships usually serve dinner at a certain time and with open seating, allowing you to sit at any table you want but at a set time. Large ships may offer only two fairly rigid, set seating times, especially for dinner; this means that your table will be preassigned and remain the same for the duration of the cruise. Increasingly, however, there are exceptions to the rule in the large-ship category. The ships of Norwegian Cruise Line, Oceania, Regent Seven Seas, Seabourn, Silversea, and Windstar serve all meals with open seating—dine when you want and sit with whom you want (within the restaurants' open hours and sometimes requiring reservations to be made in the morning for dinner). Princess, Holland America, Carnival, Royal Caribbean, and Celebrity have their own systems, allowing guests to choose before the cruise between traditional early or late seating, or open restaurant-style seating. Most large ships today also offer multiple alternative-dining options, featuring casual buffets and specialty restaurants, most with an additional charge of up to $45, or more if you choose a fancy Chef's Table where dishes are paired with wines ($95 on Royal Caribbean ships, for example). Special dining packages may reduce the price if you plan to visit more than one venue. See "Choosing Your Dining Options" in chapter 3 for more information on dining choices, and see the individual ship reviews in chapters 5 and 6 for ship-specific dining information.

These ships have big dining rooms and buffet areas and serve a tremendous variety of **cuisine** throughout the day, often with 24-hour food service. There may also be additional dining venues, such as pizzerias, hamburger grills, ice cream parlors or gelato shops, alternative restaurants (typically for an extra service charge), wine bars, cigar bars, champagne bars, caviar bars, and patisseries. Note that because these ships carry a lot of people, there may be lines at the buffets and in other public areas.

In most cases, there are lots of **onboard activities** to keep you occupied when you're not whale- or glacier-watching, including games, contests, and classes and lectures (sometimes by naturalists, park rangers, or wildlife experts; other times on topics such as line dancing or napkin folding). A variety of entertainment options may even include celebrity headline acts and stage-show productions, some pretty extravagant (those of Carnival come to mind).

The Small & Alternative Ships

While big cruise ships are mostly for people who want every resort amenity, small or alternative ships are best suited for people who prefer a casual, crowd-free cruise experience that gives passengers a chance to get up close and personal with Alaska's **natural surroundings** and **wildlife.**

Thanks to their smaller size, these ships, carrying only 22 to 100 passengers, can go places where larger ships can't, such as narrow fjords, uninhabited islands, and smaller ports that cater mostly to small fishing vessels. Due to their shallow draft, they can nose right up to sheer cliff faces, bird rookeries, bobbing icebergs, and cascading waterfalls that you can literally reach out and touch. Also, sea animals are not as intimidated by these ships, so you might find yourself having a close encounter with a humpback whale or watching other sea mammals bobbing in the ship's wake. You may catch excellent glimpses of land animals, too—while on a small ship in the Misty Fjords (a place big ships can't even go), Fran and her fellow passengers watched through binoculars as a brown bear shoreside stood to its full height. The decks on these ships are closer to the waterline, too, giving passengers a more intimate view than they would get from the high decks of the large cruise ships. Some of these ships stop at ports on a daily basis, like the larger ships, while others avoid ports almost entirely, exploring natural areas instead. Small ships also have the flexibility to change direction as opportunities arise—say, to go where whales have been sighted and to linger awhile once a sighting has been made.

The alternative-ship experience is all about a sense of **adventure** (usually of a soft rather than rugged sort), and it's a generally casual cruise experience: There are no dress-up nights, and food may be rather simple (although there are notable exceptions—on the luxury ships of UnCruise Adventures the chefs show a deft hand with fresh Alaskan seafood, and on Alaskan Dream ships the Asian dishes are particularly tasty). These ships have so few public areas to choose from—usually only one or two small lounges—that camaraderie tends to develop more quickly among passengers than aboard larger vessels, which can be as anonymous as a big city. **Cabins** on these ships don't usually offer TVs or telephones and tend to be small and in some cases downright spartan (though the luxury ships of UnCruise Adventures include cabins and suites with Jacuzzis and French balconies, and Lindblad's *National Geographic Quest* and American Cruise Line's *American Spirit* offer actual step-out balconies). Meals are served at a set time, with open seating (seats are not assigned), and dress codes are usually nonexistent.

None of these ships has the kind of significant exercise or spa facilities that you'll find on the big ships—your best exercise bet is usually a brisk walk around the deck after dinner—but many compensate by providing more **active off-ship opportunities,** such as hiking or kayaking. The alternative ships are also more likely to feature in-depth **lectures** on Alaska-specific topics, such as marine biology, history, and Native culture.

These smaller ships have few if any stabilizers, and the ride can be bumpy in open water—which isn't much of a problem on Inside Passage itineraries, when most of the cruising area is protected from sea waves anyway. With no elevators, these ships can also be challenging for travelers with disabilities. And the alternative-ship lines don't usually offer specific activities or facilities for children, although you will find a few families on some of these vessels.

CRUISETOURS: THE BEST OF LAND & SEA

Most folks who go to the trouble of getting to a place as far off the beaten path as Alaska try to stick around for awhile once they're there, rather than jetting home as soon as they hop off the boat. Knowing this, the cruise lines have set themselves up in the land-tour business as well, offering a number of great land-based excursions that can be tacked onto your cruise experience.

We're not just talking about an overnight stay in Anchorage or Juneau before or after your cruise; almost any cruise line will arrange an extra night of hotel accommodations for you. Enjoyable as that may be, it doesn't begin to hint at the real opportunities available in Alaska. No, the subject here is **cruisetours,** or Land + Sea Journeys, as Holland America now calls them, a total package with a cruise and a structured, prearranged, multiday land itinerary already programmed in—for instance, a 7-day cruise with a 5-day land package. There are any number of combinations, between 10 and 20 days in length.

In this section, we discuss the various cruisetour itineraries available through the lines. See chapter 9 for details on the cruisetour destinations.

Cruisetour Itineraries

Many parts of inland Alaska can be visited on cruisetour programs, including Denali National Park, Fairbanks, Wrangell–St. Elias, Nome, and Kotzebue. If you're so inclined, you can even go all the way to the oil fields of the North Slope of Prudhoe Bay, hundreds of miles north of the Arctic Circle.

Three principal tour destination areas can be combined with your Inside Passage or Gulf of Alaska cruise—two major ones, which we'll call the **Anchorage/Denali/Fairbanks** corridor and the **Yukon Territory,** and one less-traveled route that we'll call the **Canadian Rockies Route,** which is an option because of Vancouver's position as an Alaska cruise hub.

ANCHORAGE/DENALI/FAIRBANKS CRUISETOUR

A typical Anchorage/Denali/Fairbanks cruisetour package (we'll use Princess as an example because it is heavily involved in the Denali sector) might include a 7-day Vancouver-Anchorage cruise, followed by 2 nights in Anchorage and a scenic ride in a private railcar to **Denali National Park** for 2 more nights at Princess' Denali Wilderness Lodge or Mt. McKinley Princess Wilderness Lodge (or 1 night at each) before heading on to Fairbanks. On a clear day, the Mount McKinley property affords a panoramic view of the Alaska Mountain Range and its centerpiece, Denali—at 20,320 feet, North America's highest peak. A full day in the park allows guests to explore the staggeringly beautiful wilderness expanse and its wildlife before reboarding the train and heading into the Interior of Alaska, to **Fairbanks,** for 2 more nights. Fairbanks itself isn't much to look at, but the activities available in outlying areas are fantastic—the *Riverboat Discovery* paddlewheel day cruises on the Chena River and an excursion to a gold dredge are two excellent activity options in the area. Passengers on that particular cruisetour fly home from Fairbanks.

A shorter variation of that itinerary might be a cruise combined with an overnight (or 2-night) stay in Anchorage along with the Denali portion, perhaps with rail transportation into the park and a motorcoach back to Anchorage, skipping Fairbanks. Princess has cruisetours that include visits to a hitherto largely inaccessible area, **Wrangell–St. Elias National Park,** where it built the Copper River Princess Wilderness Lodge, the fifth hotel in the company's lodging network.

YUKON TERRITORY CRUISETOUR

Another popular land itinerary offered along with Alaska cruises typically involves a 3- or 4-day cruise between Vancouver and Juneau/Skagway (you either join a 7-day sailing late or get off early), combined with a land program into the **Klondike,** in Canada's Yukon Territory, then through the Interior of Alaska to Anchorage. En route, passengers experience a variety of transportation modes, which may include rail, riverboat, motorcoach, and/or air—Holland America flies passengers between Fairbanks and Dawson City. The hour-long flight saves 2 days of motorcoach travel and a hotel overnight.

Although located in Canada, the Yukon is nevertheless an integral part of the overall Alaska cruisetour picture because of its intimate ties to Alaska's gold-rush history. The overnight stops are **Whitehorse,** the territorial capital, and **Dawson City,** a remote, picture-perfect gold-rush town near the site where gold was found in 1896. Holland America offers a visit to Tombstone Territorial Park, about a 90-minute drive from Dawson City and an area of stunning scenery, Native architecture, and abundant wildlife.

CANADIAN ROCKIES CRUISETOUR

A Canadian Rockies tour is easily combined with a Vancouver-originating (or -terminating) Inside Passage or Gulf cruise. In 5-, 6-, or 7-day chunks, you can visit such scenic wonders as **Banff, Lake Louise,** and **Jasper National Park** in conjunction with an Alaska sailing.

The Canadian Rockies have some of the finest **mountain scenery** on Earth. It's not just that the glacier-carved mountains are astonishingly dramatic and beautiful; it's also that there are hundreds and hundreds of miles of this wonderful wilderness high country. Between them, Banff National Park and Jasper National Park preserve much of this mountain beauty. Other national and provincial parks make accessible more vast and equally spectacular regions of the Rockies, as well as portions of the nearby Columbia and Selkirk mountain ranges. Beautiful Lake Louise, colored deep green from its mineral content, is located 35 miles north of Banff.

Battle of the Top Players

If we talk in this section more about **Princess** and **Holland America Line** than we do about other lines, it's because their significant financial investments in land components of Alaskan tourism have allowed them to become the 800-pound gorillas duking it out for regional dominance. Other lines offer some of the same cruisetours as these two, but many buy at least some of their cruisetour components from Princess and/or Holland America's land operations. It may seem odd to have companies buying from (or selling to) competitors, but with tourism in Alaska, there's practically no other way. As recently as the early 1980s, when Holland America–Westours owned the bulk of the landtour components, Princess, its number-one rival, was also its number-one customer! Hey, a 4-month season makes for strange bedfellows.

SHOULD YOU TAKE YOUR cruisetour BEFORE OR AFTER YOUR CRUISE?

Though the land portion of both the Denali and the Yukon itineraries can be taken either before or after the cruise, we feel it's better to take the land portion pre-cruise rather than post-cruise. Why? After several days of exploring the wilderness, it's nice to be able to get aboard a ship to relax and be pampered for a while.

Because of the distances that must be covered on some wilderness cruisetour itineraries, passengers often have to be roused out of bed and ready to board the motorcoach by, say, 7:30am. And the day may seem to go on forever, with a stop to view this waterfall, or that river, or that mountain. Then, upon arrival at the next stop—in the early evening usually—the request is, "Hurry and get cleaned up for dinner." By the time you've crawled into your new bed, often quite late at night, you're beat. It's a nice kind of tired, as the saying goes, but it's tired nevertheless. After a few days of that, it's great to get on a luxurious cruise ship, unpack just once, and rise when you feel like it, comfortable in the knowledge that you haven't missed your transportation and that you'll still make it in time to have a leisurely breakfast.

That, at any rate, is the conventional wisdom, and there's more of a demand for pre-cruise land packages than for post-cruise. As the lines obviously can't always accommodate everybody on a land itinerary before the cruise (they're hoping to even out the traffic flow by having a like number of requests to go touring after the voyage), it's smart to get your bid in early.

It was partly to carve out a niche for itself and, at the same time, to lessen its reliance on the services of a competitor that Princess plunged heavily into the lodging and transportation sectors. Princess is arguably stronger in the Denali corridor than any other line, while Holland America could be said to have the upper hand in the Yukon/Klondike market. But each line offers tours to both of these areas, among other options.

Princess owns railcars (the *Midnight Sun Express*) in the Denali corridor. Holland America also owns railcars there (the *McKinley Explorer*). Both, incidentally, rely on the Alaska Railroad to pull them. Princess owns five wilderness lodges; Holland America owns city hotels (in Fairbanks, Anchorage, and Skagway) and the McKinley Chalet Resort just outside Denali National Park. Holland America Line, in a project completed in 2016, upgraded all rooms at its hotel and added some riverfront rooms as well as Denali Square, a gathering place with a restaurant and bar, shopping, and areas for lectures and performances (plus firepits!). Princess and Holland America also each have a fleet of motorcoaches. Other major lines work with private companies such as the Wilderness Express Train, with four railcars that are state-of-the-art, with business-class-style leather seats, a fine kitchen on the lower level (meals are extra, with a variety of menus), and a friendly, knowledgeable staff.

QUIZ TIME: QUESTIONS TO ASK WHEN CHOOSING YOUR CRUISE

After you've decided which itinerary and what kind of ship appeals to you, we suggest you ask yourself some questions about the kind of experience you want, and then read through the cruise-line and ship reviews in chapters 5 and 6 to see which ones match your vision of the perfect Alaska cruise vessel.

When looking at the attributes of the various ships to make your choice, some determining factors will be no-brainers. For instance, if you're traveling with kids, you'll want a ship with a good kids' program. If you're a foodie, you'll want a ship with gourmet cuisine. If you're used to staying at a Ritz-Carlton hotel when you travel, you'll probably want to cruise on a luxury ship. If you usually stay at B&Bs, you'll probably prefer one of the small ships.

Also ask yourself whether you require resortlike amenities, such as a heated swimming pool, spa, casino, aerobics classes, and state-of-the-art gym. Or do you care more about having an adventure or an educational experience? If you want the former, choose a large cruise ship; if you prefer the latter, a small ship may be more your speed.

Here are some more pertinent questions to help you narrow the field:

HOW DO YOU GET A DEAL, AND WHAT'S NOT INCLUDED? The best way to get a deal on a cruise in Alaska is usually to book early, but this is hardly a hard-and-fast rule. Virtually all the lines (with the exception of some of the small-ship lines) offer early-booking discounts. The numbers and dates may vary a bit, but the formula has been fairly standard: If you book your Alaska cruise by mid- to late February of the year of the cruise, you'll get an early-bird rate. If the cabins do not fill up by the cutoff date, that rate may be extended.

If the cabins are still not full as the cruise season begins, cruise lines typically start marketing special deals, usually through their top-producing travel agents and with savings that can run as high as 50%. In 2017, with increased interest in cruising in Alaska, last-minute fares were harder to come by. Still, you could nab a last-minute fare of $400 in May. Such bargain-basement fares generally apply to the lowest category of inside cabins, and the number of cabins offered at said prices is very limited. To get the best deal, we suggest you book your Alaska cruise, and particularly your Alaska cruisetour (because these are increasingly popular), as early as possible. (Find more on this in Chapter 3.)

Cruise fares cover accommodations, meals, shipboard entertainment, and most shipboard activities. A number of expenses are not covered in the typical cruise package, however, and you should factor these in when planning your vacation budget. Airfare to and from your port of embarkation and debarkation is usually extra (though cruise lines sometimes offer reduced rates). Necessary hotel stays before or after the cruise are also usually not included. Gratuities, taxes, and trip insurance are typically extra as well. Shore excursions are rarely included in the cruise fare (Regent Seven Seas includes a free option at each port and so does Viking Ocean Cruises, debuting in Alaska in

2019), and if you opt for pricey excursions, such as flightseeing, you can easily add $1,000 or more per person to your total. Alcohol is typically extra—though luxury lines Crystal, Regent, Seabourn, and Silversea include all drinks in the cruise fare—as are sodas and such incidentals as laundry, Internet access, telephone calls from the ship, and babysitting. Optional splurges include beauty and spa services, wine tastings, dining in alternative restaurants, select fitness classes, fancy ice cream sundaes, and photos taken by ship photographers.

Because travel agents constantly keep abreast of the latest bargains, we believe they are best equipped to advise you on the best Alaska cruise deals.

See chapter 3 for details on when to book for the best prices.

HOW MUCH TIME IS SPENT IN PORT & HOW MUCH AT SEA?
Generally, ships on 7-night itineraries spend 3 or 4 days in port and cruise in natural areas such as Glacier Bay, College Fjord, or Tracy Arm during the other days.

Coming into port, ships generally dock right after breakfast, allowing you the morning and afternoon to take a shore excursion or explore on your own. Ships usually depart in the early evening, giving you an hour or two to rest up before dinner (although some ships stay in Juneau as late as 11pm, giving you a chance to sample salmon steak, king crab legs, or similar local fare off the ship). On rare occasions, a ship might cruise through a glacier area in the morning and dock at the next port in the early afternoon, not leaving until 10 or 11pm.

On days at sea, the emphasis will be on exploring natural areas, viewing glaciers, and scanning for wildlife. Big ships stick to prearranged schedules on these days, but on small-ship, soft-adventure-type cruises, days at sea can be unstructured, with the captain choosing a destination based on reports of whale sightings, for example. Some small-ship itineraries include almost no ports, sticking instead to isolated natural areas that passengers explore by kayak or Zodiac boat or on foot.

IS THE CRUISE FORMAL OR CASUAL? If you don't care to get dressed up, select a less formal cruise, such as those offered by many of the small ships or Carnival and Norwegian, which do not have official formal nights (but may set aside a night or two for those who want to dress up). On ships such as Regent Seven Seas' *Mariner*, Viking's *Spirit*, and Windstar's *Star Legend* and the Celebrity ships, the fanciest you need to go is elegant casual. If, on the other hand, having the chance to put on your finery appeals to you, select Princess or Holland America (and, to a lesser extent, Royal Caribbean) or the posh Crystal, Seabourn, or Silversea. The ships of these lines will have casual and formal (or gala) nights, meaning women can wear anything from a sundress to an evening gown (though most show up in cocktail dresses) over the course of a week, and men will go from shirtsleeves to jacket and tie (many men are now opting for dark suits over tuxedos). All the lines also now have an option for those who do not want to dress up on formal nights—you can skip the dining room and eat casually at the buffet.

WHAT ARE THE OTHER PASSENGERS USUALLY LIKE?   Each ship attracts a fairly predictable type of passenger. Small ships bring a more physically active bunch that's highly interested in nature, but you'll find fewer families and single travelers. Larger ships cater to a more diverse group: singles, newlyweds, families, and couples over 55. Alaska sailings out of Seattle attract a younger, more family-oriented crowd. If you're looking for nightlife, you may want to look at Carnival, Norwegian Cruise Line, and Royal Caribbean among lines that cruise from this port. Disney, of course, attracts a family crowd, but also a number of adult couples. We've included information on typical passengers in the cruise-line reviews in chapters 5 and 6.

I'LL BE TRAVELING ALONE. WILL I HAVE FUN? AND DOES IT COST MORE?   A nice thing about cruises is that you're seated with other guests, so you never have to dine alone. (If you don't want to be seated with other guests, seek a ship with alternative-dining options—although a steady diet of "Table for one, please" is likely to raise a few eyebrows among your shipmates.) You also needn't worry much about finding people to talk to—the general atmosphere on nearly all ships is very congenial and allows you to find conversation easily, especially during group activities. Some ships host a party to give singles a chance to get to know one another, and some ships provide social hosts as dance partners.

The downside is that you may have to pay for the privilege of traveling solo. Because rates are based on two people per cabin, some lines charge a "single supplement" fee (aka, an extra charge) that ranges from 10% to 100% of the double-occupancy fare. As a single person, you have two choices: Find a line with a reasonable single supplement rate (such as Silversea, Regent Seven Seas, or Crystal Cruises) or ask if the line has a cabin-share program, under which the line will pair you with another single so you can get a lower fare. Some lines such as Holland America Line and Lindblad Expeditions have a single-guarantee program, which means if they can't find you a roommate (of the same sex), they'll book you in a cabin alone but still honor the shared rate. Single cabins designed and priced specifically for one person are available on some ships, including Norwegian Bliss; but be aware these cabins tend to sell out fast.

IS SHIPBOARD LIFE HEAVILY SCHEDULED?   That depends to a certain extent on you and the ship you choose. Meals are generally served during set hours, though on larger ships, you'll have plenty of alternative options if those hours don't suit you. On smaller ships, you may be out of luck if you miss a meal, unless you can charm the cook. On both large and small ships, times for disembarking and reboarding at the ports are strict: If you miss the boat, you miss the boat. (See chapter 4 for tips on what to do in this situation.) Other than these two considerations, the only schedule you'll have to follow on board is your own. It all depends on how busy you want to be.

WHAT ARE THE CABINS LIKE?   Cabins come in all sizes and configurations. See "Choosing Your Cabin" in chapter 3 for details.

WHAT ARE MEALS LIKE?   Meals are a big part of the cruise experience. The larger the ship, the more dining options you'll find. When booking on large ships that have two main dining-room seatings each evening, you'll be asked ahead of time to decide on your preferred dinner hour, with tables assigned. On Princess, Royal Caribbean, Carnival, Holland America, and Celebrity ships, you choose in advance whether to dine traditional- or restaurant-style. Norwegian, Silversea, Oceania, Regent, Seabourn, Viking, and Windstar ships have open, restaurant-style seating, meaning that you can dine when you want with whomever you choose, but you are encouraged to make reservations each morning for tables at dinner. On smaller ships, you can sit where you want, but dinner will be called for a set time. In the reviews in chapters 5 and 6, we discuss dining options for each line.

If you have any special dietary requirements (vegan, kosher, gluten-free), be sure the line is informed well in advance, preferably when you book your cruise. Almost all ships have vegetarian and low-fat options available at every meal (sugar-free desserts, too), and those that don't can usually meet your needs with some advance warning.

WHAT ACTIVITIES & ENTERTAINMENT DOES THE SHIP OFFER?
On small ships, activities are limited by the available public space and are usually up to the passengers to organize—maybe a game of Scrabble or Trivial Pursuit. There will typically also be a lecture series dealing with the flora, fauna, and geography of Alaska, usually conducted by a naturalist. These lectures are also becoming more popular on the larger ships.

The big ships have activities such as fitness, personal finance, photography, and art classes; Ping-Pong and bingo tournaments; audience-participation games; art auctions; and parties. Show productions at night are almost de rigueur. Cooking classes and demonstrations are the *in* thing. (See the general big-ship and small-ship descriptions earlier in this chapter for more information on activities and entertainment.)

DOES THE SHIP HAVE A CHILDREN'S PROGRAM?   Many parents are taking their kids with them on cruise vacations. The big ship lines have responded by adding youth counselors and supervised programs, fancy playrooms, teen centers, and even video-game rooms to keep kids entertained while their parents relax. Some lines offer special shore excursions for children and teens, and most ships provide babysitting (for an extra charge). You may even find reduced cruise fares for kids.

It's important to ask whether a supervised program will be available on your specific cruise, because sometimes the programs operate only if a certain number of children are on board. If your kids are TV addicts, you may want to make sure that your cabin has a TV. Even if it does, though, channel selection will be limited, so consider bringing along a portable DVD player and movies (or laptop with movies pre-loaded).

I HAVE A DISABILITY. WILL I HAVE ANY TROUBLE TAKING A CRUISE?   It's important to let the cruise line know about any special needs when you make your booking. If you use a wheelchair, you'll need to know if wheelchair-accessible cabins are available (and how they're equipped), as well as whether public rooms are accessible and can be reached by elevator, and whether the cruise line has any special policy regarding travelers with disabilities—for instance, whether it's required that a fully mobile companion accompany you. Based on various court cases, it's clear that when operating in U.S. waters, ships are expected to comply with the Americans with Disabilities Act (ADA). Newer ships tend to be better equipped, however, offering a larger number of cabins at various price points for passengers in wheelchairs as well as those who are sight- or hearing-impaired. But even older ships undergoing renovations are being retrofitted to provide more access.

Travelers with disabilities should inquire when booking whether the ship docks at ports or uses "tenders" (small boats) to go ashore. Tenders cannot always accommodate passengers with wheelchairs; in most cases, wheelchair-bound passengers require crew assistance to board tenders—though Holland America, for one, uses a special lift system to get passengers into the tenders without requiring them to leave their wheelchairs. Once aboard the ship, travelers with disabilities should seek the advice of tour staff before choosing shore excursions that are wheelchair-friendly. If you have a chronic health problem, check with your doctor before booking a cruise, and if you have any specific needs, notify the cruise line in advance. This will ensure that the medical team on the ship is properly prepared to offer assistance. There is another, somewhat sensitive, consideration for some would-be small-ship passengers: obesity. We mention this only because we once met, on a small ship, a charming young lady who stood a little over 5 feet tall and weighed about 250 pounds. She told us that she had been advised by the cruise line not to book passage on the ship she first chose because she wouldn't fit in the shower. Instead, the company put her on a ship for which her girth would not be a problem. Understand, please, that the cruise operator is not being judgmental. But if you don't mention such things and end up on an inappropriate ship, you're in for a miserable time. So assess the situation realistically.

WHAT IF I WANT TO TAKE A CRUISE FOR MY HONEYMOON?
One-week Alaska cruises start not only on Saturdays and Sundays, but also on Mondays, Wednesdays, Thursdays, and Fridays, which should help you find a departure date that doesn't have you dashing out of your wedding reception to catch a plane. You will want to make sure that the ship you choose has double, queen-, or king-size beds; you may also want to request a cabin with a Jacuzzi. Rooms with private verandas are particularly romantic; you can take in the sights in privacy and even enjoy a quiet meal, assuming the veranda is big enough for a table and chairs (some are not) and the weather doesn't turn chilly. If you want to dine alone, make sure the dining room has tables for two or the ship provides room service. Your travel agent can fill you in on these matters. You may also want to ask whether other honeymooners your age will be on the ship. Some ships—among them those of Princess, Royal Caribbean, Carnival, Celebrity, and Holland America—offer special honeymoon packages and sometimes honeymoon suites. Most lines provide special

perks such as champagne and chocolates if you let them know in advance that you'll be honeymooning on the ship.

CAN I GET MARRIED ON BOARD? Captains on the ships of several lines including Princess and Celebrity can officiate ceremonies at sea, but there's a catch: The ship needs to be in international waters (and not, for instance, in Alaska's Inside Passage). So if you're planning a wedding at sea, you'll want to look specifically at sailings from Seattle or San Francisco that include a day at sea (packages including cake and a champagne toast start at about $1,500, in addition to your cruise fare). You can get married while the ship is in port, but you will have to provide your own officiate. Ships without wedding chapels will usually agree to clear a public room for your nuptials and may even provide flowers and light refreshments. If you're looking to go small but with big bragging rights, lines including Holland America and Norwegian have the option of a wedding on top of a glacier in Juneau (imagine those Instagram photos!).

WILL I GET SEASICK? On Inside Passage itineraries, most of your time will be spent in protected waters with islands between you and the open sea, making for generally smooth sailing. At certain points, however, such as around Sitka and at the entrance to Queen Charlotte Strait, there is nothing between you and Japan but a lot of wind, water, and choppy seas. Ships with sailing itineraries on the Gulf of Alaska and those sailing from San Francisco, out of necessity, will spend more time in rough, open waters. Although ships that ply these routes tend to be very stable, you'll probably notice some rocking and rolling. Keep in mind: Big ships tend to be more stable than smaller ships.

Unless you're particularly prone to seasickness, you probably don't need to worry much. But if you are, medications that can help include Dramamine, Bonine, and Marezine, which are available over the counter and also stocked by most ships—the purser's office may even give them out for free. Another option is the Transderm patch, available by prescription only, which is applied behind your ear and has time-released medication. The patch can be worn for up to 3 days, but you should be aware that it comes with a slew of warnings about side effects. Some people have also had success in curbing seasickness by using ginger capsules, which are available at health food stores, or acupressure wristbands, available at most pharmacies. Our best advice is to ask for recommendations from your doctor before your cruise.

IS THERE SMOKING ON SHIPS? The short answer is yes, but on a restricted basis. The major cruise lines now ban smoking in cabins *and* on cabin balconies. Smoking is generally not allowed in shipboard theaters, show lounges, or dining rooms and may be restricted to certain bars (many ships now have cigar lounges) or even certain sides of the ship (open decks on starboard side only on Royal Caribbean vessels, for instance). Smoking is sometimes allowed in ship casinos. Celebrity, for one, prohibits smoking even on cruisetours. Small ships typically allow smoking only in certain outdoor areas. If you are a smoker, check with your line in advance. If you are not a smoker, you will no doubt be relieved by the new policies being adopted.

BOOKING YOUR CRUISE

Okay, you've thought about what type of cruise vacation you have in mind. You've decided when and for how long you'd like to travel. Read through our ship reviews in chapters 5 and 6, narrow down your focus to the lines that appeal to you, and then you'll be ready to get down to brass tacks and make your booking.

BOOKING A CRUISE: THE SHORT EXPLANATION

Cruise lines have detailed websites and brochures, or sometimes many different brochures—including e-brochures—full of beautiful glossy photos of beautiful glossy people enjoying fabulous vacations. They're colorful! They're gorgeous! They're enticing! And yes, they're confusing! It's enough to make your eyes roll to the back of your head in frustration. Don't worry, your cruise will be considerably more fun and relaxing than planning your trip.

One of the biggest areas of confusion is pricing. You'll see low starting rates on the charts, but look further and you'll realize those are for tiny inside cubicles; most of the cabins sell for much more. Sometimes the brochures have published rates that are nothing more than the pie-in-the-sky wish of cruise lines for the rate at which they'd like to sell the cruise (most customers will pay less). We strongly suggest you book your Alaska cruise as early as possible (6 or 7 months in advance if possible, but by mid-February at the latest) to ensure you get your first choice of cabin at a decent fare. Look for so-called "early-bird" fares or fares with an "early booking discount." In the past you could pretty much count on super-cheap last-minute fares too, but the tide is turning in this regard—cruise lines including Royal Caribbean and Norwegian are making concerted efforts to end the last-minute discounting practice (and encourage everyone to book early). In May and early June 2017, a very few last-minute fares started around $400 for a 7-night cruise, but most fares were from $799 and some cruises were already sold out. The availability of last-minute rates dwindled even more as the summer progressed. In fact, by June we couldn't find much below $700 per person through the end of the season, with many sailings $950 and up, or sold out. You may be one of the lucky few who are able to snag last-minute discounts, but if you don't reserve space early, you may be left out in the cold (cold in Alaska, get it?). Keep in mind that the most expensive and cheapest cabins tend to sell out first. As they say in the cruise business, ships sell out from the top and bottom first.

Deals for Past Passengers

Many of the most intense deals are marketed first to **past passengers.** So if you've cruised at all before—Caribbean, Europe, Bermuda—check with the cruise line to see if you qualify for a past-passenger deal.

So how do you book your cruise? Traditionally (meaning over the past 35 years or so), people have booked their cruises through **travel agents.** But you may be wondering: Hasn't the traditional travel agent gone the way of typewriters and eight-track tapes and been replaced by the **Internet?** Not exactly. Travel agents are alive and kicking, though the Internet has indeed staked its claim alongside them and knocked some out of business. In an effort to keep pace, nearly every traditional travel agency (and many individual agents, too) has its own website.

So what's the best way to book a cruise these days, online or with an agent? Good question. The answer depends. If you're computer-savvy, have a good handle on all the elements that go into a cruise, and have narrowed down the choices to a few cruise lines that appeal to you, trawl the online seas at your own pace and check out deals, which can be dramatic. On the other hand, you won't get the same personalized service searching for and booking a cruise online. If you need help getting a refund, arranging special meals or other matters, or deciding which cabin to choose, you're on your own. In addition, agents usually know about cruise and airfare discounts that the lines won't necessarily publicize on their websites.

However you arrange to buy your cruise, what you basically have in hand at the end is a contract for transportation, lodging, dining, entertainment, housekeeping, and assorted other miscellaneous services that will be provided to you over the course of your vacation. That's a lot of services involving a lot of people. It's complex, and like any complex thing, it pays (and saves) to study up.

BOOKING THROUGH A TRAVEL AGENT

The majority of cruise passengers still book through agents. The cruise lines are happy with this system and have only small reservations staffs themselves (unlike airlines). In some cases, if you try to call a cruise line directly to book your own passage, the line will advise you to contact an agent in your area. The cruise line may even offer a choice of names from its list of preferred agencies, and you'll often find links to preferred agencies on cruise-line websites.

This is not a bad thing. In addition to collecting commission from the cruise line, a good travel agent can save you both time and money. Booking a cruise is far more complex than booking a stay at a Marriott or even a round-trip flight to Paris. There are, in cruise planning, a lot of moving parts and decisions that need to be made. You may be the rare type who doesn't need a travel agent, but most of us are better off working with one.

Good agents, whether home-based or in an office, can give you expert advice, save you time, and (best of all) will usually work for you for free or for a nominal fee—the bulk of their fees are paid by the cruise lines. (Many agents charge a consultation fee—say, $25 or $50—which is refunded if you eventually give them the booking.) In addition to advising you about the different ships, an agent can help you make decisions about the type of cabin you need, your dining-room seating choices, whether you want to extend your vacation with any pre- and post-cruise land offerings, and travel insurance—all of which can have a big impact on your cruise experience. We have seen complaints by people who booked a really cheap inside cabin and were angry that it was "a noisy cabin." Had they asked an experienced cruise agent, they might have been advised that the cabin was cheap because it was practically in the engine room—and that simply selecting a different stateroom in the same category would have dramatically improved their cruise experience.

Having a dedicated agent you can call or e-mail can also be a lifesaver if things go south. Think of the agent as the liaison to the cruise line. Knowing what you options are and having someone in-the-know acting fast on your behalf can prove incredibly useful.

Finding a Great Agent

If you don't know a good travel agent, ask your friends for recommendations, preferably those who have cruised before. For the most personal service, look for an agent in your area or one you can easily reach on the phone, and for the most knowledgeable service, look for an agent who has cruising experience. It's perfectly okay to ask an agent questions about his or her personal knowledge of the product, such as whether he or she has ever cruised in Alaska or is personally familiar with any of the ships or cruise lines you're considering. Of course, the easiest way to be sure that the agent is experienced in booking cruises is to work with an agent at a **cruise-only agency** (that's all they book) or to find an agent who is a **cruise specialist** within a full-service agency. If you are calling a full-service travel agency, ask for the **cruise desk.** A good and easy rule of thumb to maximize your chances of finding an agent who has cruise experience and won't rip you off is to book with an agency that's a member of the **Cruise Lines International Association** (**CLIA**) (www.cruising. org; ℂ **754/224-2200**), the main industry association. Members are cruise specialists; agents accredited as Certified Cruise Counselors by CLIA have particularly extensive training. Membership in the **American Society of Travel Agents** (**ASTA**) (www.asta.org; ℂ **800/275-2782**) ensures that the agency is monitored for ethical practices, although it does not designate cruise experience. Tap into the websites of these organizations to find reliable agents in your area.

WATCH OUT FOR scams

It can be difficult to know whether the travel agency you're dealing with to book your Alaska cruise is or isn't reliable, legitimate, or, for that matter, stable. The travel business tends to attract more than its share of scam operators trying to lure consumers with incredible come-ons. If you get a solicitation by phone, fax, mail, or e-mail that just doesn't sound right, or if you are uneasy about an agent you are dealing with, call your state consumer-protection agency or the local office of the Better Business Bureau. Or you can check with the cruise line to see whether they have heard of the agency in question. Be wary of working with any company, be it on the phone or Internet, that won't give you its street address. Protect yourself by heeding the following tips:

- **Get a referral.** A recommendation from a trusted friend or colleague is one of the best ways to hook up with a reputable agent.
- **Use the cruise lines' agent lists.** Many cruise-line websites include agency locator lists, naming agencies around the country with which they do business. These are by no means comprehensive lists of all good or bad agencies, but an agent's presence on these lists is usually a good sign of experience.
- **Beware of snap recommendations.** If an agent suggests a cruise line without first asking you a single question about your tastes, beware. Because agents work on commissions from the lines, some may try to shanghai you into cruising with a company that pays them the highest rates, even though that line may not be right for you.

- **Always use a credit card to pay for your cruise.** A credit card gives you more protection in the event the agency or cruise line fails you. (Trust us! It happens occasionally.) When your credit card statement arrives, make sure the payment was made to the cruise line, not the travel agency. If you find that payment was actually made to the agency, it's a big red flag that something's wrong. If you insist on paying by check, you'll be making it out to the agency, so it may be wise to ask if the agency has default protection. Many do.
- **Always follow the cruise line's payment schedule.** Never agree to a different schedule that the travel agency comes up with. The lines' terms are always clearly printed in their brochures and usually require an initial deposit, with the balance due no later than 45 to 75 days before departure, depending on the cruise line. If you're booking 2 months or less before departure, the full payment is often required at the time of booking. However, cruise lines have been making changes in this regard, so read the fine print carefully.
- **Keep on top of your booking.** If you ever fail to receive a document or ticket on the date it's been promised, inquire about it immediately. If you're told that your cruise reservation was canceled because of overbooking and that you must pay extra for a confirmed and rescheduled sailing, demand a full refund and/or contact your credit card company to stop payment.

An Important Question to Ask Your Agent

The big thing to remember when using a travel agent: Not all agents represent all cruise lines. To be experts on what they sell, and to maximize the commissions the lines pay them (they're often paid higher rates based on volume of sales), some agents limit the cruise lines they work with. They may, for instance, represent all Royal Caribbean brands or the nine brands of Carnival Corporation. If you have your sights set on a particular line or have narrowed down your preferences to a couple of lines, you should find an agent who handles those lines. Ask the agent upfront which cruise companies they work with.

Other Ways Agents Can Help

Travel agents are frequently in contact with the cruise lines and are continually alerted by the lines about the latest and best deals and special offers. The cruise lines tend to communicate such deals and offers to their top agents first, incentives like reduced deposits, complimentary stateroom-category upgrades or onboard credits that can be applied toward shipboard costs such as beverages, shore excursions, and spa treatments. Experienced agents know how to play the cruise lines' game and get you the best deals, even if they are in the category of the not-so-obvious. For example, many cruise lines run limited promotions that allow you to book a specific category without being assigned an actual stateroom number. This is called a "guarantee cabin," or GTY, and these offers tend to be some of the most economical out there. Typically, a few weeks before your sailing your stateroom will suddenly appear on your cruise documents. You are guaranteed at least the stateroom category you booked— or better. Playing the guarantee game can really pay off if you're lucky (in an extreme case you may go from an inside stateroom to a full-blown balcony stateroom). The downside is you have limited control of the location of your stateroom once it's assigned. Because an experienced agent is familiar with the program, he or she may be able to direct you to a category on a specific ship where your chances of an upgrade are better. The cruise lines sometimes even upgrade passengers as a favor to their top-producing agents or agencies.

Depending on the agency you choose, you may run across other incentives for booking through that agent. Some agencies buy big blocks of space on a ship in advance and offer it to their clients at a group price, available only through that agency. These are called group rates, although "group" in this instance strictly means "savings"; you won't have to hang out with the other people booking through the same agency.

One word of advice: Be wary of an agent promising to give you a cash rebate. It's against the rules of most cruise lines, and they clamp down on violators (again, the most legit follow the rules!).

When booking with an experienced travel agent, you won't have to worry about missing out. The cruise lines themselves post Internet specials on their websites, and the same deals are almost always also available through travel agents. The lines don't want to upset their travel-agent partners and generally try not to compete against them.

BOOKING A SMALL-SHIP CRUISE

The small-ship companies in Alaska—**UnCruise Adventures, Alaskan Dream Cruises, American Cruise Lines,** and **Lindblad Expeditions**—all provide niche-oriented cruise experiences, attracting passengers who have a very good idea of the kind of experience they want (usually educational or adventurous, and always casual and small-scale). In many cases, a large percentage of passengers on any given cruise will have sailed with the line before. Because of all this, and because the passenger capacity of these ships is so low (22–100 passengers), in general you don't find the kinds of deep discounts often offered by the large ships. For the most part, these lines rely on agents to handle their bookings, taking very few reservations directly. All the lines have a list of agents with whom they do considerable business; just call or e-mail the cruise line and ask for an agent near you.

CRUISING ON THE INTERNET

For those who know exactly what they want (we don't recommend online shopping for first-time cruisers) and don't need the personalized care a smaller travel agency provides, there are deals to be had on the Internet. Popular sites selling cruises include mega travel agencies like **Expedia.com** and **Orbitz.com** and big agencies that specialize exclusively in cruises (**icruise. com**, **Cruise.com**, **Cruise411.com**, **VacationsToGo.com**, **7blueseas.com**, and **CruiseExpertsTravel.com** in Canada). All have phone numbers you can call or chat forums where you can ask questions (it's a good idea to get the name of anyone you deal with so you can follow up, if necessary), and some such as Expedia also have brick-and-mortar retail locations. Also selling cruises on the Web are search engines (Kayak.com) and auction sites (Allcruise auction.com, Priceline.com).

The Internet also has some good sites that specialize in providing cruise information rather than selling cruises. Two popular cruise fan sites are **Cruisecritic.com** (now owned by TripAdvisor) and **Cruiseline.com**. You'll find the websites for the various cruise companies in our cruise-line reviews in chapters 5 and 6.

CRUISE COSTS

In chapters 5 and 6, we've included the brochure rates for every ship reviewed, but as noted above, these prices may actually be higher than any passenger will pay. Prices constantly fluctuate based on special deals the cruise lines may be running. Rates are heavily influenced by the volume of travelers interested in cruising Alaska. If the sales season (Sept–Jan are the key months) fails to achieve certain predetermined passenger volume goals, the lines may start slashing rates to goose the market. The prices we've noted are for the following three basic types of accommodations: inside cabins (without windows), outside cabins (with windows), and suites. Remember that cruise ships generally have several different categories of cabins within each of these three basic divisions, all priced differently. That's why we give a range. See "Choosing Your Cabin," below, for details on cabin types.

The price you pay for your cabin represents the bulk of your cruise vacation cost, but there are other costs to consider. Whether you're working with an agent or booking online, be sure that you really understand what's included in the fare you're being quoted. Are you getting a price that includes the cruise fare, port charges, taxes, fees, and insurance, or are you getting a cruise-only fare? Are airfare and airport transfers included, or do you have to book them separately (either as an add-on to the cruise fare or on your own)? One agent might break down the charges in a price quote, while another might bundle them all together. Make sure you're comparing apples with apples when making price comparisons. Read the fine print!

It's important when figuring out what your cruise will cost to remember what extras are **not included** in your cruise fare. The items discussed in the sections below are not included in most cruise prices and will add to the cost of your trip.

Shore Excursions

The priciest additions to your cruise fare, particularly in Alaska, will likely be shore excursions. Rates on cruise-line-planned tours range from about $50 to $119 for a sightseeing tour by bus (the higher-priced tours usually include visits to museums or other local attractions or a salmon bake lunch) to $229 and up (sometimes over $600) for a thrilling excursion involving a helicopter or seaplane. If you are traveling as a family or small group, private jeep, van, or boat excursions may actually save you money. Although shore excursions are designed to help cruise passengers make the most of their time at the ports the ship visits, they can add a hefty sum to your vacation costs, so be sure to factor these expenses into your budget. Of course, whether you take any excursions at all is a personal choice, but we suggest setting aside at least $800 per person for trips in port, which might just about cover a short flightseeing trip, a kayak or jeep safari, and a bus tour. You may be able to save by booking your tours either directly with the tour company or through a private company such as the Alaskan-owned **Alaska Shore Excursions** (http://alaska-shore excursions.com), or other operators such as **CruisingExcursions.com, Viator** (www.viator.com), or **ShoreTrips** (www.shoretrips.com), which may offer the same excursions as the cruise lines at reduced prices.

Tips

Be sure to add tips for the ship's crew to your budget calculations. Crew members are usually paid low base wages with the expectation that they'll make up the difference in gratuities. Exceptions in Alaska, as far as the big ships are concerned, are Crystal Cruises, Regent Seven Seas, and Silversea Cruises, as well as Viking (arriving in 2019), which include tips in the cruise fare (but you can still leave a few bucks for your favorite crew members if you want to). On Seabourn, tips are neither required or expected (but ditto if you want to).

Because some people find the whole tipping process confusing, the big ship lines automatically add tips to guests' shipboard accounts. Carnival, Holland America, Royal Caribbean, Norwegian Cruise Line, and Princess, for instance, all add a standard tip of $12 to $16 per passenger per day. You are free to adjust the amount up or down as you see fit, based on the service you've received. The tips cover the room steward, waiter, and busperson. In practice, we find many people tend to give a little more—maybe leaving some extra cash in the cabin for the cabin steward. Additional tips to other personnel, such as the headwaiter or maître d', are at your discretion. If you have a room with a butler, slip him or her $5 a day. Most lines automatically add 15% to bar bills, so you don't have to tip your bartender. There may be an automatic tip of 15% for spa services as well. If not, you can add a tip to the bill.

On small ships, tips are typically pooled among the crew: You hand over a lump sum in cash, and they divvy it up. Because tipping etiquette on small ships varies, we include information on tipping specifics for each small-ship line on p. 151 in chapter 6, and general guidelines in "Tips on Tipping," in chapter 4.

Booze & Soda

Most ships charge extra for alcoholic beverages (including wine at dinner) and soda. Nonbubbly soft drinks, such as lemonade and iced tea, and hot drinks such as coffee and tea, are included in your cruise fare. On Disney ships, soda from fountains and at meals is free, but if you want a can, you pay extra. A can of soda will cost about $2.50, beer $3.50 and up, a glass of wine or mixed drinks $6 and up (more for the newly popular mixologist cocktails). Bottled water is extra, too, from $2 per bottle (fill up your own reusable water bottle

---

Fancy Dining Choices for a Fee

As if multicourse dining-room meals and endless buffets were not enough, cruise lines have added premium restaurant venues where, in most cases, a fee is charged to cover especially attentive service and a menu featuring extra-special cuisine. These alternative restaurants tend to be small venues done up in fancy furnishings—just the kind of place you'd want for a date night or special celebration. In most cases, the spaces are reserved for adults only. Prices vary from line to line and restaurant to restaurant. For example, you can dine for $30 per person at Disney Cruise Line's impressive Northern Italian Palo. Carnival's steakhouses serve extravagant prime aged cuts for $35. Royal Caribbean charges $95 for a Chef's Table experience, where multiple courses are presented by the ship's executive chef and accompanied by specially paired wines. If you plan on hitting several of the specialty dining spots on your ship, check and see if it offers a savings package you can book in advance.

as an alternative). A bottle of wine with dinner will run anywhere from $15 to upward of $300. If you're a big soda drinker, you'll want to consider buying a soda package that offers unlimited refills. Prices vary by cruise line, but start at around $52 for adults ($35 for kids) for a weeklong cruise. You may be required to book the package in advance of your cruise, so check the information sent from the cruise line. Some cruise lines also offer bottled water packages or wine packages (you buy, say, five bottles for a discounted price). Celebrity Cruises, Carnival, Holland America Line, Norwegian Cruise Line, and Royal Caribbean also offer all-you-can-drink alcohol and wine packages. You'll have to do the math to figure out if you can drink enough to make it worth it.

Port Charges, Local Taxes & Fees

Every ship has to pay docking fees at each port. It also has to pay some local taxes per passenger in some places. Port charges, taxes, and other fees are sometimes included in your cruise fare, but not always, and these charges can add on average between $200 and $250 to the price of a 7-day Alaska cruise. Taxes and fees imposed by the State of Alaska and ports including Juneau and Ketchikan are usually melded into this figure and not paid by passengers separately. Make sure you know whether these fees are included in the cruise fare when comparing rates.

Fuel Surcharges

Cruise lines have instituted fuel surcharges in the past, and you'll see a note that they have a right to impose such fees in their customer contracts. Last time we saw them was in 2008, when fees ranged from $8 to $11 per passenger per day, less for a third or fourth person in the cabin. If reinstated, these surcharges are a significant addition to the cruise fare.

MONEY-SAVING STRATEGIES
Early-Bird & Last-Minute Discounts

As we said earlier, in our opinion the best way to save on an Alaska cruise is to **book in advance.** In a typical year, lines offer their lowest published fares to those who book their Alaska cruise by mid-February of the year of the cruise. If the cabins do not fill up by the cutoff date, the early-bird rate, sometimes referred to as an early booking discount, may be extended, but any discount may also be lowered—meaning fares rise. For the 2018 season, we saw fares 9 months in advance for June starting under $799 on Princess and Norwegian, and even some under $699 on Celebrity and Royal Caribbean. Offers made to past cruisers presented the best discounts. If the cabins are still not full as the cruise season begins, cruise lines will probably start marketing special deals, usually through their top-producing travel agents. As we mentioned, in 2017 there were a few sporadic last-minute fares early in the season from $400, but otherwise it was hard to find anything from less than $799, with some sailings completely sold out and others with very little space available. So in our minds, it pays to book in advance and ensure that you get the ship you want and the cabin you want. One thing you might want to keep an eye out for throughout the year are sales that offer value-added perks such as free drinks or free Internet.

Shoulder-Season Discounts

You can also save by booking a cruise in the shoulder months of **May** or **September,** when cruise pricing is usually lower than during the high-season summer months. Typically, Alaska cruises are divided into budget, low, economy, value, standard, and peak seasons, but since these overlap quite a bit from cruise line to cruise line, we can lump them into three basic periods:

1. **Budget/Low/Economy Season:** May and September
2. **Value/Standard Season:** Early June and late August
3. **Peak Season:** Late June, July, and early to mid-August

Third- & Fourth-Passenger Discounts

Most ships offer highly discounted rates for third and fourth passengers sharing a cabin with two full-fare passengers, even if those two have booked at a discounted rate. You can add the four rates together and then divide by four to get your per-person rate. This is a good option for families (or very good friends) on a budget, but remember that it will be a tight fit, since most cabins aren't all that big to begin with.

Group Discounts

One of the best ways to get a cruise deal is to book as a group, so you may want to gather family together for a reunion or convince your friends or colleagues they need a vacation, too. A "group" is usually defined by the cruise lines as **at least 16 people** in at least eight staterooms. But that's not a hard and fast rule – on Princess Cruises and Seabourn, for instance, a minimum group is 10 passengers in five staterooms. Not only do the savings include a discounted rate, but at least the cruise portion of the 16th (or 10th) ticket may be free. The gang can split the proceeds from the free berth or hold a drawing for the ticket, maybe at a cocktail party on the first night. If your group is large enough, you may even be able to get that cocktail party for free, and perhaps other onboard perks as well.

Some travel agencies buy big blocks of space on a ship in advance and offer it to their clients at a group price available only through that agency. These are called group rates, although, as we mention earlier in the chapter, "group" in this case means savings, not that you have to hang out with (or even know) the other people booking through the agency.

Senior Citizen & Military Discounts

Senior citizens might be able to get extra savings on their cruise. Some lines will take 5% off the top for those 55 and older on select sailings, and the senior rate applies even if the second person in the cabin is younger. Membership in groups such as AARP is not required, but such membership may bring additional savings. Discounts may also be available for active or retired military personnel, so let your travel agent know if you fit into this category.

Other Deals

If you like your Alaska cruise so much that you decide to take a vacation with the cruise line again, consider booking your next cruise on the spot. Cruise lines cannily recognize the value in having a captive audience to whom to pitch future vacation plans. Before you sign on the dotted line, though, make sure the on-the-spot discount can be combined with other offers you might uncover later. Keep in mind that if you do choose to book on board, you can still do the reconfirmation and ticketing through your travel agent by giving the cruise line his or her name.

In addition, lines tend to offer discounted rates when they are introducing a new ship or moving into a new market. So it pays to keep track of what's happening in the cruise industry—or have your agent do so—when looking for a deal.

Finally, check each cruise line's website for the latest savings plans.

AIRFARES & PRE-/POST-CRUISE HOTEL DEALS

Also see the information on cruisetours in chapter 9.

Air Add-Ons

Unless you live within driving distance of your port of embarkation, you'll probably be flying to Vancouver, Anchorage, Seattle, or one of the other ports to join your ship. Your cruise package is not likely to include air (unless you are on Oceania or Regent Seven Seas, which do include air, or snag a special air-inclusive promotion), so you will have to make air arrangements. You are free to book your air separately, but keep in mind the lowest discount fares may not apply—especially if your cruise departs on the peak travel days of Friday or Saturday. A better option may be to take advantage of the cruise lines' air add-ons. Why? First of all, as frequent customers of the airlines, cruise lines tend to get decent (if not the best) discounts on airfare, which they pass on to their customers. They also tend to book up the prime flights. Booking air with the cruise line also allows the line to keep track of you. If your plane is late, for instance, they may actually hold the ship, though not always. When you book air travel with your cruise line, most lines will include **transfers** from the airport to the ship, saving you the hassle of getting a cab. (If you do book your air travel on your own, you may still be able to get the transfers separately—ask your agent about this.) *Tip:* Be aware that once the air ticket is issued by the cruise line, you usually aren't allowed to make changes.

The only time it really pays to book your own air transportation is if you are using frequent-flier miles and can get your air travel for free, or if you are particular about which carrier you fly or which route you take. You are more or less at the mercy of the cruise line in terms of carrier and route if you take its air deals. Princess, for one, has a program that does let you choose the airline you want to fly, but most other lines may charge a "deviation" fee if you want to fly a specific airline or route. The deadline for these requests is usually 60 days before the sailing date or, if you book later, the day your cruise reservations are made. *Tip:* If you're determined to book your own air and your travel schedule is flexible, it's often easier to get the carrier and the flight time you prefer if you choose a cruise that leaves on a Wednesday or Thursday—or other times considered nonpeak by the airlines.

On the plus side, if airfare is part of the cruise package but you choose to book your air transportation, you will be refunded the air portion of the fare.

Pre- & Post-Cruise Hotel Deals

Even if you don't take a **cruisetour** (a land trip combined with your cruise), you may want to consider spending a day or two in your port of embarkation or debarkation either before or after your cruise. (See details on exploring the port cities in chapters 7 and 8.) An advantage to arriving a day or two early is that you don't have to worry if your flight is running late. (We know seasoned cruisers who have a personal policy of always flying into their embarkation port at least a day early, to be safe; they've never missed a ship!) Plus, Vancouver, Anchorage, and Seattle—the cities into which most passengers fly—happen to be great cities to explore.

Just as with airfare, you need to decide whether you want to buy your hotel stay from the cruise line or make arrangements on your own. The cruise lines negotiate **special deals with hotels** at port cities, so you will often get a bargain by booking through the cruise line.

When evaluating a cruise line's **hotel package,** make sure you review it carefully to see what's included. See whether the line provides a **transfer** from the airport to the hotel and from the hotel to the cruise ship (or vice versa); make sure that the line offers a hotel you will be happy with in terms of **type of property and location;** and inquire if any **escorted tours, car rental deals, or meals** are included. You'll also want to compare the price against booking on your own. (See chapters 7 and 8 for information on hotels in the various ports.) *Note:* Keep in mind that cruise lines usually list rates for hotels on a per-person basis, whereas hotels post their rates on a per-room basis.

CHOOSING YOUR CABIN

Modern cruise-ship cabins (or staterooms, as some lines insist on calling them) are nothing like the small, cramped cabins found even 20 years ago. While cabins typically vary in size according to price, most contemporary cruise ships have staterooms that hover around the 150- to 180-square-foot mark and increase in size from there. Suites, obviously, offer the most personal space, but also come with the highest price—after all, you are paying for such niceties as marble bathrooms, private dining areas, and even, in the fanciest suites, your own baby grand piano (plus butler service, private elevators, and other perks that vary by line). For most of us, though, dreaming aside, a standard stateroom will be our home away from home.

Most cabins on cruise ships today have queen-size beds that can be separated into two twins upon request (or in rare cases two twins that can't be combined) and a private bathroom with shower. Some cabins have only bunk beds, but again this is rare—where you do find it, it's a bargain way for a group of friends to travel together.

There is also such thing as special cabins designed for families (or those traveling with friends), with "regular" twin beds that can be pushed together to create a queen-size bed, plus fold-down bunks and/or a double or twin sofa bed. Some of these sleep five (larger suites may sleep six or more). Families or groups of friends may also be able to book connecting cabins (although they'll have to pay for two cabins to do so). Disney takes things one step further with segmented bathrooms, so one person can take a bath or shower while someone else does his or her business in private. Cabins for travelers with disabilities are ideally located near elevators and have accessible bathrooms and showers.

In the past, solo cruisers would have to contend with paying a massive single-supplement fare. But today select ships of lines (including Holland America Line and Norwegian Cruise Line) have dedicated staterooms designed and priced for the solo traveler.

Bed Lingo

On cruise ships, "lower berths" refer to standard twin beds, while "bunks" (or "upper berths") refer to beds that passengers pull out from the wall to sleep in.

The vast majority of cruise-ship staterooms have TVs (often flatscreen), and increasingly these units are interactive—you can use your TV to book meals and activities, check menus and daily activities, and in some cases even gamble. Some cruise lines offer an on-demand service that allows you to watch movies like you would in a hotel (typically for a fee). A handful of complimentary broadcast-TV channels are usually available, typically including at least one news channel (though it may not be the one you like!), along with channels that display a live view of a camera mounted on the ship's navigation bridge, and your ship's voyage tracker, which alternates between the current weather conditions, your ship's heading and speed, and any other relevant voyage information. There may be a channel as well showing reruns of show productions and other things happening around the ship, or featuring the cruise director talking and doing interviews in a talk-show-like format.

Some staterooms come further equipped with amenities like safes, minifridges, DVD players, bathrobes, and hair dryers. A bathtub is considered a luxury on ships and is usually found only in more expensive cabins and suites—although Holland America Line has a particularly generous supply of bathtub-equipped staterooms.

Cabin Types

What kind of cabin is right for you? Price will likely be a big factor here, but so should the vacation style you prefer. The typical ship has several types of cabins, which are illustrated by floor plans in the cruise line's brochure. The cabins are usually described by **price** (highest to lowest), **category** (suite, deluxe, superior, standard, economy, and other types), and **furniture configuration** ("sitting area with two lower beds"). The cabins will also be described as being **inside** or **outside.** Simply put, inside cabins do not have windows (or even portholes), and outside cabins do. However, views from some outside cabins may be obstructed—usually by a lifeboat—or look out onto a public area; an experienced travel agent should be able to advise you on which cabin to choose if full views and privacy are important.

On the big ships, deluxe outside cabins may also come with **verandas** (also known as **balconies**), giving you a private outdoor space to enjoy the sea breezes—a great thing to have in Alaska. You can throw on your bathrobe and view the glaciers and wildlife. But remember that the verandas vary in size, so if you're looking to do more than stand on your balcony, make sure the space is big enough to accommodate deck chairs, a table, or whatever else you require. Also keep in mind that these verandas are not completely isolated— your neighbors may be able to see you and vice versa. With few exceptions, veranda cabins will not have obstructed views. It's worth reiterating that most cruise lines have completely banned **smoking** on stateroom balconies, so if you're thinking of booking one for that purpose, forget about it (there are stiff financial penalties for breaking the rules!).

Noise can be a factor that may influence your cabin choice. If you take a cabin on a lower deck, you may hear engine noises; in the front of the ship, anchor noises; and in the back of the ship, thruster noises. A cabin near an elevator may bring door opening and closing sounds (though proximity makes it easier to get around the ship), and a cabin above or below the disco may pulse until all hours of the night. Cabins near children's facilities may not be the quietest places, at least during the day. You'll also want to stay away from cabins near service areas (the doors to crew quarters open and slam a hundred times a day, as people go on and off shift). The loudest areas of a ship vary depending on how well insulated the different areas are, so if noise is a problem for you, ask what the quietest part of the ship is when you book your cabin. Be aware that noise issues in general tend to be more of a problem on older ships, especially those where public venues are right next to ship accommodations. We would say that, generally, midship on a higher deck will be the quietest part of the ship (unless, of course, it's near a disco or right below the pool deck).

Cabins on upper decks can be affected by the motion of the sea. If you're abnormally susceptible to **seasickness,** keep this in mind. Ditto for cabins in the bow. Cabins in the stern can be affected by the motion of the sea and tend to be subject to engine vibration. Cabins midship are the least affected by the motion of the sea, especially if they're on a lower deck.

If you plan to spend a lot of quiet time in your cabin, you should probably consider booking the biggest room you can afford, and you should also consider taking a cabin with a picture window or, better still, a private veranda. If, conversely, you plan to be off on shore excursions or on deck checking out the glaciers and wildlife, and using your cabin only to change clothes and collapse in at the end of the day, you might be happy with a smaller (and cheaper) cabin. Usually, cabins on the higher decks are more expensive and much nicer, with plusher amenities and superior decor, even if they are the same size as cabins on lower decks. **Luxury suites** are usually on upper decks. The top suites on some ships are actually apartment size, with lots of space to stretch out. A quirky thing about cabin pricing is that the most stable cabins during rough seas are those in the middle and lower parts of the ship.

> ### Cabin Size by Square Foot
>
> The size of a cabin is described in terms of square feet. This number may not mean a lot unless you want to mark it out on your floor at home. But to give you an idea: 120 square feet and under is low end and cramped, 180 square feet is midrange (and the minimum for people with claustrophobia), and 250 square feet and up is suite size.

On the small ships, cabins can be truly tiny and spartan, though some give the big-ship cabins a run for their money. Generally, the difference lies in the orientation of the cruise line: Those promising a real adventure experience tend to feature somewhat utilitarian cabins.

Aboard both large and small ships, keep in mind that the most expensive and least expensive cabins tend to sell out fast. Inside cabins (without windows), for example, can be real money-savers. Also keep in mind that, just as with real estate, it's sometimes better to take a smaller cabin in a nicer ship than a bigger cabin in a less pleasant ship.

CHOOSING YOUR DINING OPTIONS

It probably doesn't come as a surprise that **small ships** offer fewer dining options (typically one open-seating dining room), while big ships have a plethora of culinary delights that can range from basic room service to multi-course meals prepared under the direction of a Michelin-starred chef.

What you might not know is that there is also a world of choice when it comes to choosing *when* and *how* you'd like to dine. On big ships, gone are the inflexible dining times, assigned tables, and rigid dress codes—unless that is what you want. Most big ships now offer you a choice of going with tradition or choosing flexibility, as afforded by open seating, where you dine when you like and with whomever you like, during the restaurant's opening hours.

Small ships are the exception here, but even they offer open seating that lets you sit where you want, with whomever you want, generally at a set time.

Mealtimes & Choices

Traditional dining on most big ships means choosing between one of two predetermined dinner times; early (typically 6pm) or late (usually 8:30pm). There are advantages and disadvantages to both times, and it basically comes down to personal choice. **Early seating** is usually less crowded and the preferred time for families and seniors. The dining experience can be a bit more rushed (the staff needs to make way for the next wave of guests), but the food may be fresher. You can see a show right after dinner and have first dibs on other nighttime venues as well.

Late seating, on the other hand, allows you time for a good long nap or late spa appointment before dining. Dinner is not rushed at all, and guests tend to linger at the table until well after 10pm. Main production shows in the theater are often run twice, so you'll have opportunities to see the show (sometimes before dinner and sometimes after), and there will still be plenty of nightlife to enjoy after dinner.

Most big ships also have some form of **flexible dining,** though each cruise line gives it a different name. Holland America Line calls it "As You Wish" dining. Princess Cruises dubs it "Anytime Dining." But whatever you call it, the basic system remains the same: You are invited to dine in one of the ship's main dining rooms in an open-seating environment. You can choose who, if anyone, you want to sit with, and simply show up at any time within the published opening hours. As at a land-based restaurant, though, you might find yourself in for a wait during peak dining times and given an electronic buzzer that lights up when your table is ready.

If the idea of having to make a choice bugs you, on Norwegian Cruise Line, Oceania, Regent, Seabourn, Silversea, Viking, and Windstar *all* meals are served open seating. You dine when you want (within the restaurants' open hours, of course) and with whom you want. The catch is, particularly with Norwegian, you are best off deciding in the morning where you want to have dinner and reserving a table; otherwise, the restaurant of your choice may be full by the time you decide to eat.

The vast majority of ships today also have **alternative dining options.** Most have the casual alternative (no dressing up required) of a buffet-style restaurant, usually located on the lido deck, with indoor and outdoor poolside seating and an extensive spread of both hot and cold food items at breakfast, lunch, and dinner. Some ships also have **reservations-only restaurants,** seating fewer than 100, where—except on some luxury ships—a small fee is charged, mainly to cover gratuities.

Table Size

Your dinner companions can make or break your cruise experience. Do you mind sitting with strangers? Are you looking to make new friends? Most ships have tables configured for two to eight people. For singles or couples who want to socialize, a table with eight seats generally provides enough variety that you don't get bored and also allows you to steer clear of any individual you want to avoid (tables are assigned, not seats). Couples may choose to sit on their own, of course, but singles may find it hard to secure a table for one. A family of four may ask for a table for four or request to sit with another family at a table for eight.

You'll need to state your table-size preference in advance, unless you're going with open seating (in which case you can decide nightly whether you want to sit with other guests or not). If you are assigned to a table and change your mind once you're on board, don't worry; you'll probably have no trouble moving around. Just tell the dining-room maître d', and he or she will review the seating charts for an opening.

Special Menu Requests

The cruise line should be informed at the time you make reservations about any special dietary requirements you have. Some lines provide kosher menus, and all have vegetarian, vegan, low-fat, low-salt, gluten-free, and sugar-free options.

DEPOSITS & CANCELLATION POLICIES

You'll be asked by your travel agent to make a **deposit,** either a fixed amount or some percentage of your total cruise cost. You'll then receive a receipt in the mail from the cruise line. You'll typically be asked to pay the remaining fare usually no later than 60 to 90 days before your departure date.

Cruise lines have varying policies regarding **cancellations,** and it's important to look at the fine print in the line's brochure to make sure you understand the policy. Most lines allow you to cancel for a full refund on your deposit and payment anytime up to 75 days before the sailing, after which you have to pay a penalty. When in doubt, always ask your travel agent, call the cruise line, or do a little independent research online.

TRAVEL INSURANCE

Given today's unpredictable geopolitical situation, economic woes, and extreme weather conditions, you just never know what might occur. A cruise could be canceled, for example, because of mechanical breakdowns (such as nonfunctioning air-conditioning or an engine fire), the cruise line going out of business, or an act of war. For all these reasons—worries about travel, worries about cruise lines canceling, sudden illness or other emergencies, missed flights that cause you to miss the ship, or even if you just change your mind—you may want to think about purchasing **travel insurance.**

If you're worried about medical problems occurring during your trip, travel insurance is vital. Except for small coastal cruisers, most cruise ships have an infirmary staffed by a doctor and a nurse or two, but in the event of a dire illness, the ship's medical staff can only do so much. Therefore, you may want a policy that covers emergency medical evacuation (having a helicopter pick up a sick person on board a ship costs a bundle without insurance). You may want to consider a separate policy for medical insurance while you're away from home (especially vital if you're covered primarily by Medicare, which won't cover you in international destinations—and most ships are flagged internationally, so they don't qualify for coverage). You may also want a supplemental medical policy if you have the type of medical insurance that covers you in-network only in your home state. Canadians will want to supplement their medical insurance with third-party insurance, unless their employer already offers supplemental medical insurance.

You might also want to invest in "Trip Cancellation and Interruption Insurance." This type of insurance typically reimburses you in some way when your trip is affected by unexpected events (such as flight cancellations, dockworkers' strikes, or the illness or death of a loved one), but not by "acts of God," such as hurricanes and earthquakes (the exception being if your home is made uninhabitable, putting you in no mood to continue with your cruise plans). The policy does not reimburse you if your travel agent didn't send in your payment and goes bankrupt, so using a travel agent you're very familiar with or one who's recommended is the safest precaution you can take. (And, of course, always pay with a credit card, never a check. If a corrupt travel agent cashes it or a decent one just goes out of business, you could get screwed.)

We recommend that you book insurance directly through an insurance company. We make this recommendation because usually you can get more coverage for less money if you buy directly rather than through a cruise line or your travel agent. Also, cruise-line policies may reimburse you in future cruise credits rather than cash (and do not cover any air or hotel unless purchased from the cruise line). Note that the same company, AON Affinity (Berkely Insurance Agency), administers most policies sold by cruise lines, no matter the brand.

The cost of travel insurance policies varies from about 4% to 10% of your trip cost. Cruise-line policies tend to be on the high side—and tend to bundle coverage for trip cancellation and delay, baggage protection (which may already be covered under your homeowners insurance), medical expenses (which may already be covered by your medical insurance), and evacuation. Some policies also come with accidental death and dismemberment insurance. All this may be more than you need. The good news is you are free to

Onboard Medical Care

Large ships usually have a fully equipped medical facility and staff (a doctor and a nurse or two) on board to handle any emergency. They work in a medical center that typically keeps set office hours but is also open on an emergency basis 24 hours a day. A fee (sometimes a steep one) is charged. The staff is equipped to do some surgery, but in cases of major medical emergencies, passengers may be airlifted off the ship by helicopter to the nearest hospital.

shop around. Reputable third-party insurers include **Allianz** (www.access america.com; ☏ **800/284-8300**), **Travel Guard International** (www.travel guard.com; ☏ **800/826-4919**), and **Travel Insured International** (www.travel insured.com; ☏ **800/243-3174**). Two useful websites, **Squaremouth** (www. squaremouth.com; ☏ **800/240-0369**) and **InsureMyTrip.com**, let you easily compare various third-party insurance options. For evacuation coverage in the event of a major medical emergency, **MedJet Assist** (www.medjetassist.com; ☏ **800/527-7478**) has both short-term and annual policies.

Also be aware that travel insurance does not cover changes in your itinerary, which are at the discretion of the cruise line.

[FastFACTS] ALASKA

Area Code Almost all of Alaska is in area code **907.** Only the tiny community of Hyder, about 90 miles northeast of Ketchikan, on the Alaska/British Columbia border, uses the same area code as nearby Stewart, BC: **250.**

Banks & ATMs There are banks and automated teller machines (ATMs) in all but the tiniest towns, and in some cases on your ship as well (a nominal fee is charged).

Business Hours In the larger cities, major **grocery stores** are open 24 hours a day and carry a wide range of products (even fishing gear) in addition to food. At a minimum, stores are open Monday to Friday 10am to 6pm and Saturday afternoons, but closed on Sunday. However, many are open for longer hours, including Sundays, especially in the summer tourist season. **Banks** may close an hour earlier and, if open on Saturday, only in the morning. Under state law, **bars** don't have to close until

5am, but many communities have earlier closing times (around 2am).

Cannabis Laws As of press time, it is illegal to consume marijuana in any public place in Alaska. That said, it is legal to sell cannabis in Alaska, and you'll find shops legally selling marijuana and edibles in port cities such as Juneau, Skagway, and Ketchikan. The products are strictly forbidden on ships, per federal law (see chapter 8).

Cellphone Coverage Most of the populated portion of the state has cellular coverage. In our experience, AT&T and T-Mobile (which uses AT&T cell towers) works better in Alaska than providers such as Sprint and Verizon. Still, you may hit patches where you can't get coverage.

Emergencies Generally, you can call ☏ **911** for medical, police, or fire emergencies. On remote highways, there sometimes are 911 coverage gaps, but dialing 0 will generally get an operator, who can connect you

to emergency services. Citizens-band channels 9 and 11 are monitored for emergencies on most highways, as are channels 14 and 19 in some areas.

Holidays Besides the normal national holidays, banks and state and local government offices close on two state holidays: Seward's Day (the last Mon in Mar) and Alaska Day (Oct 18, or the nearest Fri or Mon if it falls on a weekend).

Liquor Laws The minimum drinking age in Alaska is 21. Most restaurants sell beer and wine, and a minority have full bars that serve hard liquor as well. Packaged alcohol, beer, and wine are sold only in licensed stores, but these are common and are open long hours every day. Some rural communities have laws prohibiting the importation and possession of alcohol (known as being "dry") or only the sale but not possession of alcohol (known as being "damp"). Before bringing alcohol into a Native village, ask about the law—bootlegging is a serious crime (and serious bad manners).

Newspapers   The state's main newspaper is the *Anchorage Daily News* (www.adn.com); it's available everywhere, but it's harder to find in Southeast Alaska. Seattle newspapers and *USA Today* are often available, and in Anchorage you can get virtually any newspaper.

Taxes   As of press time there is no state sales tax (though one was proposed), but most local governments have a sales tax and a bed tax on accommodations.

Telephone   We have been assured that all major calling cards will work in Alaska, but this hasn't been the case in the past. To make sure, contact your long-distance company or buy a by-the-minute card.

Time Zone   Although the state naturally spans five time zones, in the 1980s Alaska's middle time zone was stretched so almost the entire state would lie all in one zone, known as Alaska Time. It's 1 hour earlier than the U.S. West Coast's Pacific Standard Time and 4 hours earlier than Eastern Standard Time. Crossing over the border from Alaska to Canada adds an hour and puts you at the same time as the West Coast. As with almost everywhere else in the United States, daylight saving time is in effect from 2am on the second Sunday in March (turn your clocks ahead 1 hour) until 2am on the first Sunday in November (turn clocks back again).

Water   Unpurified river or lake water may not be safe to drink. Handheld filters available from sporting goods stores for around $75 are the most practical way of dealing with the problem. Iodine kits and boiling also work.

THE CRUISE EXPERIENCE

Now that you've made most of the hard decisions—choosing and booking your cruise—the rest of your vacation planning should be relatively easy. From this point on, the cruise lines take over much of the work, particularly if you've booked a package that includes air travel. Carefully read the pre-trip information sent to you by your chosen cruise line—most lines' pre-trip packets include sections that address commonly asked questions.

4

Most of this information can also be found on each cruise line's website. In this chapter, we'll add our own two cents' worth on these matters and provide some practical hints that'll help you be prepared for all you'll find in the 49th state, both aboard your ship and in the ports of call.

PACKING FOR YOUR CRUISE

Preparing for the Weather

The sometimes extreme and always unpredictable Alaska weather will be a big factor in the success of your vacation. During your summertime cruise, you may experience temperature variations from the 40s to the 80s or even low 90s (single digits to low-30s Celsius), the cooler temperatures especially near icy glaciers. The days will be long, with the sun all but refusing to set, especially in the more northern ports, and people will be energized by the extra daylight hours. You'll likely encounter some rain, but there could also be weeks of sunny skies with no rain at all. You're less likely to encounter snow, but it is a remote possibility, especially in the spring.

Weather plays a factor in what you need to pack, with the must-haves on an Alaska cruise including a raincoat, an umbrella, and comfortable walking shoes that you don't mind getting wet or muddy (if you want to go Alaskan, buy a pair of waterproof Xtratufs, otherwise known as "the Alaskan sneaker"). A swimsuit is also a must if your ship has a pool (sometimes covered, sometimes heated) or hot tubs.

Having **layers of clothing** that you can peel off if the weather is hot and add if the weather is cold is the most convenient approach.

If you are bringing a bunch of electronic gadgets—cellphones, cameras that need recharging, an iPad, a laptop—consider packing a power strip. Most cabins usually have fewer than two electrical outlets. We also bring a portable charger for use if our cellphone runs low on shore excursions.

Essentials

What you choose to pack is obviously a personal choice, but here's a checklist of items that everyone should bring along:

- A waterproof jacket or raincoat (big enough to fit a sweater or fleece pullover underneath)
- Two sweaters or fleece pullovers, or substitute a warm vest or sweatshirt
- A warm hat and gloves, plus a baseball cap or other sun hat
- Two to four pairs of pants or jeans
- Two pairs of walking shoes (preferably waterproof)
- Sunscreen (SPF 15 or higher)
- Bug spray (Alaska has 55 different kinds of mosquitoes, although the Inside Passage ports in the south are not as affected as the areas farther north)
- Sunglasses
- Binoculars (some small ships stock them for free guest use, but on the bigger ships, it will cost you—if they even have pairs for rent)
- Your cellphone or a real camera, preferably with a telephoto or zoom lens, and a drypack to protect the camera (you may also want to bring a crappy second camera that you don't mind getting wet)
- Extra flash cards and batteries for your camera
- Formal wear (with accessories) if your ship has formal nights (not all do)
- Semiformal wear if your ship has informal nights (not all do)

Alaska's Climate, by Months & Regions

ANCHORAGE: SOUTHCENTRAL ALASKA

	MAY	JUNE	JULY	AUG	SEPT
Avg. high/low (°F)	56/40	63/48	65/52	64/50	55/42
Avg. high/low (°C)	13/4	17/9	18/11	18/10	13/6
Avg. hours of light	17	19	18	15	13
Avg. sunny days	11	10	9	9	9
Avg. rainy days	5	7	11	15	15
Avg. precipitation (in.)	.71	1.04	1.9	2.89	2.56

JUNEAU: SOUTHEAST ALASKA

	MAY	JUNE	JULY	AUG	SEPT
Avg. high/low (°F)	57/41	62/47	64/50	63/49	56/44
Avg. high/low (°C)	14/5	17/8	18/10	17/8	13/7
Avg. hours of light	17	18	17	15	12
Avg. sunny days	8	8	8	9	6
Avg. rainy days	17	15	17	17	20
Avg. precipitation (in.)	3.4	3.1	4.2	5.3	6.7

Packing for Formal, Informal & Casual Events

Some people agonize over what to pack for a cruise, but there's no reason to fret. Except for the addition of a formal night or two, a cruise vacation is really no different than any resort vacation. And in some cases, it's much more casual. Don't feel you have to go out and buy "cruise wear." Sweatshirts, jeans, and athletic wear are the norm during the day. Dinner is dress-up time on most ships, although nearly all offer more casual alternatives such as the buffet. And the small adventure-type ships are all casual, all the time.

Generally, ships describe proper dinner attire as formal, informal, or semiformal (the two latter terms mean the same thing in this case), smart casual or country club casual, or casual. There are usually either two formal nights and two informal (or semiformal) nights during a weeklong cruise or two formal nights and the rest smart casual or all smart casual/country club casual; check with your line for specifics. Although the term has gotten somewhat more relaxed in recent years, **formal** generally means a dark suit or jacket with tie for men (very few still wear a tuxedo) and a nice cocktail dress, long dress, or dressy pantsuit for women. **Informal** (or **semiformal**) is a jacket, tie, and dress slacks, or a light suit, for men, and a dress, skirt, and blouse, or pants outfit for women (the ubiquitous little black dress is appropriate here). **Smart casual** or **country club casual** is pretty much the same as informal without the tie. **Casual** at dinner means a sports shirt or open-collar dress shirt with slacks for men (some will also wear a jacket), and a casual dress, pants outfit, or skirt and blouse for women. In other words, for casual nights, dress as you would to go out to dinner at a midrange restaurant. In all cases, don't be surprised if some people ignore the dress code altogether.

> ### Cleaned & Pressed
>
> Many ships offer dry-cleaning and laundry services (for a fee, of course; look for deals where they will wash whatever you can squeeze into a laundry bag for a set price, usually around $29), and some offer either free or coin-operated laundry facilities (the latter requiring quarters or tokens that you can get at the reception desk). Using these services can save you a lot of packing. Check the line's brochures for details.

MONEY MATTERS

Few forms of travel are as easy as a cruise, at least as far as money is concerned. That's because you've already paid the lion's share of your all-inclusive vacation by the time you board the ship.

When you check in for a large-ship cruise, either at the terminal or online, the cruise line will ask for a major credit card to charge your onboard expenses (although most lines now allow you to also process this information in advance online). They will typically preauthorize your account (with your credit card company) for $50 to $70 per person per day, an amount refunded if you don't spend it. On all cruises, you also have the option of paying your account with cash, traveler's checks, or, in some cases, a personal check. Check the cruise line's brochure for specific rules on this. You may be asked to leave a deposit if you are paying with cash, usually $250 to $350 per person for a 1-week sailing. You should let the cruise line know as early as possible if you wish to pay with cash or checks (some lines like to know at the time you make your cruise reservations). One thing to keep in mind is that if you plan to put down a deposit in cash and you're departing out of Vancouver in Canada, you need to have enough U.S. dollars—the accepted currency of the ships in Alaska—with you before leaving home. The ATMs in Vancouver, as you might expect, dispense Canadian dollars, not U.S. dollars.

Whether you check in online (which the lines are encouraging to speed up the process) or at the terminal, the staff at the check-in counter will give you a special **ship charge card** (sometimes called a "signature card") that you use for the length of your cruise. From this point on, on most ships, your time aboard is virtually cashless, except for any gambling you do in the casino. On many ships, you can even put your crew tips on your credit card, though on some you're expected to use cash (more on tipping later in this chapter). The same electronic card, by the way, also will likely serve as your cabin key. In lieu of the card, the newest phenomenom is a wearable device (such as Princess Cruises' Ocean Medallion on select ships), which serves as your room key, charge mechanism, and more.

On most small ships, things aren't so formal. Because there are so few passengers, and because the only places to spend money aboard are at the bar and the small gift counters, the staff will just mark down your purchases and you'll settle your account at the end of the week.

In all cases, you will need some cash on hand for port stops: to pay for cabs, make small purchases, buy sodas and snacks, tip your tour guides, and so on. Having bills smaller than $20 is useful for these purposes (especially some $1 bills). At all the ports described in this book (even in most cases in the Canadian ones), U.S. dollars are accepted (businesses set their own exchange rate, and your change may be in Canadian dollars) as are major credit cards. Museums may require Canadian dollars, or not. If you prefer to deal in Canadian currency in Canada, most ports will have exchange counters, banks, and ATMs. Ships in Alaska do not typically offer currency-conversion services.

Some ships have their own ATMs aboard, most often located, not surprisingly, in the casino. These give out U.S. dollars (a fee will be involved).

It's recommended that you not leave large amounts of cash in your room. All ships have some sort of safes available, either in-room or at the purser's desk, and passengers are wise to use them. You should also store your plane ticket and passport or ID papers there.

Budgeting

Before your trip, you may want to make a tentative budget. It's a good idea to set aside money for **shore excursions** ($800 per person if you plan to do

THE COST OF COMMON CRUISE INCIDENTALS	US$
Alternative dining (service charge)	15.00–95.00
Babysitting (per hour)	
Group	6.00–8.00
Private	15.00–19.00
Beverages	
Beer (domestic/imported)	3.50–7.00
Latte	3.25–4.25
Mineral water	2.00–3.95
Mixed drink (more for fine liquors)	5.95–15.00
Soft drink	2.50–4.00
Wine with dinner (per bottle)	15.00–300.00
Cruise-line-logo souvenirs	3.00–60.00
E-mail (per minute)	0.40–0.75
Haircuts	
Men's	29.00–45.00
Women's	52.00–79.00
Laundry/Dry-cleaning	2.00–10.00 per item
Massage (50 minutes)	119.00–169.00
Phone calls (per minute)	4.95–12.00
Photos	9.95–24.00

several) and **tips** ($12–$16 per passenger per day). You might also want to budget in such extras as **bar drinks, dry cleaning, phone calls, massage and other spa services, salon services, babysitting, photos taken by the ship's photographer, wine at dinner, souvenirs,** and costs for any other special splurges your particular ship might offer (items at the caviar bars or cigar bars, time on the golf simulator, and so on). Above are some rough prices for the more common incidentals.

We suggest you keep careful track of your onboard expenses to avoid an unpleasant surprise at the end of your cruise. Fortunately, most of the big ship lines now make this easy, with access to your tab via your interactive TV or at computer terminals in the atrium (on smaller ships you can stop by the purser's desk and ask).

On big ships, a final bill will be slipped under your door on the last night of your cruise. If everything is okay and you're paying by credit card, you don't have to do anything but keep the copy. If there's a problem on the bill, or if you are paying by cash, traveler's check, or personal check, you will have to go down to the purser's or guest-relations desk and wait in what will likely be a very long line. On small ships, you usually settle up directly with the purser on the last full day of the cruise.

VERY IMPORTANT PAPERS

About 1 month (and no later than 1 week) before your cruise, you should receive in the mail, and/or downloadable as online files, your **cruise documents,** including airline tickets (if you purchased them from the cruise line), a boarding document with your cabin and dining choices on it, boarding forms to fill out, luggage tags, and your prearranged bus-transfer vouchers from the airport to the port (if applicable). Also included will likely be a description of shore excursions available for purchase either on board or, in some cases, in advance, as well as additional material detailing things you need to know before you sail. Most lines also now allow you to download this information online.

All this information is important. Read it carefully. Make sure that your cabin category and dining preference are as you requested, and also check your airline tickets to make sure everything checks out in terms of flights and arrival times. Make sure that there is enough time to arrive at the port no later than an hour before departure time, and preferably a lot earlier. Be sure to carry these documents in your carry-on rather than in your luggage, since you can't board without them.

Important Rule

A Department of Homeland Security regulation requires cruise ships to deliver a final passenger manifest at least an hour before sailing, and most lines are now requiring passengers to check in at least 1½ hours before sailing and to complete a check-in form online (with your name, address, and passport or other ID information) at least 3 days prior to sailing. If you do not complete the form, you may be required to show up at least 3 hours before your sailing so that the cruise line has time to prepare and transmit your information. If you don't comply, you may be denied boarding—with no refund.

Passports & Necessary Identification

Whereas a photo ID and birth certificate used to suffice, you are now required to have a valid **passport** for all Alaska cruises that begin or end in Canada. On cruises that begin and end in the same port in the U.S. (from Seattle or Juneau, for instance), a government-issued birth certificate and government-issued photo ID (such as a driver's license) will suffice—though cruise lines highly recommend a passport, because if for some reason you need to leave the cruise early at a Canadian port you may be in for a big hassle. If you are not a U.S. citizen but live in the United States, you will have to carry your alien registration card and passport. Foreign-born travelers who do not reside in the U.S. will be required to show a valid visa to enter the U.S. through Canada. For more information about passports and to find your regional passport office, consult the **Department of State website** (http://travel.state.gov) or call the **National Passport Information Center**'s automated service at ℰ **877/487-2778.**

Even if your cruise doesn't visit Canada, you'll still be required to show photo ID when boarding the ship; in this case, however, a driver's license is sufficient.

GETTING TO THE SHIP & CHECKING IN

Before you leave for the airport, attach to each of your bags one of the luggage tags sent by the cruise line. Make sure to correctly fill in the tags with your departure date, port, cabin number, and so forth. You can find all this info in your cruise documents. Put a luggage tag on your carry-on as well.

Airport Arrival

If you booked your air travel and/or transfers with the cruise line, you should see a **cruise-line representative** holding a card with the name of the line either when you get off the plane or at the baggage area. (If you're arriving on a flight from the United States to Vancouver, you will need to clear Customs and Immigration. Follow the appropriate signs. The cruise-line rep will be waiting to greet you *after* you've cleared.) Check in with this person. If you are on a precruise package, the details of what to do at the airport will be described in the cruise line's brochure.

When you arrive at your gateway airport, you will be asked by a cruise-line representative to identify your luggage, which will then go straight to the ship for delivery to your cabin. It won't necessarily go on the same bus as you, and it may not (almost certainly *will* not) be waiting for you when you board, but it'll arrive eventually, have no fear. Make certain that your bags have the cruise line's tags on them, properly filled out, before you leave the airport for the ship.

You'll have to turn over to the bus driver the **transportation voucher** received with your cruise documents, so do have it handy.

If you're flying independent of the cruise line, claim your luggage at the baggage area and proceed to the pier by cab, rental car, or whatever other transportation you have arranged. And again, remember to put the luggage tags provided by the cruise line on your bags at this point if you haven't already, because when you get to the pier, your bags will be taken from you by a porter for loading onto the ship. The porter who takes your bags may expect a tip of $1 per bag (some will be more aggressive than others in asking for it).

On the question of identifying your luggage, don't rely simply on appearances; one Samsonite looks just like another, even though yours may have a distinctive yellow ribbon on its handle. Check the ID tags as well! There's nothing worse than boarding a cruise that starts with 2 days at sea with somebody else's luggage and only the clothes on your back.

WHAT TO DO IF YOUR FLIGHT IS DELAYED

First of all, tell the airline personnel at the airport that you are a cruise passenger and that you're sailing that day. They may be able to put you on a different flight. Second, have the airline folks call the cruise line to advise them of your delay—your cruise documents should include an emergency

Where's My Luggage?!

Don't panic if your bags aren't in your cabin when you arrive: Getting all the bags on board is a rather slow process—on big ships, as many as 8,000 bags need to be loaded and distributed. If it's close to sailing time and you're concerned, call guest relations or the purser's office. If your luggage really is lost rather than just late, the cruise line's customer-relations folks will track it down and arrange for it to be delivered to the ship's first port of call.

number. Keep in mind that you may not be the only person delayed, and the line just may hold the ship until your arrival.

MISSED THE BOAT? HERE'S WHAT TO DO

Don't panic. Go directly to the cruise line's port agent at the pier (the name, phone number, and address of the port agent should be listed in your cruise documents). You may be able to get to your ship via a chartered boat or tug, assuming that the vessel isn't too far out at sea by that time. (Be aware that if you do follow in a small boat, you'll have to transfer from it to a moving ship at sea—not an exercise to be taken lightly!) Or you may be put up in a hotel for the night and flown or provided with other transportation to the next port the next day. If you booked your flight on your own, you will likely be charged for this service.

At the Pier

Most ships start embarkation in the early afternoon and depart between 4 and 6pm. You will not be able to board the ship before the scheduled embarkation time, usually about 3 or 4 hours before sailing, and even then it's likely that you'll have to wait in line; unless, that is, you're sailing on a small ship carrying very few passengers. If you've booked a suite, you may get priority boarding at a special desk. Special-needs passengers may also be processed separately. Ship personnel will check your boarding tickets and ID and collect any documents you've been sent to fill out in advance. You will then be given a boarding card and your cabin key. (On some lines, your key may be waiting in your cabin, and on select ships of Princess Cruises you may get a device you can wear or keep in your pocket in lieu of a key.)

You have up to 90 minutes before departure to board (see "Important Rule," above), but boarding earlier has its advantages, like getting first dibs on spa-treatment times. Plus, if you're early enough, you can eat lunch on the ship.

Protocol for establishing your **dining-room table assignment,** if one is required (you may instead have open seating), varies by ship. You may be given your assignment in advance of your sailing (shown on your tickets), you may be advised of your table number as you check in, or a card with your table number may be waiting for you in your cabin. If you do not receive an assignment by the time you get to your cabin, you will be directed to a maître d's desk, set up at a convenient spot on board. This is also the place to make any changes if your table assignment does not meet with your approval.

KEEPING IN TOUCH WITH THE OUTSIDE WORLD

Getting the News & Staying in Touch

Newshounds don't have to feel out of touch on a cruise ship. In addition to what you can find online, most big ships offer CNN or Fox News on in-room TVs, and nearly every ship—even small ships without TVs—will post the latest news from the wire services outside the purser's office (some lines, such as Seabourn and Silversea, also have a complimentary app that allows you to peruse newspapers and magazines from around the world electronically). You may even find excerpted news from leading newspapers delivered daily to your cabin (if you are British, you may also be able to get British news).

Most ships provide the opportunity to make satellite phone calls, but these can be exorbitantly expensive—usually anywhere from $4.95 to $12 per minute. You should be able to use your cellular phone in most of the more populated areas of Alaska (see "Fast Facts: Alaska" in chapter 3). Check with your cellular provider for details. Many ships have added service that allows you to use your cellphone at sea, although you will have to pay what can be expensive roaming rates—again, check with your provider for details (and smartphone users should be aware that even if you have calling capability, your e-mail service and Internet access may not work). On land and near shore you'll also want to monitor to make sure your phone does not pick up a Canada signal (as indicated by a roaming symbol) unless you are indeed in Canada, in which case you'll want to make sure you understand any fees from your cellular provider associated with coverage in Canada (if this happens and you are still in Alaska, call your provider and ask them to remove any roaming charges). If you don't have a cellphone, consider buying a prepaid phone card to use at a public phone on shore.

Another alternative is, of course, the Internet. While Internet access has been historically both frustratingly slow and shockingly expensive, there have been great improvements in recent years. If you don't book a package, you'll find that rates range from about 40¢ to 75¢ per minute. You'll save money with a plan—paying in advance for 4 hours of usage or even unlimited Wi-Fi access throughout your cruise (plans vary by line, so check with your ship's Internet cafe to see what plans are available; special discounts may be offered if you sign up on the first day of your cruise). Carnival, for example, has packages based on your usage habits: A week of connecting to social media for e-mail, Facebook, and Twitter will only run you $5 per day; or you can splurge on a Premium package and Skype and stream videos for $25 per day. Select Royal Caribbean ships have a rate of $15 per device, per day, for unlimited use. Some of the small ships and luxury lines provide free e-mail access, though on small ships it's not likely to be high speed. Cruise-line sale promotions may let you choose free Internet as a value-added perk (and if you're a member of a line's frequent cruiser program, you may also find some free Internet time among the perks). Most of the port cities you'll be visiting have coffee shops with Wi-Fi; ditto with some bars and most hotel lobbies. Local libraries in Alaska also offer free Internet access, and often have computer terminals you can use if you don't have your own device.

Sending Mail

If you want to send mail from the ship, the purser's office should have postage stamps and a mailbox.

VISITING THE PORTS OF CALL

Here's where the kind of ship you chose for your cruise, and the itinerary, comes into play. On a big ship, you will likely visit the popular ports of Skagway, Juneau, and Ketchikan (and possibly Sitka or Victoria, depending on your itinerary) and have several days at sea to enjoy the glorious glaciers, fjords, and wildlife, as well as participate in shipboard activities and relax. On a smaller ship, you may also visit several smaller ports of call and head into wilderness areas that cannot accommodate larger vessels—such as the tricky Wrangell Narrows, the winding, 22-mile channel you go through to get to Petersburg.

On **days in port,** you need a plan for what you want to see on land (more on that in this section). On **days at sea,** you will probably want to be out on deck much of the time looking for whales and listening to the commentary of glacier and wildlife experts. There will be plenty of shipboard activities offered, but these may be reduced at certain times—for instance, when the ship is scheduled to pass one of the famous glaciers.

Nearly every ship in Alaska has naturalists and other Alaska experts on board to share their expertise on glaciers, geography, plant life, and wildlife. Sometimes these experts are on for the entire cruise and give lectures complete with slides or films; other times they are National Park Service rangers who come on board at glacier sites (particularly in Glacier Bay) to provide commentary, usually over the ship's PA system. Depending on the ship, local fishermen, Native Alaskans, teachers, photographers, librarians, historians, and anthropologists may come aboard to teach about local history and culture.

Cruise lines carefully arrange their itineraries to visit places that have a little something for everyone, whether your interest is nature, museum hopping, bar hopping, or no hopping at all. You can take in the location's ambience and natural beauty, learn about the local culture and history, eat local foods, and enjoy sports activities. And you'll have the opportunity to shop to your heart's content.

Shore Excursions

When the ship gets into port, you'll have the choice of going on a shore excursion organized by the cruise line or going off on your own. The

---

Religion on the High Seas

Religious services depend, of course, on the ship and the clergy on board. Most ships have a nondenominational service on Sunday and a Friday-night Jewish Sabbath service, usually run by a passenger. On Jewish and Christian holidays, clergy are typically on board large ships to lead services, which are usually held in the library or conference room. If you are looking for a daily Catholic Mass, you may have to visit churches at the ports.

shore excursions are designed to help you make the most of your limited time at each port of call, to get you to the top natural or historical attractions, and to make sure you get back to the ship on time. But shore excursions are also a moneymaking area for the cruise line, and they can add a hefty sum to your vacation costs. Whether you choose to take one of these prearranged sightseeing trips is a matter of both personal preference and budgetary concerns; you should in no way feel that you must do an excursion in every port. Our picks of some of the best shore excursions in Southeast and Southcentral Alaska, as well as in Vancouver and Victoria, are included with all the port listings in chapters 7 and 8, along with advice on exploring on your own.

At most ports, the cruise lines have **guided tours** to the top sights, usually by bus. The most worthwhile tours take you outside the downtown area or include a meal, a dance or music performance, or a crafts demonstration (or sometimes all the above). Each bus has a guide, and the excursion price includes all incidental admission costs. The commentary is sometimes hokey, other times educational.

In most Alaska ports, it's easy to explore the downtown area on your own. There are advantages to independent exploration: Walking around is often the best way to see the sights, and you can plan your itinerary to steer clear of the crowds. In some ports, however, there's not much within walking distance of the docks, and it may difficult to find a cab or other transportation. In these cases, the cruise line's excursion program may be your best and most cost-effective option. For instance, a typical **historical tour** in Sitka will take in the Russian St. Michael's Cathedral in the downtown area plus two great sights a little way out of downtown: Sitka National Historic Park, with its totem poles and forest trails, and the Alaska Raptor Rehabilitation Center, where injured bald eagles and other birds of prey are nursed back to health. The tour may also include a Russian dance performance by the all-female New Archangel Dancers. Although you could visit the church on your own, it's a long walk to the park and another long walk to see the eagles—so with limited time in port you may find yourself having to choose among the attractions, or looking for a shuttle bus, or springing for a pricey cab fare, and still not seeing all the attractions included in the shore excursion.

There are plenty of active shore excursions in Alaska, such as **mountain-bike trips, fishing, snorkeling,** and **kayak voyages,** all of which get you close to nature and afford stunning views. These trips are generally worth taking. They usually involve small groups of passengers, and by booking your activity through the cruise line, you have the advantage of knowing that the vendors have been prescreened: Their prices may be higher than those offered by the outfitters that you'll find once you disembark at the port, but you can be assured that the outfitters the cruise lines work with are reputable (and they also assume responsibility for getting you back to the ship well before departure).

For those who enjoy trips in small planes or helicopters and are willing to pay for the experience (they are on the pricey side), **flightseeing trips,** offered as shore excursions at many of the ports of call, are a fascinating way to see the Alaskan landscape; again, the cruise lines work with specific vendors.

That said, in some cases you can lock in the exact same tour your cruise line is selling you (with the exact same outfitter) at a lower price by cutting out the middleman (the line) and going straight to the source (the outfitter). The trick is finding the same operator, which takes a fair amount of legwork online, and maybe some phone calls, too (or ask your travel agent to do the work). But it's doable, and can result in significant savings—if you're getting 20% off, for instance, it can add up quickly, particularly if you're booking a whole family on a pricey tour (for four people on a tour priced at $400 per person, you've saved $320). If you try the direct route, keep in mind that a fair number of the outfitters in Alaskan towns won't budge from quoting you the same price whether you book on the ship or off. It's no secret that cruise lines discourage their preferred outfitters from undercutting them by taking bookings directly from cruisers at lower prices, and the last thing an outfitter in Alaska wants is to be put on the naughty list of a cruise line that's one of its biggest customers. The outfitters that do offer you a discount often ask you not to mention it to anyone back at the cruise line—lest they find themselves in the hot seat.

As for tracking down the operators that cruise lines use, the secret is to examine in great detail the tour you're interested in on your cruise line's website, noting the wording of the description and even the photos you find there, and then comparing that to the descriptions and photos of tour options you'll find on the websites of Alaska's main port towns such as Juneau and Skagway (in many cases, you'll find an exact match). In some of the small towns, such as Skagway, it's fairly obvious once you do a little digging which particular outfitter does what for the cruise lines. Keep in mind that some of the port towns, such as Skagway, are so small that they might only have one operator offering such activities as climbing tours, biking, and the like, so no matter where you book, you're probably going to end up with the same folks.

There are also private companies that specialize in selling shore excursions at a discount. (See chapter 3 for details.)

Another savings option is getting a group together and doing a private shore excursion—the cruise line arranges a guide just for you and others you want to invite along. In Juneau, Princess Cruises, for instance, can arrange for you and up to 11 other guests to go out with a captain on a private boat to see whales, the 3½-hour outing priced from about $2,000 (for the group). It's the best of both worlds: You get to see what you want to see with an experienced guide, and you may actually save money compared to the price of individual excursions.

Regular shore excursions usually range in price from about $50 to $119 for a bus tour to $229 and up for flightseeing by floatplane and even more by helicopter (and $600 and up if you add in thrills such as dogsledding on a glacier). You may be in port long enough to book more than one option or take an excursion and still have several hours to explore the port on your own. You may well find that you want to do a prearranged shore excursion at one port and be on your own at the next.

The best way to decide which shore excursions you want to take is to do some research in advance of your trip. In addition to our descriptions in chapters 7 and 8, which detail the most common and popular excursions offered in the various ports, your cruise line has descriptions of shore excursions online and will probably send you a booklet or PDF with options for your specific sailing. Then compare and contrast. Because the most popular shore excursions tend to sell out fast, you are best off booking online before your trip. But if you wait until you are on board, you'll find a shore-excursion order form in your cabin, at the purser's desk or shore-excursion desk, or at the shore-excursion lecture offered the first day of your cruise. To make your reservations, check off the appropriate places on the shore-excursion order form, sign the form (include your cabin number), and drop it off as directed, probably at the ship's shore-excursion desk or at the purser's office. Your account will be automatically charged, and tickets will be sent to your cabin before your first scheduled tour. You may also be able to book excursions on your interactive TV, or through the cruise line's onboard app (if there is one). Tickets will include such information as where and when to meet for the tour. Carefully note the time: If you are not at the right place at the right time, the tour will likely leave without you.

Bottom line: The most popular excursions (such as flightseeing trips) sell out fast. For that reason, you're best off booking your shore excursions online before your cruise or at least by the first or second day of your cruise.

Arriving in Port

When the ship arrives in port, it will either dock at the pier or anchor slightly offshore. You may think that when the ship docks right at the pier, you can walk right off, but you can't. Before the gangway is open to disembarking passengers, lots of papers must be signed, and local authorities must give their clearance, a process that can take as long as 2 hours. Don't even bother going down to the gangplank until you hear an announcement saying the ship has been cleared.

If your ship anchors rather than docks (as may be the case in Sitka, for instance), you will go ashore in a small boat called a launch or tender, which ties up next to your ship and shuttles passengers back and forth all day. Getting on the tender may require a helping hand from crew members, and the waves may keep the tender swaying, sometimes requiring passengers to literally jump to board. (The tenders, by the way, are part of the ship's ample complement of lifeboats, lowered into the water, usually four at a time, for the day in port.)

Whether the ship is docked or anchored, you are in no way required to get off at every port of call. The ship's restaurants will remain open, and there will still be activities, though usually on a limited basis.

Tips for Your Port Visits
THE ESSENTIALS: DON'T LEAVE THE SHIP WITHOUT 'EM

You must bring your **ship boarding pass** (or shipboard ID or wearable device) with you when you disembark or you will have trouble getting back on board. (You probably have to show it as you leave the ship anyway, so forgetting it will be hard.) You may also be required to show a photo ID (such as your passport or driver's license). And don't forget to bring a little cash—although your ship operates on a cashless system, the ports do not. Many passengers get so used to carrying no cash or credit cards while aboard the ship that they forget them when going ashore.

WATCH THE CLOCK

If you're going off on your own, whether on foot or on one of the alternate tours or transportation options that we've listed, remember to be very careful about timing. You're generally required to be back at the dock at least a half-hour before the ship's scheduled departure. Passengers running late on one of the line's shore excursions needn't worry: If an excursion runs late, the ship accepts responsibility and won't leave without the late passengers.

If you're on your own, however, and miss the boat, immediately contact the cruise-line representative at the port. (Most lines list phone numbers and addresses for their port agent at each stop in the newsletter delivered to your cabin daily; be sure to take it ashore if you are going any distance from the ship!) You'll probably be able to catch your ship at the next port of call, but you'll have to pay your own way to get there.

TIPPING, PACKING & OTHER END-OF-CRUISE CONCERNS

A few tips that should save you time and aggravation at the end of your cruise:

Tips on Tipping

Tipping is a subject that some people find confusing. First, let's establish that you are expected on most ships to tip the crew at the end of the cruise—in particular, your cabin steward, server, and busperson—and *not* to tip is bad form. Big-ship lines have made the process easier, adopting a system whereby tips of $12 to $16 per passenger per day are automatically added to your shipboard account. You can visit guest services or the purser's desk and ask to increase or decrease the amount, depending on your opinion of the service you received. Other lines may suggest that you tip in cash, but most allow you to tip via your shipboard account. Bar bills usually automatically include the tip (usually 15%), but if the dining-room wine steward, for instance, has served you exceptionally well, you can slip him or her a few bucks, too.

If there is no automatic tip, the cruise line will give suggested tip amounts in the daily bulletin and in the cruise director's debarkation briefing, but these are just suggestions—you can tip more or less, at your own discretion. Keep in mind, though, that stewards, servers, and buspersons are often extremely underpaid and that their salaries are largely dependent on tips. Many of these crew members support families back home on their earnings.

We think the **minimum tip** you should consider is $4.50 per passenger per day for your room steward and your waiter, and $3 per passenger per day for your bus person/assistant server. That's a total of up to $84 per passenger for a 7-night cruise (you don't have to include debarkation day). Some lines recommend more, some a little less. You should tip more for good service. You'll also be encouraged to tip the dining room maître d', the headwaiter, and other better-salaried employees. Whether to tip these folks is your decision. If you have a cabin with butler service, tip the butler about $5 per person per day, provided he has been visible throughout your cruise (if he hasn't, reduce that amount). The captain and his officers should not be tipped—that would be like tipping your doctor.

Crystal, Regent Seven Seas Cruises, Viking, Seabourn, and Silversea Cruises include tips in the cruise fare (or otherwise don't require tips), although some people choose to tip key personnel anyway—it's really up to you. Small-ship lines have their own suggested tipping guidelines. (See chapter 6.)

If you have spa or beauty treatments, you can tip at the time of service (just add it to your ship account; be aware some ships add 15% automatically). Most ships now automatically add a gratuity to bar tabs, but if not, you can hand a bartender a buck if you like. Otherwise, tips are usually given on the last night of your cruise. On some ships (especially small ships), you may be asked to submit your tips in a single sum that the crew will divide among itself after the cruise, but generally, you reward people individually, usually in little preprinted envelopes that the ship distributes.

If a staff member is particularly great, a written letter to a superior is always good form and may earn that person an employee-of-the-month honor, and maybe even a bonus.

Settling Your Shipboard Account

On big ships, your shipboard account will close just before the end of your cruise, but before that time, you will receive a preliminary bill in your cabin. If you are using a credit card, just make sure the charges are correct. If there is a problem, you will have to go to the purser's office, where you will likely encounter long lines (so allow some time). If you're paying by cash or traveler's check, you'll be asked to settle your account during the day or night before you leave the ship. This will also require that you go to the purser's office. A final invoice will be delivered to your room before departure.

On small ships, the procedure will be simpler. Often you can just mosey over to the purser's desk on the last evening, check to see that the bill they give you looks right, and sign your name.

Luggage Procedures

With thousands of suitcases to deal with, big ships have established the routine of requiring guests to pack the night before they disembark if they don't want to carry their bags off the ship themselves. You will be asked to leave your bags (except your carry-on) in the hallway before you retire for the night—usually by midnight. The bags will be picked up overnight and placed in the cruise terminal before passengers are allowed to disembark. It's important to make sure that your bags are tagged with the luggage tags given you by the cruise line toward the end of your cruise. These are not the same tags you arrived with; rather, they're color-coded to indicate deck number and debarkation order—when you can get off the ship. Remember the color, because that's the way the bags will be arranged in the cruise terminal (head to the blue section to find your blue-tagged luggage, for example). If you need more tags, alert your cabin steward or the purser's staff. You also have the option of carrying your own bags off if they aren't too heavy for you to do so.

If you booked your air travel through the cruise line, you may be able to check your luggage for your flight at the cruise terminal (or even on board the ship for a small fee). Make sure you receive your luggage claim checks. You may even be able to get your flight boarding passes at the cruise terminal, saving you a wait in line at the airport. A bus will then take you to the airport.

If you're signed up for a **post-cruise tour,** special instructions will be given to you by the cruise line.

Debarkation

You won't be able to get off the ship until it is cleared by Customs and other authorities, a process that usually takes 90 minutes or more. So if a ship is scheduled to arrive in port at 7am, don't expect to just walk off at 7am. If you are flying home the day of disembarkation, make sure you give yourself plenty of time to get off the ship, through Customs, and to the airport. In general, we don't recommend booking flights before noon on disembarkation day; it's not worth the stress. In most cases, you'll be asked to vacate your cabin by 8am and wait in one of the ship's lounges (you can grab breakfast first). As we mentioned, everyone will get colored tags indicating their departure time (the same tags indicating where you will find your bags in the cruise terminal). If you have a flight home on the same day, you will disembark based on your flight departure time. Passengers with mobility problems and those who booked suites typically are disembarked first. If you have independent travel plans and are not heading to the airport, you may be asked to linger until those with flights disembark—though if you don't mind handling your own luggage you may find more flexibility on when you can leave. If you have booked a land package through the cruise line, transportation will be waiting to take you from the ship to your hotel.

Customs & Immigration

If your cruise begins or ends in Canada, you'll have to clear Canadian Customs and Immigration, which usually means simply that your name goes on a list that is reviewed by authorities. You must fill out a Customs declaration form, and you may be required to show your passport.

When disembarking in U.S. ports after starting out from Vancouver, non–U.S. citizens (including green-card holders) will be required to meet with U.S. Immigration authorities, usually in a lounge or theater, when the ship arrives at the port. Bring your passport receipt; all family members must attend.

The U.S. Customs & Border Protection Service has a preclearance program at the airport in Vancouver. This means you go through Customs before boarding your flight home (you don't have to do it when you arrive back in the U.S.).

THE CRUISE LINES: THE BIG SHIPS

H ere's where the rudder hits the road: It's time to choose the ship that will be your home away from home for the duration of your Alaska cruise.

As we said earlier, your biggest decision is whether you want to sail on a big ship or a small ship. So that you can more easily compare like with like, in this chapter we'll deal with the big and midsize ships; in chapter 6, we discuss the small ships.

For some years, the ships in Alaska have been getting bigger and bigger. In terms of total tonnage, **Princess** ships still lead. Indeed, five of the seven vessels the company is sending to Alaska in 2018 are more than 100,000 tons, putting them among the biggest cruise ships in the world. The largest, the 113,000-ton *Ruby Princess* and its sister ship *Emerald Princess,* are capable of carrying 3,080 passengers each, and the *Grand Princess*, *Golden Princess,* and *Star Princess* are not far behind.

There are other megaships: **Celebrity Cruises'** *Solstice* measures 122,000 tons and carries 2,850 passengers, while the line's two other ships in the region both are in excess of 90,000 tons. **Royal Caribbean** has two ships in the region: the 90,000-ton, 2,112-berth *Radiance of the Seas* and the 137,000-ton, 3,114-passenger *Explorer of the Seas*. In a bold move, **Norwegian Cruise Line** is sending its newest ship to Alaska in 2018: the 167,000-ton, 4,004-passenger *Norwegian Bliss*, as well as the 93,000-ton *Norwegian Pearl* and the 93,502-ton *Norwegian Jewel*.

And, as in past years, even Caribbean-focused **Carnival Cruise Lines** is positioning one ship in Alaska, the 88,500-ton, 2,124-passenger *Carnival Legend.*

For those looking for a slightly more intimate experience, midsize-ship-focused **Holland America Line** has seven vessels in Alaska this year. The largest of the lot—the *Westerdam, Noordam, Eurodam,* and *Niew Amsterdam*—are "only" a little in excess of 80,000 tons and carry fewer than 2,000 passengers apiece, while several other Holland America ships, such as the *Volendam,* are around 60,000 tons. (By today's standards, such ships are definitely midsize!)

Disney Cruise Line arrived in Alaska in 2011, and has returned every year since. The family-friendly operator's 83,000-ton,

1,754-passenger *Disney Wonder* once again will sail to Alaska in 2018, this time out of Vancouver, BC (the line has switched back and forth between Vancouver and Seattle as its Alaska base).

Another line that is returning for 2018 is **Oceania Cruises,** which offers a more upscale (and pricey) experience than the likes of Princess and Holland America. Consider it a step up from the mass-market lines, as is **Viking Ocean Cruises,** which is sending a ship to Alaska for the first time. Lovers of ultra-luxury, meanwhile, can choose between **Regent Seven Seas, Seabourn,** and **Crystal.** They're small compared to most of the vessels we mention here; however, they're a good bit bigger than the ships in the next chapter, and they have a full range of big-ship amenities, so we've kept them in with the big guys. Similarly, French cruise line **Ponant** is another newcomer to the region, and their ships are small, too, but offer lots of amenities and a chic style. Ponant's focus is on longer, expedition-style itineraries.

And at press time, Cunard announced that the venerable British line (known for afternoon tea, formal nights, and proper pubs), in bringing the 2,068-passenger *Queen Elizabeth* to Alaska in 2019. The ship, which launched in 2010 as the smallest vessel in the fleet, will sail four 10-night round-trip sailings out of Vancouver in May and June.

The beauty of some of the latter-day megaships is that they're designed so that you won't feel as if you're sharing your vacation with thousands of others. They offer lots of nooks and crannies in which to relax and hide far from the maddening crowd, so to speak.

The evolution of cruise ships is almost worth a chapter all by itself, but we'll address it here in shorter order. A few decades ago, major cruise lines operated ships that ranged from about 20,000 to 40,000 gross registered tons (GRT). These were considered "big" ships. The cabins had portholes or, at best, picture windows that didn't open. The ships had one dining room, with two seatings for lunch and dinner, and a snack bar/buffet as pretty much the only alternative. Many had large numbers of inside cabins, and all the cabins, inside and outside, tended to be rather basic (in some cases, downright spartan). Only the very best half-dozen or so suites on some had private balconies.

Things began changing in the 1980s, when ships began getting bigger—and debuting with not just a few but rows of balcony cabins. As the demand for cruises grew—stoked in part by the popular TV show *The Love Boat*—the lines also began looking for ways to make life at sea more enjoyable for their passengers, adding everything from larger showrooms with more sophisticated acts to more deck-top amenities. Advances in shipbuilding technology allowed them to move up from 45,000 tons to 70,000 tons and, by the middle of the 1990s, more than 100,000 tons, adding ever more onboard attractions (from miniature golf courses to climbing walls) along the way. But the growth of cruise ships wasn't over. Early last decade, lines such as Cunard and Royal Caribbean rolled out ships as big as 160,000 tons, and in 2009 Royal Caribbean upped the ante again with the unveiling of the 225,282-ton *Oasis of the Seas,* by far the biggest ship ever built—until Royal Caribbean just kept topping itself. In April 2018, the line will launch the 230,000-ton *Symphony of the Seas*, the new world title holder. (***Note:*** None of these biggest-of-the-big vessels—aimed primarily at the Caribbean market—sail in Alaska.)

All the new ships, but especially those built in this century, have more technologically advanced showrooms, million-dollar collections of original art, better-trained and higher-paid entertainment directors, flashy and extensive children's and teens' centers—and alternative dining facilities. Lots and lots of alternative dining facilities! Nowadays the roster of available food choices on cruise ships would do credit to the Manhattan telephone directory. Depending on your ship, you may have Italian, Tex-Mex, Cajun, Asian fusion, top-flight steakhouse, French, even good old British fish-and-chips to choose from. More and more cruise ships are also going to an "open seating" policy (come when you like, eat with whom you like). On some ships, it is even possible nowadays to eat dinner in a different restaurant every night of your cruise.

The ships featured in this chapter vary in size, age, and amenities, but they share the common thread of having scads of activities and entertainment. You will not be roughing it: On these ships, you'll find swimming pools, health clubs, spas, nightclubs, movie theaters, shops, casinos, multiple restaurants and bars, special kids' playrooms (in most cases, special club spaces for teens as well), sports decks, virtual golf, computer rooms, martini and cigar bars, as well as the aforementioned quiet spaces where you can get away from it all. Onboard activities generally include games, contests, classes, and lectures, plus a variety of entertainment options and show productions, some very sophisticated. There's usually a vast array of shore excursions (for which you will have to pay extra). Cabins vary in size and amenities but are generally roomy enough for the time you'll be cruising. And with all the public rooms and activities, you won't be spending much time in your cabin, anyway.

SOME COMPONENTS OF OUR CRUISE-LINE REVIEWS

People feel very strongly about ships. For centuries, mariners have imbued their vessels with human personalities, usually referring to an individual ship as "her." In fact, an old (really old) seafaring superstition holds that women should never be allowed aboard a ship because the ship, being a woman herself, will get jealous. It's a fact that people bond with the ships aboard which they sail. They find themselves in the gift shop loading up on T-shirts with the ship's name emblazoned on the front. They get to port and the first question they ask other cruisers they meet is "Which ship are you sailing on?" They engage in a (usually) friendly comparison, and both parties walk away knowing in their hearts that their ship is the best. We know people who have sailed the same ship a dozen times or more and feel as warmly about it as they do their summer cottage. That's why, when looking at the reviews, you'll want to look for a ship that says "you."

Each of our cruise-line review begins with a quick word about the line in general and a short summation of the kind of cruise experience you can expect to have aboard that line. The text that follows fleshes out the review, giving you a feel for the kind of vacation the cruise line will provide.

There is a saying in the industry that nobody should cruise just once. On any voyage, a ship could encounter bad weather. On any given day at sea, the only seat left in the show lounge might be behind an unforgiving pillar. Or a technical problem might affect the enjoyment of the onboard experience. In travel there is liable to be an occasional snafu. Your hotel room may not be available, even though you have a valid confirmation number. Your flight might be canceled. The luxury car you thought you rented might not be on the lot, and all that's available is a miniature subcompact. But you don't stop flying, you don't refuse to stay in a hotel ever again, and you don't stop renting cars. Nor should one unforeseen problem on a cruise ship cause you to swear off the product forever. Give it another go, on a different cruise line if you prefer. If you still haven't had the enjoyable experience that millions of others have discovered, then, and only then, is it perhaps time to abandon hope of becoming a cruise aficionado.

The individual ship reviews following the general cruise-line description then delve into the nitty-gritty, providing all the details on the ships' accommodations, facilities, amenities, comfort levels, and upkeep.

We've listed some of the ships' vital statistics to help you compare: ship size, year built and year most recently refurbished, and number of cabins and crew. Size is listed in tons. Note that these are not actual measures of weight but gross register tons (GRTs), a measure of the interior space used to produce revenue on a ship. One GRT equals 100 cubic feet of enclosed, revenue-generating space. Among the crew/officers statistics, an important one is the **passenger/ crew ratio,** which tells you, in theory, how many passengers each crew member is expected to serve and, thus, how much personal service you can expect.

Note: When several vessels are members of a class—built on the same design, with usually only minor variations in decor and attractions—we've grouped the ships together into one class review.

Stars
THE RATINGS

To make things easier on everyone, we've developed a simple ratings system that covers those things that vary from vessel to vessel—quality and size of the cabins and public spaces, comfort, cleanliness and maintenance, decor, number and quality of dining options, gyms/spas (and for the small adventure lines that don't have gyms and spas, a slightly different system; see p. 152), and children's facilities—plus a rating for the overall enjoyment of the onboard experience. We've given each ship an overall **star rating** (for example, ★★★) based on the combined total of our poor-to-outstanding ratings, translated into a 1-to-5 scale:

1	=	Poor	4	=	Excellent
2	=	Fair	5	=	Outstanding
3	=	Good			

In instances when the category doesn't apply to a particular ship (for example, none of the adventure ships have children's facilities), we've simply noted "not applicable" (N/A) and absented the category from the total combined score, as these unavailable amenities will be considered a deficiency only in certain circumstances (for instance, if you plan to travel with kids).

Now for a bit of philosophy: The cruise biz today offers a profusion of experiences so different that comparing all ships by the same set of criteria would be like comparing a Park Avenue apartment to an A-frame in Aspen. That's why, to rate the ships, we've used a sliding scale, rating ships on a curve that compares them only with others in their category. Once you've determined what kind of experience is right for you, you can look for the best ships in that category based on your particular needs.

Itineraries

Each cruise-line review includes a chart showing itineraries for each ship the line has assigned to Alaska for 2018. Often a ship sails on alternating itineraries—for instance, sailing southbound from Seward or Whittier to Vancouver, BC, one week and doing the same route in reverse the next. When this is the case, we've listed both and noted that they alternate. These one-way cruises are known as Gulf of Alaska cruises, as opposed to Inside Passage cruises, which generally are round-trip out of either Seattle or Vancouver, BC. (Some longer round-trip cruises depart from San Francisco.) All itineraries are subject to change. Consult the cruise-line websites or your travel agent for exact sailing dates.

The variety of cruise itineraries and of ports of embarkation (and debarkation, for that matter) also demonstrates the maturation of the cruise industry and growth in demand for the product. Not so long ago, just about the only thing you could do in Alaska cruising was a Vancouver-to-Vancouver Inside Passage loop; very few lines had one-way Gulf itineraries. It was simply easier for the ship operators to stick with the tried and true. People wanted it. Ships' crews got into a rhythm—arrive in Vancouver, BC, at 8am, discharge passengers, take on new ones, and start all over again. But demand began to outstrip the available berths. San Francisco became an attractive alternative, then Seattle. People who had done the Inside Passage round-trip began to demand a new experience—a cruise across the Gulf. Princess and Holland America, sister companies in the Carnival Corp. family that had invested heavily in a physical presence in Alaska (hotels/lodges, motorcoaches, railcars for land tour add-ons in the Denali Park corridor between Anchorage and Fairbanks), began to see that route as the way to go. Princess tweaked the itinerary further, using Whittier rather than Seward as the northern terminal of its Gulf cruises because it was closer to Anchorage. (Not much, but when you're on vacation, every minute counts!) Royal Caribbean Cruises also has invested heavily in Denali railcars and motorcoaches for its Royal Caribbean International and Celebrity brands. Those lines that do not have a strong investment in Alaska land components still tend to stick with the Vancouver, BC, or Seattle-originating round-trip.

For your convenience, we've listed the **cruisetours and add-ons** you can book with your cruise, and we've provided brochure prices for these as well where possible—though some lines make their plans (and set their prices) early, others do not. Therefore, at press time, some of the numbers were not available.

Prices: Don't Get Sticker Shock

We've listed the prices for cabins and suites. We stress that all the prices listed reflect the line's **brochure rates,** so depending on how early you book and any special deals the lines are offering, you may get a rate substantially below what we've listed. (Discounts can run as high as 60% or thereabouts.) Rates are per night for a 7-night cruise, per person, and are based on double occupancy. If the ship does not sail 7-night itineraries, we've noted that and given per diem rates for whatever itineraries it does sail.

Our rates are based on the basic types of accommodations:

o Inside cabin (without windows)
o Outside cabin (with windows)
o Suite

Remember that cruise ships generally have several different categories of cabins within each of these three basic divisions, all priced differently, which is why, on some ships, you'll see a rather broad range in each category.

Please keep something else in mind. As they say in the business, **"Buy as much cruise as you can afford."** If you go in with the attitude that you refuse to buy anything but the least-expensive inside cabin, you may be doing yourself a disservice. The idea that "Oh, I'm not going to spend any time in my cabin anyway, so what does it matter if it's inside or outside, big or small?" isn't really valid. You *will* spend time in your cabin, and sometimes having no exposure to the outside world can be awfully claustrophobic. You may find that for a few hundred dollars more, you can upgrade to an outside room. Or if you're planning to pay for an outside cabin, you may discover that you could reserve a room with a balcony if you dug just a little deeper into the purse. This is not to suggest you have to go deeply into debt to buy the best—just that you should investigate the possibility of buying something a little better.

CARNIVAL CRUISE LINES

Carnival Place, 3655 NW 87th Ave., Miami, FL 33178-2428. www.carnival.com. © **888/ CARNIVAL** (227-6482).

Pros

o **Entertainment.** Carnival's entertainment is among the industry's best, with each ship boasting a large cast of dancers and singers who perform lively production numbers in a big theater, along with jugglers and numerous live bands, as well as a big casino. Most recently, the line added the Punchliner Comedy Club, with comedians performing in a dedicated space. Unfortunately, Carnival Live, an onboard concert series that brings in big names to perform on the ships when they're in port, is not offered on Alaska sailings.

- **Children's program.** Carnival has long had one of the best children's programs in the industry, and it keeps getting better. Four years ago, the line joined up with Dr. Seuss Enterprises to expand its kiddie offerings with Seuss-themed activities fleetwide. Carnival's Alaska cruises, moreover, include Alaska-specific activities thrown into the mix, including a special series of shore excursions designed for teens.

Cons

- **Service.** The international crew doesn't provide the type of service typically found on higher-end brands, but that's not the point here, is it?
- **Crowds.** This is a big ship with lots of people on board, and you are occasionally aware of that fact, like when you have to wait in line to get off at a port.

THE LINE IN A NUTSHELL Almost the definition of mass market, Carnival is the Big Kahuna of the industry, boasting a modern fleet of flashy megaships that cater to a fun-loving crowd. Nonstop entertainment (if you have the energy after a busy day of cruising) is the name of the game on board.

THE EXPERIENCE Carnival ships are known for spectacularly glitzy decor that some people love and others find overwhelming (and that's putting it nicely). Translating the line's warm-weather, fun-in-the-sun experience to Alaska has meant combining the "24 hours of good times" philosophy with opportunities to experience the natural wonders of the state, so you may find yourself bellying up to the rail with a multicolored umbrella drink to gawk at a glacier. The casino is nearly always hopping, although the festive atmosphere is a little more subdued in Alaska than on the line's Caribbean sailings. This, of course, is either a plus or a minus, depending on your taste. Carnival does not pretend to be a luxury experience. It doesn't claim to have gourmet food (although it's routinely praised for serving some of the best meals of any mass-market ship), and it doesn't promise around-the-clock pampering. The motto is "fun," and with a big focus on entertainment, friendly service, and creative cruise directors (who can be corny sometimes, but at least they're lively), that's what Carnival delivers.

THE FLEET With 25 ships, Carnival has the biggest cruise fleet in the world, but only one, the 2,124-passenger *Carnival Legend,* sails in Alaska. It has plenty of activities, great pool and hot-tub spaces (some covered for use in chillier weather), a big oceanview gym and spa, and more dining options than your doctor would say are advisable.

PASSENGER PROFILE Overall, Carnival has some of the youngest demographics in the industry. But it's far more than age that defines the line's customers. Carnival executives are fond of using the word "spirited" to describe the typical Carnival passenger, and indeed, it's right on target. The line's many fans increasingly come from a wide range of ages as well as

Carnival Fleet Itineraries

SHIP	ITINERARIES
Carnival Legend	7-night Inside Passage: Round-trip from Seattle, visiting Skagway, Juneau, Ketchikan, and Victoria, and cruising Tracy Arm Fjord (May–Sept)

occupations, backgrounds, and income levels, but what they share is an unpretentious, fun-loving, and outgoing demeanor. This is a line for people who don't mind at all that their dinner will be interrupted by the loud music and flashing lights of a dance show starring their waiters. If anything, the typical Carnival passenger will want to jump right into the fray. On Carnival, you'll find couples, a few singles, and a good share of families (in fact, the line carries more than 700,000 kids a year—the most in the cruise industry). But the bottom line is this is not your average sedentary, bird-watching crowd. Passengers want to see whales, but they also want to dance the Macarena.

DINING OPTIONS Food is bountiful, and the cuisine is traditional American: Red meat is popular on these ships. In addition, delicious preparations of more "nouvelle" dishes include broiled Chilean sea bass with truffle butter or smoked turkey tenderloin with asparagus tips. Alaska sailings include fresh salmon. For those seeking healthier options, there's a gourmet Spa Carnival Fare menu, and pasta and vegetarian choices are also served nightly.

Until recently, meals were always served at assigned tables, with two seatings per meal. But the line has rolled out an alternative, eat-when-you-want dining option called Your Time Dining. Passengers must sign up for Your Time Dining in advance, in lieu of fixed seatings.

The casual lunch buffets include international (Italian, Indian, and so on, with a different cuisine featured daily), deli, rotisserie, and pizza stations; the breakfast buffet has everything from made-to-order eggs to cold cereals and pastries. Many passengers prefer to eat their meals in the buffet rather than in the main dining room. The *Carnival Legend* also adds the special treat of a truly superb reservations-only steakhouse, where, for a fee of $35 per person, you can dine on a great steak and other upscale culinary choices.

ACTIVITIES If Atlantic City and Las Vegas appeal to you, Carnival will, too. What you'll get is fun—lots of it, professionally and consistently delivered and spangled with glitter. Cocktails inevitably begin to flow before lunch. You can learn to country line dance or play bridge, take cooking lessons, and watch first-run movies. Among the offerings on Alaska sailings is a photo safari in Juneau led by a professional photographer; newly launched in 2017 are ice-carving demonstrations, an Alaska-themed photo booth, and Alaska-themed trivia games. In addition, onboard art classes allow guests to create pictures of whales or the Northern Lights to commemorate their trip. Plus, there are always the onboard staple activities of eating, drinking, and shopping, and Alaska-specific naturalist lectures are delivered daily. Once in port, Carnival lives up to its "more is more" ethos by providing more than 120 shore excursions in Alaska, divided into categories of easy, moderate, and adventure. Internet cafes as well as Wi-Fi are available (75¢ a minute, with a 10-minute minimum; fees start at $5 per day for the social media package).

CHILDREN'S PROGRAMS   For children ages 2 to 11, Camp Ocean features some 200 marine-themed activities as well as a host of other kid-pleasing fun, allowing Mom and Dad some downtime. In Alaska, these activities include everything from Native American arts-and-crafts sessions to lectures conducted by wildlife experts. On the *Carnival Legend,* parents of little kids can request beepers so they can keep in touch. Carnival also offers Circle "C," programs for 12- to 14-year-olds, and Club O2 for teens ages 15 to 17, each with dedicated facilities and separate staffs.

ENTERTAINMENT   Carnival consistently has the most lavish entertainment extravaganzas afloat, spending millions on stage sets, choreography, and acoustical equipment that leave many other floating theaters in their wake. The *Carnival Legend* has a cast of flamboyantly costumed dancers and singers, plus magicians, jugglers, and acrobats. Carnival also has stage shows called Playlist Productions featuring interactive high-tech LED screens and shorter, more frequent performances. Passengers can even join a lip-synching competition on board, in collaboration with Spike TV's *Lip Sync Battle* show, as well as game shows in collaboration with Hasbro.

SERVICE   As we said before, Carnival service isn't exactly "refined" in the way you'd find on a luxury line, but it is certainly friendly and professional. A Carnival ship is a well-oiled machine, and you'll get what you need—but not much more. When you board the ship, for instance, you're welcomed by polite staff at the gangway, given a diagram of the ship's layout, and then pointed in the right direction to find your cabin on your own, carry-on luggage in tow. On Carnival, gratuities of $12.95 per passenger per day are automatically charged to your shipboard account, but you can increase or decrease the amount by visiting the guest services desk on board.

An onboard laundry service (for washing and pressing only) charges by the piece; it also has a handful of self-service laundry rooms with irons and coin-operated washing machines and dryers. Dry cleaning is not available.

CRUISETOURS & ADD-ON PROGRAMS   None.

Carnival Legend

The Verdict

The *Carnival Legend* is glitzy Vegas, with more bars and lounges than you'll be able to visit. The dining room is two decks high, and it offers such cool extras as a reservations-only steakhouse and a wedding chapel.

Specifications

Size (in Tons)	88,500	Crew	930
Passengers (Double Occ.)	2,124	Passenger/Crew Ratio	2.3 to 1
Space/Passenger Ratio	41.7	Year Launched	2004
Total Cabins/Veranda Cabins	1,062/682	Last Major Refurbishment	2014

Frommer's Ratings (Scale of 1–5) ★★★★

Cabin Comfort & Amenities	4	Dining Options	4
Ship Cleanliness & Maintenance	4	Gym, Spa & Sports Facilities	4.5
Public Comfort/Space	4	Children's Facilities	5
Decor	4	Enjoyment Factor	4

THE SHIP IN GENERAL The *Carnival Legend* is big and impressive, even if some find the interior a bit over-the-top (it may actually grow on you after a few days on board). Rooms are themed around "great legends of the world," from Medusa and the Colossus of Rhodes to Sherlock Holmes and unicorns, with all sorts of (sometimes clashing) materials, from ebony paneling to faux stone walls, and lots of flash. In other words, legendary Carnival designer Joe Farcus has shown little restraint. Love it or not, you'll certainly be wowed.

CABINS Some 80% of the cabins on this ship boast ocean views; of those, 80% have private balconies, a big plus in a market like Alaska where views are the main draw. Cabins are larger than those you'll find on other lines in the same price category and are mostly furnished with twin beds that can be converted to king. (A few have upper and lower berths that cannot be converted.) All cabins come with a TV, a wall safe, and a telephone; oceanview cabins also come with bathrobes and coral-colored leather couches with nifty storage drawers underneath. Connecting cabins are available for families or groups traveling together. Suites are offered at several different levels, each with separate sleeping, sitting, and dressing areas, plus double sinks, a bathtub, and a large balcony. Sixteen cabins are wheelchair-accessible. Carnival features the Carnival Comfort Bed sleep system with plush mattresses and fluffy duvets (no more scratchy wool blankets for this line).

CABINS & RATES

CABINS	PER DIEM RATES	SQ. FT.	FRIDGE	HAIR DRYER	SITTING AREA	TV
Inside Passage						
Inside	$117–$147	185	yes	yes	no	yes
Outside	$145–$178	220–260*	yes	yes	yes	yes
Suites	$307–$340	340–430*	yes	yes	yes	yes
Gulf of Alaska						
Inside	$117–$147	185	yes	yes	no	yes
Outside	$145–$178	220–260*	yes	yes	yes	yes
Suites	$307–$340	340–430*	yes	yes	yes	yes

Includes veranda

PUBLIC AREAS The ship's soaring atrium spans 11 decks. There are dozens of bars and lounges, including a piano bar, a sports bar, and a jazz club. A lobby bar provides live music and a chance to take in the vast dimensions of the ship. A particularly fun room is the two-level disco; depending on your particular Alaska sailing, it may be hopping until dawn or simply hosting a few stragglers late at night. A better hangout spot, we think, is the **RedFrog**

Pub, a Caribbean-inspired watering hole featuring Carnival's own private label draught beer, ThirstyFrog Red, and live musicians nightly.

The ship, which is part of the line's Spirit class, consciously offers the best features of the line's earlier Fantasy-class ships, including an expansive outdoor area with four swimming pools (a retractable dome over the main pool lets you take a dip no matter what the weather), four whirlpools, and a waterslide; a high-tech children's play center with computers and a wall of video monitors; a multilevel oceanview fitness facility; numerous clubs and lounges; and a variety of eating and entertainment options. Among the interesting features is a wedding chapel, as well as a mostly outdoor promenade (if you are doing a full tour around the ship, you have to take a few steps inside). The ship also has ultramodern engines and waste treatment and disposal systems to make it more environmentally friendly. And the *Carnival Legend* offers more space per passenger than most ships in the Alaska market.

The hundreds of onboard activities for which Carnival is famous, including Vegas-style shows and casino action (the ship's **Club Merlin** casino, named after the legendary wizard, is one of the largest at sea), keep passengers on the *Carnival Legend* on the fast track to that famous and oft-mentioned fun. It's up to you to find time to stop and catch the scenery, which you can do both from the generously sized open-deck spaces and from some (but not many) indoor spaces. For kids, there's a children's playroom, children's pool, and video arcade. The *Carnival Legend's* library doubles as an Internet cafe, though the clicking of computers may be annoying to those who want to read a book. Shoppers will find plenty of enticements at the ship's shopping arcade.

Carnival passengers also have the capability of using their personal cellphones anywhere at sea.

DINING OPTIONS The ship's handsome atrium is topped with a red stained-glass dome that is part of the **Golden Fleece** steakhouse, a reservations-only ($35 per person supplement) restaurant. Some people might consider the dinner-only spot a little pricey, but this is not your run-of-the mill restaurant filling tables with two or three changes of customers in the evening. Rather, it's an intimate room in which passengers are encouraged to linger and savor a truly elegant and enjoyable experience. The two-level main dining room is lined with glass cases containing displays of fine china. A 24-hour poolside pizzeria and 24-hour room service keep you from getting hungry.

POOL, FITNESS, SPA & SPORTS FACILITIES The ship has three pools, including one with a retractable dome, as well as a children's splash pool. A freestanding waterslide is on the top deck. For adults, the outdoor **Serenity Lounge** is a welcome escape from both the crowds and the kids. Best of all, there's no fee to hide away on one of the comfy upgraded lounge chairs there. The gym has an interesting tiered design and more than 50 exercise machines, as well as a spacious aerobics studio. Windows keep you from missing the Alaska scenery. The spa has a dozen treatment rooms and an indoor sunning area with a whirlpool. The ship also has three additional whirlpools and a jogging/walking track (10 laps = 1 mile).

CELEBRITY CRUISES

1050 Caribbean Way, Miami, FL 33132. www.celebritycruises.com. ☏ **800/647-2251** or 305/262-8322.

Pros

- **Spectacular spas and gyms.** Beautiful to look at and well stocked, the spas and gyms on *Celebrity Solstice, Celebrity Infinity,* and *Celebrity Millennium* (and Celebrity's other non-Alaska megaships) are among the best at sea today and set the standard followed by other lines.
- **Fabulous food.** Celebrity cuisine is rated high among mainstream cruise lines.
- **Innovative everything.** Celebrity's entertainment, art, service, spas, and cuisine are some of the most groundbreaking in the industry. Its ships were among the first in the industry to display major art collections on board, and its menus have long recognized the need for vegetarian, low-sodium, heart-conscious, and other healthy dishes.

Cons

- **Occasional crowding.** Pack a couple thousand people onto a ship (pretty much any ship), and you'll get crowds at times, such as during buffets and when disembarking.
- **So-so kids' programs.** While Celebrity ships offer a full day of activities for children, kids' facilities and programs are less elaborate and enticing than those found on more family-focused mainstream lines such as Carnival, Princess, and Disney.

THE LINE IN A NUTSHELL With a premium fleet that's among the best designed in the cruise industry, Celebrity offers a great experience: classy, tasteful, and luxurious. You'll be pampered at a relatively reasonable price.

THE EXPERIENCE Each of the Celebrity ships is spacious and comfortable, mixing modern and Art Deco styles and boasting an astoundingly cutting-edge art collection. The line's genteel service is noticeable: Staff members in our experience are polite and professional and contribute greatly to the cruise experience. Dining-wise, Celebrity shines, offering innovative cuisine that's a cut above the fare served by some of the other mainstream lines.

Celebrity gets the "best of" nod in a lot of categories: The Canyon Ranch Spa on the line's megaships is tops for mainstream lines, the art collections fleetwide are the most compelling, and the onboard activities are among the most varied. Like all the big-ship lines, Celebrity has lots for its guests to do, but it focuses on mellower pursuits and innovative programming.

It's interesting to note that Celebrity (and its sister company, Royal Caribbean International) was an early champion of the new Alaska port of Icy Strait Point. The port is growing—it was created from a cannery dock—and lies between Juneau and Glacier Bay, with a prime vantage point for whale- and wildlife-watching and easier access to the Alaskan wilderness.

THE FLEET   Celebrity's current Alaska fleet comprises one of the line's most celebrated ships, the *Celebrity Solstice* (122,000 tons, 2,850 passengers), launched in 2008, and the somewhat older *Celebrity Millennium* (91,000 tons, 2,138 passengers) and sister ship *Celebrity Infinity* (91,000 tons, 2,170 passengers). All three ships have a high degree of decorative panache and just the right combination of elegance, artfulness, excitement, and fun.

PASSENGER PROFILE   The typical Celebrity guest is one who prefers to pursue his or her R&R at a relatively relaxed pace, with a minimum of aggressively promoted group activities. The overall atmosphere leans more toward sophistication and less to the kind of orgiastic Technicolor whoopee that you'll find aboard, say, a Carnival ship. Celebrity passengers are the type who prefer wine with dinner and maybe a tad more decorum than on some other ships, but they can kick up their heels with the beer-and-pretzels crowd just fine if the occasion warrants. Most give the impression of being prosperous but not obscenely rich, congenial but not obsessively proper, animated and fun but not the type to wear a lampshade for a hat. You'll find everyone from kids to retirees, with a good number of couples in their 40s.

DINING OPTIONS   Celebrity's cuisine, plentiful and served with style, is extra special and leans toward American/European. This means that dishes are generally not low-fat, although the line has eliminated trans fats and in 2013 brought in healthy-eating organization SPE Certified to consult on and certify dozens of dishes in Celebrity's main restaurants. Also, guests in AquaClass cabins have access to **Blu** restaurant, a complimentary specialty restaurant that offers spa-inspired fare (think muesli made tableside at breakfast; and "clean" dishes, such as grilled calamari with lemon confit, for dinner), plus an extensive list of sustainable and biodynamic wines. The company's dining program is under the leadership of Cornelius Gallagher, a highly talented and experienced chef who has worked with, among other notables, Daniel Boulud.

Celebrity's Alaska cruises serve an array of Pacific Northwest regional specialties, and vegetarian dishes are featured at both lunch and dinner. If three meals a day in both informal and formal settings are not enough for you, Celebrity has one of the most extensive 24-hour room-service menus in the industry, plus themed lunch buffets and one to two (depending on the itinerary length) special brunches. Meals in the alternative dining rooms on *Infinity, Millennium,* and *Solstice,* served on a reservations-only basis, generally are worth the extra charges of up to $50 per person; in some cases, they are among the best romantic restaurants at sea.

You can dine formally in the dining room or informally at buffets for breakfast and lunch, with a sushi bar and made-to-order pastas and pizzas served nightly in the **Oceanview Cafe.** Dinner is served at two seatings in the main dining room. Five years ago, the line also introduced Celebrity Select Dining, the option of open seating in the dining room; you choose either traditional or open seating before your cruise. The **AquaSpa Cafe,** in a corner of the Solarium pool area, serves low-cal treats, including raw veggie platters,

Celebrity Fleet Itineraries

SHIP	ITINERARIES
Celebrity Solstice	7-night Tracy Arm Fjord: Round-trip cruises from Seattle visiting Ketchikan, Juneau, Victoria, BC, and Skagway, in addition to cruising the Inside Passage and beside Sawyer Glacier (May–Sept)
Celebrity Infinity	7-night Hubbard Glacier: Round-trip cruises from Vancouver, BC, visiting Ketchikan, Hubbard Glacier, Icy Strait Point or Sitka, Juneau, and the Inside Passage (May–Aug)
Celebrity Millennium	7-night North- and Southbound Glacier Cruise: Sails from Vancouver, BC, to Seward and reverse, visiting Juneau, Skagway, Icy Strait Point, Ketchikan, and Hubbard Glacier (May–Sept)

poached salmon with asparagus tips, vegetarian sushi, and pretty salads with tuna or chicken (this is a hidden secret worth finding).

ACTIVITIES The line offers a laundry list of activities through its all-encompassing enrichment program. A typical day might involve a Rosetta Stone language course, a game of bridge, a culinary demonstration, a chef's cook-off, distinct wine tastings in partnership with the renowned Riedel Crystal, an art auction, and a volleyball tournament. Lectures on the various ports of call (some by Smithsonian speakers), the Alaskan environment, glaciers, and Alaskan culture are given by resident naturalists, who also provide commentary from the bridge as the ships arrive in port and at other times are available for one-on-one discussions with passengers. Celebrity iLounge, the brand's chic version of the Internet cafe, allows e-mail access with discount packages that give you access to Wi-Fi across the ship for everywhere from 1 hour to the full cruise, and even rates that permit acccess to streaming video

The line was among the first to offer an Acupuncture at Sea program.

CHILDREN'S PROGRAMS For children, Celebrity ships employ a group of counselors who direct and supervise a camp-style children's program with activities geared toward different age groups. Though not as elaborate as the kids' facilities on the ships of some other mainstream lines, Celebrity's ships offer kids' play areas and a separate lounge area for teens that, among other things, now feature Xbox-themed spaces for organized Xbox-related activities and games. Private and group babysitting are both available.

ENTERTAINMENT Although entertainment is not generally cited as a reason to sail with Celebrity, the line's stage shows are none too shabby. You won't find any big-name entertainers, but you also won't find any obvious has-beens either—there's just a whole lot of singin' and dancin'. If you tire of the glitter, you can always find a cozy lounge or piano bar to curl up in, and if you crave a little more action, the disco and casino stay open late.

SERVICE In the cabins, service is efficient and so unobtrusive that you might never see your steward except at the beginning and end of your cruise. In the dining rooms, service is polite, professional, and cheerful. Five-star service can be had at the onboard beauty salon or barbershop, and massages can be scheduled at any hour of the day in the spa. Laundry, dry cleaning, and valet services are also available. If you stay in a suite, you really will be treated like royalty, with a tuxedo-clad butler at your beck and call. The butler will serve you afternoon tea (or free cappuccino or espresso) and bring pre-dinner hors d'oeuvres. And yes, the butler will gladly shine your shoes, too, at your request. For those who can't quite afford a suite, Concierge Class rooms come with such perks as fresh fruit, a choice of pillow types, and over-size towels.

On Celebrity ships, gratuities of $13.50 per passenger per day are automatically charged to your shipboard account ($14 per person per day for those staying in Concierge Class and AquaClass cabins; $17 per person per day for those in suites), but you can increase or decrease the amount by visiting the guest relations desk on board.

CRUISETOURS & ADD-ON PROGRAMS Celebrity offers a variety of cruisetours in conjunction with its sailings on *Celebrity Millennium* and *Celebrity Infinity,* ranging in length from 9 to 13 nights. All of Celebrity's cruisetours include a combination of travel through the interior of Alaska in deluxe motorcoaches and the company's Wilderness Express glass-domed railcars, at least 1 night visiting Denali National Park, and the expert advice of a tour director who travels with customers for the entire journey. For vacationers seeking the ultimate cruisetour experience, a 19-night package includes a 6-night pre- or post-cruise Canadian Rockies land tour, a 7-night Alaska cruise, and a 6-night pre- or post-cruise Alaska land tour.

Celebrity Solstice

The Verdict

This ship is a true winner, combining the kind of luxury you'd expect at a great contemporary hotel with all the leisure, sports, and entertainment options of megaships. If this ship was a high school senior, it'd be heading to Harvard. It is best in its class.

Specifications

Size (in Tons)	122,000	Crew	1,250
Passengers (Double Occ.)	2,850	Passenger/Crew Ratio	2 to 1
Space/Passenger Ratio	43	Year Launched	2008
Total Cabins/Veranda Cabins	1,426/1,216	Last Major Refurbishment	2016

Frommer's Ratings (Scale of 1–5) ★★★★★

Cabin Comfort & Amenities	5	Dining Options	5
Ship Cleanliness & Maintenance	5	Gym, Spa & Sports Facilities	5
Public Comfort/Space	4.5	Children's Facilities	4
Decor	5	Enjoyment Factor	5

THE SHIP IN GENERAL *Celebrity Solstice* is one of Celebrity's most stunning ships. Stylish and contemporary, the line's first *Solstice*-class vessel (there are now five) features interiors created by noted designer Adam Tihany, including a dramatic, two-level dining room that features a soaring glass wine tower; a pool deck with a sleek South Beach vibe; a sumptuous spa; and some of the most enticing specialty restaurants at sea. It also boasts the industry's first deck-top "lawn club" with a half-acre of live grass—a place for outdoor games such as bocce that has proven a hit with customers. In 2016, the ship also received a multimillion-dollar refresh.

CABINS   Celebrity took its cabins up a notch with the debut of the *Solstice*-class ships, where cabins are about 15% larger, on average, than those on earlier classes of Celebrity ships. Even the smallest inside cabins are a respectable 183 square feet and boast relatively large bathrooms (with touches such as footrests in showers), sitting areas with sofas, and entertainment units. Slightly smaller are the ship's 70 oceanview cabins without balconies, which measure 176 square feet, while the majority of oceanview cabins with balconies measure 192 square feet, not including 53 square feet of outdoor space on their balconies (floor-to-ceiling sliding glass doors lead to the outside). Suites come in several sizes and offer such accoutrements as whirlpool tubs, DVD players, and walk-in closets. The fanciest suites also have whirlpools on the veranda. The two apartment-size Penthouse Suites (1,291 sq. ft. each, not including their balconies) feature bedrooms with walk-in closets, marble-lined master baths with whirlpool tubs and separate showers, living rooms with dining areas, a baby grand piano, and a full bar with lounge seating. Thirty cabins are wheelchair-accessible, including several suites.

CABINS & RATES

CABINS	PER DIEM RATES	SQ. FT.	FRIDGE	HAIR DRYER	SITTING AREA	TV
Inside	$135–$200	183	yes	yes	no	yes
Outside	$200–$315	176–192	yes	yes	yes	yes
Suites	$435–$665	251–1,291	yes	yes	yes	yes

PUBLIC AREAS   A highlight of *Celebrity Solstice* is the **Lawn Club,** a half-acre hideaway at the top of the ship that features a broad expanse of live grass and such outdoor games as lawn bowling. It's a cruise-ship rarity, for sure, and a hit with passengers. The Lawn Club is home to a small putting green and, perhaps most notably, an outdoor glass-blowing studio where passengers can watch periodic glass-blowing demonstrations. Snacks are available at the **Patio on the Lawn,** and the adjacent **Sunset Bar** is a haven. Down below, on the ship's interior decks, there's also a grand shopping boulevard, casino, champagne bar, theater, beauty salon, library, Celebrity iLounge, children's center, teen room, arcade, and more. For those who like to shop, the ship has a Tiffany & Co. boutique and a Michael Kors shop, too.

DINING OPTIONS   Designer Adam Tihany designed the ship's dramatic, two-story main dining room, the 1,429-seat **Grand Epernay,** which features a soaring glass wine tower. It serves elaborate multicourse dinners nightly in two seatings and is also open for breakfast and lunch. In addition, the ship has a wide array of alternative dining venues that, alas, come with fairly steep extra charges, including the Tihany-designed, 132-seat Italian steakhouse **Tuscan**

Grille ($45 per person); the contemporary **Qsine** restaurant ($45 per person); and the 76-seat **Murano** ($50 per person), which serves international cuisine. Located near the top of the vessel is the **Oceanview Cafe,** the ship's casual buffet eatery. With 632 seats, it's not only spacious but also one of the most diverse buffets at sea, with a wide range of choices. The ship also has **Sushi on Five** (with a la carte pricing) and the upscale **Cafe al Bacio** and **Gelateria,** which serves gourmet coffees, pastries, and gelato at an extra charge.

After dinner, **Michael's Club,** decorated with leather chairs and men's club coziness, offers piano entertainment. More than half a dozen other bars are spread around the ship, including a **Martini Bar** and a separate wine bar called **CellarMasters** that boasts a state-of-the-art "Enomatic" wine-serving system.

POOL, FITNESS, SPA & SPORTS FACILITIES *Celebrity Solstice* is home to one of the most lovely spas at sea, run by Canyon Ranch. It features the **Persian Garden,** a tranquil area that includes a coed sauna and steam room, tropical rain shower, and heated relaxation chairs that face the sea (passengers can pay a daily or weekly fee for access). Nearby is the adults-only **Solarium,** a soaring, glass-enclosed space with plush chairs, a lap pool, and two whirlpools. The ship also has a striking main pool area with a pool and four hot tubs and a South Beach vibe. For exercise fans, a very large, well-equipped fitness center near the spa has dozens of cardio and weight machines, and a jogging track is up on one of the ship's top decks (8 laps = 1 mile). The top decks also have facilities for basketball, volleyball, and paddle tennis.

Celebrity Millennium • Celebrity Infinity

The Verdict

Recent overhauls have breathed new life into these older vessels, which remain a solid option for cruisers looking for a stylish, contemporary experience.

Specifications

Size (in Tons)	90,940/90,940	Crew	999/999
Passengers (Double Occ.)	2,158/2,170	Passenger/Crew Ratio	2 to 1
Space/Passenger Ratio	46	Year Launched	2000/2001
Total Cabins/Veranda Cabins	975/590	Last Major Refurbishment	2016/2015

Frommer's Ratings (Scale of 1–5)   ★★★★½

Cabin Comfort & Amenities	4	Dining Options	4.5
Ship Cleanliness & Maintenance	5	Gym, Spa & Sports Facilities	4
Public Comfort/Space	4	Children's Facilities	3.5
Decor	4	Enjoyment Factor	4

THE SHIPS IN GENERAL When *Celebrity Millennium* and *Celebrity Infinity* debuted in 2000 and 2001, respectively, they were considered among the most spectacular ships afloat. While no longer the belles of the ball at Celebrity (that distinction now goes to the line's new Edge-class ships, the first of which sails in December 2018), they're still elegant vessels with a lot to offer—particularly after massive overhauls in recent years. The ships now boast several new eateries and other features that first debuted on Solstice class ships as well as revamped cabins that reflect the latest in cruise-ship style.

CABINS   The smallest inside cabins are 170 square feet and boast minibars, sitting areas with sofas, and entertainment units with flatscreen TVs. Premium oceanview cabins measure 191 square feet, and large oceanview cabins with verandas are indeed large—271 square feet, with floor-to-ceiling sliding glass doors leading outside. Suites come in several sizes and offer such accoutrements as whirlpool tubs, DVD players, and walk-in closets. The fanciest suites also have whirlpools on the veranda. The two apartment-size Penthouse Suites (1,432 sq. ft. each), designed to evoke Park Avenue aeries, have all the above plus separate living and dining rooms, a foyer, a grand piano, a butler's pantry, a bedroom, exercise equipment, and—sure to be a favorite accessory—motorized drapes. Twenty-six cabins are wheelchair-accessible.

CABINS & RATES

CABINS	PER DIEM RATES	SQ. FT.	FRIDGE	HAIR DRYER	SITTING AREA	TV
Inside	$85–$175	170	yes	yes	yes	yes
Outside	$140–$235	170–191	yes	yes	yes	yes
Suites	$435–$585	251–1,432	yes	yes	yes	yes

PUBLIC AREAS   Like all Celebrity ships, the *Millennium* and *Infinity* have stylish, contemporary decor, with a splash of old-world charm. The dramatic, three-deck-high **Grand Foyer,** with its sweeping staircase, is the heart of each vessel's interior. It's home to the guest relations and shore-excursion desks, a concierge, and the Captain's Club for frequent Celebrity cruisers. From the Grand Foyer, passengers can stroll up to Deck 4, the hub of the ship's evening entertainment, with bars, eateries, and other venues including the photo gallery. The **Emporium,** a shopping area, is one more deck up on Deck 5, and Deck 6 is home to a Celebrity iLounge, an iMac-lined Internet cafe developed in partnership with Apple and also used for (extra-charge) technology classes that focus on Apple products. The *Millennium* also has a two-story library, **Words,** on Decks 8 and 9, with the floors connected by a spiral staircase. A top spot for looking out over the ocean is the **Sky Observation Lounge,** a lounge at the front top of the ship with floor-to-ceiling windows. There's also a casino on board (isn't there always?).

DINING OPTIONS   The ships have two-tier dining rooms that feature live music by a pianist or a quartet. Each also offers a gourmet dining experience in a wonderfully intimate alternative restaurant, **Tuscan Grille** (reservations required; $45 surcharge per person for dinner). Dinner is served in the main dining room in two seatings, as well as in the **Oceanview Cafe** and the **AquaSpa Cafe. Qsine,** a playful, food-as-art eatery, was first unveiled in 2010 on the line's *Celebrity Eclipse,* and **Blu,** the Mediterranean-themed specialty restaurant for AquaClass passengers, debuted on *Solstice* in 2008. Qsine costs

$45 per person; Blu comes with no extra charge for passengers in AquaClass spa cabins and a small charge (currently $5) for passengers in suites. Each ship also has a **Sushi on Five** (which has a la carte pricing) and a **Cafe al Bacio and Gelateria** (both venues first appeared on *Celebrity Solstice*).

After dinner, if you upgraded to a top-tier cabin, consider **Michael's Club**— the private lounge for suite guests—decorated like the parlor of a London men's club and devoted to the pleasures of live jazz and piano entertainment and fine Cognac. Several other bars are tucked into the nooks and crannies of the ships, including an ice-topped **Martini Bar** and a separate wine bar called **Cellar-Masters** that boasts a state-of-the-art "Enomatic" wine-serving system.

POOL, FITNESS, SPA & SPORTS FACILITIES   Spa aficionados, listen up: The *Millennium* and *Infinity* will not disappoint. Each of the ships' 25,000-square-foot spa complexes provides a range of esoteric hydrotherapy treatments; a suite of beautiful New Age steam rooms and saunas; and a huge free-of-charge thalassotherapy whirlpool. In addition, there is the usual array of massage and beauty procedures, plus some unusual ones, such as an Egyptian ginger-and-milk treatment. Next door to the spa is a very large, well-equipped cardio room and a large aerobics floor. On the top decks are facilities for basketball, volleyball, quoits (a game akin to horseshoes), and paddle tennis; a jogging track; a golf simulator; two pools; four whirlpools; and a multitiered sunning area. The swimming pool features a waterfall.

CRYSTAL CRUISES

11755 Wilshire Blvd., Suite #900, Los Angeles, CA 90025. www.crystalcruises.com. 📞 **866/446-6625.**

Pros

○ **Fabulous food.** Crystal has a special place in our hearts. For years they were the only luxury line serving food at sea that was just as good as the best restaurants on land. Today, that tradition of excellence continues.
○ **Amazing service.** Crystal continues to wow us with their undeniably attentive and thoughtful service.

Cons

○ **Less all-inclusive.** Regent Seven Seas, which also has a ship in Alaska, has done an excellent job of redefining the luxury market's definition of all-inclusive. Crystal includes wine and spirits and complimentary Wi-Fi but has yet to include gratuities, airfare, shore excursions, or pre-cruise hotel stays.

THE LINE IN A NUTSHELL   Crystal has expanded a lot in the last 3 years, from a small-focus cruise line with best-in-class luxury ships to a luxury lifestyle brand that also has a yacht, river ships, and a custom-designed jet. Up next? Polar ice breakers. That said, the ocean-going luxury ships—of which there are two, *Crystal Symphony* and *Crystal Serenity*—remain the core of the business. And, after a 5-year hiatus, Crystal Cruises returned to Alaska in 2016. Both will be fully renovated before serving their next seasons in

Crystal Cruises Fleet Itineraries

SHIP	ITINERARIES
Crystal Symphony	7-night Glaciers & Gold: From Vancouver, BC, to Anchorage/Whittier, visiting Ketchikan, Juneau, and Skagway, and cruising Tracy Arm and Hubbard Glacier (June)
Crystal Symphony	7-night Alaska & the Yukon: From Anchorage/Whittier to Vancouver, BC, visiting Sitka, Juneau, Skagway, and Ketchikan, and cruising Hubbard Glacier (June)
Crystal Symphony	14-night Alaskan Grandeur: Round-trip from Vancouver, BC, visiting Ketchikan, Juneau, Hoonah, Skagway, Anchorage/Whittier, Sitka, Prince Rupert, and Victoria, and cruising Tracy Arm and Hubbard Glacier, the Outside and Inside Passages, and the Gulf of Alaska (June)

Alaska: In 2018, *Crystal Symphony* will sail in June, and in 2019 *Crystal Serenity* plans sailings in May to September.

THE EXPERIENCE   Both service and food are exemplary on this more formal line, which has both maintained its elegant evenings and elevated the art of customer service at sea to a level that is truly intuitive. Mention that you love the peanut butter parfait at dinner one night, say, and you may find warm peanut butter cookies delivered to your cabin the next day. Look like you're struggling with your bow tie on formal night, and your butler will offer to tie it for you. Return from a shore excursion with muddy sneakers? They will most likely be left sparkling clean by your bedside during turndown service.

THE FLEET   As the Crystal fleet expanded into river ships and yachting, the ocean-going ships began to feel a bit neglected. Updated in bits and pieces, these once unbeatable ships felt disjointed and looked dated. The good news: *Crystal Symphony* has already been given a full luxury overhaul, and *Crystal Serenity* is going into dry dock in October 2018 for its own multimillion-dollar refurbishment.

PASSENGER PROFILE   The sophisticated, well-traveled passengers on these ships tend to be a bit younger than those on other luxury lines, particularly on shorter and more active itineraries. While other luxury lines are more likely to see primarily retirees, Crystal often has a more balanced mix of empty nesters and the retired, all of whom seem to appreciate that this is one of the last lines to offer Black Tie Optional evenings on board.

DINING OPTIONS   Food is a real focus on all of the line's vessels, and the attention to detail across the ships is unparalleled. While some lines bring in Celebrity chefs to up both the profile of its food game *and* its food, Crystal has long quietly delivered impeccably executed fare, from the main dining room to the buffet to the specialty restaurants.

ACTIVITIES   Crystal tends to bring onboard celebrity entertainers and speakers. You'll also find wine tastings and card games as well as Tai Chi and fitness classes. Computer University@Sea offers courses on everything from photo retouching to designing your own website; the Creative Learning Institute offers classes in art, digital filmmaking, and dancing.

CHILDREN'S PROGRAMS   The Crystal focus is largely on adults, but for those passengers who travel with children, each ship comes with a well-stocked kids' playroom. The Fantasia area (ages 3–12 years old) has arts and crafts and Sony Playstations, while the Waves area (13–17 years old) is largely a video arcade. Some times of the year these spaces are for independent day but in the summertime, when the ship is in Alaska, all sailings are supervised. Kids can also sign up for scavenger hunts, fashion shows, and pajama parties.

ENTERTAINMENT   There seems to be live music everywhere on this ship: The **Palm Court** has a dance floor and the **Stardust Lounge** hosts the Crystal Ensemble. The **Avenue Saloon** has a baby grand and is easily the place to be before dinner. **Pulse** nightclub offers karaoke and a DJ. And, on formal nights, the **Crystal Cove** has a string quintet and dancing.

SERVICE   Service on board is truly legendary, and Crystal is famous for giving butlers the discretion to do whatever needs to be done to wow guests. The line includes gratuities in the cruise fare, so no additional tips are expected.

CRUISETOURS & ADD-ON PROGRAMS   Crystal has had them in the past, but had not announced its plans at press time.

Crystal Symphony • Crystal Serenity

The Verdict

These identical luxury ships may be the best choice for food lovers in Alaska—we've had entire week-long sailings where everything from our morning eggs to our late-night dessert was unfathomably flawless.

Specifications

Size (in Tons)	51,044/68,870	Crew	545/655
Passengers (Double Occ.)	848/980	Passenger/Crew Ratio	1.55 and 1.49 to 1
Space/Passenger Ratio	60.2/70.3	Year Launched	1995/2003
Total Cabins/Veranda Cabins	623/537	Last Major Refurbishment	2017/2018

Frommer's Ratings (Scale of 1–5)   ★★★★½

Cabin Comfort & Amenities	5	Dining Options	5
Ship Cleanliness & Maintenance	5	Gym, Spa & Sports Facilities	5
Public Comfort/Space	4	Children's Facilities	1
Decor	4	Enjoyment Factor	5

THE SHIPS IN GENERAL   *Crystal Symphony* and *Crystal Serenity* hold just under 1,000 passengers, making them the largest of the luxury vessels in Alaska or anywhere else in the world. And while many feared that their size would affect personalized service, that's just not been our experience. We've never felt like a number here: Instead, our butlers and waiters have learned our names and preferences so quickly we wish we knew their secret. For devotees, the size also means that you get more dining and entertainment options—and more privacy—than you would find on a smaller luxury vessel, which tend to feel like intimate small towns that have comparable strengths (a feeling of community) and weaknesses (for some, limited options and claustrophobia).

CABINS   During dry-dock renovations, Crystal is pulling some staterooms and redesigning them as Penthouses and Penthouse Suites. As a result, the passenger capacity will go down a bit for each ship. Still, even staterooms that have picture windows instead of verandas will retain a certain degree of posh-ness—with Frette bathrobes, kimonos, and slippers, as well as custom Etro bath products in gorgeous gemstone-hued containers, Egyptian cotton linens, and electronic "DO NOT DISTURB" signs that may just be the only ones of their kind on the Alaskan waters. The throws on the couches are mohair, the head-boards are leather, and there are fresh flowers, fresh fruit, and stocked mini-bars as well as 24-hour room service. (In suites, you can even have dinners served course by course on your veranda from the main dining room or one of the specialty restaurants.)

CABINS & RATES

CABINS	PER DIEM RATES	SQ. FT.	FRIDGE	HAIR DRYER	SITTING AREA	TV
Outside	$305–$697	202–367	yes	yes	yes	yes
Suites	$331–$1,882	202–982	yes	yes	yes	yes

PUBLIC AREAS   The **Palm Court,** home to afternoon tea and a sort of "living room" space for the ship, is being entirely redesigned. The ship also has the small **Crystal Casino,** a cigar bar, a nightclub, and a clubby piano bar called **Avenue Saloon** that tends to draw crowds for pre- and post-dinner drinks. The Creative Learning Institute is designed for classes and the Com-puters@Sea area hosts large computer courses. The **Galaxy Lounge** shows review-style shows, and the **Hollywood Theater** serves warm popcorn with their films. There's a well-stocked library and equally well-executed self-service laundry rooms. The **Vintage Room** offers wine-tasting classes as well as gorgeous (though pricey at $1,000 per person!) wine-pairing dinners. The lounges around the ship do a lovely job of serving pre-dinner hors d'oeuvres with your cocktails, too.

DINING OPTIONS   The ship's main dining space, the **Crystal Dining Room,** has two menus: a modern one full of trendy, contemporary choices and a classic one with all the stalwarts that long-time cruisers—and less adventur-ous, traditional types—have come to know and love. It will be renamed Waterside after dry dock and go from a two-seating format with assigned tables to a more modern open-seating style, though the fine bone china and crystal will remain. Crystal is also well-known for offering kosher meals with advanced notice, as well as catering well to special diets. Celebrating a big wedding anniversary or important birthday? Ask in advance, and they'll make your favorite meal, using your own family recipes.

Dry-dock renovations will also update the dated decor of the stellar Northern Italian restaurant **Prego;** the restaurant will be renamed but the delectable house-made pastas are going nowhere. The same goes for the excellent

Japanese restaurant and sushi bar helmed by Iron Chef Nobu Matsuhisa. It's currently called Silk Road, but will reemerge, its decor refreshed, as **Umi Uma** after dry dock. The food is already perfection—we can't imagine a more flawlessly executed sushi bar at sea. (If you're a fan, be sure to ask what's in from port that's not on the regular menu—we were once rewarded with a gorgeous tray of toro, rich tuna belly.) The Lido Café, the line's buffet, is also being redone and renamed: It will be **Marketplace** during the day and convert at night into **Churrascaria,** a Brazilian steakhouse with gauchos wielding swords of juicy meat. A new restaurant, **Silk,** will serve family-style Chinese dishes, from dumplings to noodles, in an alfresco space that will feel just right with a wrap or jacket on a bright Alaskan summer night. There's also a poolside grill and an ice cream bar stocked with Ben & Jerry's most popular flavors.

POOL, FITNESS, SPA & SPORTS FACILITIES   The pool on these ships, unlike those on some competitors, feels ample for the number of people on board, as do the number of (comfy teak) deck chairs and Balinese-style day-beds on deck. In addition, the ships have lovely *feng shui*–inspired spas, impressively state-of-the-art gyms, and wide and walkable promenade decks. Look for putting greens, shuffleboard, and paddle tennis as well.

DISNEY CRUISE LINE

P.O. Box 10238, Lake Buena Vista, FL 32830. www.disneycruise.com. ✆ **888/325-2500.**

Pros

○ **Great children's programs.** Would you expect anything less from Disney? In both the size of facilities and the range of activities, this is a line that's hard to beat.
○ **Disney-quality entertainment.** The line presents family-oriented musicals that are some of the best onboard entertainment at sea.
○ **Family-style cabins.** It's rare in the cruise business to find so many large, family-friendly cabins that can sleep three, four, or even five people.

Cons

○ **Limited adult entertainment.** Forget about a night out gambling—this is one of just a few ships at sea without a casino. There's an adult-only night entertainment area on board, but it's often quiet.
○ **Crowded pools.** Disney ships are kid magnets, and that can have a downside on sunny days when children come out of the woodwork to hit the pools.
○ **The cost.** Compared to other big ship lines such as Carnival and Norwegian, Disney is pricey, running at least a few hundred dollars more per person for a week. In short, you pay a premium for The Mouse.

THE LINE IN A NUTSHELL   Disney's cruising arm isn't large (just four ships), but the company is the Big Kahuna when it comes to family-geared cruising. Though a number of big lines including Royal Caribbean, Carnival, and Norwegian Cruise Line have long offered wonderful programs for children, it was Disney that first set out to create a family vacation that would be as relaxing for parents as for their offspring. If you love Disney's resorts on land, you'll love the company's ships.

THE EXPERIENCE   Both classic and ultra-modern, the line's ships are like no others in the industry, designed to evoke the grand transatlantic liners of old but also boasting some truly innovative features, such as extra-large cabins for families and a trio of restaurants through which passengers rotate on every cruise. Disney is known for entertainment, of course, and its ships don't disappoint, with Disney-inspired shows. The vessels also boast separate adult pools and lounges and the biggest kids' facilities at sea, which is now, following a 2016 dry dock, known as **AquaLab.** In many ways, the experience is more Disney than it is cruise; on the other hand, the ships are surprisingly elegant and well laid out, with little Disney touches sprinkled all around.

THE FLEET   The 1,754-passenger *Disney Wonder* is the line's only ship in Alaska. The streamlined vessel is chock-full of activities for kids, with great pools (including one shaped like Mickey's head) and adult-only areas, too.

PASSENGER PROFILE   Disney's ships attract a wide mix of passengers, from honeymooners to seniors, but as one might expect, a big percentage is made up of young American families with children. (This isn't a big line for foreign passengers, though you'll see a few.) Because of the allure to families with younger children, the average age of passengers tends to be lower than aboard most other cruise ships. Many adult passengers are in their 30s and early to mid-40s. The bulk of the line's passengers are first-time cruisers, and because the line attracts so many families (sometimes large ones), many of its bookings are for multiple cabins.

DINING OPTIONS   Disney offers a traditional fixed-seating plan for dinners, but with a twist. Each of its ships has three main restaurants—each with a different theme—among which passengers (and their servers) rotate over the course of a cruise. On one night, passengers dine on dishes such as roasted duck or rack of lamb in a green peppercorn sauce in the nautical-themed **Triton's** restaurant. And then it's on to **Animator's Palate,** a bustling eatery with a gimmick: It's a sort of living animation cell, with walls decorated with black-and-white sketches of Disney characters that over the course of the meal gradually become filled in with color. Video screens add to the illusion, and even the waiters' outfits change during the evening. The 2016 dry dock refreshed this space, and now passengers can participate in the same sort of animation show that takes place in the restaurant on newer vessels. The ship also got the new **Tiana's Place** restaurant in 2016, which has a New Orleans–themed menu, character meet-and-greet moments with Tiana herself (who comes around to all the tables) and a jazz show that gets the little ones dancing by the stage. Our advice: Stay for the beignets; they're the best part of the meal.

You'll have to pay extra ($30 per person) to dine in the romantic, adults-only Italian specialty restaurant, **Palo,** which serves both dinner and a sea-day brunch that comes with a buffet of decadent baked breakfast treats you won't want to miss. Breakfast and lunch are served in several restaurants, both sit-down and buffet. **Pluto's Dog House,** on the main pool deck, serves up kid-friendly basics such as chicken fingers, fries, burgers, and nachos; nearby **Goofy's Galley** offers wraps, fresh fruit, and other more healthful fare. One notable feature of Disney ships that sets them apart from other big, mass-market vessels is that soft drinks are included in the fare, and you'll find self-serve soda machines around the pool deck and in the buffet area.

ACTIVITIES   Disney offers an array of activities similar to other big-ship lines, with one big exception: There's no casino. (Disney executives apparently decided a casino just didn't fit with the line's family-friendly image.) Besides lounging at the pool, the array of options on board includes basketball, Ping-Pong, and shuffleboard tournaments; sports trivia contests; weight-loss, health, and beauty seminars; bingo, Pictionary, and other games; wine tastings; and singles mixers (though these family-focused cruises aren't the best choice for singles). Each ship also has a spa and gym, and enrichment activities include galley tours; backstage theater tours; informal lectures on nautical themes and Disney history as well as current Disney productions; animation and drawing classes; and home entertainment and cooking demonstrations. On Disney cruises to Alaska, special cooking demonstrations highlight cuisine such as wild Alaskan salmon and halibut. All these activities come at no extra charge except for wine tastings, which cost $15 per person. There also are dance classes and movies, and all voyages include a captain's cocktail party with complimentary drinks once per cruise, where the master of the ship and (this being Disney) a gaggle of characters make an appearance.

CHILDREN'S PROGRAMS   Disney's kids' facilities are, famously, the most extensive at sea, spreading across a good part of an entire deck (what the ship lacks in casino space it makes up for with extra kids' space). The ships carry dozens of children's counselors who look after groups split into five age groups. Broken up into several areas, the children's zone generally is open between 9am and midnight. The **Oceaneer Club,** for ages 3 to 12, is a kiddie-size playroom themed around Captain Hook. Kids can climb and crawl on the bridge, ropes, and rails of a giant pirate ship, as well as on jumbo-size animals, barrels, and a sliding board; play dress-up from trunks full of costumes; dance with Snow White and listen to stories by other Disney characters; or play in the kiddie computer room on PlayStations. The interactive **Oceaneer Lab** offers kids ages 3 to 10 a chance to work on computers, learn fun science with microscopes, do arts and crafts, hear how animation works, and direct their own TV commercials. This ship also has the popular "Marvel Super Hero Academy," where kids can learn about bravery, for example, from Captain America. Other newer additions are "Andy's Room," a *Toy Story*–themed play space, and a *Frozen*-themed playroom where children can take part in a coronation ceremony.

Also on *Disney Wonder* is **Edge,** an exclusive hangout for tweens (ages 11–13). The club is located on Deck 2, midship. For teens, the *Wonder* has a hangout called Vibe that has two separate rooms, one with video screens for movies and the other a disco with a teens-only Internet center. Dance parties, karaoke, trivia games, improv comedy lessons, and workshops on photography are offered for teens on every voyage.

Disney Fleet Itineraries

SHIP	ITINERARIES
Disney Wonder	7-night Inside Passage: Round-trip from Vancouver, BC, visiting Skagway, Juneau, and Ketchikan, and cruising Tracy Arm Fjord (June–Sept)
Disney Wonder	5-night Inside Passage: Round-trip from Vancouver, BC, visiting Ketchikan and cruising Tracy Arm Fjord (June–Sept)
Disney Wonder	9-night Inside Passage: Round-trip from Vancouver, BC, visiting Ketchikan, Skagway, Icy Strait Point, and Juneau, and cruising Tracy Arm Fjord and Hubbard Glacier (June–Sept)

One thing Disney doesn't do is private babysitting. Instead, there's the **It's a Small World** nursery for kids ages 3 months to 3 years ($9 per hour for the first child, $8 per each additional child; hours vary depending on the day's port schedule, and space is limited, so book well in advance). No other lines offer such extensive care for babies.

Disney also offers youth activities exclusive to Alaska sailings. While the ship sails through Tracy Arm Fjord, kids can participate in "Base Camp" on the upper deck. Games, crafts, and activities in Alaska-themed stations entertain children while immersing them in the splendor of the region. During port days, adventure guides specifically for children and teens introduce them to the unique cultural and natural aspects of each Alaskan port.

ENTERTAINMENT Family-friendly entertainment is one of the highlights of being on a Disney ship, and as one might expect, Disney characters and movies often are front and center in the onboard productions. Performances by Broadway-caliber entertainers in the nostalgic **Walt Disney Theatre** include "Disney Dreams: An Enchanted Classic," a musical medley of Disney classics from *Peter Pan* to *The Lion King;* and "Golden Mickeys," a tribute to Disney films through the years that combines song and dance, animated films, and special effects. Best of all: the new "Frozen: A Musical Spectacular" stage show, which is designed to wow kiddos and parents alike with special effects that include snow falling in the theater.

Family game shows (including a trivia contest called "Mickey Mania") and karaoke take place in the **Studio Sea family nightclub.** Adults 18 years and older, meanwhile, have their own play zone, an adults-only entertainment area in the forward part of Deck 3 with three themed nightclubs. There, the **Crown and Fin** offers a pub-style atmosphere and a wide selection of beers. The **Cadillac Lounge** is sexier, with superbly executed cocktails. (Look for gorgeous presentations, such as the Alexander cocktail, served with an atomizer so that you can spritz extra cognac on your drink.) Another nightspot is the **Promenade Lounge,** where live music is featured daily. The **Buena Vista Theatre** shows movies day and evening.

SERVICE Just as at its parks, Disney's cruise ships feature staff that come from around the globe. Service in the dining rooms is efficient and precise, but leans toward friendly rather than formal. The crew keeps the ship exceptionally clean and well-maintained. Overall, things run very smoothly.

Services include laundry and dry cleaning. (The ship also has self-service laundry rooms and 1-hr. photo processing.) Tips can be charged to your onboard account, for which most passengers opt, or you can give them out in the traditional method, as cash. Disney suggests a gratuity of $28 per person per week for the dining room server, $21 for the assistant server, and $28 for the cabin steward. Disney also recommends tipping the dining room head server $7.

CRUISETOURS & ADD-ON PROGRAMS   None.

Disney Wonder

The Verdict

Whether you're a Disney fanatic or just someone looking for a heavily family-focused experience while sailing in Alaska, this is your ship. Just keep in mind you'll be paying a bit of a "Disney premium" for the privilege.

Specifications

Size (in Tons)	83,000	Crew	950
Passengers (Double Occ.)	1,754	Passenger/Crew Ratio	1.8 to 1
Space/Passenger Ratio	47.3	Year Launched	1999
Total Cabins/Veranda Cabins	877/362	Last Major Refurbishment	2016

Frommer's Ratings (Scale of 1–5)   ★★★★½

Cabin Comfort & Amenities	5	Dining Options	5.5
Ship Cleanliness & Maintenance	5	Gym, Spa & Sports Facilities	3
Public Comfort/Space	4	Children's Facilities	5
Decor	5	Enjoyment Factor	5

THE SHIP IN GENERAL   This sleek homage to ocean liners of old carries 1,754 passengers at "double occupancy"—the standard industry measuring stick for passenger capacity that assumes two people per cabin. But with all the kids packing into rooms with their parents, the double occupancy rating for this particular vessel is less indicative of the crowds that will be on many sailings. Built to be family-friendly, many cabins can hold four or even five people (some two-bedroom family cabins can hold up to seven!), and theoretically, the *Disney Wonder* could carry 2,700 people if every possible berth was filled. Though service is a high point of a Disney cruise and the ships are well laid out, the large number of passengers means some areas of the ship can feel crowded at times, notably the kids' pool area and the buffet eatery.

CABINS   As noted above, the *Disney Wonder* is all about family-friendly cabins, and the rooms on the ship have a number of features that make them unusually appealing to parents with kids. In addition to being able to hold up to five people in some cases (a rarity in the cruise world), cabins are about 25% larger on average than the industry standard. All 877 cabins have at least a sitting area with a sofabed to sleep families of three. Some cabins also have one or two pull-down bunks to sleep families of four or five. Nearly half have private balconies. One-bedroom suites have balconies and sleep four or five comfortably; two-bedroom suites sleep up to seven. Outside cabins that don't have balconies have large-size porthole windows.

One big twist aimed at families: The majority of cabins have two bathrooms—a sink and toilet in one and a shower/tub combo and sink in the other, making both getting out the door in the morning and bedtime rituals much simpler for families with several children.

As for decor, it's virtually identical from cabin to cabin, combining modern design with nostalgic ocean-liner elements such as a steamer-trunk armoire for kids, globe- and telescope-shaped lamps, map designs on the bedspreads, and a framed black-and-white shot of Mr. and Mrs. Walt Disney aboard the fabled ocean liner *Rex*. Warm wood tones predominate, with Art Deco touches in the metal and glass fittings and light fixtures.

CABINS & RATES

CABINS	PER DIEM RATES	SQ. FT.	FRIDGE	HAIR DRYER	SITTING AREA	TV
Inside	$273–$295	184–214	yes	yes	yes	yes
Outside	$311–$333	214–304	yes	yes	yes	yes
Suites	$1,017–$1,927	614–1,029	yes	yes	yes	yes

PUBLIC AREAS The *Disney Wonder* has several theaters and lounges, including an adults-only area with three venues: a piano/jazz lounge, a disco, and a sports bar. A family-oriented entertainment lounge called **Studio Sea** offers game shows, karaoke, and dancing; the **Promenade Lounge** has classic pop music in the evenings; and a 24-hour Internet cafe has eight flatscreen stations. The **Cove Cafe** is a comfy place for gourmet coffee (for a price) or cocktails in a relaxed setting with books, magazines, Internet stations, Wi-Fi, and TVs. A 270-seat cinema shows mostly recent-release Disney movies. The ship also has a jumbo 336-square-foot screen attached to the forward funnel outside on Deck 9 that shows classic Disney animated films. The children's facilities, as you'd expect, are the largest of any ship at sea. In preparation for its Alaska sailings, the *Disney Wonder* received a new venue in dry dock called **Outlook Cafe.** Located high atop Deck 10, the 2,500-square-foot observation lounge is designed as a place for passengers in Alaska to relax with a drink as they peer out through floor-to-ceiling, curved-glass windows. A spiral staircase connects Outlook Cafe with the existing Cove Cafe one deck below.

DINING OPTIONS Disney's unique rotation dining system has passengers tasting three different eateries at dinner over the course of their cruise, with an adults-only specialty restaurant also available by reservation. Exclusive to Alaska sailings, Disney adds Alaska-themed items to menus and holds a weekly Taste of Alaska dinner featuring Alaskan king crab legs, honey-mustard-marinated Alaskan salmon, and juniper-spiced elk tenderloin. At breakfast and lunch, the buffet-style spread in *Wonder*'s **Beach Blanket** restaurant offers deli meats, cheeses, and rice and vegetable dishes, as well as a carving station, a salad bar, and a dessert table with yummy chocolate chip cookies. Though the culinary offerings are par for the course in the cruise business, an oft-heard critique of the buffet area is that it's too small for the number of people on board and poorly designed for passenger flow, resulting in bottlenecks—particularly during the morning rush.

Options for grabbing a bite by the pool include **Pinocchio's Pizzeria, Pluto's Dog House** (for hot dogs, hamburgers, chicken tenders, fries, and more), and an ice-cream bar (which also includes a generous selection of toppings). There's 24-hour room service from a limited menu but no midnight buffet.

POOL, FITNESS, SPA & SPORTS FACILITIES   The pool deck has three pools: **Mickey's Kids' Pool,** shaped like the mouse's big-eared head, with a great big white-gloved Mickey hand holding up a snaking yellow slide (expect a crowd at this pool!); **Goofy's Family Pool,** where adults and children can mingle; and the **Quiet Cove Adult Pool,** with whirlpools, gurgling waterfalls, a teak deck and lounge chairs with plush cushions, a poolside bar, and the Cove Cafe coffee spot. For families with young children, adjacent is a splash pool with circulating water for diaper-wearing babies and toddlers. It's the only one at sea; the lines' official party line is no diaper-wearing children allowed in any pool (and that includes Pull-Ups and swim diapers).

Just behind the pool at the stern is a spa and gym. The Steiner-managed **Vista Spa & Salon** is impressive, with attractive tile treatment rooms and a thermal suite with a sauna, a steam room, a misting shower, and heated contoured tile chaise lounges. Among the many treatments is a selection geared to teens.

The *Disney Wonder* has an outdoor **Sports Deck** with basketball and paddle tennis. It also has shuffleboard and Ping-Pong, and joggers and walkers can circuit the **Promenade Deck.**

HOLLAND AMERICA LINE

450 Third Ave. W., Seattle, WA 98119. www.hollandamerica.com. ✆ **877/932-4259** or 206/286-3900.

Pros

o **Expertise that comes with experience.** Holland America's ships may be young, but the line sure isn't. Formed in 1873 as the Netherlands-America Steamship Company, it's been around more than 145 years, a lot of time to learn a little about operating oceangoing vessels.

o **Warm interiors.** Holland America ships, especially the more recent ones, tend to be understated, inviting, and easy on the eye; nothing garish here.

o **Line enhancements.** A $300-million-dollar fleet-wide program includes some pretty cool partnerships, including one with Oprah Winfrey that brought the celebrity herself on board an Alaska sailing in 2017.

Cons

o **Sleepy nightlife.** If you're big on late-night dancing and barhopping, you may find yourself partying mostly with the entertainment staff, although the line has been offering more for night owls in recent years. If you're looking for a lot of late-night action, you're probably better off on one of the bigger, more bustling ships operated by rivals Norwegian, Carnival, or even Princess.

THE LINE IN A NUTSHELL More than any other cruise company in Alaska, Holland America Line (HAL) has managed to hang onto some of its seafaring history and tradition with its moderately priced, classic, casual yet refined, ocean-liner-like cruise experience. The line also has somewhat smaller, more intimate vessels than its main competitors, Princess and Celebrity.

THE EXPERIENCE In Alaska terms, everybody else is an upstart when it comes to the cruise and even land tour business. The line calls itself Alaska's most experienced travel operator, and the key to that claim is HAL's 1971 acquisition of the tour company Westours, founded in 1947 by the late Charles B. "Chuck" West, often called "Mr. Alaska" and widely recognized as the absolute pioneer of tourism to and within the state.

Cruising with HAL is less hectic than cruising on most other ships. The line strives for a less intrusive, sometimes almost sedate, presentation, although it has brightened up its entertainment package—with offerings including a partnership with New York City's Lincoln Center and one with blues club B.B. King, as well as a multimedia production that's designed with BBC Earth called "Alaska in Concert." Overall, the ships tend to be more evocative of the days of grand liners, with elegant, European styling and displays of nautical artifacts.

One problem that always faces cruise lines is ensuring that their newly built vessels—invariably outfitted with all the latest bells and whistles—don't overshadow their existing, older fleetmates. The company's Signature of Excellence product- and service-enhancements program is aimed at elevating the quality of the dining, service, and enrichment programs on older ships.

Under the Signature of Excellence program, HAL spends much of its upgrade dollars on such items as new amenities in cabins: massage showerheads, lighted magnifying makeup mirrors, hair dryers, extra-fluffy towels, terrycloth robes, upgraded mattresses, and Egyptian-cotton bed linens. Passengers in all rooms are welcomed with a complimentary fruit basket. Suites have plush duvets on every bed, a VCR/DVD player, access to a well-stocked library of DVDs, and a fully stocked minibar.

In 2017, Holland America announced that they were transforming the Crow's Nest bars into destination-focused lounges called **Explorations Central,** aka EXC. In these new spaces—expected to be in place on all ships by May 2019—you'll find interactive maps, real-time data, travel books, and a shore excursions desk with guides trained to make personalized tour suggestions.

Another focus has been on branded partnerships to offer passengers the chance to try new things. America's Test Kitchen is a show kitchen with free cooking demonstrations several times during each cruise, where video cameras allow you to watch every move the chefs make. For those who prefer a more hands-on experience, cooking classes cost $39 per person. (The classes are limited to about 12 people and highly popular, so sign up early on your cruise.)

Another branded offering on Holland America vessels are the "Digital Workshops Powered by Windows," which offer free sessions on a variety of topics related to camera basics and photo editing, moviemaking, PC security, and more. "Techsperts" trained by Microsoft are on hand.

THE FLEET Over the years, Holland America Line has picked up a lot of "stuff": Holland America Line Tours (formed by the merger of Westours and Gray Line of Alaska); Westmark Hotels; the *MV Ptarmigan* day boat that visits Portage Glacier outside Anchorage; a fleet of railcars (some built in the Old West style, but with better viewing opportunities, and some built in a more contemporary style); an almost completely new fleet of motorcoaches; and a lot more. Today, all of this is managed by HAP, which stands for Holland America-Princess and is a joint venture between the two lines, both of which are owned by Carnival Corporation.

The company's *S*-class ships—the 1,258-passenger *Maasdam* (1993) and 1,350-passenger *Veendam* (1996)—are virtual carbon copies of the same attractive, well-crafted design, with a spritz of glitz here and there. The 1,432-passenger *Volendam* officially debuted in 1999, and the 1,432-passenger *Zaandam* debuted in 2000. Brighter and bolder than the earlier ships, the *Volendam* and *Zaandam* share many features of the *S*-class ships, though they are slightly larger in size (nearly 62,000 tons, as opposed to approximately 56,000) and carry more passengers (1,432, against the *S* class's 1,260). The 1,380-passenger *Amsterdam* is 62,735 tons and is one of two flagships in the fleet. (The other is the *Amsterdam*'s sister ship, the *Rotterdam*.) The *Westerdam* (2004), *Oosterdam* (2003), and *Noordam* (2006) represent the Vista class in Alaska, each at 82,350 tons and carrying 1,916 to 1,972 passengers—sister ship *Zuiderdam* (2000) is cruising elsewhere. The company's smallest ship is the luxurious *Prinsendam,* just 38,000 tons and with a passenger capacity of 835. The Signature-class ships include the 2,104-passenger *Eurodam* (2008) and the 2,106-passenger *Nieuw Amsterdam.*

Holland America has never shown any inclination to plunge into the 100,000-plus-ton megaship market. Keeping the size down allows HAL to maintain its high service standards and a degree of intimacy while offering all the amenities of its larger brethren.

PASSENGER PROFILE Holland America's passenger profile used to reflect a somewhat older crowd than on other ships. Now the average age is dropping, thanks to both an increased emphasis on the line's Club HAL program for children and some updating of the onboard entertainment offerings. HAL's passenger records in Alaska show a high volume of middle-age and older vacationers (the same demographic as aboard many of its competitors' ships), but on any given cruise, records are also likely to list a hundred or more passengers between the ages of, say, 5 and 16. This trend gathered its initial momentum a few years ago in Europe, a destination that, parents seem to think, has more kid appeal. It's spilled over into Alaska more recently, mainly thanks to the cruise line's added emphasis on generational travel with programs such as Club HAL, America's Test Kitchen, B.B. King, and family reunion travel, a growing segment of the market.

The more mature among Holland America's passengers are likely to be repeat HAL passengers. They are usually not Fortune 500 rich—they are looking for solid value for their money, and they get it from this line.

DINING OPTIONS Years ago, HAL's meals were as traditional as its architecture and its itineraries—almost stodgy. But today the variety of dishes on the menu matches those of other premium lines, and the quality of the food is generally good throughout the fleet. Vegetarian options are available at every meal. We've also found that HAL does a particularly good job of catering to special diets, ranging from vegan to kosher to gluten-free. On menus in the main dining room, look for selections from top chefs such as Elizabeth Falkner and David Burke, who advise the line as members of its Culinary Council.

The kids' menu usually includes spaghetti, pizza, hamburgers, fries, and hot dogs. In addition, a few variations on what's being offered to the adults at the table are often served.

Buffets are offered at the **Lido Restaurant** as an alternative to breakfast, lunch, and dinner in the main dining room (a large percentage of passengers dine in the Lido for breakfast and lunch, occasionally leading to some serious waiting times for tables and on lines during those times). **Canaletto** is a waiter-service casual Italian restaurant open for dinner on the Lido Deck, for a $15 extra charge (reservations recommended). For a fancier meal, the **Pinnacle Grill** is the line's excellent steak and seafood venue on all the ships, priced at $35 for dinner and $10 for lunch; reservations are required—and it's money well spent. One night a cruise, the Pinnacle Grill hosts the Sel de Mer pop-up dining experience ($49 per person, and totally worth it), featuring the cuisine of the stand-alone French seafood restaurant located on the line's *Koningsdam*.

ACTIVITIES Young hipsters need not apply. Holland America's ships are heavy on more mature, less frenetic activities and light on boogie-till-the-cows-come-home, party-hearty pursuits. You'll find good cooking classes by America's Test Kitchen and music to dance to or listen to in the bars and lounges (piano bars are lively), plus health spas, and all the other standard activities found on most large ships: photography classes, golf-putting contests (on the carpet in the lobby), art auctions, and the like. All ships provide Internet access for 75¢ a minute; less if you buy a multi-minute package.

Local travel guides sail on all Alaska-bound ships as part of the new Explorations Central program, often referred to as EXC. The guides bring their knowledge of local culture, history, art, and flora and fauna, giving lectures and interacting one-on-one with guests. The program also includes food and beverage events, including an Alaskan Brewing Company beer tasting and Pacific Northwest wine tastings. In addition, a Tlingit cultural interpreter from Hoonah boards each ship at Glacier Bay and Hubbard Glacier to give talks explaining the origins of the Huna people—a tribe that has called Glacier Bay home for centuries. At the glaciers, there is also commentary by National Park Service employees.

CHILDREN'S PROGRAMS Club HAL is more than just one of those half-hearted give-'em-a-video-arcade-and-hot-dogs-at-dinner efforts. This children's program has expert supervisors, a fitness center, and dedicated kids' rooms and teen club rooms (adults, keep out!).

Holland America Fleet Itineraries

SHIP	ITINERARIES
Eurodam, Amsterdam	7-night Alaskan Explorer: Round-trip from Seattle, visiting Juneau, Glacier Bay, Sitka, Ketchikan, and Victoria, BC (May–Sept)
Zaandam	14-night Alaskan Adventurer: Round-trip from Seattle, visiting Ketchikan, Juneau, Icy Strait Point, Anchorage, Homer, Kodiak, Sitka, and Victoria, BC, and scenic cruising in Tracy Arm and at Hubbard Glacier (May–Sept)
Volendam/ Westerdam/ Noordam/ Nieuw Amsterdam	7-night Inside Passage: Round-trip from Vancouver, BC, visiting Juneau, Skagway, Ketchikan, and Glacier Bay or Tracy Arm Fjord (May–Sept)
Noordam/ Westerdam	7-night Glacier Discovery: North- and southbound between Vancouver, BC, and Seward/Anchorage, visiting Juneau, Ketchikan, Skagway or Haines, and Glacier Bay (May–Sept)

Kids' activities are arranged in three divisions, by age (3–7, 8–12, and teens). The youngest group might have, say, crafts and games; there's golf putting and disco parties for 'tweens, and, for the older kids, a chance to try their hand at karaoke and sports tournaments. When more than 100 kids are on board, a Talent Show is presented.

ENTERTAINMENT The line has been making great strides in entertainment over the past decade, bringing in Broadway veterans to play the main theaters of its ships as well as top-notch illusionists, comedians, and musicians in addition to the performers associated with Lincoln Center and B.B. King. The change, to a large extent, reflects the tastes of the younger passengers who are starting to book in greater numbers with HAL. Overall, the quality of the professional entertainers on HAL ships has perceptibly improved over the past decade. And then there are the amateurs! Each week includes a crew talent show in which the international staff members perform their countries' songs and dances. Even if that sounds a bit corny, try it—many of the staff members are fabulous! Your fellow passengers might also be quite the surprise—HAL ships offer live karaoke and an *American Idol*–style competition that sometimes deliver professional-caliber performances.

SERVICE The line employs primarily Filipino and Indonesian staff members who are generally gracious and friendly without being cloying.

On one occasion, one of our contributors somehow managed to get his baggage on board a Holland America ship in Vancouver, BC—while the keys to the bags were lying on the bedside table at home 1,000 miles away! The cabin steward refused to let him break the locks and ruin the rather expensive (and brand-new) luggage. Instead, he called an engineer, and together they toiled patiently with a variety of tools—and a huge ring of keys—until, about a half-hour after boarding, they managed to free the offending locks. Luggage saved—and score one for the HAL service spirit!

Onboard services on every ship in the fleet include laundry and dry cleaning. On Holland America ships, a gratuity of $13.50 per person per day is automatically charged to your shipboard account ($15 per person per day if you're in a suite), but you can increase or decrease the amount by visiting the guest services desk on board.

CRUISETOURS & ADD-ON PROGRAMS As might be expected of a cruise line that owns its own land-tour company in Alaska (Royal Caribbean and Princess also own tour companies in the market), HAL offers a variety of land arrangements in combination with its cruises, and they are extensive. Newly dubbed Land + Sea Journeys in 2014, HAL's cruisetours range from 10 to 20 days in length, including a 3- to 7-day cruise, a 1- to 3-day visit to Denali National Park, and, in some cases, a few days visiting the Yukon Territory. In a big change that started in 2014, the line's tours that visit the Yukon include a 1-hour flight to the region from Fairbanks that replaces up to 2 days of motorcoach travel and a hotel overnight (in our eyes, a great improvement!). It's just the latest innovation when it comes to tours to the Yukon for Holland America, which has been a tourism pioneer in the region. While other lines have focused their land-tour options on the Anchorage-Denali-Fairbanks corridor and the Kenai Peninsula, Holland America also has poured resources into the Yukon and is the clear leader there; if you want to see the Yukon as part of your Alaska trip, Holland America is your line.

Another notable land-tour change that also began in 2014 at Holland America was a new schedule for the McKinley Explorer domed railcars the line uses to bring customers from Anchorage to Denali and back, with departures from Anchorage now occurring later in the morning and return trips from Denali now coming back earlier, with arrival back in Anchorage before dinnertime. The Holland America–owned Westmark hotels are used on the company's tours in Fairbanks, Anchorage, and Skagway. Prices for Land + Sea Journeys vary widely depending on the type of cabin chosen for the cruise portion of the trip, level of hotel for the land portion, and length of the trip. Starting fare for 2018 for a 10-day trip is $1,098 per person.

Amsterdam • Volendam • Zaandam

The Verdict

More than a decade after debuting, these three markedly similar vessels remain an attractive choice for cruisers looking for a midsize vessel in the Alaska market.

Specifications

Size (in Tons)	62,000	Crew	615
Passengers (Double Occ.)	1,380/1,432/1,432	Passenger/Crew Ratio	2.2/2.3/2.3 to 1
Space/Passenger Ratio	43	Year Launched	2013/1999/2000
Total Cabins/Veranda Cabins	716/197	Last Major Refurbishment	2017/2017/2018

Frommer's Ratings (Scale of 1–5)

★★★★

Cabin Comfort & Amenities	4	Dining Options	3.5
Ship Cleanliness & Maintenance	4.5	Gym, Spa & Sports Facilities	4
Public Comfort/Space	4	Children's Facilities	4
Decor	4	Enjoyment Factor	4

THE SHIPS IN GENERAL Holland America pulled out all the stops on these ships. The centerpiece of the striking triple-decked, oval atrium on the *Volendam,* for instance, is a glass sculpture by Luciano Vistosi, one of Italy's leading practitioners of the art—and that's just part of the ship's $2-million art collection, which reflects a flower theme. On the *Zaandam,* the focal point of the atrium is a 22-foot-tall pipe organ that is representative of the ship's music theme, which is filled out by a collection of guitars signed by rock musicians, including the Rolling Stones, Iggy Pop, David Bowie, and Queen (an attempt to attract a younger clientele?). Apart from the artwork and overall decorating motifs, there aren't many differences among these magnificent vessels; they really are virtually indistinguishable from one another. The *Zaandam* may look just the teeniest bit brighter than the *Volendam* and the *Amsterdam,* but hardly enough to make a real difference. Most recently, these ships received a branded Lincoln Center stage where the Explorer's Lounge used to be.

CABINS The 197 suites and deluxe staterooms on each ship have private verandas, and the smallest of the remaining 523 cabins is a comfortable 182 square feet. All cabins come with sofa seating areas. The suites and deluxe rooms also have DVDs, whirlpool tubs, and minibars. Twenty-one cabins on the *Amsterdam* are equipped to accommodate wheelchairs; twenty-two cabins apiece on *Zaandam* and *Volendam* are so equipped. On each ship, 28 cabins, in several categories, are wheelchair-accessible.

CABINS & RATES

CABINS	PER DIEM RATES	SQ. FT.	FRIDGE	HAIR DRYER	SITTING AREA	TV
Amsterdam						
Inside	$157–$171	182	no	yes	yes	yes
Outside	$171–$200	197	yes	yes	yes	yes
Suites	$368–$428	292–1,159	yes	yes	yes	yes
Volendam						
Inside	$143–$157	182	no	yes	yes	yes
Outside	$157–$186	187	yes	yes	yes	yes
Suites	$243–$486	292–1,159	yes	yes	yes	yes
Zaandam						
Inside	$129–$150	182	no	yes	yes	yes
Outside	$142–$164	197	yes	yes	yes	yes
Suites	$279–$564	292–1,159	yes	yes	yes	yes

PUBLIC AREAS Each ship has five entertainment lounges, including the main two-tiered showroom. The **Explorations Central,** a combination night-club and observation lounge, is a good place to watch the passing Alaska scenery during the day. Each ship also has a casino, a children's playroom, a cinema, a library, an arcade, and an Internet center.

DINING OPTIONS   All three ships have an alternative restaurant, the **Pinnacle Grill** (a staple on all HAL ships), which features steak and seafood, available on a reservations-only basis ($35 per-person supplement for dinner; $10 per person for lunch). These restaurants are designed with an artsy bistro vibe, with drawings and etchings on the walls. A second alternative option is Italian eatery **Canaletto,** which comes with a $15 per-person charge. During the day, though, we find ourselves headed straight to the poolside grill, **Dive-In.**

POOL, FITNESS, SPA & SPORTS FACILITIES   The gym is downright palatial on these ships, with dozens of state-of-the-art machines surrounded by floor-to-ceiling windows and an adjacent aerobics room. The spa and hair salon are not quite as striking. Three pools are on the Lido Deck, with a main pool and a wading pool under a retractable glass roof that also encloses the cafelike **Dolphin Bar.** A smaller and quieter aft pool is on the other side of the Lido buffet restaurant. On the Sports Deck is a pair of paddle-tennis courts as well as a shuffleboard court. Joggers can use the uninterrupted Lower Promenade Deck for a good workout.

5 | Westerdam • Noordam

The Verdict

These sister ships are nearly identical, each well-equipped to support HAL's position as a force in the Alaska market.

Specifications

Size (in Tons)	82,300	Crew	817
Passengers (Double Occ.)	1,916/1,972	Passenger/Crew Ratio	2.3 to 1
Space/Passenger Ratio	44	Year Launched	2004/2006
Total Cabins/Veranda Cabins	958/640	Last Major Refurbishment	2017/2015

Frommer's Ratings (Scale of 1–5)   ★★★★

Cabin Comfort & Amenities	4	Dining Options	3.5
Ship Cleanliness & Maintenance	5	Gym, Spa & Sports Facilities	4
Public Comfort/Space	4	Children's Facilities	4
Decor	4	Enjoyment Factor	4

THE SHIPS IN GENERAL   These sister ships are nearly identical, with just a couple exceptions: *Westerdam* has the Explorations Central lounge as well as a unique "Rijksmuseum at Sea" installation. The thoughtful layout prevents bottlenecks at key points—outside the dining room, for instance, and at the buffet and the pool area. Both ships have the line's B.B. King blues club and the Lincoln Center partnership. Art worth about $2.5 million, according to HAL, is well displayed throughout each of the vessels, and the decor reflects Holland's (and Holland America's) contribution to the development of cruising and, indeed, of ships as a trade and transportation medium. The nautical pieces on display are plentiful but never overwhelming.

CABINS   Nearly 85% of the ships' cabins have ocean views; 67% of them have verandas. The smallest of the inside cabins is just 151 square feet, and the standard outside rooms start at 185 square feet. Suites here go up to 1,318 square feet, making them some of the biggest in the HAL fleet. Tastefully decorated in quiet colors, all rooms have Internet/e-mail dataports, ample drawer and closet space, and quality bathroom fittings. *Noordam* has DVD players and *Westerdam* has interactive TVs; both ships have minibars.

CABINS & RATES

CABINS	PER DIEM RATES	SQ. FT.	FRIDGE	HAIR DRYER	SITTING AREA	TV
Westerdam						
Inside	$128–$171	151–185	yes	yes	yes	yes
Outside	$171–$200	171–185	yes	yes	yes	yes
Suites	$400–$471	389–1,318	yes	yes	yes	yes
Noordam						
Inside	$128–$186	151–185	yes	yes	yes	yes
Outside	$197–$311	171–185	yes	yes	yes	yes
Suites	$347–$526	398–1,318	yes	yes	yes	yes

PUBLIC AREAS   The ships include a disco; a two-level main dining room; a library; an alternative, reservations-requested restaurant; and seven lounges/ bars, including an observation lounge/nightclub. And each ship has not one, but two showrooms—a three-level main showroom (sadly, with some rather obstructed sightlines) and a more intimate "cabaret-style" venue for smaller-scale performances.

The **Club HAL** children's facilities are extensive and have both indoor and outdoor components. The ships have two interior Promenade Decks, affording walkers protection against the elements—very useful in Alaska!

Wheelchair users are well catered to on these vessels. Besides the 28 cabins specially designed for them, the ship has wheelchair elevators dedicated for use in boarding the tenders in port, two tenders equipped with special wheelchair-accessible platforms, and accessible areas at virtually all public decks, bars, and lounges.

The ships have well-equipped casinos, offering passengers the chance to try their luck at stud poker, slots, craps, and roulette. Dozens of original works of art, with combined values ranking in the millions, dot the public areas. Each of the ships also features **Explorations Cafe,** a coffeehouse environment in which passengers can browse the Internet, check e-mail, or just read the *New York Times*—transmitted electronically to the ships daily.

DINING OPTIONS   Both of these ships have HAL's signature **Pinnacle Grill** (for a supplemental charge) and a more casual buffet. There is also 24-hour room service for those who prefer in-cabin dining.

POOL, FITNESS, SPA & SPORTS FACILITIES The main pool on the Lido Deck has a retractable dome—a feature that has proven popular on other ships in Alaskan waters. A couple of hot tubs and a smaller pool complement the main pool. A huge spa, complete with the usual array of treatments and services, occupies part of the Lido Deck.

Eurodam • Nieuw Amsterdam

The Verdict

The biggest of the HAL ships in Alaska, these two are nevertheless intimate and offer some of the best experiences on the fleet.

Specifications

Size (in Tons)	86,273/86,700	Crew	876
Passengers (Double Occ.)	2,104/2,106	Passenger/Crew Ratio	2.4 to 1
Space/Passenger Ratio	41	Year Launched	2008/2010
Total Cabins/Veranda Cabins	1,052/718 and 1,053/718	Last Major Refurbishment	2018/2017

Frommer's Ratings (Scale of 1–5)   ★★★★

Cabin Comfort & Amenities	4	Dining Options	3.5
Ship Cleanliness & Maintenance	5	Gym, Spa & Sports Facilities	4
Public Comfort/Space	4	Children's Facilities	4
Decor	4	Enjoyment Factor	4

THE SHIPS IN GENERAL Part of the line's Signature class, these two ships have the most updates of any of the fleet in Alaska, yet aren't much larger than *Westerdam* and *Noordam*, the Vista-class ships in the region. Both have the updated **Explorations Central** lounge (the former Crow's Nest lounge), with such new features as interactive maps and an interactive bridge displaying real-time data.

CABINS All rooms are spacious and tastefully decorated. All have interactive On Demand TV programs and minibars.

CABINS & RATES

CABINS	PER DIEM RATES	SQ. FT.	FRIDGE	HAIR DRYER	SITTING AREA	TV
Eurodam						
Inside	$143–$200	141–284	yes	yes	yes	yes
Outside	$177–$243	169–267	yes	yes	yes	yes
Suites	$451–$471	273–1,357	yes	yes	yes	yes
Nieuw Amsterdam						
Inside	$140–$186	141–284	yes	yes	yes	yes
Outside	$171–$214	169–267	yes	yes	yes	yes
Suites	$400–$528	273–1,357	yes	yes	yes	yes

PUBLIC AREAS The ships include a disco; a two-level main dining room; a library; an alternative, reservations-requested restaurant; two showrooms;

and seven lounges/bars. On the *Nieuw Amsterdam* you'll find the Explorations Central, designed to provide lots of cool information about the cruise and its ports, while on *Eurodam* that space is still the Crow's Nest, a combination lounge and nightclub that remains a popular space day and night. Either way the space includes the **Exploration Café,** a coffeehouse designed for browsing the Internet, checking e-mail, or reading the *New York Times*—transmitted electronically to the ships daily. Both ships also feature cooking classes designed by America's Test Kitchen, B.B. King clubs for blues music, as well as music produced in partnership with New York's Lincoln Center. The ships have full casinos, too, and also show the line's BBC Earth programming. The Club HAL children's facilities are extensive, and both ships have two interior Promenade Decks, great for long walks during inclement weather.

Wheelchair users are well catered to on these vessels. Besides the 28 cabins specially designed for them, the ships have wheelchair elevators dedicated for use in boarding the tenders in port, two tenders equipped with special wheelchair-accessible platforms, and accessible areas at virtually all public decks, bars, and lounges.

DINING OPTIONS Both ships have HAL's signature **Pinnacle Grill** (for a supplemental charge), the fabulous **Dine-In** poolside grill, the **Sel de Mer** French seafood pop-up restaurant ($49 per person), a more casual buffet, and complimentary 24-hour room service. Afternoon tea is popular on these ships as is the Asian **Tamarind** restaurant, which also has a sushi bar.

POOL, FITNESS, SPA & SPORTS FACILITIES The main pool on the Lido Deck has a retractable dome—a welcome feature in Alaska, where even in summer temperatures can be too chilly for an outdoor swim. There are also a couple of hot tubs and a smaller pool as well as a huge spa.

NORWEGIAN CRUISE LINE

7665 Corporate Center Dr., Miami, FL 33126. www.ncl.com. ⓒ **866/234-7350** or 305/436-4000.

Pros

o **Flexible dining.** Norwegian's dining policy lets you sit where and with whom you want, dress as you want (within reason), and dine when you want (dinner is served 5:30–10pm; guests must be seated by 9:30pm) at a wide variety of restaurants, including one that's open 24 hours. Room service is also available.

o **Smoke-free zones.** Norwegian promotes a smoke-free environment for those who want it, and all dining rooms are smoke-free.

Cons

o **Few quiet spots.** Other than the library, there's not a quiet room to be found indoors, but Norwegian has added adult quiet zones at its pool decks.

o **Crowded dining areas.** The most popular of the alternative restaurants can get booked up early.

5

THE BIG SHIPS | Norwegian Cruise Line

THE LINE IN A NUTSHELL   The very contemporary Norwegian Cruise Line offers an informal and upbeat Alaska program on three large ships: the 12-year-old *Norwegian Pearl,* 13-year-old *Norwegian Jewel,* and the brand-new *Norwegian Bliss.*

THE EXPERIENCE   Norwegian excels in activities, alternative dining, and a lack of regimentation. Recreational and fitness programs are among the best in the industry. The line's youth programs for kids and teens are also top-notch. The company offers what it calls "Freestyle Cruising," which makes life a whole lot easier for passengers. Norwegian was, in fact, the pioneers of the concept in the North American cruise market. One of the main components of Freestyle Cruising is freedom in when, where, and with whom passengers dine. Guests can eat in their choice of a variety of restaurants pretty much any time between 5:30 and 10pm (you must be seated by 9:30pm), with no prearranged table assignment or dining time. Other features of Freestyle Cruising are that daily service charges are automatically charged to room accounts, dress codes are more relaxed (resort casual) at all times, and at the end of the voyage, passengers can remain in their cabins until their time comes to disembark, rather than huddling in lounges or squatting on luggage in stairwells until their lucky color comes up. Freestyle Cruising has since been copied, to whatever extent possible, by other lines operating in the U.S.

Naturally, with each new ship in a line's fleet, there usually comes innovation. In this case, the 4,000-passenger *Norwegian Bliss* was designed with the first deck-top racetrack and a waterslide that juts out over the edge of the ship. It's the largest ship in the region.

THE FLEET   *Norwegian Jewel* joined the fleet in 2005 and is a tad smaller than the newer *Norwegian Pearl.* Both ships have lots of windows for great viewing. Though these ships are relatively large and have plenty of public areas, some of the cabins are on the small side, and others have insufficient closet space. The *Norwegian Bliss* is significantly larger and features the line's wide array of eateries, plus a few new ones.

PASSENGER PROFILE   In Alaska, the overall demographic tends to be more toward older, affluent retirees than on the line's warmer-climate sailings, but you'll find an increasing number of younger couples and families as well, attracted by the line's flexible dining policy and relaxed dress code, not to mention the fun new activities on *Norwegian Bliss.*

DINING OPTIONS   The cruise line has long handled the business of dining in an innovative way, with an extensive number of alternative restaurants (albeit often at an extra charge) in addition to two traditional (and subsequently smaller) main dining rooms. And you can dress pretty much however you like, too—guests are allowed to wear blue jeans, shorts, and T-shirts in the evenings at the buffets, outdoor barbecues, and 24-hour venues (there is one optional formal night for those who want to dress up). As on all ships, breakfast and lunch are available either in the dining room, on an open-seating basis, or in the buffet up top, where passengers can help themselves, dress

5

Norwegian Cruise Line

THE BIG SHIPS

Norwegian Fleet Itineraries

SHIP	ITINERARIES
Norwegian Pearl	7-night Inside Passage/Glacier Bay: Round-trip from Seattle, visiting Juneau or Icy Strait Point, Skagway, Ketchikan, and Victoria, BC (May–Sept)
Norwegian Jewel	7-night Inside Passage/Sawyer Glacier: Round-trip from Seattle, visiting Ketchikan, Juneau, Skagway, and Victoria, BC (May–Sept)
Norwegian Jewel	7-night Glacier Bay from Vancouver: Northbound from Vancouver, BC, to Seward, visiting Ketchikan, Juneau, Skagway, and Glacier Bay (May–Sept)
Norwegian Sun	7-night Sawyer Glacier from Seward: Southbound from Seward to Vancouver, BC, visiting Ketchikan, Juneau, Skagway, Glacier Bay, Hubbard Glacier, Sawyer Glacier, and Icy Strait Point (May–Sept)
Norwegian Bliss	7-night Inside Passage/Glacier Bay: Round-trip from Seattle, visiting Juneau, Skagway, Ketchikan, and Victoria, BC, and cruising Sawyer Glacier (June–Sept)

pretty much as they please, and enjoy a more relaxed meal—chefs manning cooking stations at the buffet prepare food right in front of your eyes. In addition to the main dining rooms, both ships have a variety of other food options—more than a dozen a piece. Included in the mix, depending on the ship, are French; sushi, sashimi, and teppanyaki; Brazilian-style *churrascaria* (steakhouse); and a signature steakhouse for which reservations are strongly recommended. All specialty restaurants now have delicious signature dishes. Pricing for the specialty restaurants is known to bounce around a bit as the line manages crowds by adjusting prices—they're now a la carte, but it's typical to pay $15 to $30 extra per person to dine in many of the eateries.

ACTIVITIES   In Alaska, the line has a destination lecturer or two on the history, landscape, and culture of the state; wine-tasting demonstrations; art auctions; dance classes and a fitness program; daily quizzes; crafts; board games; and bingo, among other activities. Passengers also tend to spend time at sports activities, which include basketball and mini-soccer. The ships all have Internet cafes and Wi-Fi, with package rates available. In addition, Alaska sailings feature some 130 options for shore excursions, including Dogsledding & Glacier Flightseeing Helicopter, Whale-Watching and Wildlife Quest, and the Historic Gold Mine, Panning & Salmon Bake.

CHILDREN'S PROGRAMS   Norwegian ships tend to be very family-friendly: There's at least one full-time youth coordinator per age group, a kids' activity room, video games, an ice-cream stand, and group babysitting for ages 3 and up, plus a visit from a park ranger for ships that sail to Glacier Bay National Park.

ENTERTAINMENT   Entertainment is a Norwegian hallmark, with Broadway-style productions that are surprisingly lavish and artistically ambitious (we were especially excited to see the production of "Jersey Boys" on *Norwegian Bliss*). Show rooms also feature magic, comedians, and tribute bands. The three ships boast the Norwegian fleet's big, splashy casinos, and Norwegian's ultra-hip theme party—"White Hot Night"—keeps the ship lively into the wee hours.

SERVICE Generally, room and bar service fleetwide is speedy and efficient, and the waitstaff is attentive and accommodating. In the alternative dining rooms, service can be somewhat slow if it's a large group at one table, but at least on the *Norwegian Pearl,* they have made great strides in improving this. With the introduction of the line's flexible dining program, additional crew members, mostly waiters and kitchen staff, were added to each ship. To eliminate tipping confusion, the line automatically adds a charge of $16.99 per passenger per day in suites and $13.99 per passenger per day in all other cabin categories to shipboard accounts. These also can be prepaid at the time of booking, and you are free to adjust the amount up or down as you see fit based on the service you receive. Full-service laundry and dry cleaning are available.

CRUISETOURS & ADD-ON PROGRAMS Norwegian offers five cruisetours before the 7-day southbound cruise or after the 7-day northbound cruise: the Fairbanks Denali Express, Anchorage Denali Express, Denali/ Alyeska Explorer, Denali by Rail Explorer, and the Authentic Alaska. All cruisetours are fully escorted by local Alaskan guides, feature 1 or 2 nights in Denali, and include a scenic Alaska Railroad adventure and transfers.

5 | Norwegian Pearl

The Verdict

Norwegian's newest ship in Alaska is an evolutionary step forward with such features as bowling. It's the perfect ship for those who like lots of things to do and places to eat without much regimentation.

Specifications

Size (in Tons)	93,530	Crew	1,099
Passengers (Double Occ.)	2,394	Passenger/Crew Ratio	2.2 to 1
Space/Passenger Ratio	37	Year Launched	2006
Total Cabins/Veranda Cabins	1,197/360	Last Major Refurbishment	2017

Frommer's Ratings (Scale of 1–5)   ★★★★

Cabin Comfort & Amenities	4	Dining Options	5
Ship Cleanliness & Maintenance	4	Gym, Spa & Sports Facilities	4
Public Comfort/Space	4	Children's Facilities	4.5
Decor	4	Enjoyment Factor	4

THE SHIP IN GENERAL Launched in December 2006, *Norwegian Pearl* was the line's first ship to have a bowling alley, among other new features. In February 2017, the ship emerged from dry dock with the line's "Norwegian Edge" improvements, with a cleaner, more modern look.

CABINS *Norwegian Pearl* has 1,197 cabins, 360 of which have balconies. The smallest of the rooms is about 143 square feet, average for this new breed of ship—not big, but not cramped, either. As part of the 2017 dry dock, cabins got new carpets, furniture, and TVs as well as USB ports and a cool blue color scheme. The ship's biggest accommodations—the spectacular, three-bedroom Garden Villa—runs to a staggering 4,390 square feet. In dry dock, the Haven area of top-tier suites, which has its own courtyard with a pool, also received cabanas. Twenty-seven rooms are wheelchair-accessible. One oft-voiced complaint in some of the lower-end cabins is an age-old Norwegian bugaboo: not enough closet and drawer space. (That doesn't apply, of course, to the suites, and most assuredly not to the Garden Villa.) This should not be an issue for a 1-week Alaska cruise when there are two people to a cabin.

CABINS & RATES

CABINS	PER DIEM RATES	SQ. FT.	FRIDGE	HAIR DRYER	SITTING AREA	TV
Inside	$128–$163	143	no	yes	no	yes
Outside	$154–$342	161	no	yes	yes	yes
Suites	$264–$1,271	285–4,390	some	yes	yes	yes

PUBLIC AREAS Public areas are bright and airy, if just a tad too colorful. The **Library,** on the other hand, is a tastefully decorated, relaxing space and the only quiet room on the ship. *Pearl* has a vast array of eating and drinking spots. Other spaces include a huge casino, with wonderfully fair, Las Vegas–type odds. The main showroom, the two-story **Stardust Theater,** holds about 1,100 in comfy seating, with good sightlines from either floor (and an air-conditioning flow from the back of each chair, helping to keep the room nice and cool). With its massive stage and loads of technological bells and whistles, the Stardust pulls off some pretty ambitious Broadway-style revues. **Splash Academy** and **Entourage,** for ages 3 to 17, have trained supervisors and are fully equipped with TVs, PlayStation 3, Wii, a disco floor, foosball tables, an air hockey table, a nursery, and a sleep/rest area.

DINING OPTIONS In addition to its two main dining rooms (**Indigo** and the **Summer Palace**), the ship houses several other eateries in keeping with Norwegian's promise of providing maximum dining flexibility, including a French bistro; an Italian trattoria; a Brazilian *churrascaria* complete with *passadors* (meat carvers); a signature steakhouse; eateries for teppanyaki, sushi, tapas, and more; and the **Blue Lagoon,** open 24 hours a day. Norwegian switched from a fixed fee for specialty restaurants to a la carte pricing in 2016. Colorful electronic signage around the ship lets guests know which restaurants are full and which ones have space. Even late in the afternoons, it's often possible to book a table in any restaurant for prime or near-prime dining times.

POOL, FITNESS, SPA & SPORTS FACILITIES *Pearl* has an adult pool, six hot tubs, a kiddie pool, a spa with exceptional thermal offerings highlighted by the large thalassotherapy pool, and a salon. Active types should check out the **Body Waves** fitness center; the jogging/walking track; the rock-climbing wall; the bowling alley; and the court used for basketball, volleyball, mini-soccer, and tennis. Also nice in this day and age is the Deck 7 promenade, which goes around the entire ship (2⅔ laps to a mile).

Norwegian Jewel

The Verdict

The first of Norwegian's popular *Jewel*-class series of ships is lively and fun, with lots of restaurants and nightspots to keep cruisers busy in the evening.

Specifications

Size (in Tons)	93,502	Crew	1,100
Passengers (Double Occ.)	2,376	Passenger/Crew Ratio	2.2 to 1
Space/Passenger Ratio	39	Year Launched	2005
Total Cabins/Veranda Cabins	1,163/510	Last Major Refurbishment	2014

Frommer's Ratings (Scale of 1–5)   ★★★★

Cabin Comfort & Amenities	4	Dining Options	5
Ship Cleanliness & Maintenance	4	Gym, Spa & Sports Facilities	4
Public Comfort/Space	4	Children's Facilities	3.5
Decor	4	Enjoyment Factor	4

THE SHIP IN GENERAL From the outside, the *Norwegian Jewel* looks a lot like its slightly younger sister, the *Norwegian Pearl,* and it's similar on the inside, too, with a few key differences—the most notable being the lack of a bowling alley In 2016, the ship went through a major refurbishment that brought on board the line's O'Sheehan's pub and the Sugarcane mojito bar as well as refreshment to a variety of other onboard spaces.

CABINS Almost 540 cabins have a private balcony. The inside cabins are smallish, ranging from 142 to 150 square feet. Suites have floor-to-ceiling windows, refrigerators, and private balconies. All cabins are equipped with TVs, telephones, small dressing tables, soundproof doors, individual climate control, and sitting areas that are actually big enough to stretch out in. Closet and drawer space is quite limited, so pack lightly. The ship has 27 wheelchair-accessible cabins, including suites, all featuring collapsible shower stools mounted on shower walls; all toilets feature collapsible arm guards and lowered wash basins.

CABINS & RATES

CABINS	PER DIEM RATES	SQ. FT.	FRIDGE	HAIR DRYER	SITTING AREA	TV
Inside	$107–$154	142–150	yes	yes	no	yes
Outside	$150–$334	160–205	yes	yes	some	yes
Suites	$278–$2,499	285–4,891	yes	yes	yes	yes

PUBLIC AREAS Norwegian boasts that the *Jewel* has 16 eateries and 13 bars and nightspots, an unusually large number for a ship its size—all part of the line's "freestyle" concept of offering passengers lots of choices. The *Jewel*'s two main dining rooms (**Azura** and **Tsar's Palace**) offer traditional (that is to say, multicourse) meals and a range of lighter fare, but dining doesn't involve the traditional assigned seating found on some other lines ("If it's 8pm, it must be dinnertime"). Instead, the ship follows a no-reservations, come-as-you-please format in a wide variety of restaurants.

Public rooms include a casino, a conference center, a disco, a library, a karaoke bar, a martini bar, a champagne and wine bar, a beer and whiskey pub, and a three-level show lounge. For kids, in addition to the scheduled Nickelodeon activities, there's a children's playroom (**Splashdown Academy Youth Center**), teen center (**Entourage**), and a video arcade.

DINING OPTIONS   Rest assured, you won't go hungry on the *Jewel*. The unusually wide (for a cruise ship) assortment of restaurants available at night includes **Le Bistro,** a French eatery; **Chin Chin,** serving Asian cuisine; a sushi bar; the line's signature **Cagney's Steakhouse; the Teppanyaki Room;** and an Italian eatery. As if that weren't enough, the **Blue Lagoon** serves hamburgers, hot dogs, soups, salads, and pizza 24 hours a day. The **Garden Cafe** buffet includes a kids' buffet section with small seats and tables. *A caveat:* As on other Norwegian ships, while the *Jewel's* main dining rooms come at no extra charge, most of the specialty restaurants have a la carte pricing.

POOL, FITNESS, SPA & SPORTS FACILITIES   The *Jewel* is well equipped for the sporty and active vacationer. In addition to the fitness center, there are heated pools (two main pools with a waterslide and a children's pool), hot tubs, a jogging/walking track (3½ laps is 1 mile), and an array of sports facilities, including a basketball/volleyball/tennis court. Adults can take advantage of quiet zones poolside. The **Body Waves Fitness Center & Mandara Spa,** located on Deck 12, is well stocked with Jacuzzis, hydrotherapy baths, and saunas—not to mention facilities for couples to take treatments together.

Norwegian Bliss

The Verdict

The line's biggest, flashiest ship is full of new features that many cruisers can't wait to check out.

Specifications

Size (in Tons)	167,800	Crew	2,100
Passengers (Double Occ.)	4,004	Passenger/Crew Ratio	1.9 to 1
Space/Passenger Ratio	415	Year Launched	2018
Total Cabins/Veranda Cabins	2,043/1,476	Last Major Refurbishment	N/A

Frommer's Ratings (Scale of 1–5)   N/A

Not available at press time.

THE SHIP IN GENERAL   This may be the third ship in the line's "Breakaway Plus" class, but it's the biggest ship sailing in the region and the first ship from a mainstream line to ever debut in Alaska. As such, *Norwegian Bliss*'s arrival on the scene in Alaska in 2018 is big news. With every ship the mainstream lines seem to up the ante in activities and entertainment, and *Norwegian Bliss* is no exception: With this ship, the line launches some exciting new features: from a stage-show production of "Jersey Boys" to new dining concepts (an all-dessert restaurant? Awesome!) to a pretty impressive-looking water park. A key feature that is especially great for Alaska is the giant new Observation Lounge, which is forward-facing and offers passengers the same view the captain enjoys up on the bridge.

CABINS More than 80% of the cabins on *Norwegian Bliss* are outsides (with ocean views), but only 40% have verandas. That said, the ship has the line's famous "studio cabins," which are designed for individuals traveling alone. Sure, they're small, but they have a shared lounge (a great place to meet other solo travelers), some have "virtual" windows, and all enable cruisers to avoid the dreaded single supplement, which can make cruising for one so unaffordable. The ship also has the line's well-loved Haven area, a ship-within-a-ship concept with its own concierge, restaurant, and sundeck, as well as spa cabins that offer complimentary access to the ship's thermal suite.

CABINS & RATES

CABINS	PER DIEM RATES	SQ. FT.	FRIDGE	HAIR DRYER	SITTING AREA	TV
Inside	$150–$250	135–201	some	yes	no	yes
Outside	$207–$400	160–425	yes	yes	some	yes
Suites	$288–$1,099	430–1,458	yes	yes	yes	yes

PUBLIC AREAS Starting at the top, this is a ship that's as much inspired by amusement parks as by resorts. On deck is an electric go-kart racetrack, a laser-tag park, and a waterpark that's home to Ocean Loops, which carries riders out over the side of the ship. There are also racing slides, a kiddie splash area, two pools, and six hot tubs. The ship has almost a dozen bars, too—including a whiskey bar, a mojito bar, and a cigar lounge—as well as a theater, a comedy club, lots of spaces for kids and teens, a casino, and shopping.

DINING OPTIONS Variety is one of the line's strengths, and outside of the main dining rooms, which have open seating, *Norwegian Bliss* offers an impressive range of specialty restaurants. Besides the line's stalwarts—a **Cagney's Steakhouse, La Cucina,** a teppanyaki grill, and more—there are also some favorites from *Norwegian Escape,* which took dining to a new level for the line. We love **Food Republic** (a sushi bar and modern fusion spot with memorably good bulgogi tacos and pastrami dumplings); **District Brew House** (an undeniably cool pub—not something we ever say about cruise ship bars, we assure you!—with more beers to choose from than your local beer joint); and even **Margaritaville,** with well-executed quesadillas and fish tacos. Here, too, is **Ocean Blue,** the upscale seafood restaurant that made a splash on *Norwegian Getaway* and *Norwegian Breakaway. Norwegian Bliss* also has some original, upscale spots we can't wait to try, including **Los Lobos** (Mexican), **Q** (barbecue), and **Coco's** (an all-dessert restaurant). Note that, like the other Norwegian ships, all of the specialty restaurants are priced a la carte. The ship also has the line's first full **Starbucks** location.

POOL, FITNESS, SPA & SPORTS FACILITIES The ship's sprawling **Mandara Spa** is home to treatment rooms; a thermal suite (with salt, steam, and snow rooms); a gym; a salon; and even a classy-looking barbershop for men. There are also two adults-only deck areas: **Spice H20,** which is complimenatary, and **Vibe Beach Club** ($25 day pass; $99 weekly pass).

OCEANIA CRUISES

7665 Corporate Center Dr., Miami, FL 33126. www.oceaniacruises.com. ℂ **855/335-2390.**

Pros

o **Excellent dining.** Whether you're dining in the main dining room or in one of the two specialty restaurants, food is a focus at Oceania.

o **Small ship size.** The relative small size of the ships makes for an intimate, warm experience without masses of people.

o **Longer itineraries than the industry norm.** In the case of Alaska, the line offers 10- and 12-day trips (in addition to 7-day trips), giving you plenty of time to fully experience the destination.

o **Pretty public rooms.** Many public rooms, including the library, the Grand Bar, and the main atrium, are as pretty as any at sea.

Cons

o **Cabin size.** Cabins are relatively small.

o **Low ceilings.** In some areas, the ship's low ceilings make for a somewhat cramped feeling; in the case of the main dining room, it gets quite noisy.

THE LINE IN A NUTSHELL   Oceania Cruises entered the cruise industry in 2003 when it launched *Regatta,* formerly the *R Two* from Renaissance (which went belly-up after 9/11). It was an interesting beginning for *Regatta,* along with its sister ship, *Insignia,* formerly the *R One,* as the ships were being positioned above the premium lines and below the luxury lines. It was essentially a new category they called "upper premium," and it's been very successful, with Oceania adding a third former Renaissance ship to the fleet in 2005 (*Nautica,* formerly the *R Five*) and two new-builds, *Marina* and *Riviera,* in February 2011 and May 2012, respectively. In 2016, *Sirena*—another former R-class ship—joined the fleet and was updated extensively. Both Oceania and Regent Seven Seas Cruises are part of Norwegian Cruise Line Holdings.

THE EXPERIENCE   Oceania truly offers a deluxe or, said another way, upscale, experience. There's little glitz or hoopla on board, and the hallmarks of the line are dining, service, and itineraries. The no-charge specialty restaurants are way above the norm. One of the line's biggest strengths is the size of its first three vessels (one of which, *Regatta,* is Oceania's only ship in Alaska). At 30,277 tons and carrying 684 guests, these ships are small-to-midsize by today's standards. It's an informal setting (Oceania calls it "country-club casual") without crowds and lines. Oceania is a relative newcomer to Alaska, only entering the market in 2011. After a 1-year hiatus, the line returned in 2013, and in 2018 *Regatta* will offer 15 sailings in the region with 10 different itineraries.

THE FLEET   *Regatta*'s size is excellent for Alaska, making it easier to navigate closer to the highlights. Carrying only 684 passengers, *Regatta* offers a midsize alternative to the much larger premium ships and provides plenty of upscale features at way-lower cruise fares than the luxury lines. In 2014, *Regatta,* along with sister ships *Insignia* and *Nautica,* underwent a major multimillion-dollar refurbishment that brought new furnishings and decor to all public rooms, suites, and cabins. The overhaul (the largest for the vessel since it joined the Oceania fleet) also included the addition of a number of the popular features found on Oceania's newer ships, such as the Italian-style **Baristas** coffee bar serving Illy espresso drinks and a transformed **Terrace Café** that now boasts a state-of-the-art grill.

PASSENGER PROFILE   The basic profile is one of couples in their 50s and 60s, but Oceania's ships are equally comfortable for both younger and older cruisers. The line is appropriate for those looking for a somewhat informal cruise, where dining and excellent service take a higher priority than glitz, glamour, and nonstop activity. Historically, itineraries have been very port-intensive, with few sea days, so a busy shipboard agenda has never been a priority to passengers.

DINING OPTIONS   Food is a focus at Oceania, which offers menus overseen by celebrated chef Jacques Pépin and multiple gourmet eateries. Even Oceania's smallest vessels offer an Italian restaurant and steakhouse in addition to a main restaurant, and the food at all three is superb. While you'll pay extra for drinks on Oceania, one of the premium aspects of sailing with the line is that none of its restaurants come with an extra charge, in contrast to the norm on ships operated by the likes of Princess, Holland America, and Royal Caribbean. Another nice feature of Oceania's longer sailings is that entrees and featured items are not repeated, allowing the galley staff to show off their skills with great variety. Pépin, the line's Executive Culinary Director, works with Oceania's chefs to develop exciting and exotic dishes as well as more traditional ones. For those who want more, Oceania's ships also offer afternoon tea service, ice cream and sundae bars, and complimentary 24-hour room service. Alternatives include Canyon Ranch Spa Cuisine and kosher meals upon request as well as extensive vegan and vegetarian options at every meal.

ACTIVITIES   Oceania does not go out of its way to provide an extensive list of things for passengers to do, in keeping with its informal style and port-intensive sailings. It offers lectures on the destination and the ports of call. The beautiful library has loads of reading selections. Weather permitting, the private cabanas are a great place to hang out and watch the scenery unfold. Dance classes and cooking lessons are part of a sea-day's agenda. And there's plenty of live music around the ship to enjoy.

CHILDREN'S PROGRAMS   While kids may be on board, it's mostly up to their parents to entertain them. Oceania's ships have no facilities specifically for kids and really don't cater to them. That said, in 2013 Oceania introduced the Alaska Explorer Youth Program for select Alaskan sailings, a program designed for children ages 5 to 13 that is supervised by experienced youth counselors. It includes games, activities, and Alaska-inspired events.

Oceania Cruises Fleet Itineraries

SHIP	ITINERARIES
Regatta	11-day trip from San Francisco to Vancouver, BC, visiting Astoria, Ketchikan, Juneau, and Sitka; with scenic cruising of the Inside Passage, Hubbard Glacier, and Outside Passage (May)
Regatta	10-day round-trip Vancouver, visiting Wrangell, Icy Strait, Haines, Sitka, Ketchikan, and Victoria; with scenic cruising of the Inside Passage and Hubbard Glacier (June)
Regatta	7-day trip from Vancouver, BC, to Seattle, visiting Sitka, Ketchikan, and Prince Rupert; with scenic cruising of the Inside Passage, Tracy Arm Fjord, Sawyer Glacier, and Outside Passage (June)
Regatta	10-day round-trip Seattle, visiting Ketchikan, Juneau, Skagway, Icy Strait, Sitka, and Victoria; with scenic cruising of the Inside Passage, Hubbard Glacier, and Outside Passage (June)
Regatta	7-day round-trip Seattle, visiting Ketchikan, Sitka, and Prince Rupert; with scenic cruising of the Inside Passage, Outside Passage, Tracy Arm Fjord, and Sawyer Glacier (June & Aug)
Regatta	10-day round-trip Seattle, visiting Ketchikan, Juneau, Haines, Sitka, and Victoria; with scenic cruising of the Inside Passage, Hubbard Glacier, and Outside Passage (July)
Regatta	11-day round-trip Seattle, visiting Ketchikan, Sitka, Skagway, Icy Strait, Juneau, Wrangell, and Victoria; with scenic cruising of the Inside Passage, Hubbard Glacier, and Outside Passage (Aug)
Regatta	10-day trip from Seattle to Vancouver, BC, visiting Ketchikan, Icy Strait, Juneau, Skagway, Sitka, and Victoria; with scenic cruising of the Inside Passage, Hubbard Glacier, and Outside Passage (Sept)
Regatta	10-day round-trip Vancouver, BC, visiting Ketchikan, Juneau, Skagway, Sitka, Wrangell, and Victoria; with scenic cruising of the Outside Passage, Hubbard Glacier, and Inside Passage (Sept)
Regatta	11-day trip from Vancouver, BC, to San Francisco, visiting Ketchikan, Juneau, Sitka, Wrangell, Victoria, and Astoria; with scenic cruising of the Inside Passage, Hubbard Glacier, and Outside Passage (Sept)

ENTERTAINMENT   Show lounges on Oceania ships, including the Alaska-based *Regatta,* are relatively small and limit what performers can do. But *Regatta* has an eight-piece orchestra for shows and musical entertainment, a small team of performers, and cabaret acts. Depending on the cruise, there may be a string quartet, flamenco guitarist, concert pianist, jazz combos, local and regional folk ensembles, and the occasional headline entertainers.

SERVICE   The *Regatta*'s crew complement of 400 (European officers and international crew) does a great job, and the passenger-to-crew ratio of 1.7 to 1 is right there with the top luxury lines. Service is warm and friendly without being overbearing. In the dining room and bars, staff is particularly skillful at getting to know passenger names. In the main dining room, service can be a bit rushed (they do need to turn over the tables) and, because many of the tables are a bit close to each other, a bit informal. It's a much more relaxed experience in the alternative restaurants. Cabin service is excellent, and those rooms with butler service get extra pampering.

5

THE BIG SHIPS | Oceania Cruises

CRUISETOURS & ADD-ON PROGRAMS For those who have never been to Alaska before, a land trip before or after the cruise is virtually a must. Oceania's brochure includes a 5-day pre-cruise tour package from Anchorage that includes a combination of rail and bus travel; all transfers and hotels as well as most meals are included in the pricing. The price for this 4-day program is $2,299 per person, double occupancy. Oceania also offers hotel packages in San Francisco, Vancouver, and Seattle for pre/post stays. Prices depend on number of days booked.

Oceania Regatta

The Verdict

Having recently emerged from a major makeover, *Regatta* is a terrific midsize ship carrying 684 passengers in a decidedly upscale, informal atmosphere. Dining and service are key elements in this nonglitzy ship, with very classy decor and features. The ship is a great midpoint between the more heavily populated premium ships and the more expensive luxury ships.

Specifications

Size (in Tons)	30,277	Crew	400
Passengers (Double Occ.)	684	Passenger/Crew Ratio	1.7 to 1
Space/Passenger Ratio	44	Year Launched	1998
Total Cabins/Veranda Cabins	342/232	Last Major Refurbishment	2014

Frommer's Ratings (Scale of 1–5)　　　★★★★½

Cabin Comfort & Amenities	4.5	Dining Options	4.5
Ship Cleanliness & Maintenance	5	Gym, Spa & Sports Facilities	4.5
Public Comfort/Space	4.5	Children's Facilities	N/A
Decor	4.5	Enjoyment Factor	4.5

THE SHIP IN GENERAL *Regatta*, a midsize 30,277-ton vessel, carrying only 684 passengers, is an upper premium vessel, offering a great compromise between the bigger premium ships and the more expensive luxury ships. The space ratio (the industry measure that tells you how spacious a ship will be based on the amount of inside room per person) is 44, a nice midpoint in today's market. It's a calm experience, where passengers mostly fend for themselves without relying on the ship to keep them active every minute of every day. It's mostly a couples' experience that is decidedly not for kids. The decor of the ship is old-world country-club classy in a mix of styles—with some public rooms such as the library, **Grand Bar,** and the simply gorgeous atrium/staircase. A major overhaul of the vessel in dry dock in 2014 brought all-new furniture and decor to public areas and cabins, with top-tier Owner's and Vista suites getting brand-new bathrooms with oversize walk-in showers and marble and granite vanities. Other changes included the addition of a classic, Italian-style **Baristas** coffee bar (a staple of Oceania's newer ships); new steam and changing rooms in the **Canyon Ranch SpaClub;** a mini-golf course, new shuffleboard courts, and a selection of deck games; and a **Sports Deck** atop the ship offering magnificent vistas of the sea. New original artwork, in line with the celebrated collection on *Marina* and *Riviera,* was also added.

CABINS   The 342 rooms break down into 16 different pricing categories. Realistically, however, the ship offers eight types of rooms. At the top end of the spectrum are the six Owner's Suites and four Vista Suites, located fore and aft on Decks 6, 7, and 8. Including their verandas, these rooms range from 786 to nearly 1,000 square feet. The 52 Penthouse Suites are all on Deck 8 and measure 322 square feet including the veranda. These categories come with butler service.

The three categories of Concierge Level Veranda Staterooms on Deck 7 and the two categories of Veranda Staterooms on Deck 6 all measure 216 square feet, including the veranda. The four categories of Deluxe Ocean View State-rooms on Decks 3, 4, 6, and 7 are 143 or 165 square feet. The 28 Inside Staterooms measure 160 square feet.

Naturally, the larger rooms come with the most amenities. For example, butler service comes with penthouses on up. Jacuzzis, 42-inch plasma TVs, a laptop computer, and more are in the Owner's and Vista suites; living room areas and bathtubs are in the Penthouse Suites; and large flatscreen TVs and premier services (such as priority restaurant reservations and debarkation) are found in the concierge-level rooms. The refreshed rooms have a more modern look similar to what is found on Oceania's newer vessels and come with queen or twin Tranquility Beds, vanity desk, breakfast table, 20-inch flatscreen TVs with DVD player, security safe, goose-down pillows, Egyptian-cotton linens, plush towels, Grohe handheld shower head, full length mirror, and more.

CABINS & RATES

CABINS	PER DIEM RATES	SQ. FT.	FRIDGE	HAIR DRYER	SITTING AREA	TV
Inside	$350	160	yes	yes	yes	yes
Outside	$400	165	yes	yes	yes	yes
Outside w/ Veranda	$460	216	yes	yes	yes	yes
Penthouses/ Suites	$600–$850	322–1,000	yes	yes	yes	yes

PUBLIC AREAS   Beyond the very attractive reception area on Deck 4 with a concierge and shore excursion desk, the rest of the public areas cover Decks 5 and 9 through 11. Deck 5 starts with the **Lounge** at one end, where all perfor-mances and most activities take place, including cooking demos, dance classes, lectures, and more. At the other end is the **Grand Dining Room.** Midship has the casino, shops, and two great bars: the martini bar and lounge, with an exten-sive list of beverage options and, often, live music before and after dinner; and the lovely **Grand Bar,** adjacent to the main dining room—comfy seating and excellent service make this a great spot before meals. Deck 9 has the **Canyon Ranch SpaClub** at one end with salon, fitness center, treatment rooms, and steam rooms/lockers. Tucked in nearby are the Internet facility and the card room. At the other end is the **Terrace Café.** In between, naturally, is the pool area. It's not a huge pool, but it has two whirlpools, plenty of seating, and comfy loungers. On the side opposite **Waves Grill** is the **Patio,** a wonderful, relaxing space. Deck 10 offers up the forward-looking **Horizons Bar** at one end and **Toscana/Polo Grill** at the other. Just outside the alternative restaurants is the **Library,** perhaps the most beautiful room of its kind to be found anywhere at sea. Forward on Deck 11 is the sundeck; at the very front end are the private cabanas. They're a bit pricey, but for scenic days in Alaska, they book up fast.

DINING OPTIONS *Oceania Regatta* features four primary places to dine. First is the **Grand Dining Room** on Deck 5. It holds about 340 passengers, all open seating, for breakfast, lunch, and dinner. The dining room has plenty of tables for two, but for optimum privacy, try and snag a table along the wall or window. Table settings include Versace bone china, Riedel crystal, and Christofle silverware. Menus, all prepared under the auspices of famed chef Jacques Pépin, are a delight; not one of the nightly international-cuisine entrees and specialties is repeated during a cruise. In addition to the regular menu, Canyon Ranch Spa Cuisine as well as vegetarian and kosher options are available. The two alternative restaurants, **Polo Grill,** offering steaks, chops, and seafood (98 seats), and Toscana (96 seats), for Italian dining, are terrific. There's no extra charge, but reservations are required. Casual dining is available for all meals in the **Terrace Café,** which has 154 seats inside and 186 seats outside. The eatery offers up buffets (with some custom-made items) for breakfast and lunch and converts to a really nice alternative for evenings, with tapas, pasta, sushi, and other dishes. The aft, outdoor section is a great location for scenery watching on summer evenings in Alaska, when it stays light so late. In addition, there's 24-hour room service at no charge, sunrise continental breakfast in the **Horizon** lounge, and pizza.

POOL, FITNESS, SPA & SPORTS FACILITIES The **Canyon Ranch SpaClub,** a nautical branch of Arizona's famous Canyon Ranch, offers up a wide range of spa and salon services including its signature Canyon Stone Massage, Thai Massage, and Total Elegance Facial. Special treatments for men are on the menu. It also offers wellness lectures and lifestyle analysis, holistic sessions, a thalassotherapy pool, steam rooms, private spa deck with daybeds, personal fitness training, yoga and Pilates, aerobics, and step and strength-training classes. The smallish pool is ship-center on Deck 9, while the short jogging track goes around part of Deck 10.

PONANT

420 Lexington Ave., Suite 2838, NY, NY 10170. us.ponant.com. ℂ **888/400-1082.**

Pros

- **French connection.** For Francophiles, the French-speaking crew, French wine, and French fare are all part of the charm.
- **French partnerships.** You'll find everything from Veuve Cliquot Champagne to Fragonard room spray and Ladurée macaroons on board.

Ponant Fleet Itineraries

SHIP	ITINERARIES
Le Boréal	16-night Fire & Ice in the Arctic: Cruises from Nome to Seward, stopping in a variety of Russian and American ports
L'Austral, Le Soléal	14-night In the Wake of Pioneers: Cruises from Nome to Vancouver, BC, stopping at Ukivok Shoal or Savoonga, Saint Matthew Island, Saint George Island, Dutch Harbor, Delarof Harbor, Unga Island, Geographic Harbor, Sitka, Hoggatt Bay, Prince Rupert, Alert Bay, and Seymour Narrows
Le Soléal	12-night Magnificent Volcanoes of the Aleutian Islands: Cruises from Petropavlovsk-Kamtchatski to Juneau, stopping at Kiska Island, Davidof Island, Adak Island, Dutch Harbor, Delarof Harbor, Geographic Harbor, Hidden Harbor, Holgate Glacier, Tsaa Fjord, Inian Islands, and Elfin Cove
Le Soléal	12-night Wildlife & Forests of Alaska: Cruises from Seward to Vancouver, BC, stopping at Barry Arm Fjord, College Fjord, Cordova, Hubbard Glacier, Elfin Cove, Inian Islands, Red Bluff Bay, the Brothers, Kake, Endicott, Petersburg, Wrangell Narrows, Rudyerd Bay, Twin Island, Pine Island, and Seymour Narrows

Cons

o **French connection.** For non-Francophiles, the sometimes heavy (if wonderfully authentic) French fare (foie gras and duck confit, anyone?) may be too much after a day of hiking or kayaking in the American wilderness.

THE LINE IN A NUTSHELL   This 30-year-old French-owned line has five ships—some yachts, some tall-masted sailing vessels—that travel the world in style. The line only started sailing to Alaska in 2015 and currently has three ships with Alaskan itineraries.

THE EXPERIENCE   Ponant ships have the kind of chic decor you might expect from a French line, and the vessels bring with them a sense of French culture wherever they go. The crew speaks English, but Americans who speak some French—and are open to learning more—may be more comfortable in the environment than those with no French language skills.

THE FLEET   The line's five ships are a mixed lot. The 64-passenger *Le Ponant* is a sailing ship, complete with tall white sails that billow in the wind. The line's four other ships are intimate yacht-style vessels, holding 244 to 264 passengers.

PASSENGER PROFILE   While the line does get a lot of French passengers, on this particular itinerary you're more likely to see a mix of North American and European travelers. Guests tend to be age 55 and up, well-traveled, and fans of French culture and gastronomy. As these are expedition-style itineraries, passengers tend toward the active and outdoorsy, if not downright athletic.

DINING OPTIONS   You have two dining choices: the main dining room and the **Grill.** The dining room serves everything from French butter to French breads, cheeses, and pastries. The buffet-style Grill is more casual. Low-fat, vegetarian, and gluten-free choices are available upon request.

ACTIVITIES   While still on the small side, these ships have a few more bells and whistles than their even smaller brethren in the region, including pools and more substantial workout rooms. In addition to a library (with computers) and lounge, each ship has a theater and a small spa with multiple treatment rooms.

CHILDREN'S OPTIONS   Children less than 3 years old are not invited on board, and children age 3 to 8 are allowed on a case-by-case basis. (Parents must make a request in writing to the line and be willing to sign a liability waiver.) That said, those who do board will find a small kid's club with games and a Wii console.

ENTERTAINMENT   In the theater during the day, you can hear lectures or see presentations from naturalists. In the evenings, the same space offers shows, films, and musical performances. Cabins also have On Demand movies.

CRUISETOURS & ADD-ON PROGRAMS   None.

Le Boréal • L'Austral • Le Soléal

The Verdict

These three yachts feel French, from the crew to the food, wherever they are in the world.

Specifications

Size (in GRTs)	10,944	Crew	140
Passengers (Double Occ.)	264	Passenger/Crew Ratio	2 to 1
Space/Passenger Ratio	41	Year Launched	2010/2011/2013
Total Cabins/Veranda Cabins	132/T24	Last Major Refurbishment	N/A

Frommer's Ratings (Scale of 1–5)   ★★★★½

Cabin Comfort & Amenities	4.5	Dining Options	4
Ship Cleanliness & Maintenance	5	Gym, Spa & Sports Facilities	4
Public Comfort/Space	4.5	Children's Facilities	2
Decor	4.5	Enjoyment Factor	4.5

THE SHIPS IN GENERAL   These small ships do rather unusual itineraries that take guests farther afield than many other lines, to smaller coves and fjords. So for many travelers the focus here is on the destinations rather than the ships themselves, despite the fine food and wine on board and the chic atmosphere. (Think black and white photography, Swarovski crystal lights.)

CABINS   Decor in the upscale cabins is simple and elegant with orchids in the rooms and modern treats such as iPod charges and flatscreen TVs.

CABINS & RATES

CABINS	PER DIEM RATES	SQ. FT.	FRIDGE	HAIR DRYER	SITTING AREA	TV
Le Boréal, L'Austral, and Le Soléal						
Outside	$672–$866	194	yes	yes	no	yes
Suite	$1,173–$2,447	291	yes	yes	yes	yes

PUBLIC AREAS   Each ship has a theater, a library, a lounge, a pool on deck, and a small kids' club. It's a well-designed vessel, but with itineraries this special, most people are happy to maximize their time on land.

POOL, FITNESS, SPA & SPORTS FACILITIES   All three ships have small spas, salons, and workout rooms. The spa has a salon as well and uses Sothys Paris skincare products.

PRINCESS CRUISES

2844 Ave. Rockefeller, Santa Clarita, CA 91355. www.princess.com. ✆ **800/PRINCESS** (774-6237) or 661/753-0000.

Pros

o **Good service.** The warm-hearted Italian, British, and Filipino service crew does a great job. On a Princess cruise a few years ago, one barman with a glorious Cockney accent (which we noted he could mute or emphasize at will) was a huge hit with our group, dispensing one-liners, simple magic tricks, and drinks with equal facility. We've met others on Princess ships with the same gift for making passengers feel welcome without being overly familiar.
o **Private verandas.** Virtually all the line's Alaska ships have scads and scads of balconies, some of them in as many as 75% of the cabins.

Cons

o **Average food.** The ships' cuisine is perfectly fine if you're not a foodie, but if you are, you'll find that it's pretty banquet-hall-esque.

THE LINE IN A NUTSHELL   The company strives, successfully, to please a wide variety of passengers. It offers more choices in terms of accommodations, dining, and entertainment than nearly any other line.

THE EXPERIENCE   If you were to put Carnival, Royal Caribbean, Celebrity, and Holland America in a big bowl and mix them all together, you'd come up with Princess Cruises' megaships. The Princess fleet appeals to a wider cross-section of cruisers by offering loads of choices and activities, plus touches of big-ship glamour, along with the private balconies, quiet nooks, and calm spaces that characterize smaller, more intimate vessels. Aboard Princess, you get a lot of bang for your buck, attractively packaged and well executed.

Although its ships serve every corner of the globe, nowhere is the Princess presence more visible than in Alaska. Through its affiliate, Princess Tours, the company owns wilderness lodges, motorcoaches, and railcars in the 49th state, making it a major player in the Alaska cruise market, alongside Holland America and, increasingly, Royal Caribbean Cruises' two brands, Celebrity and Royal Caribbean International. All of its seven ships in Alaska offer an impressive number of onboard activities designed excusively for this part of the world, from visits by Alaskan storytellers, Iditarod winners, and husky dog puppies to Alaska-focused lecurers. Princess even has a special shore excursion that allows you to go fishing and then "cook your catch" back on board. Princess also operates spectacular wilderness lodges, including the

River Princess Wilderness Lodge at Cooper Landing near Wrangell–St. Elias National Park.

In 2004, Princess became the first line to use the rather nondescript Whittier as the northern terminus for its Gulf cruises instead of the more commonly used Seward, and it has done so ever since. Whittier's primary advantage over Seward is that it's about 60 miles closer to Anchorage. Passengers bound for rail tours of Denali National Park are able to board their trains right on the pier instead of taking a bus to Anchorage and then embarking on their rail carriages. The inauguration of the service was yet another effort by a cruise line to gain a competitive edge over its Alaska rivals. The battle for the minds and wallets of the public is being fought as much on land as at sea these days. With so many ship lines striving to attract new passengers or persuade old ones to come back, every little bit helps. The competition goes on, to the benefit of the traveling public. Princess Cruises is now a member of the same group that owns Holland America and Carnival, both of them highly visible in the Alaska cruise market.

THE FLEET   Princess's fleet in Alaska in 2018 comprises seven ships. New in Alaska is a 12-night round-trip excursion from Los Angeles on the *Star Princess*. In November 2017, Princess began rolling out its Ocean Medallion program across the fleet. This new technology that tracks your preferences is designed to customize your cruise for you and save your selections for future sailings. As of May 2018, *Island Princess* will be the first of the Alaska ships to have Ocean Medallion, just in time for the Alaska season.

PASSENGER PROFILE   Typical Princess passengers are likely to be between about 50 and 65 and are often experienced cruisers who know what they want and are prepared to pay for it. But the line also is popular with families, particularly multi-generation families, thanks to its solid children's programs and a-little-something-for-everyone vibe.

DINING OPTIONS   In general, Princess serves meals that are good, if hardly gourmet. But you've got to give it points for at least trying to be flexible: About a decade ago, Princess implemented a new fleetwide dining option known as Anytime Dining. Basically, this plan allows passengers to sign up for the traditional first or second seating for dinner, or for a come-as-you-please restaurant-style dining option. The latter allows you to eat dinner anytime between 5:30pm and midnight, though you must be seated by 10pm. Passengers who choose the restaurant-style option may request a cozy table for two or bring along a half-dozen shipmates, depending on their mood that evening. It's also possible to eat all your meals in the **Horizon Court** cafe on all Princess ships in Alaska. If you don't go to the main dining room, though, you may miss one of Princess's best features: its pastas. The newest ships also have several alternative-dining restaurant options, including a steakhouse called **Crown Grill,** and it's our experience that meals at these restaurants are well worth the price of admission of $29 per person.

ACTIVITIES   Princess passengers can expect enough onboard activity to keep them going from morning to night if they so desire, and enough hideaways to let them do absolutely nothing if that's their thing. The line doesn't

Princess Fleet Itineraries

SHIP	ITINERARIES
Coral/Golden/ Island/Star	7-night Gulf of Alaska: North- and southbound between Vancouver, BC, and Whittier/Anchorage, visiting Ketchikan, Juneau, and Skagway, and cruising Glacier Bay and College Fjord or Hubbard Glacier (May–Sept)
Emerald/Ruby	7-night Inside Passage: Round-trip from Seattle, visiting Ketchikan or Icy Strait Point, Juneau, Skagway, Tracy Arm Fjord or Glacier Bay National Park, and Victoria, BC (May–Sept)
Grand	10-night Inside Passage: Round-trip from San Francisco, visiting Juneau, Skagway or Icy Strait Point, Ketchikan, and Victoria, BC, plus cruising Tracy Arm Fjord or Glacier Bay (May–Sept)
Star	12-night Inside Passage: Round-trip from Los Angeles, visiting Juneau, Skagway, Ketchikan, and Victoria, BC, plus cruising Glacier Bay (May–Sept)

go out of its way to make passengers feel that they're spoilsports if they don't participate in the amateur-night tomfoolery or learn to fold napkins. These activities are usually there, along with the inevitable bingo, shuffleboard, and the rest, but they're low-key.

Specifically in Alaska, the line has naturalists and park rangers on board to offer commentary. It also brings on local entertainers, celebrities, and historians to enhance passengers' Alaska experience; for instance, Iditarod winner Libby Riddles sometimes speaks to passengers aboard ship.

Internet access is provided on all the ships, and packages that bring the cost down are available for those who use the Internet extensively—for instance, $69 for 120 minutes, $99 for 240 minutes, and $159 for 460 minutes.

CHILDREN'S PROGRAMS For well over a decade now Princess has sought to broaden its appeal and distance itself from its old image as a staid, adults-only line, and all the ships are now well-equipped for children and clearly on a mission to cater to families. Each ship has a spacious children's playroom and a sizable area of fenced-in outside deck for kids only. Supervised activities are held year-round for ages 3 to 17, clustered in three groups. Teen centers have computers, video games, and a sound system. Wisely, these areas are placed as far away as possible from the adult passengers.

ENTERTAINMENT From glittering Vegas-style shows to New York cabaret-singer performances to a rocking disco, this line provides a terrific blend of musical delights. You'll always find a cozy spot where some soft piano or jazz music is being performed. You'll also find entertainers such as hypnotists, puppeteers, and comedians, plus karaoke for you audience-participation types. The ship hosts a couple of afternoon sessions of that ubiquitous cruise favorite, the Newlywed and Not-So-Newlywed Game. Each ship also has a wine bar selling caviar by the ounce and vintage wine, champagne, and iced vodka by the glass. The Princess casinos are sprawling and exciting places, bound to excite gamblers with their lights and action. Good-quality piano-bar music and strolling musicians, along with dance music in the lounge, are part of the pre- and post-dinner entertainment.

For years, Princess has had a connection to Hollywood—this is the *Love Boat* line, after all! It's the only line we know of where you can watch yesterday's and today's television shows on your in-room TV. Also shown are A&E, Biography, E! Entertainment TV, Nickelodeon, Discovery Channel, BBC, and National Geographic productions. Like several other lines, Princess also shows recently released movies.

SERVICE Throughout the fleet, the service in all areas—dining room, lounge, cabin maintenance, and so on—tends to be of consistently high quality. An area in which Princess particularly shines is the efficiency of its shore-excursion staff. Getting 2,600-plus people off a ship and onto motorcoaches, trains, and helicopters—all staples of any Alaska cruise program—isn't as easy as this company makes it look. All of the Princess vessels in Alaska have laundry and dry-cleaning services, as well as their own self-service laundromats. On Princess ships, a $13.50 per-person per-day service charge ($14.50 for passengers in minisuites and Club class; $15.50 for passengers in suites) is automatically added to your bill. If you want to raise or lower that amount, you can do so at the passenger services desk.

CRUISETOURS & ADD-ON PROGRAMS Princess has an array of land packages in Alaska in conjunction with its Gulf of Alaska and Inside Passage voyages. Virtually every part of the state is covered, from the Kenai Peninsula to the Interior to the Far North. The land portions come in 3- to 8-night segments, all combinable with a 7-, 10-, or 12-night cruise. Four types of land itineraries—Denali Explorer, On Your Own, Off the Beaten Path, and Connoisseur (escorted)—are offered in conjunction with Princess's five wilderness lodges.

Coral Princess • Island Princess

The Verdict

These two vessels—part of the line's Coral class—are plenty big, but such is the sophistication of marine architecture nowadays that passengers don't feel as if they're living with a couple of thousand others: There are lots of places to get away from it all.

Specifications

Size (in Tons)	91,627	Crew	895/900
Passengers (Double Occ.)	2,000/2,200	Passenger/Crew Ratio	2.2 to 1
Space/Passenger Ratio	44	Year Launched	2003
Total Cabins/Veranda Cabins	1,000/527 and 987/527	Last Major Refurbishment	2016

Frommer's Ratings (Scale of 1–5)   ★★★★

Cabin Comfort & Amenities	4	Dining Options	4
Ship Cleanliness & Maintenance	4	Gym, Spa & Sports Facilities	5
Public Comfort/Space	4	Children's Facilities	4.5
Decor	4	Enjoyment Factor	4

THE SHIPS IN GENERAL   Roominess is the key here, and the impressive passenger-to-space ratios make these ships stand out.

The ships reflect the marine-design inventiveness that is becoming more obvious with the arrival of every new ship. Each ship has a 9-hole putting green, a world-class art collection, spacious kids' and teens' centers, a wedding chapel, a cigar lounge, a martini bar (the last two features have become almost standard on new ships), and much more. In addition, in November *Island* received the new Camp Discovery youth and teen center, with activities related to Discovery Channel programming. Decor is tasteful and rich, with lots of teak decking, stainless steel and marble fittings, and prominent use of light shades of gray, blue, and brown in the plush furnishings.

CABINS   These ships have a remarkable number of outside rooms (almost 90%) and a huge number of private balconies—727, or more than 7 out of 10 of the outside units. The smallest accommodations are about 160 square feet, and the largest, the 16 top suites, stretch to 470 square feet, including the veranda. In between, the *Coral* and *Island* offer rooms with square footage ranging from 217 to 248. Don't assume when making a reservation that a minisuite will necessarily come with a veranda, however; the ships have eight minisuites without that amenity, so if you want one, be sure to specify that when you make your reservation. In 2016, the line designated a block of the minisuites as Club class, and those come with a reserved dining area, priority embarkation and disembarkation, and a liquor set-up in your cabin. In addition, both ships have the Princess Luxury Beds, expertly designed to offer the best possible night's sleep. Twenty of the cabins (16 outside, 4 inside) are configured for wheelchair use. These are very spacious—between 217 square feet and 248 square feet.

CABINS & RATES

CABINS	PER DIEM RATES	SQ. FT.	FRIDGE	HAIR DRYER	SITTING AREA	TV
Inside	$125–$192	156–166	yes	yes	no	yes
Outside	$216–$308	217–248	yes	yes	no	yes
Suites	$417–$583	280–470	yes	yes	yes	yes

PUBLIC AREAS   In keeping with the trend these days, the *Coral* and *Island* each have a comfy cigar bar and a martini lounge—the **Churchill Lounge** and the **Crooners Bar,** respectively. The nautical-themed **Wheelhouse Bar** is a warm, inviting place to spend after-hours. Also appealing but more frenetic is the **Explorers Lounge,** which functions as an after-dinner disco. The huge casino is a London-themed room. An Internet cafe, a wedding chapel, children's and teens' centers, and a putting green are located on the top deck.

DINING OPTIONS   These ships have two main dining rooms and several smaller alternative dining areas: **Sabatini's,** an elegant Italian eatery with a $29-per-head charge (well worth the price); the **Bayou Cafe** ($29 per head), serving Creole food; a patisserie; a couple of cafes; a poolside hamburger grill; and a poolside pizza bar. The variety of dining options allows passengers to eat pretty much when they want and be as formal or as relaxed as they wish.

POOL, FITNESS, SPA & SPORTS FACILITIES Each ship has four pools and five whirlpool tubs. The fitness center is a large, well-stocked, airy room with absolutely the last word in equipment. The Lotus Spa has one of the widest arrays of massage and beauty treatments afloat, including oxygenating facials, an "aromaflex" package that combines the ancient healing therapies of massage and reflexology, and a treatment that involves the placing of heated, oiled volcanic stones on key energy points of the body to release muscular tension and promote relaxation.

Grand Princess • Star Princess • Ruby Princess • Emerald Princess • Golden Princess

The Verdict

Despite their size and megacapacity, you usually won't feel the crush of all those other guests, thanks to plenty of opportunities to "get away from it all."

Specifications

Size (in Tons)	107,517–113,561	Crew	1,100–1,200
Passengers (Double Occ.)	2,600–3,080	Passenger/Crew Ratio	2.4–2.6 to 1
Space/Passenger Ratio	38–42	Year Launched	1998/2001/2002/ 2007/2008
Total Cabins/Veranda Cabins	1,297/518– 1,542/682	Last Major Refurbishment	2009/2009/2011/ 2009/2015

Frommer's Ratings (Scale of 1–5)   ★★★★½

Cabin Comfort & Amenities	4.5	Dining Options	4
Ship Cleanliness & Maintenance	4	Gym, Spa & Sports Facilities	4
Public Comfort/Space	4.5	Children's Facilities	4
Decor	4.5	Enjoyment Factor	4.5

THE SHIPS IN GENERAL With more than a dozen decks apiece, these ships are taller than the Statue of Liberty (from pedestal to torch). Inside and out, the vessels—all similar in layout—are a marvel of size and design. They have massive white, boxy bodies, with two of the ships featuring a spoilerlike aft poking up into the air that offers a slightly bizarre, space-age profile (still on the *Golden* and *Star,* the feature was removed from the *Grand*). But the ships' interior designs are well laid out and easy to navigate. Amazingly, the ships seldom feel crowded—a tribute to the growing sophistication and creativity of the marine architecture community.

The ships provide an amazing variety of entertainment, dining options, and recreational activities. They have five restaurants each (plus a pizzeria and outdoor grill), four swimming pools, and three show lounges, as well as expansive deck space. *Grand* and *Star* both have the **Camp Discovery Youth**

and Teen Center. SHARE, the impressive restaurant from celebrated L.A. chef Curtis Stone, opened in *Ruby* and *Emerald* in January 2016.

Even the ships' medical centers are grand, boasting high-tech "teleradiology" equipment that enables doctors to transmit X-rays to land-based experts.

CABINS   Even the smallest of these ships' inside cabins are quite adequate, at about 160 square feet; standard outside units, sans balcony, go from 158 to 206 square feet; and larger oceanview rooms run between 232 and 285 square feet, including the balcony. All rooms have twin beds that easily convert to queens, along with refrigerators, TVs, spacious closets, robes, safes, and plenty of drawer space. The larger of the outside rooms comes with a small writing desk. Minisuites give you 323 to 370 square feet (including the balcony), and the suites range from 515 to about 800 square feet—again, including the balcony—and feature a tub and shower (regular balcony cabins and non-balcony cabins have only shower stalls). The rooms are tastefully decorated with subdued, hidden lighting, soft furnishings in quiet colors, and eye-catching (though not gallery-quality) art. The ships have 25 to 31 wheelchair-accessible cabins. (The **Skywalkers** disco on a couple of the ships even has a wheelchair lift up to the elevated dance floor.)

Nearly two-thirds of each of the ships' cabins have balconies. *But be forewarned:* The verandas are tiered, as they are on so many new ships these days, so passengers in levels above may be able to look down on you. They may be labeled "private," but they're actually rather exposed. Don't do anything out there you wouldn't want the neighbors to see! TV stations available (geography permitting) include CNN, ESPN, Nickelodeon, BBC programming, and TNT (as well as the inevitable *Love Boat* reruns).

CABINS & RATES

CABINS	PER DIEM RATES	SQ. FT.	FRIDGE	HAIR DRYER	SITTING AREA	TV
Inside	$133–$175	160	yes	yes	no	yes
Outside	$250–$317	168–257	yes	yes	no	yes
Suites	$483–$608	341–687	yes	yes	yes	yes

PUBLIC AREAS   Hey, where'd everyone go? Thanks to the smart layout of the vessels, with lots of small rooms rather than a few large rooms, passengers are dispersed rather than concentrated into one or two main areas; you'll have no problem finding a quiet retreat.

The public areas have a contemporary and upscale appeal, thanks to pleasing color schemes and the well-designed use of wood, marble, and brass. Two full-time florists on each vessel create and care for impressive flower arrangements and a large variety of live plants.

The piazza-style atrium in the *Golden Princess* serves as a central meeting point on the ship and is home to casual, cafelike seating. It's ringed by the **International Cafe,** where you can pick up a specialty coffee or a pastry, and a wine bar called **Vines.**

Besides the three—count 'em—main dining rooms, each ship has two principal alternative eateries: either **Sabatini's** or **SHARE** (depending on the ship) and the **Crown Grill,** for steaks and seafood. Other options include the casual **Horizon Court,** the **Trident Grill** (poolside), the **International Café,** and a pizza counter. The ships' restaurants are on the small side, designed that way so you don't feel like you're dining with a crowd and to maintain good acoustics (although you may also feel like the ceiling is closing in on you a bit).

Gamblers will love the sprawling and dazzling 13,500-square-foot casino, among the largest at sea. Near the casino, two lounge areas are ideal for whiling away a few moments before attacking the gaming tables.

The most striking design features on the *Star* and *Golden* (once a staple of the *Grand*-class design) are the discos, which jut out over the stern and are suspended—scarily, in our opinion—some 155 feet above the water. It's really quite spectacular. If you're scared of heights, of course, don't even think of looking down; you're so far above the water that it's (literally!) breathtaking. Smoke machines and other high-tech gizmos add to the spooky effect at night. During the day, its banquettes make a particularly cozy spot to snuggle up with a good book.

All five ships have an Internet cafe, and all but *Grand* have a library.

DINING OPTIONS   The principal alternative eating areas are **Sabatini's** and the **Crown Grill.** At Sabatini's, the $25 cover charge gets you the finest Italian food at sea—and gobs of it. The $25-a-head Crown Grill is a traditional steakhouse with steaks and seafood.

POOL, FITNESS, SPA & SPORTS FACILITIES   The ships have something like 1.7 acres of open deck space apiece, so it's easy to find a quiet place to soak in the sun. Each has multiple great swimming pools, including one with a retractable glass roof that doubles as a sort of solarium (of special importance in Alaska), another touted as a swim-against-the-current pool (although, truth be told, there really isn't enough room to do laps if others are in the water with you), and a third, aft under the disco, that feels miles from the rest of the ship (and is usually the least crowded). There are also multiple whirlpool tubs.

On the forward sundeck on each of the vessels, surrounding the lap pool and its tiered, amphitheater-style wooden benches, is the large **Lotus Spa,** which almost appears to be separate from the rest of the ship. Personally, we find the layout to be a bit weird: For instance, there are no showers in the dressing area. The complex includes a very large oceanview salon and an oceanview gym, which is surprisingly small and cramped for a ship of this size (although it has an unusually large aerobics floor).

Other active diversions: basketball, paddle tennis, and a 9-hole putting green.

REGENT SEVEN SEAS CRUISES

7665 Corporate Center Dr., Miami, FL 33122. www.rssc.com. © **844/473-4368.**

Pros

o **Overall excellence.** The line has excellent food, open seating for meals, generally fine service, great accommodations, and creative shore excursions. *Seven Seas Mariner* will undergo a major refurbishment in spring

2018 before the Alaska season, part of the line's $125-million fleetwide initiative.

- o **Great room service.** It's about the best we've found on a ship, with the food served promptly, fresh, and course-by-course or all at once—your choice.
- o **The most all-inclusive rates at sea.** Regent has a fleetwide policy on all departures that includes specialty dining, Wi-Fi, liquor and wine, shore excursions, and even transfers and airfare.

Cons

- o **Sedate nightlife.** Although the line upgraded its evening entertainment, many guests, exhausted after a full day in port, retire early, perhaps to watch a movie, leaving only a few night owls in the disco and other lounges.

THE LINE IN A NUTSHELL Regent's guests travel in style and extreme comfort. Its brand of luxury is casually elegant and subtle, its cuisine among the best in the industry. The line operates three midsize ships geared toward affluent and worldly travelers. This year marks the line's 18th full season in Alaska, and it'll be deploying the refurbished, 490-passenger *Seven Seas Mariner* to the region for the third year in a row.

THE EXPERIENCE The Regent Seven Seas experience means outstanding food, service, and accommodations in an environment that's a little more casual than some of its luxury competitors; there is, for instance, no formal dress night during its 7-night Alaska program. The line also moved to being ultra-all-inclusive in 2009, with shore excursions included in the cruise fare (excluding the more exclusive Regent Choice tours). The *Mariner*—no stranger to Alaska, as it was deployed there in 2016 and 2017—is one of the most intimate and comfortable ships at sea, providing its passengers with large suites and spacious public areas.

THE FLEET All suites on the ship have balconies—a very big deal in a place where whale-watching is always on the agenda and glacier calving is a sight to see. Like the rest of the fleet, the entire ship has an elegant yet comfortable modern design and a graceful yet casual onboard atmosphere.

PASSENGER PROFILE Regent tends to attract travelers from their 50s to their 70s (sometimes even in their 30s and 40s) who have a high household income but don't like to flaunt their wealth. The typical guest profile is someone who is admirably well-educated, well-traveled, and inquisitive. The travelers may also be a mixed bunch.

DINING OPTIONS Regent's cuisine would gain high marks even if it were on land. Service by professional waiters adds to the experience, as do little touches such as Versace china and fresh flowers on the tables. The complimentary wines served with meals are generally quite good; there's very little reason to want to trade up (however, the wines available at extra cost are actually fairly priced).

Regent Seven Seas Cruises Fleet Itineraries

SHIP	ITINERARIES
Seven Seas Mariner	7-night Gulf of Alaska: North- and southbound between Vancouver, BC, and Seward/Anchorage, visiting Ketchikan, Juneau, Skagway, and Sitka, plus cruising the Inside Passage and Hubbard Glacier (May–Aug)
Seven Seas Mariner	10-night Inside and Outside Passage: Northbound (May) and southbound (Sept) between San Francisco and Vancouver, BC, visiting Astoria, Ketchikan, Juneau, Sitka, and Skagway, plus cruising Hubbard Glacier
Seven Seas Mariner	10-night Inside Passage and Gulf of Alaska: Southbound from Seward to Vancouver, BC, visiting Ketchikan, Wrangell, Juneau, Skagway, Icy Strait, Sitka, and Victoria, plus cruising Hubbard Glacier (June and Sept)
Seven Seas Mariner	11-night Inside and Outside Passage: Round-trip from Vancouver, BC, visiting Ketchikan, Wrangell, Skagway, Prince Rupert, Juneau, Sitka, and Victoria, plus cruising Hubbard Glacier (June)
Seven Seas Mariner	11-night Inside Passage and Gulf of Alaska: Northbound from Vancouver, BC to Seward, visiting Ketchikan, Wrangell, Juneau, Skagway, Icy Strait, Sitka, Victoria, and a maiden call on Kodiak, plus cruising Hubbard Glacier (Aug)

ACTIVITIES The line assumes that, for the most part, guests want to entertain themselves on board, but that doesn't mean there isn't plenty to do, considering the ships' relatively small size. The line's Alaska cruises offer lectures by local experts; golf instruction; card and board games; art auctions; blackjack and bingo; Ping-Pong tournaments; and big-screen movies with popcorn. Bridge instructors are even on board for select sailings.

CHILDREN'S PROGRAMS The line in general is adult-oriented, but on Alaska sailings the Club Mariner Youth Program is staffed with trained counselors and offers Alaska-focused activities for ages 5 to 12.

ENTERTAINMENT The small size of Regent ships limits the line's ability to provide entertainment as lavish as that of its big-ship competitors; however, the two-tiered showroom offers well-presented, medium-scale productions with high-quality performers, cabaret acts, and headliners including comedians and magicians and sometimes symphony orchestra members and other musical groups.

SERVICE The senior dining-room staff on Regent vessels generally has had experience at fine hotels as well as on ships. (They provide service so good that you don't really notice it.) A small but telling point about bar service: During one cruise, just about all the staff members in the public lounges remembered our favorite drinks after just one meeting. Room stewards and butlers do an excellent job in the suites, and bar service is outstanding. The ship also provides dry cleaning and full- and self-service laundry. On Regent ships, gratuities for the staff are included in the fare and not expected.

CRUISETOURS & ADD-ON PROGRAMS The Discover Denali program features prominently in Regent Seven Seas Cruises' pre- or post-cruise land packages, and the line offers 4-night packages originating in Seward or Anchorage. with rates starting at $2,499 per guest. A 5-night Canadian Rockies by Rocky Mountaineer land program presents an ever-changing landscape

Regent Seven Seas Cruises

THE BIG SHIPS

of beautiful mountains, rivers, and forests aboard the award-winning train; those rates start at $3,399 per guest. The line also includes a free one-night luxury hotel stay at the beginning of all Alaska cruises in Anchorage for guests booked in Concierge Suites and higher.

Seven Seas Mariner

The Verdict

Seven Seas Mariner offers all-suite, all-balcony accommodations. Private balconies and spacious public decks make watching the glaciers and wildlife go by both easy and supremely comfortable.

Specifications

Size (in Tons)	48,075	Crew	445
Passengers (Double Occ.)	700	Passenger/Crew Ratio	1.5 to 1
Space/Passenger Ratio	68	Year Launched	2001
Total Cabins/Veranda Cabins	350/350	Last Major Refurbishment	2018

Frommer's Ratings (Scale of 1–5)   ★★★★★

Cabin Comfort & Amenities	5	Dining Options	4.5
Ship Cleanliness & Maintenance	5	Gym, Spa & Sports Facilities	5
Public Comfort/Space	5	Children's Facilities	N/A
Decor	4.5	Enjoyment Factor	5

THE SHIP IN GENERAL   The 700-passenger *Seven Seas Mariner* offers an enormous amount of public space per person for a ship this size, and its roomy accommodations give everyone lots of private space as well. Daytime activities are not extensive, as the itineraries are mostly port-intensive, but that seems to suit the clientele just fine.

CABINS   This is one ship that doesn't skimp on space: All rooms are balcony suites, and even the smallest are a whopping (by cruise standards!) 301 square feet. The largest are a remarkable 2,002 square feet, including two balconies that total an additional 798 square feet. All suites have separate living-room areas, and the top levels of suites have dining areas as well. Cabins come with queen-size beds that convert to twins, walk-in closets, marble bathrooms with showers and separate tubs (or larger shower stalls instead), and On Demand entertainment, safes, phones, 24-hour room service, and refrigerators stocked with complimentary bottled water, soft drinks, and beer. The larger suites come with butler service and upgraded amenities, including iPod players and a personalized liquor bar. Four of the suites are wheelchair-accessible.

CABINS & RATES

CABINS	PER DIEM RATES	SQ. FT.	FRIDGE	HAIR DRYER	SITTING AREA	TV
Suites	$685–$2,799*/ $799–$2,190**	301–2,002	yes	yes	yes	yes

* per-guest fares based on 7-night cruise

** per-guest fares based on 11-night cruise

PUBLIC AREAS French-designed and -built, the *Seven Seas Mariner* has an eclectic interior that's elegant yet comfortable. The ship has a number of intimate evening bar/lounges, including the **Observation Lounge,** with its live piano music; the **Stars Night Club,** with DJ-chosen dance tunes; the **Mariner Lounge; Coffee Connection;** and the **Connoisseur Bar,** a haven for cigar smokers. The casino has blackjack, roulette, Caribbean stud poker, craps, and slots. Shoppers can indulge at a few small but classy boutiques selling clothes, jewelry, and your usual array of cruise-line logo items. The library computer area has books, games, and computer terminals and guests without their own laptop, tablet, or smartphone can use the complimentary Wi-Fi there.

DINING OPTIONS Regent Seven Seas Cruises completely transformed the main dining room experience in the line's signature **Compass Rose** restaurant, and now guests can customize their dinners, selecting from more than a dozen different meat and seafood items and have them prepared to taste, garnished with a sauce of choice, and paired with side dishes of their choosing. Additionally, each evening the ship's executive chef creates nightly specials, and the dessert menu features international cheeses (served with port, as all alcohol is included on board) and handmade ice cream as well as pastries, cakes, crumbles, and soufflés.

The ship also has the more casual **La Veranda** for guests looking for a buffet at breakfast and lunch; in the evening the space is transformed into Sette Mari at La Veranda, the line's casual Italian restaurant. An enlarged pool grill serves a nice range of lunch fare such as bratwursts, custom-made hamburgers, and paninis. You can also dine at a couple other specialty restaurants where there's no charge, but reservations are a must: **Prime 7,** serveing steaks, chops, Alaskan king crab, and lobster; and the French restaurant, **Chartreuse,** offering elegant and modern takes on Parisian cooking.

POOL, FITNESS, SPA & SPORTS FACILITIES The **Canyon Ranch SpaClub** is a classy operation, and there's virtually no product push during or after treatments. The five treatment rooms and beauty salon offer the normal range of services (treatments aren't cheap, though). The gym and aerobics area do not feel crowded despite their size. Three heated whirlpools head the pool, and the pool deck has an enormous amount of open deck space. Recreational facilities include a golf driving cage, putting green, a paddle-tennis court, a jogging track, table tennis, bocce court, and shuffleboard.

ROYAL CARIBBEAN INTERNATIONAL

1050 Caribbean Way, Miami, FL 33132. www.royalcaribbean.com. ℂ **866/562-7625.**

Pros

o **Great spas and recreational facilities.** Royal Caribbean's Alaska ships all have elaborate health-club and spa facilities, a covered swimming pool, and large, open sundeck areas.

s (Scale of 1–5)			★★★★
es	4	Dining Options	4.5
enance	4	Gym, Spa & Sports Facilities	4.5
	4	Children's Facilities	4
	4	Enjoyment Factor	4

ENERAL *Radiance of the Seas* was among Royal Carib-
of the 21st century, as well as among the first vessels in a
inued the line's tradition of being an innovator in the indus-
lude billiards rooms with custom-made, self-leveling tables
big waves) and a revolving bar in the disco. The ship is
d guests that they are at sea; with that goal in mind, it fea-
huge expanses of glass (adding up to more than 3 acres)
iew the passing Alaskan scenery. That includes the 12-story
hich are made of glass and offer scenic ocean views. You
views from the Internet cafe!

ghtly more upscale than the line's other vessels—Royal
to have borrowed a page from sister company Celebrity. It
arble, and lots of nice fabrics and artwork, adding up to a
or that lets the views provide most of the visual drama.

s on *Radiance* are larger than those on earlier Royal Carib-
mallest is 165 square feet—and more come with verandas
vessels. All rooms are equipped with an interactive flat-
ne, Wi-Fi service, vanity table, refrigerator/minibar, and hair
come with a veranda, sitting area with a sofa bed, dry bar,
nd bathtub and double sinks. The Royal Suite has a separate
(king-size bed) and living room, a whirlpool bathtub, and a
. Family staterooms and suites can accommodate five. Fif-
h ship are wheelchair-accessible.

RATES	SQ. FT.	FRIDGE	HAIR DRYER	SITTING AREA	TV
213.85	162–201	yes	yes	yes	yes
443.14*	167–194	yes	yes	yes	yes
754.42	299–532	yes	yes	yes	yes

The ship is full of little surprises, including the aforemen-
om and a card club with five tables dedicated to poker. Of
d even more gaming options in the massive Art Nouveau–
Royale (although dice players will be disappointed by the
odds). Bookworms will want to check out the combo book-
ouse.

cushy bars and lounges include champagne and piano bars.
ocean views, you can gaze down into the atrium, eight decks
ortholelike window in the floor of the **Crown & Anchor**

○ **Great observation areas.** The Viking Crown Lounge and other glassed-in areas make excellent observation rooms for gazing at the Alaskan sights.

○ **Quality entertainment.** Royal Caribbean spends big bucks on entertainment, which includes high-tech show productions.

Cons

○ **Crowds.** As with some other big ships, you almost need a map to get around, and you'll likely experience the inevitable lines for buffets, debarkation, and boarding of buses during shore excursions.

THE LINE IN A NUTSHELL   This bold, brash, innovative company now in its 45th year has the largest passenger capacity in the industry on the biggest ships. Royal Caribbean International introduced the concept of the megaship with its *Sovereign of the Seas* in 1988, and the industry hasn't been the same since. The mass-market style of cruising that Royal Caribbean sells aboard its megaships is reasonably priced and has nearly every diversion imaginable.

THE EXPERIENCE   The ships are more informal than formal and are well run, with a large team of friendly service employees paying close attention to day-to-day details. Dress is generally casual during the day and informal most evenings, with two formal nights on a typical 7-night cruise. The contemporary decor on Royal Caribbean vessels doesn't bang you over the head with glitz like, say, that of the Carnival line; it's more subdued, classy, and witty, with lots of glass, greenery, and art. All the Royal Caribbean vessels feature the line's trademark Viking Crown Lounge, an observation area located in a circular glass structure on the upper deck (in some cases, encircling the smokestack). Another popular trademark feature is the ships' nautically themed Schooner bars. The range of what's available on different Royal Caribbean ships does vary somewhat depending on age, size, and design.

THE FLEET   Royal Caribbean owns most of the largest ships in the world—the largest of which, the 6,870-passenger *Symphony of the Seas*, debuts in April 2018. And big is coming to Alaska. At press time, the line announced that it would be sending one of its Quantum-class ships to the 49th State for the 2019 season: the 4,180-passenger *Ovation of the Seas*, being redeployed from Australia to sail Alaska cruises north from Seattle. The ship, which debuted in 2016, has both skydiving and surfing simulators as well as bumper cars and the towering North Star ride, which offers a vantage point from 300 feet above the ship inside a glass-walled capsule.

The two other vessels the line sends to Alaska only carry around 2,000 passengers. Introduced in 2001 as the first new category of ship for the line and revitalized in 2011, the 2,143-passenger *Radiance of the Seas* has many innovations, including a billiards room with self-leveling pool tables. For 2018, it's joined in Alaska by 3,114-passenger sister ship *Explorer of the Seas*.

PASSENGER PROFILE   The crowd on Royal Caribbean ships, like the decor, tends to be a notch down on the flashy scale from what you'll find on Carnival and perhaps a notch up from those on, say, Princess or the Holland

Royal Caribbean Fleet Itineraries

SHIP	ITINERARIES
Radiance of the Seas	7-night Gulf of Alaska: North- and southbound between Vancouver, BC, and Seward, visiting Ketchikan, Juneau, Skagway, Icy Strait Point, and Hubbard Glacier (May–Aug)
Explorer of the Seas	7-night Inside Passage: Round-trip from Seattle, visiting Juneau, Victoria, BC, and the Inside Passage (May–Aug)

America Line. Guests represent an age mix from 30 to 60, and an increasing number of families are attracted by the line's fine-tuned kids' programs.

DINING OPTIONS Food on Royal Caribbean has been upgraded and improved in recent years, and occasionally a dish will knock your socks off. The dining rooms have two seatings with assigned tables at dinner, as well as the more flexible My Time Dining program for dinner (open seating at breakfast and lunch). Every menu contains selections designed for low-fat, low-cholesterol, and low-salt dining as well as vegetarian and children's dishes. On both the *Explorer* and *Radiance,* you also have the option of dining on a reservations-only basis at **Chops Grille,** a classy steakhouse, or at an upscale Italian eatery. The line levies a range of prices for its specialty restaurants, typically from $6.95 to $95 per person (including **Johnny Rockets** and **Chefs Table**), but in our experience, the food soars above what's served in the dining room. On *Radiance,* casual table-service dining is enjoyed at **Rita's Cantina** for dinner as an alternative for those who don't want to sit in the dining room. On both ships, buffet-style breakfast, lunch, and dinner are available in the **Windjammer,** on Deck 11. A basic menu is available from room service 24 hours a day, and during normal dinner hours, a cabin steward can bring you anything being served in the dining room that night. Royal Caribbean bans smoking in the dining rooms on all its vessels.

ACTIVITIES On the activity front, Royal Caribbean has plenty of the standard cruise-line fare (crafts classes, bingo, shuffleboard, deck games, line-dancing lessons, wine-and-cheese tastings, cooking demonstrations, and art auctions). But if you want to take it easy and watch the world go by or scan for wildlife, nobody will bother you or cajole you into joining an activity. Port lectures are given on topics such as Alaskan wildlife, history, and culture. The ships also have an extensive fitness program called Vitality.

CHILDREN'S PROGRAMS Children's activities are some of the most extensive afloat and include a teen disco, children's play areas, and the Adventure Ocean and teen programs, which have a full schedule of scavenger hunts, arts-and-crafts sessions, and science presentations—so many activities, in fact, that kids get their own daily activity programs delivered to their cabins. Royal Caribbean also provides teen-only spaces on board every ship in its fleet. After *Radiance* was revitalized as part of the line's fleetwide revitalization program, a Royal Babies and Tots nursery was added, designed by Fisher-Price and Crayola, for kids 6 to 36 months of age and up ($8 per hour per child).

ENTERTAINMENT Royal incorporates sprawling, high-tec rooms, some with a wall of vid as good as that of any other m dinner and continues late, late in acts, sock hops, toga parties, tale oke. The Vegas-style shows are come to expect—these large-cas ship. Royal Caribbean uses 10 bands and other lounge acts keep

SERVICE Overall, service in t modating, and efficient. You're l polishing the brass in a stairwe Caribbean's are no strangers to c be able to get to you exactly wh armies of personnel required to m a miracle that staffers appear as m and dry-cleaning services are avai service laundromat. Royal Carib folios of passengers who have not passengers can modify these pa line's recommended daily gratui to the dining room staff and $3. and housekeeping staff ($6.10 fo typically depending on the catego

CRUISETOURS & ADD-ON F two 12-day cruisetours. **Kantish** Denali's unspoiled wilderness w kayaking and biking at Eklutna National Park and Preserve to Fa backcountry lodge after the cruise **Fly Over** gives passengers the ch its natural habitat in the Katmai Denali or Anchorage, before or af

Radiance of the Seas

The Verdict

So what if you need a map to find your way a to the superb spa, the self-leveling billiards ta

Specifications

Size (in Tons)	90,090
Passengers (Double Occ.)	2,143
Space/Passenger Ratio	43
Total Cabins/Veranda Cabins	1,056

Cabin Comfort & Amer
Ship Cleanliness & Mai
Public Comfort/Space
Decor

THE SHIP IN G
bean's first ships
new class that co
try. Highlights in
(in case there ar
designed to remi
tures rooms with
through which to
lobby elevators,
can even get oce

The ship is s
Caribbean seems
features wood, n
pretty, low-key d

CABINS Roo
bean ships—the
than on the earli
panel TV, teleph
dryer. Suites als
stereo and DVD,
bedroom (with a
baby grand pian
teen rooms on e

CABINS & RATE

CABINS	PER DIEM
Inside	$212.99
Outside	$424.42
Suites	$610.24

* with balcony

PUBLIC AREA
tioned billiards
course, you'll f
inspired **Casino**
less-than-friend
store and coffe

The numerou
If you tire of th
below, from a

Lounge. The **Viking Crown Lounge** holds the disco and its revolving bar, as well as an intimate cabaret area. A three-level theater recalls the glacial landscapes of not only Alaska, but the North Pole as well.

The ship also has a show lounge, a library, a shopping mall, and a conference center. For kids, children's centers are equipped with computer and crafts stations; teens get their own hangout. There is also a video arcade.

DINING OPTIONS   The elegant two-level main dining room features a grand staircase, but it's a rather noisy space. Buffet breakfasts and lunches are provided in the **Windjammer,** which also offers casual dinners with waiter service at night. In addition, the ship features several reservations-only restaurants that come with a cover charge: **Chops Grille,** serving steaks and chops, is a favorite; it's $35 per person for dinner and $19 per person for lunch. A recent overhaul also brought **Chef's Table, Samba Grill, Rita's Cantina, Izumi, Boardwalk Dog House, Giovanni's Table,** and **Park Cafe,** all a big step up from the ship's regular dining. Park Cafe offers an assortment of gourmet deli selections in the solarium.

POOL, FITNESS, SPA & SPORTS FACILITIES   For the active sort, there is a rock-climbing wall and a 9-hole minigolf course designed as baroque gardens, of all things. The ship has a nice spa (with sauna and steam rooms); an oceanview fitness center with dozens of machines (including 18 Stairmaster treadmills); a jogging track; sports courts (including basketball); golf simulators, for those who like to play virtual golf; and three swimming pools—one outside, one enclosed, and the third a teen/kiddie pool with slide. Whirlpools can be found in the solarium and near the outdoor pools.

Explorer of the Seas

The Verdict

Part of the important Voyager-class series, this ship was a step forward in amusement-park-inspired cruising when it was first built almost 20 years ago.

Specifications

Size (in Tons)	137,208	Crew	1,180
Passengers (Double Occ.)	3,286	Passenger/Crew Ratio	2.7 to 1
Space/Passenger Ratio	35	Year Launched	2000
Total Cabins/Veranda Cabins	1,642/652	Last Major Refurbishment	2015

Frommer's Ratings (Scale of 1–5)   ★★★★

Cabin Comfort & Amenities	4	Dining Options	4.5
Ship Cleanliness & Maintenance	4	Gym, Spa & Sports Facilities	4.5
Public Comfort/Space	4	Children's Facilities	4
Decor	4	Enjoyment Factor	4

THE SHIP IN GENERAL   Big and bustling, this ship has a lot to offer families (especially those with children of different ages or multigenerational groups) as well as big groups of friends. While it doesn't have some of the great dining found on newer ships, it offers plenty of activities to keep you busy.

CABINS & RATES

CABINS	PER DIEM RATES	SQ. FT.	FRIDGE	HAIR DRYER	SITTING AREA	TV
Inside	$204.53–$217.10	160–191	yes	yes	yes	yes
Outside	$385.53–$387.96*	164–179	yes	yes	yes	yes
Suites	$481.24–$673.53	277–1,188	yes	yes	yes	yes

with balcony

PUBLIC AREAS   This ship has a lot of the features that defined the line for years: an ice-skating rink, a mall-like **Royal Promenade** (home to shopping and parades), a theater with 3D movies, the FlowRider surfing simulator, a large main pool with outdoor movies, and a solarium with a smaller, more peaceful pool. The wide variety of bars (15, to be exact) include a proper British-style pub and the **Schooner Bar,** home to live music. In addition, this is a ship that's filled with impressive artwork, so keep your eyes peeled for memorable pieces.

DINING OPTIONS   The *Explorer* has so many choices you'll never have to eat in the same place twice. There's sushi (**Izumi**), a burger diner with dancing waiters (**Johnny Rockets**), a buffet (**Windjammer**), Italian (**Giovanni's Table**), and a steakhouse (**Chops Grille**). Looking for a fun date night? Consider the Mystery Dinner Theater experience. The ship has 24-hour room service, and continental breakfast is complimentary.

POOL, FITNESS, SPA & SPORTS FACILITIES   The ship's main pool feels like a party, with children running around with soft-serve cones and movies up on the big screen. The smaller, glassed-in **Solarium,** a greenhouse-style space with its own pool, works well in Alaska, where sunshine and heat are never guaranteed. The **Vitality spa** goes beyond massages and facials to offer medi-spa choices and has treatment rooms, a salon, and a fitness center. The ship also has miniature golf, an arcade, and a rock-climbing wall.

SEABOURN CRUISE LINE

450 Third Ave. West, Seattle, WA 98119. www.seabourn.com. © **866/755-5619.**

Pros

o **Expedition-style luxury voyages.** Seabourn deploys its "Ventures by Seabourn" experiences in Alaska, wherein a dedicated expedition team provides topical lectures, guided hikes, Zodiac discovery tours, and even specialized kayak adventures.

o **Off-the-beaten-path itineraries.** Seabourn's Alaska cruises visit places that few other ships of this caliber do. You'll get to visit the big ports like Juneau and Ketchikan, but your experiences in Wrangell or the First Nations community of Klemtu, British Columbia, may be even more memorable.

- **Attention to detail.** Expect the best of the best with this line, including lavish deck parties, custom Molton Brown toiletries, and cuisine curated by star chef Thomas Keller. Guests sailing to Alaska with Seabourn also receive complimentary parkas!

Cons

- **Quiet nightlife.** After a day of Alaska adventures, most guests retreat to their cabins for some down time.

THE LINE IN A NUTSHELL After nearly 2 decades away, Seabourn sailed back into Alaska in 2017 with the ultra-sleek *Seabourn Sojourn*. For such a monumental occasion, Seabourn pulled out all the stops, crafting itineraries that were part expedition cruise, part luxury cruise, and wholly unique. The line also introduced a British Columbia–centric focus, and to date, *Seabourn Sojourn* is the only luxury line to call on the First Nations community of Klemtu and the port of Alert Bay, and, for 2018, offer a scenic cruise off Bella Bella at the edge of British Columbia's Great Bear Rainforest.

THE EXPERIENCE The good life is well represented aboard Seabourn's ships. Every room is a suite, and all beverages (with the exception of the most premium, top-shelf pours) are available gratis. There's no need to tip on board (that's included, too), and consummate service is Seabourn's hallmark. Expect staff members to know your name, remember your drink, and treat you warmly at every turn. In Alaska, Seabourn has developed an immersive program of adventurous "Ventures by Seabourn" excursions that bridge the gap between luxury and expedition cruising. These come at an extra cost, but it's well worth it to go kayaking among the glaciers in Endicott Arm or cycling through Alaska's backcountry. Who says sophistication can't be fun?

THE FLEET Seabourn's small, yacht-like ships were all launched after 2009, making the line's fleet of five (soon to be six) luxury ships one of the youngest in the industry. Intimate, quiet, and comfortable, Seabourn lavishes guests with personalized service, spacious cabins, and superb cuisine.

In the summer, *Seabourn Sojourn* makes her home in Alaska, with sailings between Vancouver and Seward. Launched in 2010, the 458-guest ship sparkles like new, carrying a fleet of sea kayaks and motorized Zodiac rafts for explorations into the hidden Alaska that eludes larger ships.

PASSENGER PROFILE Well-heeled and well-traveled, Seabourn's sophisticated guests are used to the five-star treatment, but are interesting and congenial. You might find yourself engaged in dinner conversation about safaris in South Africa or a sailing on the Irrawaddy. While parents taking their adult (and like-minded) children on board aren't uncommon, kids are. Seabourn doesn't actively cater to families with young children, and Seabourn's guests like it that way.

DINING OPTIONS Seabourn's partnerships with culinary wizard Thomas Keller, launched in 2016, have proven to be superbly successful, and the *Seabourn Sojourn* space formerly occupied by Restaurant 2 has been refitted as **The Grill by Thomas Keller.** Considering that a meal at Keller's Per Se

Seabourn Itineraries

SHIP	ITINERARIES
Seabourn Sojourn	12-night Ultimate Alaska & Inside Passage: Round-trip Vancouver, BC, visiting Ketchikan, Sitka, Inian Islands, Icy Strait Point, Juneau, Tracy Arm (or Endicott Arm), Wrangell, Misty Fjords, Rudyerd Bay, Prince Rupert, Klemtu, Bella Bella, and Alert Bay (June & Sept)
Seabourn Sojourn	14-night Ultimate Glacier & Fjord Adventure: Seward to Vancouver, BC, visiting Resurrection Bay, Holgate Glacier, Aialik Glacier, Chiswell Islands, Kenai Fjords, Inian Islands, Icy Strait Point, Juneau, Haines, Tracy Arm (or Endicott Arm), Wrangell, Misty Fjords, Rudyerd Bay, Ketchikan, Prince Rupert, Klemtu, Bella Bella, and Alert Bay (June–Sept)
Seabourn Sojourn	11-night Ultimate Alaskan Sojourn: Vancouver, BC, to Seward, visiting Ketchikan, Rudyerd Bay, Misty Fjords, Wrangell, Sitka, Tracy Arm (or Endicott Arm), Haines, Juneau, and Icy Strait Point (July–Aug)
Seabourn Sojourn	20-night Alaska & America's Gold Coast: Vancouver, BC, to Los Angeles, visiting Ketchikan, Sitka, Icy Strait Point, Juneau, Tracy Arm (or Endicott Arm), Wrangell, Misty Fjords, Rudyerd Bay, Prince Rupert, Klemtu, Bella Bella, Alert Bay, Vancouver, Seattle, Victoria, San Francisco, Monterey, and Santa Barbara (Sept)

restaurant in New York would set you back $600, dinner at this complimentary reservations-only dining venue is a must.

The Restaurant serves up delicious fare from an uncomplicated menu each evening, and is often open for breakfast and lunch as well. In Alaska, Seabourn goes to great pains to feature local foods, like British Columbia salmon and king crab. More casual fare can be had at the **Colonnade,** with its relaxed dress code and rotating themed-menus that run the gamut from French to Italian and everything in between.

ACTIVITIES You're not going to find ice-skating rinks or rock-climbing walls on Seabourn's ships, but you will find plenty of lectures, along with popular cruise diversions such as afternoon tea, nightly production shows, and live music. There's also a fold-out marina on the stern of the ship that houses sea kayaks and Zodiac rafts for (extra-cost) shore excursions. In Alaska, Seabourn modifies its popular "Caviar in the Surf" beach party and takes it up to the ship's pool deck, where guests can enjoy Caviar on the Ice.

CHILDREN'S PROGRAMS Seabourn doesn't actively cater to kids.

ENTERTAINMENT Low-key and quiet, the entertainment on board primarily consists of mingling with your fellow guests over cocktails and live music offered in multiple venues during the evening hours. Seabourn has upped the game on its nightly production shows, however—a performance of "An Evening with Tim Rice" on our voyage through Alaska on *Seabourn Sojourn*'s maiden season is one of the most original and well-performed production shows we've seen at sea.

SERVICE Perhaps Seabourn's greatest asset, service is polished and precise while remaining friendly and personable. Expect to be addressed by name throughout your voyage. We were even recognized by name in the terminal in Vancouver, before we'd even stepped aboard. Tipping is never required on

Seabourn—gratuities for all staff members, including the Ventures by Seabourn team, are included in the cost of the voyage.

CRUISETOURS & ADD-ON PROGRAMS   Optional 5-day pre/post Seabourn Journey to Denali National Park. Seabourn limits this to just 20 guests per group, so you'll want to call and book this one in advance.

Seabourn Sojourn

The Verdict

An all-around winner, with stunning interior design and plenty of floor-to-ceiling windows and open deck spaces from which to admire Alaska's majesty. A refit in the fall 2017 added new features, and *Seabourn Sojourn*'s high passenger-to-space ratio means things never get crowded.

Specifications

Size (in Tons)	32,000	Crew	335
Passengers (Double Occ.)	450	Passenger/Crew Ratio	1.3 to 1
Space/Passenger Ratio	71	Year Launched	2010
Total Cabins/Veranda Cabins	225/199	Last Major Refurbishment	2017

Frommer's Ratings (Scale of 1–5)   ★★★★★

Cabin Comfort & Amenities	5	Dining Options	5
Ship Cleanliness & Maintenance	5	Gym, Spa & Sports Facilities	5
Public Comfort/Space	5	Children's Facilities	N/A
Decor	5	Enjoyment Factor	5

THE SHIP IN GENERAL   The second of Seabourn's trendsetting Odyssey-class ships, *Seabourn Sojourn* is one of the most graceful ships afloat. Exterior decks cascade forward and aft, while public rooms are bright, airy, and filled with floor-to-ceiling windows. Modern design touches, including plenty of glass, accent lighting, and bold colors, give *Seabourn Sojourn* a warm, cozy feeling that works well in Alaska.

CABINS   A touch of the good life is available in every cabin aboard *Seabourn Sojourn*. All cabins are suites and all have ocean views, and the majority feature private balconies. Ocean View Suites, the entry-level accommodation aboard *Seabourn Sojourn*, have oversize picture windows, a separate seating area, and a bed that can be arranged as either a queen or two twins. A fully stocked minibar, flat-panel TV with video-on-demand, and a vanity/desk area round out these 295-square-foot rooms. Essentially identical are the Veranda Suites, which add a substantial private balcony to the mix. Both Ocean View and Veranda suites feature marble-clad bathrooms complete with a separate tub and shower, along with custom-designed Molton Brown toiletries.

If you're willing to splurge, you'll be rewarded nicely. Top-of-the-line suites range from the 534-square-foot Penthouse Suites to the amazing 1,352-square-foot Signature Suites, which feature a six-person dining room, guest bathroom, pantry with a dedicated wet bar, and the option to combine the suite with the adjacent suite for even more space.

Wintergarden Suites have large windows with ocean views, plus a balcony that cantilevers attractively out over the side of the ship for amazing sightseeing vistas. In addition to 914 square feet of living space, these suites come with some pretty nice perks, including a personal visit from the Hotel Manager and an invitation to visit the Captain on the bridge when the ship is in port.

For the spa lover, *Seabourn Sojourn*'s Penthouse Spa Suites are heavenly. Measuring 536 to 539 square feet, these rooms have gargantuan balconies that are nearly 200 square feet and come equipped with complimentary access to the serene area at the Spa at Seabourn, along with a second minibar loaded with healthy beverages and snacks, Molton Brown spa products, L'Occitane room fragrances, and even a calming soundtrack that can be piped into the room. Guests booking this category also have the services of a dedicated Spa Concierge. You may never want to leave your suite.

CABINS & RATES

CABINS	PER DIEM RATES	SQ. FT.	FRIDGE	HAIR DRYER	SITTING AREA	TV
Suites	$331–$1,182	295–1,682	yes	yes	yes	yes

PUBLIC AREAS   *Seabourn Sojourn* is just plain beautiful. At the heart of the ship is Seabourn's trademark soaring spiral-staircase atrium. Topped with a massive skylight, it is the conduit to all of the ship's public areas and one of the most photographed spots on board. One of the ship's most unique features is **Seabourn Square,** located all the way aft on Deck 7. This attractive, wood-paneled space combines a coffeeshop and attractive seating areas (plenty of books and Internet workstations) with the more traditional guest relations desks, which are inset—literally—into a square in the center of the room. The Future Cruise Consultant is tucked away on the starboard side, next to a book exchange and the ship's onboard shops.

In Alaska, it's tough to beat the views from the forward-facing **Observation Lounge,** which, as you might expect, tends to get crowded during scenic cruising. Afternoon tea is served here, and at night live piano music gives the lounge a classy after-dinner vibe. Down on Deck 5, **The Club** is *Seabourn Sojourn*'s other watering hole, though it doesn't typically open until evenings after 5pm, but does offer live music each evening "until late." During the day, the room is repurposed in Alaska as the staging point for the Ventures by Seabourn team. The only room that doesn't quite work is **The Grand Salon,** which suffers from poor sightlines due to a number of support columns that tend to get in the way, especially if you're seated at the back of the room. A small **Casino** is located on Deck 5, adjacent to The Club, but it was mainly forgotten about on our Alaska sailing.

DINING OPTIONS   The showstopper of *Seabourn Sojourn*'s dining world is **The Restaurant.** Located amidships on Deck 4, this simply named space is one of the grandest dining venues at sea, topped only by the Britannia Restaurant aboard Cunard's *Queen Mary 2*. Vertical rectangular windows provide for unusually breathtaking views, and additional light is let into the room via a center partition that extends all the way up into Deck 5. High ceilings, soft lighting, and excellent service are on the menu here for breakfast, lunch, and dinner. Open seating is the rule of the day, though it is always up to you whether you wish to dine alone or with others. You'll want to dress nicely for dinner here, but Seabourn's relaxed dress code means you won't need to don a suit and tie every night. In Alaska, dinner menus features highlighted dishes designed by superstar chef Thomas Keller, along with regional specialties like British Columbia salmon and Alaskan king crab.

Restaurant 2 was transformed into **The Grill by Thomas Keller** at the end of *Seabourn Sojourn*'s first Alaskan season. Featuring a new menu and a swanky new look, The Grill is designed to provide a classic American chophouse experience. In addition to steak, expect to find favorites like lobster thermidor and tableside preparation for many dishes. There's no extra fee to dine here, but you will want to make reservations well in advance—this is the hottest ticket on board. It's open for dinner only.

All the way aft on Deck 8 is **The Colonnade,** the go-to spot for a casual breakfast or lunch. You can either dine indoors (it's a beautiful space, with a surprising variety of seating options, including high-top counters and low, cozy tables), or eat outside on the aft-facing veranda, which can accommodate a whopping 124 guests. At dinner, themed menus, with delectable dishes from Thomas Keller's Ad Hoc restaurants, turn The Colonnade into a specialty restaurant of sorts, with reservations required but no cover charge, in keeping with Seabourn's all-inclusive policy. You can also dine outdoors poolside at **The Patio** (home to the Thomas Keller burger, of course), and complimentary room service is available around the clock.

POOL, FITNESS, SPA & SPORTS FACILITIES   A large swimming pool and two hot tubs are located amidships on Deck 8, but arguably the most popular hot tub on board *Seabourn Sojourn* in Alaska is the one that's tucked away at the very tip of the bow on Deck 5. Typically open while in port or on scenic cruising days, this is the place to be when you're sailing through Misty Fjords.

The **Spa at Seabourn** is tucked away on Deck 9 aft and comes with all the usual treatments, plus a full-service salon. What you might not expect, however, is the **Kniepp Walk Pool,** with relaxing loungers facing the stern of the ship. A well-stocked fitness center has a motion studio with a Kinesis Wall and a Thai massage area. High up on Deck 11 forward, a putting green is bordered by two shuffleboard courts, neither of which tend to be used all that much in Alaska.

SILVERSEA

333 Ave. of the Americas, Suite 2600, Miami, FL 33131. www.silversea.com. ℂ **800/722-9955.**

Pros

o **All-around excellence.** The no-tipping policy is always a hit, and the cuisine, open seating for meals, exemplary service, and great accommodations make Silversea well worth the money for those who want something special.

- **Surprisingly little formality.** Considering the economic status of most of the passengers, there's very little stuffiness.
- **A huge number of private verandas.** More than 80% of the suites on the *Silver Shadow* have this desirable feature.

Cons
- **Not a great deal of nightlife.** Although the ship has a show lounge, it's not really big enough for anything overly lavish. The line in recent years has been de-emphasizing production-type shows in favor of more low-key, concert-style performances by vocalists and other musicians.

THE LINE IN A NUTSHELL   There's no argument: Silversea is a very worthy member of the small number of operators of truly luxurious small-to-midsize ships. The *Silver Shadow*, the main ship of the Silversea fleet that cruises to Alaska, underwent a refurbishment in 2017 that's left it looking shiny and new.

THE EXPERIENCE   Silversea represents the last word in elegance and service. Spacious accommodations, all oceanview suites, no tipping expected, free beverages (alcoholic and otherwise), swift and caring baggage handling—these are the hallmarks of the Silversea line.

THE FLEET   The 382-passenger *Silver Shadow,* which joined the fleet in 2000, is one of nine Silversea ships, and the only one, other than the line's expedition ship *Silver Explorer,* that cruises to Alaska. *Silver Shadow*'s twin, the *Silver Whisper,* entered service the following year. The others are the smaller and virtually identical *Silver Cloud* (1994) and *Silver Wind* (1995), as well as the somewhat bigger *Silver Spirit* (2009). In 2013, the company rolled out a small, 100-passenger expedition ship in the Galapagos, the *Silver Galapagos,* and in 2014 added a third expedition vessel, the 120-passenger *Silver Discoverer.* In spring 2017, the line launched the spacious new *Silver Muse.*

PASSENGER PROFILE   Guests tend to be in their mid-40s and up. They are generally well educated, with definite ideas on just what luxury means in accommodations, cuisine, and service. And they have the means to pay for it!

DINING OPTIONS   Food is one of Silversea's strengths—both in preparation and in presentation—not only in the main dining room (known simply as **The Restaurant**), but also in the breakfast/lunch buffets in **La Terrazza.** That room doubles as a low-capacity candlelit Italian restaurant with a "slow-food" philosophy in the evening.

Silversea serves very acceptable complimentary wine with dinner (and at other meals), but if you must upgrade to something really, really expensive (Opus One and Dom Perignon are a couple choices that come to mind), you should expect to pay the going rate. There are many mid-priced options by the bottle as well.

ACTIVITIES   In past years, Silversea has significantly enhanced its onboard enrichment program. Naturalists, historians, well-known authors, award-winning chefs, and wine experts host excellent sessions, often targeted toward

Silversea Fleet Itineraries

SHIP	ITINERARIES
Silver Shadow	7-night Inside Passage: North- and southbound between Vancouver, BC, and Seward, or round-trip from Vancouver, visiting Ketchikan, Sitka, Sawyer Glacier, Hubbard Glacier, Juneau, and Skagway (May–Sept)
Silver Explorer	19-night Alaska Expeditions: Round-trip from Nome to a variety of Russian Federation ports (July)
Silver Explorer	12-night Alaska Expeditions: Round-trip from Nome to a variety of Russian Federation ports (July–Aug)

the specific cruising location. The line has also introduced a Cooking School with state-of-the-art cooking theaters that allow chefs to present a variety of specialized cooking classes and demonstrations on every cruise.

CHILDREN'S PROGRAMS There are youth counselors on Silversea ships based on the number of children on board; activities are defined accordingly.

ENTERTAINMENT It's just not possible to stage extravagant song-and-dance presentations on ships of the small size that Silversea operates, but the Alaska-based *Silver Shadow* sails with a team of six vocalists and musicians who do an excellent job nonetheless as they put on several shows every week in the main theater. Outside the main showroom, there's usually a small combo for dancing (no disco, please!). The library has an ample supply of books.

SERVICE The finest compliment that anyone can pay the Silversea staff is that they provide the kind of service that you just don't notice. It has a self-service laundry and remarkably speedy valet service, including laundry and dry cleaning. On Silversea ships, gratuities for the staff are included in the fare and not expected.

CRUISETOURS & ADD-ON PROGRAMS Silversea offers a small number of pre- and post-cruise land packages ranging from 2 to 4 nights. The shortest, for passengers who are interested in wildlife, is a 2-night program called Flight to Bear Country that takes passengers by floatplane to Redoubt Bay, where bears are frequently sighted. It costs from $1,529 per person, based on double occupancy. On the longer side is a 4-night trip to Denali National Park that starts at $1,899 per person, based on double occupancy.

Silver Shadow

The Verdict

If this ship had a movie equivalent, it would have to be Jack Nicholson's *As Good as It Gets*.

Specifications

Size (in Tons)	28,258	Crew	295
Passengers (Double Occ.)	382	Passenger/Crew Ratio	1.3 to 1
Space/Passenger Ratio	74	Year Launched	2000
Total Cabins/Veranda Cabins	194/168	Last Major Refurbishment	2017

Cabin Comfort & Amenities	5	Dining Options	5
Ship Cleanliness & Maintenance	5	Gym, Spa & Sports Facilities	4
Public Comfort/Space	4.5	Children's Facilities	N/A
Decor	4.5	Enjoyment Factor	5

THE SHIP IN GENERAL The *Silver Shadow* has one of the highest space-to-passenger ratios in the industry—technically, determined as 74. That's a rather esoteric measurement that's arrived at by dividing the ship's gross tonnage (the volume of its interior space) by the lower berth capacity. It's complicated, but take our word for it—this ship is plenty spacious. The *Silver Shadow* takes Silversea's concept of luxury cruising to exceptional heights, with walk-in closets, dressing tables with hair dryers close at hand, real marble double-vanity basins, bathtubs and separate showers, and DVD units in every stateroom. Butler service is provided for all suites (in other words, in all rooms). Wi-Fi access is available throughout the ship.

CABINS All outside, all suites. All but a few have private verandas; the smallest of the units—there are only a handful—have none. But they're a roomy 287 square feet, with picture windows. From there the sizes go up and up, ranging from 345 square feet to 1,435 square feet. Every suite comes with convertible twin-to-queen beds, a minibar (stocked), and safes. Two of the suites are wheelchair-accessible.

CABINS & RATES

CABINS	PER DIEM RATES	SQ. FT.	FRIDGE	HAIR DRYER	SITTING AREA	TV
Outside Suites	$540–$2,017	287–1,435	yes	yes	yes	yes

PUBLIC AREAS The *Silver Shadow*'s two-level showroom is not the biggest we've ever seen, but it has good sightlines, and it's a pleasant place to while away an hour after dinner. The small cigar bar is known as the **Connoisseur's Corner.** The casino provides the usual array of money-speculating ventures: roulette, blackjack, and a few slots. Have a drink in the casino or in a bigger room simply called **The Bar,** a great gathering spot with live music in the evening. The best place for a drink may well be the really small **Lampadina,** just off the casino. The rear-facing **Panorama Lounge** has dancing to a range of musical styles, from ballroom and dinner dancing to rock-'n'-roll classics to the latest club mixes. The ship's forward-facing **Observation Lounge** on the top deck is a quiet sanctuary for a game of chess or backgammon, conversation, reading, or watching the scenery. The ship also has a fully equipped eight-computer Internet center, a card room, an upscale boutique, and an H. Stern jewelry store.

DINING OPTIONS The *Silver Shadow* has four dining venues. **The Restaurant,** the main dining room, serves breakfast, lunch, and dinner in elegant style. A more casual, buffet-style breakfast and lunch are served at the indoor/

outdoor **La Terrazza**—and in the evening, this spot becomes a lovely specialty Italian restaurant (reservations required; no cover charge). **Le Champagne,** developed in collaboration with Relais & Châteaux, offers seasonally inspired menus showcasing regional specialties prepared with fresh, locally sourced items in an intimate setting on Deck 7 next to La Terrazza (reservations are absolutely necessary, with a cover charge of $40 per person). **The Grill,** the ship's outside poolside cafe, has burgers, sandwiches, and salads at lunch and turns into a wonderful alfresco grill at night. The Grill features an interactive Black Rock experience: A preheated volcanic rock is brought to your table, allowing you to cook such delicacies as steak, veal, pork, lamb, salmon, fish, or prawns exactly to your liking right in front of you. Of course, there's 24-hour room service, and meals can be served course-by-course if so desired.

POOL, FITNESS, SPA & SPORTS FACILITIES The spa is, like most of the other public rooms, small when measured alongside those of its mega-ship competition. But even with just four treatment rooms, it provides the same range of hydrotherapy, massage, and beauty treatments; men's and women's saunas; and more. The line recently introduced a Wellness Program that combines daily activities, including yoga, Pilates, and meditation classes, with suggestions from its light and low-carb lunch and dinner menus. For fitness buffs, there is a fitness center and a small jogging track. The beauty shop provides pedicures, manicures, and facials as well as hair styling. The one pool and two hot tubs, surrounded on two levels by lots of lounge chairs, are just right for a ship this size.

Silver Explorer

The Verdict

This was the first luxury expedition ship, and it's still a comfortable yet intimate way to see Alaska.

Specifications

Size (in Tons)	6,072	Crew	118
Passengers (Double Occ.)	144	Passenger/Crew Ratio	.85 to 1
Space/Passenger Ratio	46.71	Year Launched	1989
Total Cabins/Veranda Cabins	66/28	Last Major Refurbishment	2017

Frommer's Ratings (Scale of 1–5)

★★★★★

Cabin Comfort & Amenities	5	Dining Options	5
Ship Cleanliness & Maintenance	5	Gym, Spa & Sports Facilities	4
Public Comfort/Space	4.5	Children's Facilities	N/A
Decor	4.5	Enjoyment Factor	5

THE SHIP IN GENERAL Expect a study in contradictions: The all-inclusive *Explorer* is a hybrid expedition vessel and luxury ship. On one hand every room is a suite and there's a lovely afternoon tea service every day, and on the other hand the ship is an ice-class vessel, designed for handling the rugged Arctic. And although you won't find formal nights on this Silversea ship, the *Explorer* sails with a fleet of Zodiacs (and boots for wet landings), and brings champagne and strawberries on its excursions.

CABINS   While all cabins on board the vessel are suites, they start off with portholes and work their way up to having picture windows and then French balconies before getting to actual verandas. That said, all are decked out in the type of luxuries you'd expect to see on a fancy wedding registry, from Pratesi sheets to Bulgari bath products, Etro robes and slippers, and down duvets. You can choose from a menu of nine types of pillows, just like on the line's bigger ships. All of the rooms have butler service, as well as safes, minibars, filtered water, blow dryers, and even elegant personalized stationery.

CABINS & RATES

CABINS	PER DIEM RATES	SQ. FT.	FRIDGE	HAIR DRYER	SITTING AREA	TV
Outside Suites	$720–$2,510	157–728	yes	yes	yes	yes

PUBLIC AREAS   The *Explorer* has a library, an observation lounge, and the **Panorama** lounge. Classes (cooking demos, wine tastings) are occasionally offered, but most passengers are early to bed and early to rise in order to be fresh for the day in port. Dinner is the main event at night—evenings are quiet—while daytime educational lectures are a hot ticket.

DINING OPTIONS   There are just two options on board: **The Restaurant** and **The Grill,** and both have open seating. At night, The Grill, which is alfresco, showcases lava rocks on which you cook your own dinner; a more casual menu of burgers and salads is served during the day.

POOL, FITNESS, SPA & SPORTS FACILITIES   Both the gym and the spa are small on this ship.

VIKING OCEAN CRUISES

5700 Canoga Ave., Suite 200, Woodland Hills, CA 91367. www.vikingcruises.com. © **855/884-5464.**

Pros

o **A grown-up experience.** The line has no children's programs. All activities are geared toward sophisticated, well-traveled passengers.

o **All-inclusive fares.** Viking includes everything from shore excursions to Wi-Fi as well as beer and wine at meals—even the spectacular thermal area in the **LivNordic spa** is complimentary to all guests.

o **Gorgeous design.** The Scandinavian look and feel of the ship is beautifully executed—you may disembark wishing you could bring everything from the chairs to the window coverings home with you.

Cons

o **Quiet evenings.** The line's evening entertainment feels sleepy, and many guests head back to their—admittedly palatial—cabins after dinner.

THE LINE IN A NUTSHELL You won't find flashing lights or Vegas-inspired decor choices here, and Viking's guests love the effortlessly chic and subtle interior design. The line, which is part of the newer ocean arm of a company well known for European river cruises, operates three midsize ocean ships, largely sailing the Baltic and the Mediterreanean. The year 2019 will be the line's first season in Alaska.

THE EXPERIENCE The Scandinavian-inspired experience is more than just best-in-class decor and an unforgettable spa: The Northern European food is also impressive, from open-faced smoked-salmon sandwiches at lunch to waffles with brown cheese and berries at breakfast. Equally impressive is the attention to detail in the accommodations.

THE FLEET Viking is new to the Alaska market, and the ocean line itself is only 3 years old. The ships have primarily sailed in Europe, then the Caribbean, and are just starting to make their way farther afield.

PASSENGER PROFILE Viking attract travelers from their 40s to their 70s, largely low-key but well-traveled empty-nesters and retirees. They flock here for the style, but also for the value offered by the line.

DINING OPTIONS Viking's chefs go out of their way to pick up local ingredients at the market, and fresh choices often appear on the lunch buffet, which offers a variety of well-executed continental dishes. In **Mamsen's** café, you can get Scandinavian specialties for breakfast, lunch, afternoon snacks (don't miss the gorgeous cakes!), and late-night treats, including a rich pea soup that's sure to feel just right on a chilly Alaskan night. The ships also have an afternoon tea service, a poolside grill, and room service. The two alternative dining restaurants are included in the fare. **Manfredi's** is truly one of the best Italian restaurants at sea—we always go in thinking we'll "order less this time" and then find ourselves thoroughly seduced by the menu once again. **The Chef's Table** completely revamps its menu every few days; one night it may be Chinese, with handmade dumplings; the next night, Norwegian cuisine.

ACTIVITIES Spending the day in the bright gym or at the gorgeous spa is the right way to go on this ship. The thermal suite—with a stunning in-wall fireplace, wood-lined saunas, cold bucket-style shower, and snow room—may just be the best at sea, and it's complimentary. Afternoon tea, served in the lovely glassed-in **Wintergarden** (with finger sandwiches and sweets presented on tiered trays along with steaming pots of high-quality tea), is the highlight of any sea day for many passengers—so do go early if you want a table, especially if you have a preference for being near (or far) from the live music. The line's Alaska cruises offer lectures by local Alaska experts, and many passengers engage in card and board games. The **Kitchen Table** is a special space that allows passengers to follow a chef to a local market, and

Viking Ocean Cruises Fleet Itineraries

SHIP	ITINERARIES
Viking Orion	10-night Inside Passage: North- and southbound between Vancouver, BC, and Seward/Anchorage, visiting Ketchikan, Juneau, Skagway, and Sitka, and cruising Icy Strait (May–Aug)
Viking Orion	22-night North Pacific Passage: From Tokyo, Japan, to Vancouver, BC, visiting a variety of ports in Japan, Russia, Alaska, and Canada (May)

then return here to help with the preparation of an elaborate shared feast. (At $199 per person, it's a pricey afternoon for a couple, but so worth it.) Other than that, activities are limited, but most passengers prefer it that way, napping on deck or reading a tome from one of the many themed libraries on board. And, because Wi-Fi is included in the fares, you'll see many passengers using their phones or tablets on deck.

CHILDREN'S PROGRAMS   This adult-oriented line has no programming or facilities for children.

ENTERTAINMENT   The ship's small size means limited (and less strong) evening entertainment. Most passengers make a night of pre- (and sometimes post-) dinner cocktails so that they can be up bright and early to visit the next day's port. That said, the **Star Theater** showcases local performers and also hosts review-style musical shows. Movies shown in the theater come with pillows, blankets, and freshly popped popcorn. **Torshavn,** the ship's intimate jazz lounge/piano bar, hosts cabaret-style performances and sometimes late-afternoon spirits tastings. Before and after dinner, trios and quartets perform in the open lobby area to the cocktail crowd.

SERVICE   The excellent room stewards do a great job, and bar service is also spot-on. On Viking ships, gratuities for the staff are automatically charged at a rate of $15 per day.

CRUISETOURS & ADD-ON PROGRAMS   The line offers three pre- and post-cruise tour options: a 2-night, pre-cruise tour in Vancouver for $499 per person; a 2-night, post-cruise tour in Anchorage for $599 per person; and a 5-night, post-cruise tour in Denali for $3,299 per person, including visits to Anchorage and Talkeetna.

Viking Orion

The Verdict

Viking Orion is a fantastic addition to the Alaska market: a brand-new ship from a fairly new line, offering a sophisticated option for cruisers looking for peace and quiet as well as quality.

Specifications

Size (in Tons)	47,800	Crew	550
Passengers (Double Occ.)	930	Passenger/Crew Ratio	1.69 to 1
Space/Passenger Ratio	51.4	Year Launched	2018
Total Cabins/Veranda Cabins	465/465	Last Major Refurbishment	None

Frommer's Ratings (Scale of 1–5)

★★★★★

Cabin Comfort & Amenities	5	Dining Options	4
Ship Cleanliness & Maintenance	5	Gym, Spa & Sports Facilities	5
Public Comfort/Space	5	Children's Facilities	N/A
Decor	5	Enjoyment Factor	5

THE SHIP IN GENERAL The 930-passenger *Viking Orion* is a luxurious vessel that's identical to her four predecessors. The amount of public space per person is enormous for a ship this size, and its spacious cabin design gives everyone lots of private room to move around in, too. Shore excursions—such as gold prospecting in Juneau and visiting a Tlingit Village in Icy Strait Point—are included, but you can also sign up for additional, upgraded adventures, such as riding a floatplane through Misty Fjords to see glaciers up close.

CABINS Every room comes with a private veranda, king-size beds, tons of storage space, well-appointed bathrooms with heated floors, refrigerators stocked with complimentary bottled water and soft drinks, as well as snacks, safes, soft robes and slippers, phones, and 24-hour room service. All cabins come with QuietVox audio systems, for use on the included guided tours. You can order full meals from the dining room menu, served in-suite. The smallest of the staterooms is 270 square feet, and even those have thoughtful touches, such as bedside tables with bookmarks provided as well as USB ports (a feature you would think would be common on ships but remains elusive). The largest of the suites—the single Owner's Suite—is a whopping 1,448 square feet and includes an in-suite sauna.

CABINS & RATES

CABINS	PER DIEM RATES	SQ. FT.	FRIDGE	HAIR DRYER	SITTING AREA	TV
Cabins	$440–$480	270–338	yes	yes	yes	yes
Suites	$700–$1,060	405–757	yes	yes	yes	yes

PUBLIC AREAS The *Viking Orion* has a bright, gorgeously designed interior that's elegant, spacious, and comfortable. Best of all, it's also playful—look carefully at the birch-tree patterns in the elevators and you may see trolls laughing from behind a branch. The ship has a number of intimate lounges, including the airy, greenhouse-style **Wintergarden** (home to afternoon tea with live music); the **Explorer's Lounge,** with its fur throws and fireplaces, a cozy place to warm up after a day in Alaska; the **Atrium Lounge,** with a coffee bar and a living-room-style feel; and **Torshavn,** a jazz club. Shoppers should visit the classy boutique selling clothes and jewelry from carefully chosen artisan Scandinavian designers; the well-curated spa gift shop (home to hats hand-knit by a Norwegian granny); and a sundries shop that carries salted black licorice.

DINING OPTIONS The design of the main dining room, **The Restaurant,** is equally elegant, with just as much of a Scandinavian influence. **Compass Rose** serves breakfasts that include Swedish shrimp salad on pumpernickel, smoked Norwegian salmon, broiled kippers with onions, and stunning bowls of mixed berries with marscapone cheese. Lunches and dinners are as beautifully presented, with a strong Continental leaning, if not always as flawlessly executed. Look for savory soufflés, consommés, and salads to start, followed by entrees such as seared liver and onions or filet mignon. The buffet, called the **World Café,** has similar Continental fare, offering cold cuts, soups, and a carving station that might include, say, roast beef with vegetables and potatoes—if it's nice outside you can take your food onto the Aquavit Terrace and dine by the ship's lovely infinity pool. The **Pool Grill,** by the larger main pool, offers exactly what you would expect: burgers, veggie burgers, grilled fish, and even surprisingly good chili dogs. At night we try to dine in **Manfredi's** and **The Chef's Table** as much as possible. While the room service menu is extensive, we usually opt for **Mamsen's** when we're hungry outside of meal times—it's hard to pass up the café's fresh, authentic Scandinavian fare.

POOL, FITNESS, SPA & SPORTS FACILITIES   The bright gym and aerobics area do not seem to get crowded despite their size. The spa and sunny beauty salon offer the normal range of services plus a few Scandinavian specialties, such as the playful "sauna night," which involves—get this—running back and forth between the snow room and the steam room and getting hit with branches to improve your circulation. (It's more fun than it sounds, and it's only $39.) The central pool is flanked by heated whirlpools and an enormous amount of open deck space; its glass magrodome can be closed when the temperature drops. A small infinity pool often remains empty, probably because few passengers want to swim right next to people dining at the buffet. No matter: It's a truly elegant water feature, even if it is underused during the day. In addition, a small sports deck at the front of the ship has a quiet, Astroturf-lined putting green and bocce court, and a shuffleboard court.

WINDSTAR CRUISES

2101 4th Ave., Suite 210, Seattle, WA 98121. www.windstarcruises.com. ℭ **877/203-5729.**

Pros

o **Casual all day long.** The line doesn't have formal nights, so you can leave the jackets and ties at home.

o **Fair fares.** It may be a former Seabourn ship, but rates are much lower.

Cons

o **Tiny pool.** The ship's pool is very small—which generally isn't a big deal in Alaska, but if you get a warm, sunny day you may wish for more space.

THE LINE IN A NUTSHELL   This fleet of small ships spreads out across the globe, but 2018 will be the first time Windstar has cruised in Alaska since 1998.

Windstar Cruises Fleet Itineraries

SHIP	ITINERARIES
Star Legend	12-night Alaskan Splendors: From Vancouver, BC, to Anchorage/Seward, visiting Ketchikan, Misty Fjords, Wrangell, Sitka, Icy Strait Point, Tracy Arm, Juneau, Haines, Metlakatla, and Kenai Fjords National Park (May–Aug)
Star Legend	12-night Islands and Inlets of the Inside Passage: Round-trip cruises from Vancouver, BC, visiting Ketchikan, Icy Strait Point, Tracy Arm, Juneau, Wrangell, Misty Fjords, Metlakatla, Prince Rupert, and Greenville Channel (July–Aug)
Star Legend	13-night Japan and North Pacific Crossing: From Tokyo, Japan, to Anchorage/Seward, visiting Miyako, Hakodate, and Kushiro (May)
Star Legend	14-night Wonders of Alaska and Canada: From Anchorage/Seward to Vancouver, BC, visiting Kenai Fjords National Park, Icy Strait Point, Haines, Tracy Arm, Juneau, Sitka, Wrangell, Misty Fjords, Ketchikan, Metlakatla, Prince Rupert, and Greenville Channel (May–Aug)
Star Legend	16-night Aleutians and North Pacific Crossing: From Anchorage/Seward to Tokyo, Japan, visiting Homer, Kodiak, Sand Point, Dutch Harbor, Kushiro, and Miyako (Sept)
Star Legend	27-night Alaska Crossing to Japan: From Vancouver, BC, to Tokyo, Japan, visiting Ketchikan, Misty Fjords, Wrangell, Sitka, Tracy Arm, Haines, Juneau, Kenai Fjords National Park, Anchorage/Seward, Homer, Kodiak, Sand Point, Dutch Harbor, Kushiro, and Miyako (Aug)

THE EXPERIENCE Windstar's passengers may be well traveled, but they are also down to earth and unassuming—in addition to no formal nights, you won't find any airs here. And, on a ship with just 212 passengers, liking the other guests is fairly important. Windstar ships operate a bit like a small town; if you're the social type, you should expect to recognize a lot of faces, and maybe even know a lot of names, before you disembark.

THE FLEET Windstar doubled its fleet in 2013 when it purchased three sister ships from Seabourn. Today, the line once known for its sailing ships has a mixture of those and these all-suite yachts. While many long-time Windstar fans prefer to watch the sails be raised—the moment does have its majesty—we find these power yachts handle the weather a bit more smoothly.

PASSENGER PROFILE Windstar attract travelers from their 40s to their 70s, largely well-traveled empty-nesters and retirees traveling in pairs. (You'll also see the occasional younger couple, often on their honeymoon.) This is the first time the line has sailed in Alaska in 20 years, so for devoted loyalists it's a great opportunity to check the destination off your list.

DINING OPTIONS Windstar ships are small and don't have the volume of options you find on larger vessels. Most people eat dinner in the main dining room just about every night. Recently, the line partnered with the James Beard Foundation, and now dining-room menus feature signature dishes of award-winning chefs. Lunch and breakfast are offered in the **Veranda,** a cafe that offers additional a la carte options and at night morphs into a candlelit reservations-only dinner restaurant. One night per sailing the line creates an elaborate cookout on deck—and for many repeat guests this is the highlight of the sailing. (Unless you're on a French Polynesia cruise, and then the afternoon on the private island wins.)

ACTIVITIES These ships are fairly destination-focused, and daytime activities may be limited to aerobics classes, wine tastings, and port talks. In the lounge, passengers read, play board and card games, and work on the giant puzzle set out at the beginning of the sailing.

CHILDREN'S PROGRAMS The line is adult-oriented, but these sailings could be a great choice for families with older kids who are intrigued by nature and animals.

ENTERTAINMENT The small size of this ship means limited evening entertainment. Look for pre-dinner performances by a musical duo. After dinner, you'll find team trivia, a crew talent show, and a fairly competitive game show one evening.

SERVICE The excellent room stewards are dedicated, and bar service is also well done. How good are the waiters on *Star Legend*? When we asked for hot sauce one night, our waiter went down to his cabin and brought us some his mother had made for him—he didn't think the ship's brand would be hot enough for us. The spa team is impressive, too: A woman doing our manicure noticed how dry our nails were and insisted on giving us some cuticle oil to use.

CRUISETOURS & ADD-ON PROGRAMS None.

Star Legend

The Verdict

Star Legend is a former Seabourn power yacht that retains its intimate look and feel, albeit at a lower price point. This is a great new option in a region that's well suited to small-ship sailing.

Specifications

Size (in Tons)	9,961	Crew	153
Passengers (Double Occ.)	212	Passenger/Crew Ratio	1.4 to 1
Space/Passenger Ratio	1:47	Year Launched	1991
Total Cabins/Veranda Cabins	414/6	Last Major Refurbishment	2017

Frommer's Ratings (Scale of 1–5)   ★★★★

Cabin Comfort & Amenities	3	Dining Options	4
Ship Cleanliness & Maintenance	5	Gym, Spa & Sports Facilities	4
Public Comfort/Space	4	Children's Facilities	N/A
Decor	4	Enjoyment Factor	4

THE SHIP IN GENERAL The ship went into dry dock in late 2017 before sailing to Alaska from Asia, allowing Windstar to update the so-called "soft goods" (carpets, linens) and add a fleet of Zodiacs and kayaks. This is a ship designed to get into small ports and explore parts of Alaska that few ships can reach—which suits the already outdoorsy line just fine. In addition, in Alaska the port talks and other destination lectures are done by speakers who double as expedition leaders on land.

CABINS   The cabins feel a bit dated—no USB ports here and surprisingly few U.S. outlets as well. The TVs still come with DVD players rather than an On Demand system, with a modest selection of movies to choose from in the library. The cabins are spacious, however, and the bathrooms have bathtubs, a rare luxury at sea. In addition, some staterooms have French balconies, but only the Owner's Suites have full ones.

CABINS & RATES

CABINS	PER DIEM RATES	SQ. FT.	FRIDGE	HAIR DRYER	SITTING AREA	TV
Suites	$308–$766	275–575	yes	yes	yes	yes

PUBLIC AREAS   On small ships like this one, it takes little time to get to know the public spaces. There's a theater, a show lounge, and a forward lounge that serves as a coffee bar and card room during the day as well as an observation lounge with deck access. (It's ideally designed for whale-spotting moments.) A small gift shop has a surprising array of goods, from candy to bathing suits and sturdy little carry-ons made of sails that go for several hundred dollars. In true Windstar fashion, the bridge is always open—you're welcome to visit the captain whenever you like—another rare treat in these waters.

DINING OPTIONS   The **Amphora** dining room is primarily used for dinner, and it's a well-designed space. The **Veranda** cafe is a buffet at breakfast and lunch (one day we were excited to see a spread of Indian food, while the next there were treats that had been picked up in port the day before). After dark, this place becomes **Candles;** while its dinner menu can feel a little basic, the setting is gorgeous—especially when you're sailing out of port.

POOL, FITNESS, SPA & SPORTS FACILITIES   The small gym hosts several classes during the day, from stretching and yoga to Zumba, but its limited number of exercise machines go fast during peak hours. The spa and salon are also small, but generally accommodate whatever treatment you might want. The ship's small central pool and hot tub probably don't serve passengers well in the Caribbean or Mediterranean, but suffice in chilly Alaska. That said, another, less-central hot tub on a lower deck on the bow of the ship is easily the best spot for sailaways on this vessel—it becomes more discovered as the sail proceeds, so it's the perfect place to toast on embarkation night.

THE CRUISE LINES: THE SMALL SHIPS

Big ships show you Alaska from a vibrant, resortlike atmosphere; small ships let you see it from the waterline, with no distraction from anything un-Alaskan: no glitzy interiors, no big shows or loud music, no casinos, no crowds. The largest of these ships carry only 100 passengers, the smallest a mere 10. On these small ships you're immersed in the 49th state from the minute you wake up to the minute you fall asleep.

The vessels listed in this chapter allow you to visit more isolated parts of the coast. Thanks to their smaller size and shallow draft (the amount of hull below the waterline), they can go places larger ships can't, plus they have the flexibility to change their itineraries as opportunities arise—say, to go where whales have been sighted or to watch black bears frolic on the shore. (Keep in mind, though, that ships are prohibited from "stalking" wildlife for too long: They must keep their distance and break off after a relatively short while.)

Depending on the itinerary, small-ship ports of call might include popular stops such as Juneau, Sitka, or Ketchikan; lesser-visited areas such as Elfin Cove or Warm Springs Harbor; or a Tlingit Native village such as Kake. The one thing you can be confident of is that all itineraries will include **glacier viewing** and **whale-watching.** Most of the itineraries also have time built in for passengers to explore the wilder parts of Alaska and for ferrying passengers ashore for hikes in wilderness areas. In some cases, the ships also carry **sea kayaks** and **Zodiac** inflatable boats for passenger use—allowing a type of exploration not available on most of the big ships in Alaska.

Rather than glitzy entertainment, you'll likely get informal and informative **lectures** and sometimes **video presentations** on Alaskan wildlife, history, and Native culture. In most cases, some shore excursions are included in the cruise fare. Meals are served in open seatings, so you can sit where and with whom you like—and time spent huddled on the outside decks scanning for whales fosters great camaraderie among passengers. It must be noted, though, that the size of the ships precludes any kind of spacious dining rooms.

Generally, they're quite small—some would say cramped. And on most of the smaller ships, room service is not an option (unless you are sick, of course).

Cabins on these ships don't always have TVs or telephones, and they tend to be tiny and sometimes spartan. (See individual reviews below for exceptions.) Many lack e-mail access. Most small ships have no stabilizers, so the ride can get bumpy in rough seas—but because the vessels tend to spend most of their time in the somewhat protected waters of the Inside Passage, this is not usually a major concern. But it can be a problem in open seas.

Another drawback of small ships is that they generally are not wheelchair-friendly; small ships are not a good choice for travelers with mobility issues. Small ships also may not be the best choice for families with children, unless those kids are avid nature buffs and able to keep themselves entertained without a lot of outside stimuli.

Reading the Reviews

In this chapter, you'll also see the following terms used to describe the various small-ship experiences:

- **Soft adventure:** These ships don't provide onboard grandeur, organized activities, or entertainment, but instead give you a really close-up Alaskan experience. Soft-adventure ships often avoid large ports.
- **Active adventure:** These ships function less like cruise ships than like base camps. Passengers use them basically to sleep and eat, getting off the ship for hiking and kayaking excursions every day.
- **Port-to-port:** These ships are for people who want to visit the popular Alaskan ports (and some lesser-known ones), but also want the flexible schedules and maneuverability of a small ship and a more homey experience than you would find aboard a glitzy big ship.

Rates

Cruise rates in these reviews are brochure rates. Some discounts may apply, including early-booking and last-minute offers (see more in chapter 3), although small-ship lines do not traditionally discount their fares as much as bigger ship lines. As in chapter 5, all rates have been calculated by nights spent on ship, based on 7-night sailings, unless otherwise indicated. Note that, in general, small ships are more expensive—often significantly so—than the large ships operating in Alaska. It costs more to provide the more intimate experience of small ships, and that extra cost is passed on to passengers.

Tipping

Tipping on small ships is not exactly standardized, as it tends to be on the big ships. None of the small lines operating in Alaska automatically adds gratuities to passenger bills. Instead, they suggest amounts that would be appropriate to leave for crew, while leaving the decision of how much to tip—or whether to tip at all—to the customer. Gratuities then are pooled among all the staff on board, from the room cleaners to the deck hands.

A NOTE ON SHIP ratings

Because the small-ship experience is so completely different from the megaship experience, we've had to adjust our ratings. For instance, because all but a tiny fraction of these ships have just one dining room for all meals, we can't judge them by the same standard we use for ships with 5 or 10 different restaurants. So we've set the default **Dining Options** rating for these ships at 3, or "good," with points deducted if a restaurant is particularly uncomfortable and points added for any options above and beyond. Similarly, we've changed the "Pool, Fitness, Spa & Sports Facilities" rating to **Adventure & Fitness Options** to reflect the fact that on small ships the focus is what's outside, not inside. Options covered in this category include kayaks, trips by inflatable Zodiac, and frequent hiking trips.

When reading the reviews in this chapter, bear in mind, too, that small-ship lines often measure their ships' gross register tonnage, or GRT (a measure of internal space, not actual weight), differently than the large lines. Some use an international standard, others a U.S. standard, so to compare ship sizes it's best to just look at the number of passengers aboard. Also note that where GRT measures are done using the U.S. standard, passenger/space measurements are impossible or meaningless.

Dress Code

The word is *casual*. You're fine with polo shirts, jeans, khakis, shorts, a fleece pullover, and a Gore-Tex shell. Having a pair of rubber sandals or old sneakers is handy, since going ashore in rubber landing crafts might require you to step out into the surf. Hiking boots are also recommended.

ALASKAN DREAM CRUISES

1512 Sawmill Creek Rd., Sitka, AK 99835. www.alaskandreamcruises.com. © **855/747-8100.**

Pros

o **Off-the-beaten-path itineraries.** With a mantra of showing customers the "true Alaska," Alaskan Dream has built itineraries around such little-visited Southeast Alaskan outposts as the Native village of Kake, as well as such iconic attractions as Glacier Bay National Park.

o **Local Alaskan flavor.** Alaskan Dream is locally owned by a family in Sitka, Alaska.

Cons

o **Tough to reach.** Most of Alaskan Dream Cruises' itineraries begin or end in Sitka, which only gets a few flights a day.

THE LINE IN A NUTSHELL Run by a local Southeast Alaska family, Alaskan Dream promises a glimpse of the "true Alaska." Its growing fleet of recently refurbished small ships take vacationers to off-the-beaten-path Native villages and little-visited natural areas across Southeast Alaska in addition to such classic hotspots as Glacier Bay.

THE EXPERIENCE   Launched in 2011 by the Allen family of Sitka, Alaska, Alaskan Dream focuses on small-ship cruises in Southeast Alaska with a local twist. The line has taken great pains to staff its vessels with local Alaskans, who bring an insider's knowledge of the region. Its itineraries include stops at several little-visited, "locals only" destinations in the region such as the Native village of Kake. Other Alaskan touches on Alaskan Dream trips include local Alaska products prominently featured on board vessels, from fresh Alaskan seafood (and other local ingredients) on the menu to the Alaskan-made beer and spirits offered at the bar to the Alaskan-crafted soaps and shampoos in every cabin. As is typical with most of the small-ship lines in Alaska, Alaskan Dream includes all excursions in the base cost of its sailings. The cruising atmosphere on the line's ships is casual, as is typical of small ships in Alaska.

THE FLEET   While this five-ship line is fairly new, its ships aren't. Alaskan Dream Cruises launched in 2011 with vessels that had sailed before in Alaska, but had been out of commission for several years. It has since added more older vessels to its fleet, all of which received major overhauls before going into service for Alaskan Dream Cruises and are well maintained by the Allen family's shipyard.

PASSENGER PROFILE   Alaskan Dream Cruises passengers tend to be well-traveled, well-educated people (most hold a bachelor's degree or higher) in search of an authentic Alaskan experience. Often they're semi-retired or retired and come from all over the world. In addition to the United States, passengers from Australia, the United Kingdom, and Germany are fairly common. The line also is drawing a growing number of multigenerational families, which led to the development of family cruises in 2013.

DINING OPTIONS   Each of the line's ships has a single communal dining room where meals are served three times a day. As is often the case on vessels with fewer than 100 passengers, there is no fixed seating, allowing passengers to sit with different people at different times. In the morning, in addition to a full breakfast, an early morning Continental breakfast is put out for early risers, and you'll always find snacks available at other times, whether a batch of muffins whipped up by the pastry chef or afternoon cookies. All of the food aboard ship is sourced locally when possible, and in Alaska meals focus on locally inspired dishes, including fresh-caught salmon and other seafood. In addition, beer from the Alaskan Brewing Company and Alaskan Distillery spirits are prominent on all three vessels. Passengers with dietary restrictions and allergies will find that the line's head chefs and crew make a great effort to be accommodating. Don't be shy about asking!

ACTIVITIES   Whether you're cruising a kayak across a remote bay or taking a walk around a Native village, most of the activities take place off the ship—and all are included in the base price of the trip. Led by naturalist and cultural heritage guides who travel with passengers on the vessel, daily outings on a typical cruise in Alaska include a mix of outdoorsy pursuits and visits to some of Southeast Alaska's small fishing towns. There is often time

Alaskan Dream Cruises Fleet Itineraries

SHIP	ITINERARIES
Chichagof Dream and Admiralty Dream	7-night Glacier Bay and Island Adventure: Round-trip from Sitka with stops in Metlakatla, Misty Fjords, Kasaan, Wrangell, Petersburg, Tracy Arm, Hobart Bay, Juneau, and Glacier Bay National Park (May–Sept)
Alaskan Dream	8-night Inside Passage Sojourn: One-way between Ketchikan and Sitka with stops in Skagway, Petersburg, Wrangell, Kasaan, Misty Fjord, Tracy Arm, Hobart Bay, Juneau, and Glacier Bay National Park (May–Aug)
Baranof Dream and Alaskan Dream	10-night Southeast Explorer: One-way between Ketchikan and Sitka with stops in Kake, Petersburg, Tracy Arm, Hobart Bay, Juneau, and Glacier Bay National Park (June–Aug)
Misty Fjord	7-night Islands, Whales & Glaciers: One-way between Ketchikan and Juneau with stops in Baranof Island, Tenakee Inlet, Icy Strait, Taku Inlet, Tracy Arm Fjord, and Frederick Sound (June–Aug)
Baranof Dream	10-night Admiralty, Baranof, and Chichagof Explorer: Round-trip from Sitka with stops in Juneau, Skagway, Icy Strait, Tracy Arm, Hobart Bay, Petersburg, Kake, and Red Bluff Bay (May–Aug)
Chichagof Dream	7-night Alaskan Family Cruise: One-way between Sitka and Juneau with stops in Saginaw Bay, Petersburg and Frederick Sound, Tracy Arm Fjord, Juneau, and Glacier Bay National Park (June–July)
Admiralty Dream	12-night Alaska's Glacier Bay and Inside Passage Voyage: One-way from Sitka to Ketchikan with stops in Skagway, Gustavus, Glacier Bay, Juneau, Tracy Arm, Hobart Bay, Kake, Petersburg, Wrangell, Kasaan, and Misty Fjords (Aug)

for two excursions on some port calls, though one is typical. Examples of popular outings on Alaska trips include a king salmon and king crab dinner at a lodge near Juneau and visits to historically and culturally significant sights in the Alaskan towns of Sitka and Petersburg.

CHILDREN'S PROGRAM   While most Alaskan Dream sailings have no formal children's program, the line in 2013 added dedicated family cruises that include daily excursions aimed at kids, young adults, and families. Activities on these trips range from classes in traditional arts to trips to wildlife sanctuaries, with dedicated youth leaders. When not leading a family-friendly expedition off the ship, youth leaders coordinate onboard activities and crafts aimed at children and families.

ENTERTAINMENT   There are no shows in the traditional sense, but in the evenings, after dinner, the ships' lounges often are the site of onboard presentations and discussions led by scientific- and cultural-expedition leaders. Passengers also gather in the lounge before dinner for hors d'oeuvres, drinks, and a recap of the day from the ship's expedition leader. Books are available for passengers to borrow from a small onboard library.

SERVICE   Alaskan Dream prides itself on hiring local Alaskans to work on its ships. Naturalists and other English-speaking crew members facilitate all off-ship and onboard activities, as well as serve meals and perform housekeeping duties. *Note:* While gratuities are not mandatory, the line suggests that passengers leave $15 per person per day to be shared among the crew.

CRUISETOURS & ADD-ON PROGRAMS As of January 2017, Alaska Dream Cruises passengers can extend their stay in Alaska through a new partnership with **John Hall's Alaska,** choosing one of two John Hall's Alaska land itineraries: the 7-night "Denali Explorer" or the 8-night "Grand Slam Alaska." The cruise-and-land-tour combos are available between June and September, and prices for the land tours start at $5,270 per person double occupancy, including a hotel night and breakfast during the transition between land and sea.

Admiralty Dream • Baranof Dream

The Verdict

These are small, Alaskan-run ships that show you the "true Alaska," including colorful Native villages. They're not true sister ships, but they are very similar.

Specifications

Size (in U.S. reg. GRTs)	95/97	Crew	21/19
Passengers (Double Occ.)	58/49	Passenger/Crew Ratio	2.8/2.6 to 1
Space/Passenger Ratio	N/A*	Year Launched	1979/1980
Total Cabins	27/25	Last Major Refurbishment	2014/2015

* These ships' sizes were measured using a different scale than the others in this book, so comparison is not possible.

Frommer's Ratings (Scale of 1–5) ★★★½

Cabin Comfort & Amenities	3.5	Dining Options	3.5
Ship Cleanliness & Maintenance	4	Adventure & Fitness Options	3.5
Public Comfort/Space	3.5	Children's Facilities	N/A
Decor	3.5	Enjoyment Factor	4

THE SHIPS IN GENERAL Built in 1979 and 1980, these two similar vessels are among the oldest sailing in Alaska, and their accommodations and public areas are relatively simple by today's standards (some might even call them spartan). That said, both were significantly renovated before going into service for Alaskan Dream, and they're well maintained. Just don't expect a lot of bells and whistles in cabins (there are no TVs, for instance, and bathrooms are tiny) or elaborate gathering areas (the single lounge and dining room on each vessel are relatively basic). Still, small-ship cruising in Alaska isn't about the ship. It's about exploring the state's spectacular scenery and wildlife in a way that big ships can't. These vessels have a shallow draft that's perfect for navigating intimate coves and passages, a spacious bow deck for viewing fjords and glaciers, a covered outside deck, and a relaxed cruising speed for optimum viewing of wilderness and wildlife. While simple, the vessels' lounges and dining rooms offer an intimate venue for getting to know your fellow travelers.

CABINS With the exception of a few large "deluxe" cabins on each of the vessels, accommodations are relatively small and simple. The typical cabin has two twin beds or a double bed that takes up a good portion of the room, a closet, built-in storage drawers under beds, and in some cases a desk with chair. Bathrooms are tiny and, in the style of expedition ships of old, often combine the toilet and shower in the same small dual-purpose space (the largest cabins have separate toilet areas as well as a desk area). There are no wheelchair-accessible rooms. In keeping with the line's "true Alaska" focus, soaps and shampoos are locally made in the state. Rooms have no TVs, and none come with balconies (windows are the norm), but passengers will find high-powered binoculars for spotting wildlife. An intercom system in the cabins allows passengers to hear expedition leaders talking about the passing scenery.

CABINS & RATES

CABINS	PER DIEM RATES	SQ. FT.	FRIDGE	HAIR DRYER	SITTING AREA	TV
Admiralty Dream/Baranof Dream						
Outside	$271–$785*	93–135/ 105–210	yes	no	some	no

* Rates are per day based on 7-night cruises.

PUBLIC AREAS   The vessels both have a similar layout, with cabins spread out among three to four passenger decks including a few at the front of an open-air top deck. Activity on board both ships revolves around a single lounge at the front (home to a daily pre-dinner social hour with hors d'oeuvres and recap from the expedition leader), and both have a main dining room toward the back of the same level. Still, in Alaska at least, the place to be often is on the ships' bow viewing decks, just below the bridge, where passengers gather to watch for whales, seals, and sea otters and to gaze at the lush green forests, soaring, snow-covered mountains, and calving glaciers of Southeast Alaska. Also offering great views is the open-air sundeck on each ship.

POOL, FITNESS, SPA & SPORTS FACILITIES   The top decks of the vessels feature several exercise machines. There are no hot tubs, pools, or other sports facilities.

Alaskan Dream

The Verdict

An intimate, yacht-like vessel for vacationers who want a truly small-scale experience.

Specifications

Size (in U.S. reg. GRTs)	93	Crew	18
Passengers (Double Occ.)	40	Passenger/Crew Ratio	2.1 to 1
Space/Passenger Ratio	N/A*	Year Launched	1986
Total Cabins	20	Last Major Refurbishment	2014

* This ship's size was measured using a different scale than the others in this book, so comparison is not possible.

Frommer's Ratings (Scale of 1–5)   ★★★½

Cabin Comfort & Amenities	3.5	Dining Options	3.5
Ship Cleanliness & Maintenance	4	Adventure & Fitness Options	3.5
Public Comfort/Space	3.5	Children's Facilities	N/A
Decor	4	Enjoyment Factor	4

THE SHIP IN GENERAL   Smaller than Alaskan Dream Cruises' two other vessels, the 38-passenger *Alaskan Dream* looks more like a large yacht than a small cruise ship—a funny-looking one, to boot, as it seems unusually tall for its length, giving it a top-heavy appearance. Technically, the vessel is a catamaran, with two parallel hulls, which means it has unusually good stability for its size. Its small footprint also means the *Alaskan Dream* can get into narrow bays and other natural areas that other vessels can't visit. *Alaskan Dream* has three indoor passenger levels that contain its 20 cabins and a handful of public areas, and an open-air observation deck at its top.

CABINS   The *Alaskan Dream*'s 20 cabins are split into four categories that range notably in size. All but six of the cabins fall within Category A, which has the least square footage; expect twin beds that take up a large portion of the room, a closet, a sink in the main part of the cabin, and a separate bathroom with toilet and shower. Slightly longer due to their location on the bottommost deck are the three Category AA cabins, and two significantly larger Vista View Suites come with a small sitting area. Even bigger is the vessel's single Owner's Suite, exactly twice the size of standard cabins.

CABINS & RATES

CABINS	PER DIEM RATES	SQ. FT.	FRIDGE	HAIR DRYER	SITTING AREA	TV
Alaskan Dream						
Outside	$271–$780*	104–208	some	yes	some	no

* Rates are per day based on 7-night cruises.

PUBLIC AREAS   The biggest of the *Alaskan Dream*'s three interior passenger decks is the bottommost Main Deck, home to the forward-facing lounge and the nearby dining room (with three passenger cabins squeezed in between the two venues). When not in one of these two areas, passengers can be found up top on the vessel's large observation deck; there is also a small covered open deck one floor below at the rear of the Bridge Deck (the Bridge and four more passenger cabins also are on this level).

POOL, FITNESS, SPA & SPORTS FACILITIES   The ship has no pools, hot tubs, or sports facilities.

Misty Fjord

The Verdict

This small ship was designed specifically to cruise in Alaska, and the hull design mimics a regional fishing-boat style.

Specifications

Size (in GRTs)	101	Crew	5
Passengers (Double Occ.)	10	Passenger/Crew Ratio	2 to 1
Space/Passenger Ratio	N/A*	Year Launched	2006
Total Cabins	5	Last Major Refurbishment	2015

* This ship's size was measured using a different scale than the others in this book, so comparison is not possible.

Frommer's Ratings (Scale of 1–5)   ★★★½

Cabin Comfort & Amenities	3.5	Dining Options	3.5
Ship Cleanliness & Maintenance	4	Adventure & Fitness Options	3.5
Public Comfort/Space	3.5	Children's Facilities	N/A
Decor	4	Enjoyment Factor	4

THE SHIP IN GENERAL   The tiny 10-passenger *Misty Fjord* feels more like a private yacht than a cruise ship. Plenty of polished teak and portholes give it an über-maritime look. Four of the cabins are on the main deck and one, the largest, is on the lower deck.

CABINS   The *Misty Fjord* has just five cabins, and all have private bathrooms—something that's not a given on a ship of this size. Lower-category cabins have bunk beds, while the more expensive options come with queen-size beds. All have lots of wood finishes and are approximately 85 square feet.

CABINS & RATES

CABINS	PER DIEM RATES	SQ. FT.	FRIDGE	HAIR DRYER	SITTING AREA	TV
Misty Fjord						
Outside	$628*	85	no	yes	no	no

* Rates are per day based on 7-night cruises.

PUBLIC AREAS   In addition to an outer deck—on which to gather for whale-watching and other wildlife viewing—the ship has a big wheelhouse, a dining area, and a lounge.

POOL, FITNESS, SPA & SPORTS FACILITIES   There are no pools, hot tubs, or sports facilities.

Chichagof Dream

The Verdict

Designed with a hull that cuts through even the iciest Alaskan waters, this ship has very generously sized bow and aft viewing areas for a vessel of its proportions.

Specifications

Size (in GRTs)	97	Crew	27
Passengers (Double Occ.)	74	Passenger/Crew Ratio	2.74 to 1
Space/Passenger Ratio	N/A*	Year Launched	1984
Total Cabins	37	Last Major Refurbishment	2016

* This ship's size was measured using a different scale than the others in this book, so comparison is not possible.

Frommer's Ratings (Scale of 1–5)   ★★★½

Cabin Comfort & Amenities	3.5	Dining Options	3.5
Ship Cleanliness & Maintenance	4	Adventure & Fitness Options	3.5
Public Comfort/Space	3.5	Children's Facilities	N/A
Decor	4	Enjoyment Factor	4

THE SHIP IN GENERAL   The 74-passenger *Chichagof Dream* is by no means a large ship, but it's big compared with many of the other ships in the fleet. It was fully renovated when it became a part of the line, with new carpeting and furniture throughout.

CABINS   Cabins are located on the upper, lounge, and main decks. Cabins in the least-expensive category have twin beds, while the more expensive options come with queen-size beds.

CABINS & RATES

CABINS	PER DIEM RATES	SQ. FT.	FRIDGE	HAIR DRYER	SITTING AREA	TV
Chichagof Dream						
Outside	$570–$827*	105–155	no	yes	no	no

* Rates are per day based on 7-night cruises.

PUBLIC AREAS   The forward-facing, floor-to-ceiling windows in the lounge have some of the best views of the water and the coastline on the ship. Passengers gather here—and in the viewing area on deck—to watch for whales and sea otters and see glaciers calving before their eyes. The vessel also has a dining room.

POOL, FITNESS, SPA & SPORTS FACILITIES   There are no pools, hot tubs, or sports facilities.

AMERICAN CRUISE LINES

741 Boston Post Rd., Ste. 200, Guilford, CT 06437. www.americancruiselines.com. ✆ **800/ 814-6880.**

Pros

o **Spacious, upscale cabins.** At more than 300 square feet, cabins on American Cruise Lines vessels are the most spacious in small-ship cruising and feature large bathrooms and picture windows.

o **Balconies.** Unlike most small ships in Alaska, American Cruise Lines' Alaska-based *American Constellation* offers a large number of cabins with balconies—a real plus in such a scenic region.

o **Modern amenities.** Newer than most other small ships in Alaska, the *American Constellation* also boasts satellite TV, DVD players, and complimentary Wi-Fi in every cabin.

Cons

o **The cost.** Starting at more than $5,000 per person per week for the smallest cabins, cruises on the *American Constellation* are among the most expensive on small ships in the region. However, almost all shore excursions are guided and included in the price.

THE LINE IN A NUTSHELL   Still relatively unknown to many Americans, American Cruise Lines is a niche operator of upscale small-ship voyages on America's waterways from the Chesapeake Bay to Puget Sound and Alaska.

THE EXPERIENCE   Founded in 1999, American Cruise Lines offers a true slice of Americana: Sailing exclusively in the United States, its ships are U.S.–built and U.S.–flagged and staffed by an all-American crew. Its original vision of offering gracious hospitality and personalized service in an intimate, small-ship setting remains the line's mantra, and the line's vessels are relatively new, modern, and environmentally friendly, with lots of upscale amenities. In addition to Alaska, American Cruise Lines vessels sail to 28 other U.S. states on 35 different itineraries. Hallmarks of the line include elegant, locally sourced cuisine, nightly entertainment (something not always found on small ships), and daily lectures from historians, naturalists, and local experts.

THE FLEET   American Cruise Lines owns and operates 10 small U.S.–flagged cruise ships, only one of which—the 175-passenger *American Constellation*, launched in 2017—sails in Alaska, which it will for the first time in 2018. The vessels range in size from the 49-passenger *American Glory* to the 175-passenger *American Constellation,* and nearly all are less than a decade old, giving American Cruise Lines one of the youngest fleets in small-ship cruising. In addition to Alaska, the vessels operate in the U.S.'s Pacific Northwest, New England, the mid-Atlantic, Southeast, and Mississippi River complex. More ships, meanwhile, are on the way as the company builds eight new vessels that will enter service in the next few years.

PASSENGER PROFILE   The line tends to attract experienced travelers who are largely well-educated, professional, and over 50 years old. In the mix are some singles and a smattering of younger passengers who share a common interest in history and cruising (and have the money to afford American Cruise Lines' high rates). The line's passengers also like to socialize, and if you do, too, you'll find plenty of fun and interesting people who make for excellent company.

DINING OPTIONS   As is typical with small ships, American Cruise Lines vessels have a single main restaurant for breakfast, lunch, and dinner daily. Each evening, before dinner, passengers enjoy complimentary cocktails and hors d'oeuvres in a lounge as they mingle with other passengers to exchange tales of the adventures of the day. Then it's off to the dining room, where every meal is open seating—there are no table reservations. This gives passengers an opportunity to move from table to table making new friends. The system works perfectly. All meals are served by waiters. There are no buffets, although a table offering a variety of tasty selections such as fruit, veggies, and assorted muffins is there as you enter the dining room. For the most part, though, breakfast, lunch, and dinner are ordered off the menu. Food in the dining room—generally your choice of appetizer, two or three entrees, and dessert selections—is well prepared and presented by waiters eager to please. You are welcome to go to the main lounge anytime for soft drinks, coffee, tea, and snacks—you won't go hungry! You can also order room service breakfast to be served on your balcony. At both lunch and dinner, wine is always on the table, included at no extra charge, and beer is also available at no charge.

American Cruise Lines Fleet Itineraries

SHIP	ITINERARIES
American Constellation	7-night Southeast Alaska: Round-trip from Juneau with visits to Haines, Skagway, Petersburg, Icy Strait/Hoonah, and Glacier Bay (June–Aug)
American Constellation	11-night Alaska Inside Passage: One-way between Seattle and Juneau with visits to Anacortes and Friday Harbor, WA; Strait of Georgia, Ketchikan, Wrangell, Petersburg, Frederick Sound, and Tracy Arm (June and Aug)

ACTIVITIES   During days in port, most activities take place off the ship. American Cruise Lines includes shore excursions in its trips, and many passengers take advantage of them. Some are quite elaborate, such as the Stikine River Tour on jet boats offered during visits to Wrangell, Alaska—you'll talk about that one for a long time. In Glacier Bay, where American Cruise Lines has a highly sought after permit to cruise, an official park ranger and native interpreter come on board in the morning and stay all day offering information, folklore, and stories about Alaska in addition to pointing out sites. If you're staying on board during a port call you can relax on deck or in one of the library lounges socializing, reading, or getting together for a friendly game of chess or bridge. Up on the top deck you can relax or work out on one of several exercise machines. On the *American Constellation,* there's even a small putting green. At the cruise director's discretion, additional activities such as wine tastings or a hot chocolate bar are arranged for passengers.

CHILDREN'S PROGRAMS   Children aren't a huge market for American Cruise Lines, and its ships don't offer programs for Junior Cruisers. Still, if you notify the company in advance that you will be bringing children on board, they will prepare special activities of interest and fun.

ENTERTAINMENT   American Cruise Lines is unusual among small-ship companies in that it always offers nightly entertainment in the main lounge of its vessels. In Alaska, the offerings can range from lectures and slide presentations covering Alaska's wildlife, geography, and history to a talk from the captain followed by a tour of the bridge to see how the ship navigates. More-lightweight evenings might include activities such as bingo, complete with silly prizes. On some nights, singers and musicians perform classic songs that everyone knows, prompting passenger singalongs. In an American Cruise Lines tradition, at some point during the evening's program, a waiter makes his way through the audience with a tray full of ice cream sundaes.

SERVICE   American Cruise Lines prides itself on its gracious hospitality, offered from an all-American crew, and passengers can expect warm, personal service. While the line says tipping is left to the discretion of its customers, passengers on weeklong cruises leave about $125 per person, on average, to be shared among the crew.

CRUISETOURS & ADD-ON PROGRAMS American Cruise Lines doesn't offer land-and-sea cruisetours in Alaska, but all Alaska sailings that depart from Juneau do include a complimentary 1-night stay at the **Historic Westmark Baranof Hotel** in Juneau the day before the cruise departs, and you also get a city tour and a Mendenhall Glacier tour before your transfer to the ship. For the cruises that sail out of Seattle, you can purchase a hotel night through the cruise line.

American Constellation

The Verdict

Looking for a brand-new, upscale small vessel with all the latest amenities, including large cabins with furnished balconies? The *American Constellation* is your ship—assuming you can afford it.

Specifications

Size (in GRTs)	4,057	Crew	60
Passengers (Double Occ.)	175	Passenger/Crew Ratio	3 to 1
Space/Passenger Ratio	457	Year Launched	2016
Total Cabins	85	Last Major Refurbishment	2016

Frommer's Ratings (Scale of 1–5)   ★★★★★

Cabin Comfort & Amenities	5	Dining Options	4
Ship Cleanliness & Maintenance	5	Adventure & Fitness Options	3.5
Public Comfort/Space	5	Children's Facilities	N/A
Decor	4	Enjoyment Factor	5

THE SHIP IN GENERAL In a market where most small ships are 20 or even 30 years old, with tiny cabins and limited onboard features, the *American Constellation* stands out. Built in 2017, it has all the modern amenities, including relatively large cabins, most with furnished 60-square-foot balconies. It's the only small ship in Alaska that's fully stabilized, which makes a big difference when you hit storms in this part of the world. Activity on board revolves around the main lounge, the **Chesapeake Lounge,** but in Alaska the place to be is often the ship's **observation decks** and **outdoor lounges,** where passengers gather to watch for whales, seals, and sea otters and gaze at lush green forests, snow-covered mountains, and calving glaciers. The top deck has a putting green and a sundeck for stunning views.

CABINS At 226 (singles cabins) to 450 square feet (suites), the *American Constellation* cabins are quite spacious for small ships, and, notably, many come with balconies (a rarity on small ships in Alaska). Each room has twin beds, two double beds, or a king-size bed as well as a closet, a desk, dresser, and two chairs. Spacious bathrooms have a full-size shower and enough room to do everything you've got to do without feeling claustrophobic. Cabin balconies are wide enough to be furnished to allow you not only to enjoy sunsets and the spectacular vistas of Alaska's Inside Passage, but have breakfast here as well. The ship has one wheelchair-accessible cabin.

CABINS	PER DIEM RATES	SQ. FT.	FRIDGE	HAIR DRYER	SITTING AREA	TV
American Constellation						
Outside	$570–$789*	302–368	no**	yes	yes	yes
Suites	$877–$951	450	some	yes	yes	yes

* Rates are per day based on 7-night cruises.
** Fridges can be placed in cabins upon request.

PUBLIC AREAS   The *American Constellation* has a small but comfortable library lounge stocked with books and magazines. It also has a dining room and several lounges, including the large shipwide main lounge, the **Chesapeake Lounge,** with sweeping views and a bar—it's always stocked with coffee, tea, soft drinks, and snacks. The ship is equipped with elevators.

POOL, FITNESS, SPA & SPORTS FACILITIES   The top decks of the *American Constellation* have several exercise machines, a sundeck, and a small putting green. The vessel has no pools or hot tubs.

LINDBLAD EXPEDITIONS— NATIONAL GEOGRAPHIC

96 Morton St., 9th Floor, New York, NY 10014. www.expeditions.com. ℭ **800/397- 3348** or 212/765-7740.

Pros

- o **Great expedition feeling.** Lindblad's programs have innovative, flexible itineraries; outstanding lecturers/guides; and a friendly, accommodating staff.
- o **Built-in shore excursions.** Rather than relying on outside concessionaires for their shore excursions (which is the case with most other lines, big and small), Lindblad Expeditions runs its own. These excursions are an integral part of its cruises and included in the cost of the cruise fare.
- o **Highly knowledgeable experts on board.** The partnership with *National Geographic* has resulted in many top *National Geographic*–affiliated photographers, explorers, scientists, and researchers joining the line's voyages. Six naturalists are on board every expedition, for a 10-to-1 passenger-to-naturalist ratio.

Cons

- o **Cost.** Cruise fares tend to be a little higher than similar adventure-focused sailings on competing lines.

THE LINE IN A NUTSHELL   In 1979, Sven-Olof Lindblad, son of adventure-travel pioneer Lars-Eric Lindblad, followed in his father's footsteps by forming Lindblad Expeditions, which specializes in environmentally sensitive, soft-adventure/educational cruises to remote places in the world, with visits to a few large ports. In 2004, Lindblad Expeditions entered into an alliance with *National Geographic*. As pioneers of global exploration, the organizations work in tandem to produce innovative marine expedition programs and promote conservation and sustainable tourism around the world. The venture lifts Lindblad's educational offerings out of the commonplace.

THE EXPERIENCE Lindblad's expedition cruises are explorative and informal, designed to appeal to the intellectually curious traveler seeking a vacation that's educational as well as relaxing. Passengers' time is spent learning about life above and below the sea (from *National Geographic* experts and high-caliber expedition leaders and naturalists trained in botany, anthropology, and biology, and geology) and observing the world either from the ship or on-shore excursions, which are included in the cruise package. Lindblad Expeditions' crew and staff emphasize respect for the local ecosystem—the company's literature calls it "Responsible Travel"—and the company has won many awards for its commitment to conservation. Flexibility and spontaneity are keys to the Lindblad experience, as the route may be altered anytime to follow a pod of whales or other wildlife. Depending on the weather and sea conditions, there are usually two or three excursions every day.

THE FLEET In 2017, the line launched its first new build, the 100-passenger *National Geographic Quest*, which sailed in Alaska. In 2018, her identical sister—*National Geographic Venture*—will sail here, too. In addition, the 62-passenger *National Geographic Sea Lion* and *National Geographic Sea Bird* (built in 1981 and 1982, respectively), nearly identical in every respect, cruise in Alaska. Both are basic vessels built to get you to beautiful spots and have a minimum of public rooms and conveniences: one dining room, one bar/lounge, and lots of deck space for wildlife and glacier viewing. Picking a cabin on these ships is simple: There are no inside cabins or suites.

PASSENGER PROFILE Lindblad Expeditions tends to attract well-traveled and well-educated, professional, 55-plus couples who have "been there, done that" and are looking for something completely different in a cruise experience. The passenger mix may also include some singles and a smattering of younger couples. Although not necessarily frequent cruisers, many passengers are likely to have been on other Lindblad Expeditions programs or share a common interest in history and wildlife.

Interestingly, Lindblad itineraries have attracted so many passengers with families that in 2018 all four ships will have the line's **National Geographic Global Explorers program,** designed to make educational moments fun and memorable for kids. Challenges include everything from mapping tours to creating short films about the trip and earning a Zodiac "driver's license."

DINING OPTIONS Hearty buffet breakfasts and lunches and sit-down dinners include a good variety of both hot and cold dishes accompanied by plenty of fresh fruits and vegetables. Many of the ingredients are obtained from ports along the way, and meals often reflect regional tastes. (In Alaska, Lindblad chefs search out sustainably caught local fish as part of an overall commitment to promoting sustainable cuisine.) Although far from haute cuisine, dinners are well prepared and well presented, served at single open seatings, which lets passengers get to know one another by moving around to different tables. Lecturers and other staff members dine with passengers.

Lindblad Expeditions Fleet Itineraries

SHIP	ITINERARIES
Sea Bird/Sea Lion	14-night Inside Passage: North- and southbound between Seattle and Sitka, visiting Gulf Island, BC, Alert Bay and Johnstone Strait, BC, Inside Passage, BC, Haida Gwaii, Misty Fjords, Frederick Sound, Petersburg, Tracy Arm/Fords Terror Wilderness Area, Juneau, Glacier Bay, and Sitka (May and Sept)
Sea Lion, National Geographic Venture, and National Geographic Quest	7-night Inside Passage: North- and southbound between Juneau and Sitka, visiting Tracy Arm, Petersburg, Frederick Sound, Chatham Strait, Glacier Bay, Icy Strait, and the Inian Islands (May–Aug)
Sea Bird	5-night Inside Passage: North- and southbound between Juneau and Sitka, visiting Tracy Arm, Lynn Canal, Haines, and Chichagof Island (May–Aug)

ACTIVITIES   Shore excursions are included in the cruise fare. During the day, most activity takes place off the ship, aboard expedition landing-craft Zodiac boats or kayaks and/or on land excursions. On board, passengers entertain themselves with the usual small-ship activities: ogling the passing scenery and keeping an eye out for wildlife, reading, and socializing. Lindblad also has an open-bridge policy—rare in the cruise industry—that gives travelers the opportunity to spend time on the bridge to interact with the captain and staff.

CHILDREN'S PROGRAMS   Family cruising to Alaska is big business, and Lindblad has stepped up to the plate with special family activities led by specially trained staff on all sailings. Activities have a nature slant, such as exploring an Alaskan rain forest or meeting with a local ranger in Glacier Bay National Park to work toward earning a "Junior Ranger" badge. Don't expect such big-ship features as a video arcade or playroom, however.

ENTERTAINMENT   Lectures and slide presentations are scheduled throughout the cruise, and documentaries or movies may be screened in the evening in the main lounge. The line's exclusive fleetwide Expedition Photography program features a Lindblad–National Geographic Certified Photo Instructor on every departure to help passengers take their photography skills to the next level. Several voyages are also specially designed photo expeditions that go deeper into geography photography with *National Geographic* photographers on board. Since 2011, Lindblad has been bringing a native Huna/Tlinglit interpreter on board its vessels in Glacier Bay to offer a local perspective on Alaska's indigenous people. The interpreter shares local stories that date back before written history that have been passed down through oral traditions and arts. Also on Lindblad's Alaska sailings, the Alaska Undersea Program brings an undersea specialist on board who makes regular dives up to 80 feet below the vessel with high-intensity lighting and a video camera to capture Alaska's underwater wonders. The fascinating footage is viewed by passengers on a plasma screen in the lounge, often in real time. Books about Alaska are found in each ship's small library.

SERVICE   Dining-room staff and room stewards are affable and efficient and seem to enjoy their work. There's no room service unless you're ill and unable to make it to the dining room. Gratuities are at your own discretion. The line says that many guests choose to give $10 per person per day.

CRUISETOURS & ADD-ON PROGRAMS The line offers 7-day pre- or post-cruise land extensions to Denali National Park for $6,190 per person double occupancy. You stay at the park's North Face Lodge, where you can hike, canoe, and fish in the park.

Sea Bird • Sea Lion

The Verdict

Get up-close and personal in Alaska on these comfortable small ships, and expect excellent commentary from knowledgeable naturalists along the way.

Specifications

Size (in U.S. reg. GRTs)	100	Crew	29
Passengers (Double Occ.)	62	Passenger/Crew Ratio	2.1 to 1
Space/Passenger Ratio	N/A*	Year Launched	1982/1981
Total Cabins	31	Last Major Refurbishment	2015

* These ships' sizes were measured using a different scale than the others in this book, so comparison is not possible.

Frommer's Ratings (Scale of 1–5)   ★★★★

Cabin Comfort & Amenities	3.5	Dining Options	3.5
Ship Cleanliness & Maintenance	4	Adventure & Fitness Options	5
Public Comfort/Space	3.5	Children's Facilities	N/A
Decor	3.5	Enjoyment Factor	4.5

THE SHIPS IN GENERAL The shallow-draft *National Geographic Sea Bird* and *National Geographic Sea Lion* are identical twins, right down to their decor and furniture. Not flashy at all, each ship has just two public rooms that are utilitarian but comfortable. In 2015, both ships went through a refurbishment that updated both the public spaces and the staterooms.

CABINS The postage-stamp cabins are tight and functional rather than fancy. Each has twin or double beds, a closet (plus drawers under the bed for extra storage), and a sink and mirror in the main room. Behind a folding door lies a Lilliputian bathroom with a head-style shower (toilet opposite the shower nozzle, all in one compact unit). All cabins are located outside and have picture windows that open to fresh breezes. The vessels have no wheelchair-accessible cabins.

CABINS & RATES

CABINS	PER DIEM RATES	SQ. FT.	FRIDGE	HAIR DRYER	SITTING AREA	TV
Sea Bird/Sea Lion						
Outside	$855–$1,477*	90–120	no	yes	no	no

* Rates are based on 7-night cruises; includes shore excursions.

PUBLIC AREAS Public space is limited to the open sundeck and bow areas, the dining room, and an observation lounge that serves as the nerve center for activities. In the lounge, you'll find a bar; a library of atlases and books on Alaska's culture, geology, history, plants, and wildlife; a gift shop tucked into a closet; and audiovisual aids for the many presentations by naturalists.

POOL, FITNESS, SPA & SPORTS FACILITIES While there is no formal gym space, the ships have two outdoor exercise machines (bicycle and tread-mill) and a 30-minute stretching class every morning on the top deck led by a wellness specialist. In addition, Lindblad's style of soft-adventure travel means you'll be taking frequent walks or hikes in wilderness areas (usually accessed via inflatable expedition landing craft) and kayaking excursions. The ships offer a full line of wellness treatments through the **LEXspa.**

National Geographic Quest • National Geographic Venture

The Verdict

Get up close and personal in Alaska on these comfortable small ships, and expect excellent commentary from knowledgeable naturalists along the way.

Specifications

Size (in U.S. reg. GRTs)	2,906	Crew	35
Passengers (Double Occ.)	100	Passenger/Crew Ratio	2.8:1
Space/Passenger Ratio	29	Year Launched	2017/2018
Total Cabins	50	Last Major Refurbishment	2017/2018

Frommer's Ratings (Scale of 1–5)   ★★★★

Cabin Comfort & Amenities	3.5	Dining Options	3.5
Ship Cleanliness & Maintenance	4	Adventure & Fitness Options	5
Public Comfort/Space	3.5	Children's Facilities	N/A
Decor	3.5	Enjoyment Factor	4.5

THE SHIPS IN GENERAL These new expedition ships have some innova-tive tools that are firsts for the region, including a SplashCam and a hydrophone, which enable passengers to both look and listen to what's going on under the sea, beneath the waves. The ships also sail with Zodiacs, kayaks, snorkeling gear, and a variety of cameras. In addition to toys, specially trained crew mem-bers are on board: a photo instructor, a videographer, an undersea specialist, and a wellness specialist. Both ships have Internet access and an elevator.

CABINS Cabins are located on three decks: the Observation Deck, Upper Deck, and Main Deck. All cabins are located outside; some have picture win-dows that open to fresh breezes while others have portholes.

CABINS & RATES

CABINS	PER DIEM RATES	SQ. FT.	FRIDGE	HAIR DRYER	SITTING AREA	TV
Outside	$941–$1,514*	136–185	no	yes	no	no

* Rates are based on 7-night cruises; includes shore excursions.

PUBLIC AREAS   Public space is limited to the partially covered sundeck (which has an outdoor grill), the dining room, the viewing platform, and an observation lounge with a bar and audiovisual facilities.

POOL, FITNESS, SPA & SPORTS FACILITIES   Each ship has a small spa with a treatment room and a small gym. That said, shore excursions are active enough that many passengers will feel like they are getting their "cardio" on land.

UNCRUISE ADVENTURES

3826 18th Ave. W., Seattle, WA 98119. www.uncruise.com. ℂ **888/862-8881.**

Pros

o **Intimate experience.** With just 22 to 84 passengers, UnCruise Adventures' vessels are the antithesis of the crowded megaships that dominate Alaskan tourism.

o **Built-in shore excursions.** Most off-ship excursions and activities (such as kayaking and skiffing, snorkeling, hiking, and paddleboarding) are included in the cruise fare, as is an open bar.

o **Night anchorages.** A great boon to light sleepers is that the routes taken allow time for the vessels to often anchor overnight, making for quiet nights and gorgeous mornings in coves and inlets.

o **Time to explore.** With few port calls and flexible schedules, UnCruise doesn't have a strict schedule to follow. Instead, itineraries are determined on-the-fly based on weather and wildlife.

Cons

o **The price.** On UnCruise's smaller ships in particular, the least expensive accommodations can start at more than $700 per person per night. At a recommended $25 to $35 per guest per day, gratuities also can add mightily to the outlay. In short, you pay for all the privacy and pampering you get.

THE LINE IN A NUTSHELL   Looking for an off-the-beaten-path adventure in Alaska? That's what it's all about at UnCruise Adventures. The line also has a history of specializing in Alaska.

THE EXPERIENCE   UnCruise Adventures fills a distinct niche, offering vacationers the chance to explore remote areas by boutique yacht and adventure ships. None of the company's seven vessels holds more than 88 passengers, and it prides itself on offering intimate, leisurely getaways into spectacular wilderness areas where close-up encounters with wildlife are a focus along with scenery, history, and culture. In Alaska, the philosophy has translated into sailings through the most beautiful and wildlife-filled corners of Southeast Alaska's Inside Passage. Itineraries mostly forego calls in Southeast Alaskan towns, allowing for more time to explore the many remote (and little-visited) bays, fjords, and glaciers of the region. A key element of UnCruise trips is unraveling the tradition of rigid cruise-ship schedules. UnCruise itineraries are flexible, and getting off the ship and interacting with the landscape in a meaningful way is a focus. In short, it's not a typical cruise; hence the line's name. It's about getting out into the wilderness of Southeast Alaska. And it just so happens that the easiest way to get people into the region's remote back bays and hidden areas is via small ships.

All ships carry kayaks and paddleboards on board, and several have snorkeling equipment. Other activities include guided hikes and searching for wildlife in motorized inflatable boats, also carried on board. And for those who don't want to participate in the most active adventure activities, sailings also offer all the creature comforts for which cruising is known, including fine food and wines and craft beers.

THE FLEET Expanding rapidly in recent years, the line now operates seven vessels that carry from 22 to 88 passengers. The entire fleet sails in Alaska.

PASSENGER PROFILE For the most part, the company targets young-at-heart, outdoorsy types who typically range from 40 to 70 years old—the kind of people, in the words of one manager, who shop at the outdoor store REI. Multi-generational families are a solid market, and UnCruise's focus on wildlife and scenery on many itineraries can be appealing to teens and even young children, although the 13-and-under set isn't allowed on *Safari Quest* except on charters. UnCruise often attracts people who have not cruised before and who are not particularly interested in a big-ship experience. Ages skew a bit younger on the line's larger ships, which offer a lower price point. The line's two smallest ships draw a slightly older crowd, as one might expect given the higher price point.

DINING OPTIONS On *Safari Quest* and *Safari Explorer*, shipboard chefs delight guests with multicourse plated meals and tasty snacks (such as fresh halibut ceviche, outstanding fresh muffins every morning, and smoked salmon). Given the opportunity, chefs barter with nearby fishing boats for the catch of the day and raid local markets for the freshest fruits and vegetables. Passengers on these ships enjoy the well-stocked bar, which during one visit had two kinds of sherry and four brands of gin alone, all of them premium; it also offered a variety of Alaskan beers. On the other ships, the dining is simpler, though still scrumptious. Passengers assemble in a single dining room for breakfast and lunch, for a mix of buffets and plated dishes. Dinner is also in the same room, but it is a three-course plated meal. A typical dinner might include a main course of roasted Pacific cod paired with a side dish of sautéed chayote and fire-roasted tomatoes, or a filet mignon with shallot tart tatin and roasted asparagus paired with an arugula salad and a preserved lemon vinaigrette and Parmesan *fricco*. The ships' galleys also work wonders when it comes to desserts, baking items from scratch on a daily basis, including a citrus tart or a pavlova (meringue cake) with kiwi and strawberry sauce. All bread, desserts, and pastries served aboard are made fresh daily; unlimited spirits, wine, and beer are served up by the bartender.

ACTIVITIES Getting outdoors is what it's all about on UnCruise's Luxury and Active Adventures. When passengers aren't eating or drinking, an expedition leader is helping them into motorized rubber rafts or kayaks to explore glaciers and icebergs and to be on the alert for whales, bears, and sea lions. Other activities include landings by raft for guided hikes through remote forests, paddleboarding, snorkeling, unforgettably frosty swims, birding, and glacier walks.

By foregoing calls in Southeastern Alaska towns such as Skagway, UnCruise ships offer much more time to explore rarely visited and sparsely populated parts of the region. Skiffs take guests up close and personal to glaciers in the Endicott Arm with Dawes Glacier and Fords Terror Wilderness, rarely visited by larger cruise ships. Extended days in Glacier Bay National Park allow passengers the rare opportunity to explore the park off the boat by hiking and kayaking. Many itineraries explore remote areas along the Chichagof and Baranof islands.

Cruises do occasionally include a stop in a town such as Wrangell or the Native community of Klawock. Billed as nontraditional port calls, these aren't the typical cruise stop, where a bus awaits to take people around. Instead, in the case of Kake, passengers can walk down to a totem-carving shed to see a totem-carving demonstration. In 2018, Haines joins the roster of UnCruise's few port calls, with guided hikes, bikes available for rides into town, and the chance to float down the Chilkat River.

The UnCruise ships carry high-quality equipment to use during outings, including top-of-the-line sea kayaks, trekking poles, reusable water bottles, binoculars, rain pants and slickers, mud boots, paddleboards, and (some, but not enough for all guests) wetsuits for water activities.

CHILDREN'S PROGRAMS UnCruise ships have no formal children's programs, but the outdoorsy focus make them a natural for animal-loving kids, and activities such as kayaking are tailored for all ages. Children ages 8 to 13 receive a discount of $500 off the regular cruise fare through the Family Discoveries Savings program. *Note:* Children must be 8 years or older to sail, unless the ship is chartered, with the exception of the *Safari Quest,* where children 12 and under are not allowed except on full-ship charters.

ENTERTAINMENT In the evening, after dinner, passengers often gather in a lounge to share discoveries made during the day. Many of UnCruise's vessels feature a small but often lively bar that serves complimentary local Alaskan craft beers on tap as well as wine and mixed drinks. Flatscreen TVs in the lounge/bar area are used to show educational videos and movies—and sometimes even videos shot by passengers. Educational presentations on such topics as whales, glaciers, and Native cultures are provided by onboard naturalists on select nights. In the evening, passengers can relax under the Alaskan night sky in the top-deck hot tubs found on all of line's ships in Alaska. Guests sailing on the *Safari Endeavour, Safari Explorer*, and *S.S. Legacy* may choose to schedule a massage with the onboard wellness director/licensed masseuse. And on most ships, passengers can view the world below from bow-mounted underwater cameras that stream video into all TVs on board. DVDs are also available for passengers to watch in their cabins.

SERVICE All of the line's ships offer top-notch service, with the most attentive on the *Safari Endeavour, Safari Quest, Safari Explorer,* and *S.S.*

UnCruise Adventures Fleet Itineraries*

SHIP	ITINERARIES
Safari Explorer, Wilderness Discoverer, Wilderness Explorer, Safari Endeavour, S.S. Legacy	14-night one-way Alaska's Inside Passage & San Juan Cruise: Seattle to Juneau (or reverse), with visits to Seattle, WA, Olympic National Park, San Juan Islands, Salish Sea, Alaska's and Canada's Inside Passages, Ketchikan, AK, Misty Fjords National Monument, Behm Canal, Ernest Sound, Petersburg, Frederick Sound, Chatham Strait, Chichagof Island, Glacier Bay National Park, Icy Strait, Haines, and Juneau (April–May, Aug–Sept)
Safari Endeavour, S.S. Legacy	14 night-Alaska Glacier Cruise Ultimate Expedition: Round-trip from Juneau, with visits to Haines, Sitka, Kake, Glacier Bay National Park, Tracy Arm, Stephen's Passage, Lynn Canal and Sergius Narrows, Icy Strait, Ideal Cove, Thomas Bay, Baranof & Chichagof islands, Peril and Neva straits, Frederick Sound, and Krestof and Nakwasina sounds (May–Aug)
Wilderness Discoverer, Wilderness Explorer	14-night Fjords of Alaska Ultimate Expedition: One-way Sitka to Ketchikan (or reverse), with visits to Juneau, Wrangell, Ketchikan, Krestof and Nakwasina sounds, Sergius Narrows, Neva, Peril and Icy straits, Chichagof Island, Glacier Bay National Park, Endicott Arm, Fords Terror, Stephen's Passage, Thomas Bay, Wrangell Narrows, Behm Canal, and Misty Fjords National Monument (April–Sept)
Safari Endeavour, S.S. Legacy	7-night Alaska's Glaciers & Whales: One-way Juneau to Sitka, with visits to Tracy Arm, Stephen's Passage, Thomas Bay, Baird Glacier, LeConte Glacier, Ideal Cove, Kake, Frederick Sound, Baranof Island, Peril Strait, Sergius Narrows, and Neva Strait (May–Aug)
Safari Endeavour, S.S. Legacy	7-night Whales, Wildlife & Glaciers: One-way Sitka to Juneau, with visits to Krestof Sound, Nakwasina Sound, Icy Strait, Glacier Bay National Park, Chichagof Island, Lynn Canal, and Haines (May–Aug)
Wilderness Adventurer, Wilderness Discoverer, Wilderness Explorer	7-night Alaska Fjords & Glaciers: One-way Juneau to Ketchikan (or reverse), with visits to Endicott Arm, Fords Terror, Stephen's Passage, Thomas Bay, Wrangell Narrows, Wrangell, Behm Canal, and Misty Fjords National Monument (May-Sept)
Wilderness Discoverer, Wilderness Explorer	7-night Northern Passages & Glacier Bay: One-way Juneau to Sitka (or reverse), with visits to Glacier Bay National Park, Icy Strait, Chichagof Island, Peril Strait, Sergius Narrows, Neva Strait, and Krestof and Nakwasina sounds (April–Aug)
Safari Explorer, Wilderness Adventurer, Safari Endeavour, S.S. Legacy	7-night Glacier Bay Small Ship Cruise: Round-trip Juneau, with visits to Glacier Bay National Park, Chatham Strait, Kuiu Island, Frederick Sound, Endicott Arm, and Dawes Glacier (April–Sept)
Wilderness Adventurer	7-night Glacier Bay National Park Adventure Cruise: Round-trip Juneau, with visits to Icy Strait, Cross Sound, Glacier Bay National Park, Lynn Canal, and Haines (April–Sept)
Safari Quest	8-night Alaska Yacht: Bears, Bergs & Bushwhacking: Round-trip Petersburg, with visits to Kake, Keku Islands, Tebenkof Bay Wilderness Area, South Baranof Wilderness Area, Chatham Strait, Frederick Sound, Admiralty Island National Monument, and Stikine-LeConte Wilderness Area (May–Aug)

* In addition to the itineraries above, many of the ships offer repositioning cruises between Seattle and Juneau. Also, UnCruise itineraries are designed to be flexible, and it's not uncommon for the ship to make a detour from one cove or bay to another as the ship's captain seeks out the best wildlife-viewing opportunities.

Legacy, where the staff-to-passenger ratio is the lowest. Naturalists and English-speaking crew members facilitate all off-ship and onboard activities, as well as serve meals and perform housekeeping duties. ***Note:*** The company suggests each passenger leave an end-of-voyage tip for the crew ($25–$35 per day), which works out to around $200 to $300 per person.

CRUISETOURS & ADD-ON PROGRAMS The line offers land-tour add-on packages into Denali National Park and an Alaskan wilderness lodge. The line also offers pre- and post-cruise stopover packages in Ketchikan, Sitka, and Juneau.

Safari Explorer • Safari Quest

The Verdict

Excellent adventure cruising at a relaxed, flexible pace; aah, a decidedly different Alaskan experience.

Specifications

Size (in GRTs)	695/345	Crew	15/10
Passengers (Double Occ.)	36/22	Passenger/Crew Ratio	2.5 to 1/2 to 1
Space/Passenger Ratio	19.3/15.7	Year Launched	1998/1992
Total Cabins/Veranda Cabins	18/2; 11/4	Last Major Refurbishment	2008/2006

Frommer's Ratings (Scale of 1–5) ★★★★½

Cabin Comfort & Amenities	4.5	Dining Options	4
Ship Cleanliness & Maintenance	4	Adventure & Fitness Options	5
Public Comfort/Space	4	Children's Facilities	N/A
Decor	4	Enjoyment Factor	5

THE SHIPS IN GENERAL More private boat than cruise ship, these two vessels are an oddity in the cruise world, and as far from the Alaska norm as it's possible to get. The bigger of the two, the *Safari Explorer,* is just 145 feet long. Inside, virtually no area is out of bounds, including the bridge; the captain will welcome your visit, provided he's not involved in some critical nautical maneuver at the time. It all leads to the feeling that you're vacationing on a friend's private floating home. These two vessels promise an intimate, virtually all-inclusive cruise to more out-of-the-way parts of the Inside Passage—and succeed admirably. The prices for these cruises are not inexpensive, but the items included and the degree of pampering make it a worthwhile investment for those seeking an "uncruise." With just 22 to 36 guests, the vessels guarantee flexibility, intimacy, and privacy. Once passenger interests become apparent, the expedition leader shapes the voyage around them. Black-bear aficionados can chug off in a motorized skiff for a better look, active adventurers can explore the shoreline in one of the yacht's kayaks, and slacker travelers can relax aboard the ship. A crew-to-passenger ratio of about one to two ensures that a cold drink, a good meal, or a sharp eagle-spotting eye is always nearby on the line's comfortable vessels.

CABINS   Sleeping quarters aren't large, but they are comfortable and clean, with beds outfitted with memory-foam Tempur-Pedic mattresses, adequate light, and art (of varying quality, if hardly museum-standard) on the walls. Bathrooms are fine, even in the standard cabins; cabins on the *Safari Quest* have showers only. On the *Safari Explorer,* six premium cabins have a combination Jacuzzi tub/shower. The top-category cabins have sliding glass doors and a step-out balcony, a small sitting area, and even a separate living room. Down below, deluxe rooms are tidy, filled with a surprising amount of natural light, and fairly spacious. All staterooms have iPod docking stations, binoculars, hair dryers, automatic nightlights and heated tile floors in the bathrooms, robes, slippers, and flatscreen TV/DVDs. Both the *Safari Explorer* and *Safari Quest* have cabins designed specifically for single occupancy and are priced accordingly. Those looking for posh accommodations and over-the-top amenities should look elsewhere. The ships have no special facilities for travelers with disabilities.

CABINS & RATES

CABINS	PER DIEM RATES	SQ. FT.	FRIDGE	HAIR DRYER	SITTING AREA	TV
Safari Quest						
Outside	$832–$1,121*	125–168	no	yes	some	yes
Safari Explorer						
Outside	$1,149–$1,692**/ $686–$1,019***	133–275	some	yes	some	yes

* Rates are per day based on 8-night cruises.

** Rates are per day based on 7-night cruises.

*** Rates are per day based on 14-night cruises.

PUBLIC AREAS   Sitting rooms are intimate and very comfy, almost as if they've been transported intact from a spacious suburban home. Four or five prime vantage points for spotting wildlife (one is a hot tub!) ensure as little or as much privacy as you desire. As an example, the back area of *Safari Quest* has a great sitting nook to get away from the "masses," and the aft outside area is great for enjoying early morning coffee. In an upscale touch, meals are served fully plated for breakfast, lunch, and dinner (a breakfast buffet is also put out for early risers). There's a sense of communal dining, with one seating in a casual room. Ships have 24-hour espresso/coffee/tea facilities, a fully stocked open bar, and a small book/DVD library.

POOL, FITNESS, SPA & SPORTS FACILITIES   Both vessels have stairsteppers and elliptical machines; sea kayaks and stand-up paddleboards for passenger use (15 on *Safari Explorer,* 8 on *Safari Quest*), plus yoga mats. Hot tubs are located on the top deck; the *Safari Explorer* also has a sauna. The best equipped is the *Explorer,* which also has a small dedicated fitness area. The wellness director/licensed masseuse on the *Safari Explorer* leads yoga classes in the early mornings and provides each passenger with a complimentary massage.

Safari Endeavour

The Verdict

The same pampering as UnCruise's other Luxury Adventures vessels, but in a somewhat bigger ship with more amenities.

Specifications

Size (in GRTs)	1,425	Crew	35-37
Passengers (Double Occ.)	84	Passenger/Crew Ratio	2.5 to 1
Space/Passenger Ratio	16.6	Year Launched	1983
Total Cabins	42	Last Major Refurbishment	2012

Frommer's Ratings (Scale of 1–5)   ★★★★½

Cabin Comfort & Amenities	4	Dining Options	5
Ship Cleanliness & Maintenance	4.5	Adventure & Fitness Options	4.5
Public Comfort/Space	4.5	Children's Facilities	N/A
Decor	4	Enjoyment Factor	4.5

THE SHIP IN GENERAL *Safari Endeavour* is the largest of UnCruise's three Luxury Adventures vessels and offers more onboard amenities than the smaller *Safari Quest* and *Safari Explorer,* including two hot tubs overlooking the back of the vessel that are hot spots, literally, for watching wildlife and passing scenery. Significantly renovated in 2012, *Endeavor* has room for more "toys" than the smaller UnCruise vessels, including a small armada of inflatable motorized boats and sea kayaks used for off-ship adventure touring, as well as two massage suites (where every passenger gets a complimentary massage once per voyage). "Casual elegance" is the phrase used to describe the onboard ambience. In addition to a stylish forward-facing lounge where passengers congregate for pre-dinner happy hours and post-dinner lectures, the ship has a small self-serve **Wine Bar,** a sauna, and a small library. Overall, this is one of the more comfortable small ships in the Alaskan market. In part, that's because UnCruise doesn't pack in the passengers. The *Safari Endeavour*'s last owner, the now-defunct Cruise West, carried up to 102 passengers on the vessel, but UnCruise had it reconfigured for just 84 people, resulting in a lot more room per person.

CABINS The *Safari Endeavour* offers five categories of well-appointed cabins that vary significantly in size (and pricing). All offer views of the ocean through outward-facing windows, and the four biggest cabins, labeled Commodore Suites, also have step-out balconies (as well as Jacuzzi tubs). All cabins have private bathrooms. Depending on the room, beds may be configured as twin, double, or queen, and in many cases are convertible. All rooms include an iPod docking station, flatscreen TV with DVD player, desk with chair, and hair dryers. The ship has no wheelchair-accessible rooms.

CABINS & RATES

CABINS	PER DIEM RATES	SQ. FT.	FRIDGE	HAIR DRYER	SITTING AREA	TV
Safari Endeavour						
Outside	$671–$1,549*/ $466–$1,376**	100–240	no	yes	some	yes

* Rates are per day based on 7-night cruises.
** Rates are per day based on 14-night cruises.

PUBLIC AREAS   For a small ship, the *Safari Endeavour* has lots of outdoor public space, including an ample outdoor bow viewing area, where passengers often congregate during wildlife sightings, and a partially covered outdoor **Sun Lounge** deck atop the vessel. In short, you won't find yourself elbowing fellow passengers for a deck-top spot for wildlife watching. Inside, the ship has a spacious forward-looking lounge with a bar (hopping at happy hour), the hub for after-dinner presentations. One deck below, the **Dining Room** is where all meals are served. The same deck is also home to a small library that's an intimate place to tuck yourself away with a good book. A self-serve **Wine Bar** built into the dining room is quite elegant. You can do a tasting while standing at the Wine Bar or pour a glass and head up to the lounge.

POOL, FITNESS, SPA & SPORTS FACILITIES   The wellness program on board consists of a smattering of fitness equipment on the top deck of the vessel (open to the air), two hot tubs, and a sauna, which is a lot more than you'll find on most small ships in Alaska. In one of the vessel's luxury touches, there are two small massage rooms where a certified massage therapist provides a complimentary massage for every passenger during cruises (the therapist also does impromptu sessions in a massage chair set up in the lounge). Each morning, weather permitting, free yoga classes also are held on deck. Of course, the highlight of a trip on this vessel is the adventure available with its wide array of equipment. A custom-made kayak launch platform is attached at the stern of the vessel, and four kayaks at a time can quickly be launched. This is also a stable platform for departing on tours on motorized skiffs carried on the ship, and on single-person paddleboards. You'll always find crew on hand to help you in and out of the equipment and make you feel comfortable. The platform also is a jumping-off point for passengers who want to take the "polar bear" plunge into Alaska's icy water during the cruise (there are always a few).

Wilderness Discoverer • Wilderness Adventurer • Wilderness Explorer

The Verdict

Looking for a way to get off the beaten path in Alaska's Inside Passage? These three small ships will bring you right into the wilderness, where bears and eagles outnumber humans.

Specifications

Size (in U.S. reg. tons)	99/89/94	Crew	26/25/26
Passengers (Double Occ.)	76/60/74	Passenger/Crew Ratio	2.9/2.4/2.8 to 1
Space/Passenger Ratio	N/A*	Year Launched	1992/1984/1976
Total Cabins	38/30/37	Last Major Refurbishment	2011/2011/2012

These ships' sizes were measured using a different scale than the others in this book, so comparison is not possible.

Frommer's Ratings (Scale of 1–5)   ★★★★

Cabin Comfort & Amenities	3	Dining Options	4
Ship Cleanliness & Maintenance	4	Adventure & Fitness Options	5
Public Comfort/Space	4	Children's Facilities	N/A
Decor	3.5	Enjoyment Factor	4.5

THE SHIPS IN GENERAL Built as expedition ships, the similar-size *Wilderness Discoverer, Wilderness Adventurer,* and *Wilderness Explorer* (the *Adventurer* is slightly shorter) are capable of nimble exploration through nature's most dramatic hideaways. The shallow draft and hull design allow easy access to Southeast Alaska's wildlife-rich shores and glacially fed inlets, and they serve as ideal launching pads for an array of daily adventure excursions. Each of the vessels carries several dozen kayaks and paddleboards that passengers can use to explore the glacier-carved coves and fjords where the ships often anchor. Several motorized rubber rafts, deployable by a large mechanical arm built at the rear of the ships, are used daily to take small groups of passengers on waterborne tours to view wildlife, waterfalls, glaciers, and other natural wonders. The boats also are used to land passengers on shore for such activities as guided hikes and tidal-zone walks. Completely gutted and rebuilt in either 2011 or 2012, the interior spaces of the ships offer contemporary colors and simple furnishings.

CABINS As is typical on small expedition ships, the cabins on these vessels are relatively spartan, though not uncomfortable. All face outward and have windows that slide open to allow in a breeze. Four large cabins added to the top deck of the *Discoverer* (labeled the Explorer category) offer a premium location for wildlife viewing and privacy as well as significantly more space—unlike standard cabins, there's room for relatively normal-size bathrooms with full-size showers. Three out of four of the Explorer cabins also have a daybed that can be made up for sleeping, turning what is normally a cabin for two into a triple. All cabins have a large closet as well as multiple wall hooks for storing adventure gear, soft overhead lighting, bedside reading lamps, a compact corner sink located on the outside of the bathroom, and functional if not luxurious beds and bedding. Hair dryers, iPod docks, and flatscreen TVs with built-in DVD players round out the amenities (a small DVD library is available for passenger use at no charge). *Note:* The ships don't get a television satellite signal, so TVs offer no cable or broadcast stations, just a handful of internal ship stations. With the exception of the Explorer category, cabins on the *Wilderness Adventurer* and *Wilderness Discoverer* have compact, expedition-ship-style bathroom facilities that combine the shower and toilet in the same small compartment (a shower curtain pulls across the toilet to keep it dry while you shower). Neither ship has wheelchair-accessible rooms.

CABINS & RATES

CABINS	PER DIEM RATES	SQ. FT.	FRIDGE	HAIR DRYER	SITTING AREA	TV
Wilderness Discoverer						
Outside	$418–$905*/ $313–$866**	81–180	no	yes	some	yes
Wilderness Adventurer						
Outside	$428–$828*	60–101	no	yes	no	yes
Wilderness Explorer						
Outside	$368–$824*/ $266–$813**	90–125	no	yes	some	yes

* Rates are per day based on 7-night cruises.

** Rates are per day based on 14-night cruises.

PUBLIC AREAS   All three vessels offer plenty of open deck space from which to watch for wildlife, including an open sundeck with tables and chairs and a bow observation area. In the ships' interiors, public space is limited to a main salon and adjacent dining area that fills part of a single deck (the two areas are adjacent on the *Wilderness Adventurer* and *Wilderness Discover* and on separate floors on the *Wilderness Explorer*). The lounges serve as the ships' hubs and offer seating and a bar serving Alaskan craft beers, wine, and mixed drinks (the bars, notably, were handmade from Alaskan yellow cedar during the ships' renovation); large flatscreen TVs; small libraries of DVDs and books on Alaskan wildlife, plants, history, and culture; and a collection of games.

POOL, FITNESS, SPA & SPORTS FACILITIES   Each ship has a hot tub (two hot tubs on *Wilderness Discoverer*) on an outside deck and several elliptical cross-trainers and exercise bikes for passenger use (also located on an outdoor deck in a covered area).

S.S. Legacy

The Verdict

New to Alaska, an *S.S. Legacy* cruise offers a unique way of seeing the wilderness: The vessel itself is a striking replica of an 1898 coastal gold-rush steamer, with Victorian-style decor.

Specifications

Size (in GRTs)	96	Crew	34–35
Passengers (Double Occ.)	88	Passenger/Crew Ratio	2.5 to 1
Space/Passenger Ratio	N/A*	Year Launched	1983
Total Cabins	44	Last Major Refurbishment	2018

* This ship's size was measured using a different scale than the others in this book, so comparison is not possible.

Frommer's Ratings (Scale of 1–5)   N/A

Not available at press time.

THE SHIP IN GENERAL   *S.S. Legacy* is the fastest ship in the UnCruise fleet, capable of cruising along at 15 knots. It's a truly one-of-a-kind experience in every way. When the ship sails into Alaska's ports, the elegant *S.S. Legacy* announces her arrival with an antique whistle—a relic from UnCruise CEO Dan Blanchard's childhood tugboat. Kayaks, paddleboards, and skiffs are on board to facilitate exploration on land. But just because the look and feel of the ship is vintage doesn't mean there aren't plenty of modern-day creature comforts: Look for fitness equipment, two massage rooms, a large A/V screen in the lounge for movies, and DVDs in the library. The ship is home to the **Pesky Barnacle Saloon,** a bar stocked with premium spirits, wines, and microbrews, as well as a whiskey parlor and wine bar area.

CABINS   The *S.S. Legacy* has six cabin categories. While they vary significantly in size and pricing, all have windows and a private bathroom with a shower. Each cabin also has an iPod docking station, a flatscreen TV with DVD player, a hair dryer, bathrobes, binoculars, reusable water bottles, and a safety deposit box. Depending on the room, beds may be configured as twin, double, or queen; in many cases they're convertible. Depending on the category, singles, doubles, triples, or quadruples can be accommodated.

CABINS & RATES

CABINS	PER DIEM RATES	SQ. FT.	FRIDGE	HAIR DRYER	SITTING AREA	TV
S.S. Legacy						
Outside	$499–$1,536*/ $836–$2,942**	81–180	no	yes	some	yes

* Rates are per day based on 7-night cruises.

** Rates are per day based on 14-night cruises.

PUBLIC AREAS   The ship has ample outdoor viewing areas, including a large one on the bow that's ideal for wildlife sightings, and a partially covered **Sun Lounge** deck. Inside, the ship has a spacious forward-looking lounge, where passengers gather for after-dinner presentations. All meals are served in the main dining room, which becomes a social place to discuss the day's events. The same deck is also home to a wine bar and the **Pesky Barnacle Saloon.**

POOL, FITNESS, SPA & SPORTS FACILITIES   The top sundeck is home to two hot tubs and fitness equipment, and another two hot tubs outside the saloon. The ship also has a dedicated massage room.

ALASKA MARINE HIGHWAY SYSTEM

7559 N. Tongass Hwy., Ketchikan, AK 99901. www.ferryalaska.com. © **800/642-0066** or 907/465-3941.

In Alaska, which has fewer paved roads than virtually any other state, getting around can be a problem. There are local airlines, of course, and small private planes—lots and lots of small private planes, some with wheels, some with skis, some with floats for landing on water. (In fact, there are more private planes per capita in Alaska than in any other state in the union.) But given the weather conditions in many northland areas for large parts of the year, airplanes are not always the most reliable way of getting from Point A to Point B.

That's why the Alaska Marine Highway System (aka the AMHS, or the Alaska Ferry) is so important. Sometimes in inclement weather even the state capital, Juneau, can't be reached by air (no roads of any consequence link it with the rest of the state), so it relies heavily on the ferryboats of the AMHS to bring in visitors, supplies, and even, now and then, the legislators who run the state.

Although the ferry system was created more than 50 years ago with the aim of providing Alaska's far-flung, often inaccessible smaller communities with essential transportation links to the rest of the state and the Lower 48, the boats have developed a following in the tourism business as well. Each year, thousands of visitors eschew luxury cruise ships in favor of basic services of the 10 vessels of the AMHS. It's of particular value to independent travelers, enabling visitors to come and go as they please among Alaska's outposts and small seaside towns, spending the night or several days to explore the trails and waterways nearby. All the AMHS ferries carry **both passengers and vehicles.**

In 2005, the Alaska Marine Highway System was designated an "All American Road" by the U.S. Department of Transportation, and it remains the only marine route with such recognition. To qualify, a road must be nationally significant and contain features that do not exist elsewhere—it must be "a destination unto itself." The marine highway's southernmost port is Bellingham, Washington. That leg of the route system, from Bellingham to Ketchikan, Alaska, quickly sells out for the summer its seats, cabins, and space for vehicles, so travelers should book early. Travelers without vehicles may fly to Ketchikan or other Alaskan towns to begin their ferry journey. The ferry network stretches 3,500 miles throughout Southeast and Southcentral Alaska and out to the Aleutian Island chain to the west of Anchorage.

Note: Because booking with the ferries can be a complex proposition, most travelers new to the ferries book their rides and related shore lodgings and excursions not directly through the ferry system but through concessionaire **Viking Travel** in Petersburg (www.alaskaferry.com; ✆ **800-327-2571**).

Pros

o **Unique way to travel.** The ferry system allows a casual and relaxing mode of transportation, with an opportunity to meet fellow travelers.

o **Lots of flexibility.** Passengers may customize their vacation package by combining various itineraries in the ferry system.

Cons

o **No doctor on board.** None of the vessels carry a doctor, so if you have health concerns, this may not be a good way to travel.

o **Space books up quickly.** The only way you will be able to find cabin and vehicle space on most of the ferries is by booking early. Don't call in May and expect to get what you want in June.

o **Spartan cabins.** Sleeping accommodations, when available, are basic—no fridge, no telephone, no TV. But cabins are clean and the mattresses comfortable, and many have a small private bathroom and shower so you need not share public facilities with other passengers.

THE LINE IN A NUTSHELL   The ferries operate in three distinct areas. Year-round service is offered in the Southeast, or Inside Passage, from Bellingham to Skagway/Haines; in Southcentral, which includes Prince William Sound, the Kenai Peninsula, and Kodiak Island; and, in the summer months, the Southwest region, which includes the Aleutian chain. The Aleutian's service is not offered during the winter because of the region's extreme weather. The seas become too rough, the fog too thick, and the cold too intense in this region for the ferries to operate safely or profitably in the winter. One of the newest ports added to the system is Gustavus, the town recognized as the gateway to Glacier Bay National Park & Preserve. Another popular summer route connects the southernmost community of Bellingham, through the Inside Passage and across the Gulf of Alaska, to Whittier, located only 60 miles south of Anchorage. See the websites **www.ferryalaska.com** and **www.alaskaferry.com** for more details on the many routes that the AMHS operates.

THE EXPERIENCE   Ferry-riding vacations are different from cruise vacations. Don't even think about the ferries if you're looking for lots of creature comforts, like fancy accommodations, gourmet food, spa treatments, or entertainment. You won't find any of the above on the sturdy vessels of the AMHS, with the occasional exception being a movie in one of the lounges. In fact, not all ferry passengers get sleeping berths—five of the 10 ferries in the fleet are considered day boats and have no bedroom accommodations at all. Even when cabins are available, some passengers roll out their sleeping bags on the top deck floor or on lounge chairs and bed down in a solarium with space heaters. Others pitch a tent in the open, using duct tape to secure their "accommodations" to the windy deck. Public showers are available.

It's in the lounges or on deck that riders may encounter the only entertainment on board, all created by passengers on a strictly impromptu basis. It might be a backpacker strumming a guitar and singing folk songs, or a father keeping his children occupied by performing magic tricks. Occasionally, spirited discussion groups will form in which all are welcome to participate. The subject might be the environment (always a hot topic in Alaska, especially now with talk of opening up the Alaska Wildlife Preserve for oil exploration), politics (Alaskan or federal), the effect of tourism on wildlife (as much a hot-button issue as the environment), or any of a thousand other topics. Occasionally, sports will be discussed—but don't look for the locals to want to talk about anything as much as dog-sledding. It's almost a religion in the 49th state—their World Series, Super Bowl, and Stanley Cup rolled into one.

Local passengers are unhappy with the ferry-system decision to close the bars aboard ship, apparently as a cost-saving decision. Passengers are prohibited from drinking alcohol in public areas (not that anyone seems to be patrolling the halls to determine what liquid is in your beverage container). While ferry passengers may bring alcohol aboard, they may open it only inside a private cabin, so passengers without a cabin have no legal place to drink alcohol.

Traveling on the ferries is comfortable, with large seats and good viewing choices. Any luggage you won't be needing aboard you may check at a luggage cart ashore, retrieving it at the next port. Be sure to ask ahead of time about the location of the dock at ports where you'll be getting off; some ferry terminals are away from the town. The dock is 5 miles from Haines (though there are shuttles) and a taxi or bus ride at Juneau. In Petersburg and Wrangell, it's an easy walk to town.

THE FLEET   Eight of the traditional Alaska Marine Highway boats are designated M/V, as in motor vessel. Two newer, catamaran-style vessels are designated FVF, for fast vehicle ferries. Below is a thumbnail description of each one. *Note:* These plans and schedules are for 2018 but may change again for 2019 and beyond as new ferries are added and others are renovated.

The 382-foot-long *Kennicott,* in service since 1998, operates some of the longest runs in the system, connecting Bellingham, Washington, with the towns of Southeast Alaska before continuing on across the Gulf of Alaska as far west as Kodiak. The *Kennicott* holds up to 499 passengers and 80 vehicles, and it has 109 cabins: 51 four-bed rooms with private bathrooms containing toilets and showers; 34 two-bed rooms with sinks but no showers or toilets (public facilities are down the hall); and 24 super-small, two-bunk "roomettes" that don't even have sinks but are far less pricey. Five of the cabins are wheelchair-accessible. The ship has a large cafeteria.

The 418-foot-long *Columbia,* the largest of the fleet, connects Bellingham with the towns of the Southeast only (unlike the *Kennicott,* it doesn't continue across the Gulf of Alaska). It holds up to 499 passengers and 134 vehicles, and it has 44 four-berth cabins and 59 two-berth cabins. Three cabins are suitable for wheelchair users. The vessel has a dining room and a cafeteria. *Columbia* can hold up to 600 passengers but for operating purposes is limited to 499.

Also sailing between Bellingham and the towns of the Southeast is the 499-passenger, 88-vehicle *Malaspina.* It has 46 four-berth cabins, 27 two-berth cabins, a cafeteria, and a solarium. For much of the summer, this vessel provides service to different communities throughout Southeast Alaska.

The 499-passenger, 88-vehicle *Matanuska* sails between Prince Rupert, BC, and the towns of the Southeast (including Juneau, Ketchikan, Wrangell, Petersburg, Sitka, and Skagway). It has 23 three-bunk cabins and 81 two-bunk cabins (one of which can accommodate a wheelchair user) as well as a cafeteria.

One of the newest vessels in the fleet is the fast ferry *Fairweather,* which operates mostly between Juneau and Sitka, sometimes stopping in Angoon. The *Fairweather* holds 250 passengers and 35 vehicles but has no sleeping quarters; it is designed purely to provide fast access between towns. Its value to locals is immense, a lifeline to many communities including small Native Alaska villages, getting residents to stores such as Costco and to the government offices of Juneau twice as fast as once was possible. Its value to tourists is that it enables them to spend less time in transit. A sister ship, the *Chenega,* is not in service primarily because of budget constraints, an issue that nearly closed the entire ferry system in 2017 and concerns residents along the ferry routes.

Sailing between the towns of Prince William Sound is the *Aurora,* which holds 300 passengers and 34 vehicles but has no cabins. It has a cafeteria and solarium.

The *Lituya,* the smallest and slowest of the ferries, has operated exclusively between Ketchikan and the nearby Native village of Metlakatla since joining the fleet in 2004. The 8-mile trip takes 45 minutes, and the cabin-less vessel carries 149 passengers and 18 vehicles. Although built with a specific local market in mind, it offers travelers an easy way to visit this off-the-beaten-path outpost.

Another vessel that will get you off the beaten path is the 300-passenger, 34-vehicle *Le Conte.* It connects Juneau with such small Southeast communities as Angoon, Gustavus (gateway to Glacier Bay National Park), Pelican, and Hoonah, and also provides service between Juneau and the communities of Haines and Skagway in North Lynn Canal. It has a cafeteria but no cabins.

The 174-passenger, 36-vehicle *Tustumena,* in Alaska since 1964, connects the towns of the Southwest from Homer west to Dutch Harbor in the Aleutians. One of its 26 cabins is adapted for wheelchair use; the ferry has a dining room.

Note: Since the quality of the ferry system continues to be a matter of debate for Alaska's state government, travelers should check in the winter to get the latest news for the coming spring/summer seasons.

PASSENGER PROFILE More than half of the passengers on the Alaska ferry system are locals traveling between towns for everything from work to sporting events (remember that many towns in rugged Alaska, such as Ketchikan and even state capital Juneau, lack roads to the outside world). But you'll also find a healthy mix of vacationers from the Lower 48 and beyond, everything from young, adventurous backpackers to retirees (who just might have their RV parked down below in the ship's hold). It's a fairly laid-back crowd and totally casual. Jeans and hiking boots (sometimes not removed for days), anoraks and backpacks—these are the basic accessories of ferry travelers in the 49th state. They are definitely not looking for luxury.

The ferries have become very popular with RVers, who use them to move their vehicles into and out of the state, saving thousands of miles of driving.

CABINS   Booking passage on the AMHS can be a complicated affair. First, you'll pay for a spot on the ship, which can be as little as $36 ($27 for ages 65 and older) for the 1-hour trip between Skagway and Haines, or as much as $772 ($666 for 65 and older) on the 1,629-mile, 4-day voyage between Bellingham and Whittier. If you want a cabin for the sailing, it can add hundreds of dollars more for a multiday trip. Children between the ages of 6 and 11 are charged roughly half the adult fare throughout the system, and children 5 and under travel free. Once you've booked basic passage and paid for a cabin, assuming you want one, you'll then have to account for what you're taking along. A kayak? A motor vehicle? A motorcycle? An inflatable boat? All of these, and more, are an additional cost. Be sure to disclose all information about what you are bringing on board and the overall length of your vehicle so that there are no surprises when you get to the ferry terminal.

In general, cabins are small and spartan, coming in two-, three- and four-bunk configurations, and either inside (without windows) or outside (with windows). For a premium, you can reserve a more comfortable sitting-room unit on some vessels. Some cabins have small private bathrooms with showers and toilets; others have sinks only, with showers and toilets located down the hall. Cabins can be stuffy, and the windowless units can be claustrophobic as well, so you may want to try to get an outside one. (If you're insistent on a balcony with your cabin when sailing in Alaska, forget about traveling on the ferries!)

Travelers who do not book ferry passage in time to snag a cabin—or purposely eschew one in an effort to save money—must spend nights curled up in chairs in lounges or in the glass-enclosed solariums found on some vessels. This being Alaska, where the frontier spirit is alive and well, some hearty travelers without cabin reservations bring sleeping bags and "camp" in the solariums or even pitch a tent out on deck—a phenomenon that is not only allowed but encouraged. Only in Alaska! If you plan to set up outside, just be sure to bring Gorilla or duct tape to secure your tent to the deck, because the wind blows like an endless gale over a ship in motion. If the vessel looks crowded, grab your spot fast to snag a choice location. No matter whether you have a cabin or not, public showers are available, although there may be lines. Lock valuables in the coin-operated lockers.

DINING OPTIONS   Only two of the 10 AMHS ferries (*Columbia* and *Tustumena*) have a full-service, sit-down dining room. The others have cafeteria-style facilities that serve hot meals and beverages, some with menus more limited than others. Travelers may want to time their arrival in port and departure for a better meal ashore. All of the boats also have vending machines that dispense snacks and drinks. Priced from $1 for a vending-machine snack to $8 and up for hot meals, food is not included in the fares (credit cards accepted).

ACTIVITIES   There are no organized activities but lots of scenic viewing on most sailings. Some vessels have small theaters that show films of general interest and documentaries on Alaska and the outdoors. Small gift shops sell magazines, books, toiletries, and Alaskan souvenirs. Some vessels even have card rooms, reading rooms, small video game arcades, and/or toddler play areas.

CHILDREN'S PROGRAMS   None.

ENTERTAINMENT   None.

SERVICE   The small American staff on each vessel works enthusiastically, but without a great deal of distinction.

CRUISETOURS & ADD-ON PROGRAMS   None. However, those seeking a change from the more popular and frequently congested, larger Inside Passage and Gulf ports find that the ferries are an ideal way to get to the less-visited parts of Alaska, where paved roads are in short supply and reliable air connections—especially when the weather turns ugly—are nonexistent. A trip on one of the ferries can deposit you in, say, Pelican, on Chichagof Island, where you can enjoy fishing and scenery and join in the banter of the local fisherfolk in Rosie's Bar, the center of activity in town. Another ferry will transport you to Tenakee Springs, a popular hot springs as far back as the gold-rush days, where you can "take to the waters" or go saltwater fishing. The ferry will get you to Port Lions, on the northeast coast of Kodiak Island at the eastern end of the Aleutian Chain, or to other areas of the Aleutians (False Pass and King Cove, for instance); to Chenega Bay, in Prince William Sound; to the Native settlements at Kake, on Kupreanof Island; and to Met-lakatla on Annette Island, among other destinations. These are not, and never will be, ports with mass appeal. No giant cruise liner will ever unload 3,000 passengers in any of them. But those who seek a taste of down-home spirit, Alaskan style, find these ports to be attractive destinations. In short, the Alaska Marine Highway System can get you to places where cruise ships just don't go. It also allows you to take a vehicle, so you can explore the interior of Alaska without driving the entire Alcan Highway both directions. In addition, riding on a ferry allows you the flexibility to explore a place for several days (as opposed to only a few hours) at your leisure—giving you time to get to know real Alaskans along the way.

PUBLIC AREAS   All of the ferries have warm, if somewhat sparse, interiors, with room for all when the weather is foul. They often have solariums with high windows for viewing the passing scenery. You're welcome to wander around on the outside decks to get some fresh Alaska air.

POOL, FITNESS, SPA & SPORTS FACILITIES   Are you kidding?

THE PORTS OF EMBARKATION

Most Alaska cruises operate either round-trip from Vancouver or Seattle, or one-way northbound or southbound between Vancouver or Seattle and Seward/Anchorage. Whittier, an unprepossessing little place that has the advantage of being 60 miles closer to Anchorage, is the northern turnaround port for Princess' cruises in the Gulf of Alaska. Another U.S. city, San Francisco, also is growing as a home port for voyages to Alaska, with round-trip and one-way sailings, including from Princess. The small adventure-type vessels sail from popular Alaska ports of call such as Juneau, Ketchikan, and Sitka (as well as Seattle). In this chapter, we'll cover the most common of these home ports: Anchorage, Seward, Vancouver, Seattle, Juneau, and Whittier.

Consider traveling to your city of embarkation at least a day or two before your cruise departure date. You can check out local attractions and, if you're traveling from afar, give yourself time to overcome jet lag.

ANCHORAGE

You'll hear it again and again: Anchorage got its start in 1914 as a tent camp for workers building the Alaska Railroad. In fact, the area's history really began much earlier. Way before those 20th-century workers showed up, the land, which stands between the Chugach Mountains and the waters of upper Cook Inlet, was home to the Dena'ina and Ahtna Athabascan people. (Learn more about their history, present, and future with a visit to the **Anchorage Museum;** see below.) Their hold on the land was upended when the Russians arrived in the 1700s, bringing diseases with them that decimated the Native population. Two centuries later the tent city rose up. Why do we mention this? Because any visit to Anchorage is enriched by a deeper sense of what came before those tents were pitched.

The city itself started to build up when military bases were installed in the 1940s. And things really took off in the 1950s, when oil was discovered on the Kenai Peninsula, to the south.

Modern-day Anchorage stretches far beyond the downtown area. While downtown has its charms (and, like any city, its problems), some of the city's most interesting and fun diversions are south of downtown. See them by renting a car or, if you just have a day, grabbing a cab.

No matter where you roam in Anchorage, the landscape makes one thing clear: This is very much Alaska—though many Alaskans who live outside the state's most cosmopolitan city like to poke fun by calling it "Los Anchorage" or saying that "Anchorage isn't far from Alaska." To the east, the Chugach Mountains watch over the city (and offer stellar hiking opportunities), and on the Tony Knowles Coastal Trail, which stretches 11 miles from downtown, moose sightings are far from rare (a good thing to keep in mind when taking a stroll or bike ride).

Getting to Anchorage

To avoid the extra day that cruising around the Kenai Peninsula adds to Gulf of Alaska itineraries, most ships don't dock in Anchorage. Instead, passengers embark or disembark south of the city in Seward or Whittier, and travel from or to Anchorage by train or motorcoach. (Most visitors use Anchorage as a hub because, thanks to the international airport, it's where Alaska connects to the rest of the world.) It's well worth spending a day or two in Anchorage before or after your cruise.

BY PLANE   If you're arriving or leaving by plane, you'll land at the **Ted Stevens Anchorage International Airport** (www.dot.state.ak.us/anc/). The facility is located within the city limits, just a 15-minute drive from downtown. Taxis run about $27 for the trip downtown; many hotels also offer free shuttles.

BY CAR   Only one road into Anchorage comes from the north, the Glenn Highway, and another leads out of the city heading south down the Kenai Peninsula. During the height of summer travel, allow extra time in case the highways are clogged with RVs or accidents block the roads.

Exploring Anchorage

INFORMATION   Visit **Anchorage** (www.anchorage.net; ✆ **907/276-4118**) maintains five information locations. The main one is the **Log Cabin Visitor Information Center** at 4th Avenue and F Street (✆ **907/257-2363**). It's open daily 8am to 7pm June through August; 9am to 4pm mid-September to mid-May; and 8am to 6pm late May and early September.

GETTING AROUND   Most car-rental companies maintain a counter at the airport. A compact car costs from about $55 a day, with unlimited mileage. (There aren't many of those $30-a-day specials that you see advertised in some other states.) Advanced bookings are strongly recommended throughout the summer. Anchorage's bus system, **People Mover** (www.peoplemover.org), is an effective way of moving to and from the top attractions and activities. Weekday service is between 6:30am and 12am (on Route 40, which goes to the airport, the buses run until 2am on weekdays). On Saturdays buses run between 8am and 8pm, and Sunday service runs 8am to 7pm. Passage costs $2 for adults, and $1 for seniors and youth ages 5 to 18 (4 and under free).

Anchorage

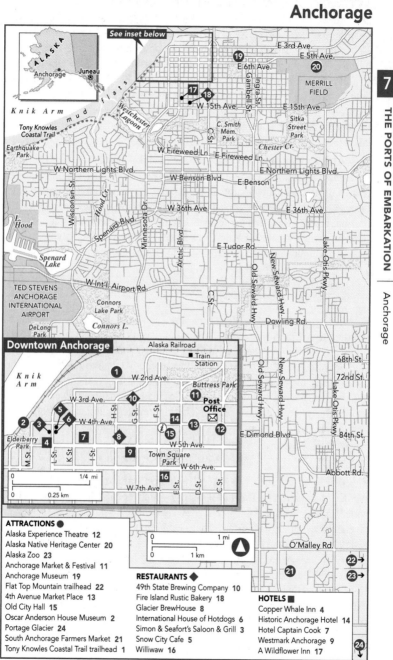

ATTRACTIONS ●
Alaska Experience Theatre **12**
Alaska Native Heritage Center **20**
Alaska Zoo **23**
Anchorage Market & Festival **11**
Anchorage Museum **19**
Flat Top Mountain trailhead **22**
4th Avenue Market Place **13**
Old City Hall **15**
Oscar Anderson House Museum **2**
Portage Glacier **24**
South Anchorage Farmers Market **21**
Tony Knowles Coastal Trail trailhead **1**

RESTAURANTS ◆
49th State Brewing Company **10**
Fire Island Rustic Bakery **18**
Glacier BrewHouse **8**
International House of Hotdogs **6**
Simon & Seafort's Saloon & Grill **3**
Snow City Cafe **5**
Williwaw **16**

HOTELS ■
Copper Whale Inn **4**
Historic Anchorage Hotel **14**
Hotel Captain Cook **7**
Westmark Anchorage **9**
A Wildflower Inn **17**

ATTRACTIONS WITHIN WALKING DISTANCE

Downtown Anchorage is equal parts business district, culture and dining destination, and, yes, haven for schlocky souvenir shops (though seriously, the T-shirt deals are worth getting in on). The best option for free fun: Walk or bike the **Tony Knowles Coastal Trail,** which runs along the water for about 11 miles from the western end of 2nd Avenue to Kincaid Park. You can hop onto the trail at several points, including Elderberry Park, at the western end of 5th Avenue. Like music? Local acts—some of them seriously good—perform at Peratrovich Park Wednesday at noon. Free concerts (plus a beer tent) take place at 5:30pm on Thursdays in Town Square Park.

The Alaska Experience Theatre ★   Think Alaska, think big. This popular attraction features Alaska-themed movie presentations shown in a 96-seat domed theater with a wraparound, planetarium-style screen that stands nearly three stories high. It is a cool introduction to some of the places you'll be touring, but be aware that the format (like IMAX) may cause motion sickness in some people. A smaller Safe-Quake Theatre shows a video about the 1964 Alaska earthquake—and seating shakes to simulate an earthquake.

333 W. 4th Ave. (at C St.). www.alaskaexperiencetheatre.com. ℂ **907/272-9076.** Admission movies $9.95, earthquake video $8.95, combo tickets $14.95 ($1 off for kids and seniors). Daily 10am–7pm.

Anchorage Market & Festival ★★   One of the signs that summer has returned to Anchorage (even if the weather doesn't make it clear) is the opening of this downtown weekend market. Though some truly schlocky stuff is sold out of a few of the tents (really, does anybody come to Anchorage to buy bad socks?), most of the vendors sell made-in-Alaska goods, from traditional ulu knives to carved-wood bears and jellies made from local flowers. The food stalls offer plenty of local yum, including smoked-salmon quesadillas and fireweed honey ice cream.

225 E St. http://anchoragemarkets.com/anchorage-market-festival/. ℂ **907/572-5634.** Summer (mid-May to mid-Sept) Sat 10am–6pm; Sun 10am–5pm (closed in winter).

Anchorage Museum ★★★   The largest museum in Alaska just got a whole lot bigger. The Rasmuson Wing, which opened in September 2017, added 25,000 feet of exhibit space, allowing curators to put more of their extensive archives on display. And, perhaps even more important to new-to-Alaska visitors, the Alaska exhibition (formerly the Alaska Gallery)—which details the history of the state from way, *way* back (and long before it became a state)—has been completely overhauled to tell the story of Alaska from multiple perspectives and new themes. The art collection, which features traditional Native arts, Western-trained artists, and modern-day artists working in everything from oil paints to animal skins, makes it clear that there is no single Alaska, that the beauty, danger, and mystery of the land runs ever so deep. Visitors who just have an hour or two should head straight to the Smithsonian Arctic Studies Center for a stunning lesson in Native cultures. Here you can view everything from waterproof clothing made from seal intestines, intricate baskets, and

THE iditarod

While there's plenty of interest in sports like football (Alaskans root for the Seattle Seahawks) and, definitely, hockey, nothing gets more attention in Alaska than long-distance dog mushing. And, of course, there's no race better known than the **Iditarod Trail Sled Dog Race**, a 1,000-plus-mile run from Anchorage to Nome that takes place in mid-March, across frozen tundra and rivers, through dense forest, over mountains and along windy coastline. Winners cover the distance in just under 9 to 10 days, which includes mandatory stopovers to rest the dogs. The current reigning family of the Iditarod is the Seaveys, with dad Mitch Seavey reclaiming the title from his son, Dallas (winner of the 2012, 2014, 2015, and 2016 races), in 2017. The event is big news here—TV anchors speculate on the mushers' strategies at the top of the evening news, and schoolchildren plot the progress of their favorite teams on maps.

The start of the race in downtown Anchorage is covered by network TV, too. The number of teams varies per year—in 2017, 64 mushers completed the race, most from Alaska, but also from places such as Canada and Norway. Each musher handles a team of 12 to 16 dogs. When the event hits Nome, the town overflows with visitors kept busy by the many local events and activities that coincide with the race. Even if the first team crosses the finish line at 3am—in 30°F (–1°C) weather, a huge crowd turns out to congratulate the musher.

Recent competitors have included a mortician, a former fashion model, a dentist, contractors, a fur trapper, and even married couples and other family members competing against each other. Some are professional mushers (who get endorsement deals), others run kennels, and some do dog sledding as a hobby. To qualify, you need to compete in three smaller races—of which there are many in Alaska.

The victors are feted and admired throughout the state as much as any sports star ever is in the lower 48. They're not compensated quite as well, mind you: First prize in the grueling event varies, but Mitch Seavey took home $571,250 and a new truck. The lead dogs are celebrated, too.

The cruise lines long ago recognized the significance of the Iditarod, even to non-Alaskans. Princess, for instance, has a contract with Libby Riddles, the first woman to win the race, in 1985. She comes aboard in Juneau with a slide show to talk about her mushing experience. The *Riverboat Discovery* is a popular day sternwheeler cruise on the Chena River in Fairbanks, an outing cruise lines include in their cruisetour itinerary if they have programs in the Denali Corridor. The boat stops on each sailing at the dog yard where the late Susan Butcher—an Alaska legend who won the Iditarod four times (1986, 1987, 1988, and 1990)—kept some of her champion dogs. The Iditarod Trail Sled Dog Race headquarters (with a small museum) is located in Wasilla, 43.5 miles north of Anchorage, and is also a part of the shore-excursion schedule of virtually all Gulf of Alaska cruise operators.

Cruise aficionados may never be in the state to see the race itself, since it takes place off cruise season—way off-season. But they are likely to see and hear plenty about it during their summer vacations.

You will have the opportunity to meet sled dogs on tours offered in several ports including in Juneau, Seward (where Mitch Seavey has an operation), and Skagway.

vibrant masks to weapons and drums. Much of the collection was under lock and key in Washington, D.C., and is displayed here for the first time anywhere. At the front of the room, grab a seat in front of one of the video monitors to learn about modern-day Native life and efforts to keep the culture and language alive. If you're traveling with kids, make a beeline for the **Imaginarium Discovery Center,** where learning is enhanced by such attractions as a saltwater touch tank (stocked with critters like starfish). The museum's **cafe** serves up surprisingly creative cuisine plus a kids' menu. Special exhibits are frequent. Do not miss the museum's gift shop (see "Shopping for Art in Alaska," below).

625 C St. (at the corner of 7th Ave.). www.anchoragemuseum.org. ℂ **907/929-9200.** Admission $15 adults, $10 seniors and students, $7 for children 3–12. May–Sept daily 9am–6pm.

The Oscar Anderson House Museum ★

Back in 1915, when Anchorage was a big tent city, butcher Oscar Anderson decided to build his family a real wood-frame house. Today this small house is listed on the National Register of Historic Places. House tours—which last about 45 minutes—give a glimpse into what Anchorage life was like in the early–20th century, with period furnishings, historic photos, and a chance to hear a tune on Oscar's player piano.

420 M St. (in Elderberry Park). www.aahp-online.net. ℂ **907/274-2336.** Admission $10 adults (13 and up), $5 children 5–12, children under 5 free. Summer Tues–Sun noon–4pm; closed in winter except for Swedish Christmas (1st and 2nd weekends in Dec).

ATTRACTIONS OUTSIDE THE DOWNTOWN AREA

The Alaska Native Heritage Center ★★★

Come to this 26-acre center to learn about 11 distinct Alaska Native cultures. It has a small museum and a theater showing an introductory film on the different cultures in the Welcome House. The building's rotunda serves as a venue for Native song and dance performances, held throughout the day. Also check out the center's workshop, where Native craftspeople demonstrate such traditional crafts as kayak-making. Outdoors, along a small lake, a walking trail takes visitors to six life-size dwellings showcasing the traditional way of life of various groups including the Athabascans and Tlingits. Cultural representatives are on hand to answer questions and share stories.

8800 Heritage Center Dr. www.alaskanative.net. ℂ **800/315-6608** or 907/330-8000. Admission $25 adults, $21 seniors and military, $17 children 7–16, free for children 6 and under; family rate (2 adults, 2 children) $71.50; combined Anchorage Museum/Native Heritage Center culture pass $30; dog cart ride $10. Summer daily 9am–5pm. Closed in winter. From the Glenn Hwy., take the Muldoon Rd. N. exit.

The Alaska Zoo ★★

Don't expect a big-city zoo. Instead, come to experience a little Eden complete with Alaskan bears, seals, otters, musk oxen, mountain goats, caribou, moose, and waterfowl. The election for the zoo's animal "president" is an annual event that is equal parts fun and fundraiser; in 2016 the winner was Denali the wolf. The zoo also cares for hurt or abandoned animals including wolf pups, a lynx, and a peregrine falcon. You'll also see decidedly non-Alaskan elephants, tigers, and the like here.

4731 O'Malley Rd. www.alaskazoo.org. ℂ **907/346-2133.** Admission $15 adults, $10 seniors, $7 children 3–17, free children 2 and under. May and Sept daily 9am–6pm, summer daily 9am–9pm. New Seward Hwy. to O'Malley Rd., then turn left and go 2 miles; it's 20 min. from downtown, without traffic.

Portage Glacier ★★★   In 1985, the National Forest Service spent $8 million building the Begich, Boggs Visitor Center at Portage. Imagine its chagrin when the glacier then started receding, moving away from the center so fast that at this point, you can't even see one from the other. You must now board a tour boat to get close to the glacier face. Portage is not the best glacier in Alaska—it's relatively small—but if you haven't had enough of them after your cruise (or want a preview beforehand), it's well worth a tour. The visitor center itself is worth a stop; it's a sort of glacier museum and an excellent place to learn about what you'll be seeing (or saw) on your cruise. Many bus tours are offered (your cruise line may give one, too), including a 5½-hour **Gray Line of Alaska** (www.graylinealaska.com; ✆ 888/452-1737) trip from Anchorage, which involves a motorcoach ride to the glacier and a 1-hour cruise across Portage Lake. On the way back, stop for lunch at Hotel Alyeska and take an optional tram ride to the top of Mount Alyeska. The cost is $79 for adults and $39 for children, and the trip is offered daily at 1:30pm in the summer.

About 50 miles south of the city on the Seward Hwy. (toward Seward). Admission $5 adults, free for children 15 and under. May–Sept daily 9am–6pm.

South Anchorage Farmers Market ★   Anchorage has been undergoing a bit of a boom on the culinary-entrepreneur front of late. Several of the companies to open storefronts in the last few years got their start—and continue to sell at—the South Anchorage Farmers Market. Top sweet eats include the ice cream from Wild Scoops and macaroons from Sweet Caribou. Stock up on locally made foods to bring back home for gifts or just to satisfy your own cravings. There's always family-friendly music to enjoy and plenty of Alaskan produce to sample.

11111 O'Malley Centre Dr. www.safm.org. Sat 9am–2pm (May–Oct). Second location behind the Dimond Center: Wed 10am–4pm (July–Sept).

The Trail of Blue Ice ★★★   Though Flattop Mountain is far better known to outsiders, the crowds and surprisingly challenging terrain there make it not-so-ideal for inexperienced hikers. Instead, we recommend heading south on the Seward Highway and turning off onto Portage Glacier Road 49 miles later. Here, you'll find the Trail of Blue Ice, an easy and very rewarding 5-mile (one-way) walk or bike ride with views of several glaciers, spruce trees and tall cottonwoods, streams where salmon sometimes run thick in summer, and mountain views galore. For more about Portage Glacier itself, see above.

At Mile 79 on the New Seward Hwy., turn left onto Portage Glacier Rd. There's trail access from five different points along the road, including from the lakefront parking lot at the Begich, Boggs Visitor Center. www.fs.usda.gov/detail/chugach/home/?cid= stelprdb5251094.

BEST CRUISE-LINE SHORE EXCURSIONS

Anchorage Flightseeing Safari (1½ hr.; $116): See Anchorage surroundings by air as a bush pilot takes you on an exciting seaplane ride to explore the Chugach Mountain Range, where views include secluded valleys and slopes with Dall sheep, and over the Cook Inlet in search of beluga whales. Longer flightseeing tours (4 hours; $276), take you over the mountains to view the fjords, inlets and tidewater glaciers of Prince William Sound.

Spencer Glacier Sightseeing & Float Trip (10 hr.; $276): This Princess Cruises tour (recommended by the Discovery Channel) takes you by rail along the Turnagain Arm, past Girdwood and Whittier and into an area you can only reach by train. The destination is Spencer Glacier, home to bears, wolves, coyotes, and moose, where you'll board a raft and float among the icebergs in the glacier-formed Spencer Lake and along the gentle currents of the Placer River.

EXCURSIONS OFFERED BY LOCAL AGENCIES

Locally owned and operated **Salmon Berry Tours** (www.salmonberrytours. com; ℂ **907/278-3572**) offers a variety of different excursions, including a 2-hour scenic drive ($49) through the city and up to a scenic overlook near Flattop Mountain for stunning photo opportunities of the Chugach Mountains as well as Anchorage itself.

Get a bit of exercise before taking a deep dive (and many a taste) of Anchorage's brewery boom. **Big Swig Tour**'s full-day "Anchorage Bike and Brew" tour features an 8-mile guided bike ride along the Tony Knowles Coastal Trail and then a behind-the-scenes guided tour (they do the driving) of several of the city's breweries ($199); www.bigswigtours.com; ℂ **907/268-0872.**

Where to Stay

Rooms can be hard to come by in Anchorage in summer, so try to arrange lodging as far in advance as possible, whether through your cruise line or on your own. It's not a cheap city: Room rates in Anchorage, before discounts, often range upward of $250. In addition to the more moderately priced properties listed below, you might try the **Westmark Anchorage** ★★, 720 W. 5th Ave. (www.westmarkhotels.com; ℂ **800 544-0970** or 907/276-7676); the **Hotel Captain Cook** ★★★, 939 W. 5th Ave. (www.captaincook.com; ℂ **800-843-1950** or 907/276-6000), with excellent views from rooms on upper levels; or the small and charming **Historic Anchorage Hotel** ★★ at 330 E. St. (www.historicanchoragehotel.com; ℂ **800/544-0988** or 907/272-4553). The town also has chain hotels.

Copper Whale Inn ★★★ This quaint bed & breakfast overlooks both the water and Elderberry Park. Inside the duo of clapboard houses are casually charming rooms of every shape and size; some in the newer building have nice high ceilings. Right at the inn, rent a bike through **Lifetime Adventures** (www. lifetimeadventures.net; $30/day) and hit the coastal trail after breakfast.

440 L St. www.copperwhale.com. ℂ **866/258-7999** or 907/258-7999. 14 units, 12 w/ bathroom. $189 double w/out bathroom; $229 double w/bathroom. Extra person $20. Lower rates in winter and shoulder seasons. Special packages available. Rates include continental breakfast. Parking $15. **Amenities:** Wi-Fi (free).

A Wildflower Inn ★★★ Housed in an older (for Anchorage) but beautifully kept home, this inn beautifully lives up to its name. Painted white with bright red shutters, the house is surrounded all summer long by a stunning array of flowers. A Wildflower Inn sits in one of Anchorage's oldest

SHOPPING FOR ART IN ALASKA

While the trinkets at the downtown souvenir shops in Anchorage and other towns and cities may tempt you, consider saving your cash for a special purchase. Anchorage has two truly excellent places where you can buy stunning examples of Native art produced by some of the state's best artists. From bentwood boxes to carved masks and beaded fur slippers, there are plenty of treasures to be found.

The best shop, the **AMNC Craft Shop** in the **Alaska Native Medical Center** (4315 Diplomacy Dr.; http://anmc.org/patients-visitors/craft-shop/; © **907/729-1122**), buys directly from the artists; if you're lucky, you might even get the chance to meet the person who made your favorite piece. Its limited hours and payment rules (cash or traveler's checks only) can be a bit challenging, however. It's open 10am to 2pm Monday to Friday and 11am to 2pm on the first and third Saturday of each month.

The museum shop in the **Anchorage Museum** (https://museumstore.anchoragemuseum.org) also stocks a tremendous selection of Native art.

Here you'll find pieces by some of the artists featured in some of the museum's galleries.

As you travel and shop throughout Alaska, watch for the two marks that designate Alaska products: a MADE IN ALASKA polar bear sticker, which means the item was at least mostly made in the state, and an **Authentic Native Handicraft from Alaska** silver hand sticker, which indicates authentic Native art. An absence of the label does not necessarily mean the item is not authentic; it may just mean the artist doesn't like labels. So if you're curious about a piece of artwork lacking a sticker, simply ask. Something priced way too low to be real? Trust your instincts. An elaborate mask, for instance, should be priced at $3,000, not $300.

Ask plenty of questions before handing over your credit card. You don't want to go home with a fake. Ask the shop owner for a biography of the artist and whether the artist actually carved the piece (rather than just lending his or her name to knockoffs). Most dealers will tell you where a work really comes from—you just have to ask.

neighborhoods, South Addition, so be sure to take a stroll around the streets to see the wild array of architectural styles. All of downtown is just a short walk away as well. Rooms come with sound- and light- reducing shades.

1239 I St. alaska-wildflower-inn.com. © **907/274-1239.** 3 units, all with bathrooms. $159–$179 May 15–Sept. 15 ($89–$99 off-season). Rates include full breakfast. Free parking. **Amenities:** Wi-Fi (free).

Where to Dine

49th State Brewing ★★ AMERICAN/BREWERY   There's no need to name names but for a long time, Anchorage residents wondered why the restaurant formerly housed in the 49th State Brewing building was so very bad. Still, they kept going because the place had one of the best outdoor dining spaces anywhere in town. Excitement spread quickly as word got around that 49th State Brewing was taking the place over to open its second location. (The original 49th State is in Healy, a short drive from Denali National Park.) The extensive menu—from nachos to crab-loaded grilled cheese and grilled king salmon—offers something for everyone (including kids), and sizable portions will keep even the biggest eaters from going hungry. But even better than the food (though the food is really good) is the beer. With an ever-rotating lineup of their own ales, porters, and so much more, it's the perfect spot to begin exploring Alaska's brewpub explosion without having to wander far from your downtown hotel. The restaurant also hosts loads of concerts and other events.

717 W. 3rd. Ave. www.49statebrewing.com. © **907/277-7727.** Reservations recommended for dinner. Main courses $11–$49 lunch and dinner. Daily 10:30–1am.

Simon & Seafort's Saloon & Grill ★★★ STEAK/SEAFOOD The amazing views of Cook Inlet and mountains in the distance is worth the visit, but so is the food. Sockeye salmon is the star of the show, along with other seafood specialties, but the prime rib should keep meat-lovers well satisfied. Locals come here (the happy hour is a good one), as do smart tourists—the friendly atmosphere and warm service enhance the experience. Light meals are available in the bar.

420 L St. www.simonandseaforts.com. © **907/274-3502.** Reservations recommended (days in advance in summer). Main courses $13–$23 lunch, $17–$65 dinner. Mon–Fri 11am–2:30pm and 4:30–10pm; Sat–Sun 10am–3pm (for brunch) and 4:30–10pm.

Snow City Cafe ★★★ REGIONAL/AMERICAN A longtime favorite of both locals and tourists, Snow City is as famous for its long wait as it is for its menu. The good news: You can reserve ahead or, if you're flying solo or just with one friend, snag seats at the counter. No reservation? Put your name in at the front desk, pour yourself a cup of coffee, and wait. It'll be worth it. Once seated, prepare for a challenging decision process. Will it be the Kodiak Benedict (poached eggs on Alaska Red King Crab cakes) or the Ship Creek

---

QUICK hits: 24 HOURS IN ANCHORAGE

Short on time? Here are tips from our local expert for your quick trip to Alaska's biggest city:

1. Have breakfast at one of the city's most-loved **bakeries** (an easy walk from downtown). The scones at **Fire Island Rustic Bakeshop** (1343 G St.; fireislandbread.com; © **907/569-0001**) are worth waking up early for.

2. Rent a **bike** and check out views as you ride the Tony Knowles Coastal Trail. You can get a bike from one of downtown's two rental shops and then hop right onto the trail.

3. Stop by the **Anchorage Museum** to take a deep dive into Alaska's history, art, and cultures.

4. Reward yourself for biking or hiking at the **International House of Hot Dogs** (415 L St.). Here you can travel the culinary world with a crazy-big variety of hot dog toppings. Up the Alaska quotient by requesting a Reindeer dog instead of the beef hot dogs you can get back home. It's open every day but Sunday.

5. Check out the city's surprisingly vibrant **local music scene.** Best downtown bets: **Williwaw** (williwaw social.com) or **free shows** put on by the city (anchoragedowntown.org).

6. Try the **local brew.** At **49th State Brewing,** round out your day in Anchorage with a local beer and chow at one of downtown's most popular spots.

Benedict (eggs on salmon cakes)? (Both are topped with house-made hollandaise.) Or how about the crabby omelette made with crab, Swiss cheese, green onions, and avocado? Or pancakes? Or … you get the picture. Make reservations and come early, or be prepared for lines that often snake out the door.

1034 W. 4th Ave. www.snowcitycafe.com. © **907/272-CITY** (2489). A limited number of reservations available on the website. Main dishes $10–$13. Mon–Fri 7am–3pm; weekends 7am–4pm (open breakfast and lunch only).

SEWARD

Okay, so your cruise begins or ends in Seward, a place that may not have been on your dream-destination bucket list. But if you have an extra day or two, consider delaying your train ride or motorcoach up to Anchorage (and the airport), and stick around. There are good reasons why the town is a favorite summer destination for plenty of Alaskans and independent travelers. This pretty little seaside town butts up against Resurrection Bay, quite the majestic waterway. It's rimmed by mountains, and its streets are lined with vintage wood-frame houses and fishermen's homes. The town is also the site of one of the state's best kids' attractions: the spectacular **Alaska SeaLife Center** (a marine research, rehabilitation, and public education center where visitors can watch scientists uncovering the secrets of nearby **Prince William Sound**). Adults who enjoy watching sea otters and other creatures tumble around will get a kick out of it, too. Feeling adventurous? Seward is an ideal spot to hop on wildlife-watching day trips by boat or begin one of a variety of road and rail trips through the beautiful **Kenai Peninsula.**

Located about 125 miles south of Anchorage, Seward traces its history back to 1793 when Russian pooh-bah Alexander Baranof first visited. Seward was hit hard on Good Friday 1964 when a massive earthquake rattled Anchorage, the peninsula, and everything in between. The villagers (there were only about 2,500 of them) watched the water in the harbor drain away after the shaking stopped and realized immediately what was about to happen: a tidal wave. Because they were smart enough to read the signs and run for high ground, loss of life was miraculously slight when the towering 100-foot wall of water struck. The town itself, however, was heavily damaged, so many of the buildings that visitors see today are of a more recent vintage. Care has been taken to rebuild them in the style of the town's earlier days, however. One of the more interesting facilities in town is the **Resurrect Art Coffee House & Gallery** (www.resurrectart.com; © **907/224-7161**), located in a converted church, built in 1916, at 320 3rd Ave. Look over the local art that lines the walls or just schmooze with other visitors and residents over coffee. It's about as relaxed and welcoming a coffee shop as you could ever imagine.

While rainy weather often gets the best of Seward, don't get cranky. The rain will pass, and even if it doesn't, you'll be able to witness firsthand how Alaskans just keep on keeping on with their plans. Slip on your raincoat and join them.

Planning to be in town on July 4th? Make sure you book a place to stay well in advance of your arrival. Seward is one of Alaska's most popular spots for

Independence Day. The main reason: The annual **Mt. Marathon Race,** which sends crazy, er, hearty adventure racers scrambling up and tumbling down the mountain (yes, Mt. Marathon) that overlooks the town. The whole town is a party on the Fourth.

Getting to Seward

Most cruise passengers arrive at Seward either by ship (at the end of their cruise) or by bus.

BY PLANE   The nearest major airport, Ted Stevens Anchorage International Airport, is 130 miles away.

BY BUS   The bus trip from the airport takes about 3 hours, passing through the beautiful Chugach National Forest. If you haven't made transportation arrangements through your cruise line, **Seward Bus Line** (www.seward buslines.net; ✆ **907/224-3608**) has one trip a day (leaving at 9:30am and 2pm) from Anchorage for $40 one-way from May 1 through September 15.

BY CAR   For those arriving by car, Seward and the Kenai Peninsula are served by a single major road, the Seward Highway.

BY TRAIN   The train ride to or from Anchorage with a stop at Seward goes through some truly beautiful scenery; it costs $105 one-way for adults ($168 round-trip) and $53 one-way for kids ($84 round-trip) on the **Alaska Railroad** (www.alaskarailroad.com; ✆ **800/321-6518** or 907/265-2494). Along the way you'll see gorges, rushing rivers, and tunnels cut through mountains. Be aware that you may have to schlep your own bags when you arrive in Seward, though some cruise lines offer buses for the short distance to the pier.

Exploring Seward

INFORMATION   The **Seward Chamber of Commerce** (www.seward. com; ✆ **907/224-8051**) operates an information booth right on the cruise-ship dock; it's open Monday to Saturday 9am to 6pm and Sunday 10am to 4pm. If you have time, stop by **Kenai Fjords National Park Visitor Center,** near the waterfront at 1212 4th Ave. (✆ **907/224-7500**), to learn about what's in the area, including nearby hiking trails. It's open daily May to Labor Day 8:30am to 7pm; off-season Monday through Friday 9am to 5pm.

GETTING AROUND   The downtown area is within walking distance of the cruise-ship dock, and you can easily cover downtown Seward on foot. For motorized transport, the city operates a complimentary shuttle from 8am to 8pm daily during the summer (look for a big yellow school bus) on cruise days. The route loops from the cruise-ship terminal through the small boat harbor and then downtown. The trip isn't much more than a mile, though, so it's a pleasant walk if the weather cooperates.

ATTRACTIONS WITHIN WALKING DISTANCE

Downtown Seward can be explored with the help of a **walking-tour map,** available from the Chamber of Commerce visitor center near the cruise-ship docks and at establishments throughout town.

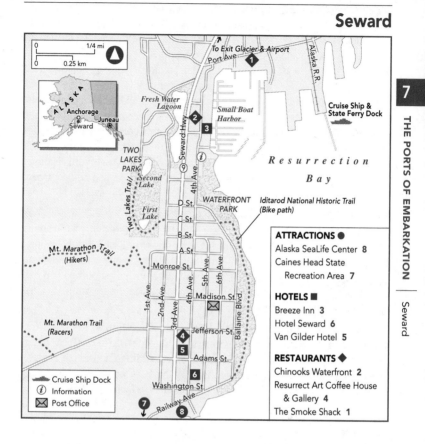

Seward

Map labels:

To Exit Glacier & Airport
Port Ave. **1**
Alaska R.R.
Fresh Water Lagoon **2 3**
Small Boat Harbor
Cruise Ship & State Ferry Dock
Anchorage
Juneau
Seward
ALASKA
TWO LAKES PARK
Second Lake
First Lake
Two Lakes Trail
Seward Hwy
4th Ave
i **9**
Resurrection Bay
WATERFRONT PARK
Iditarod National Historic Trail (Bike path)
D St.
C St.
B St.
A St.
Mt. Marathon Trail (Hikers)
Monroe St.
5th Ave
6th Ave
1st Ave
2nd Ave
3rd Ave
4th Ave
Madison St.
Ballaine Blvd
Mt. Marathon Trail (Racers)
Jefferson St. **4**
5
Adams St.
6
Washington St.
Cruise Ship Dock
i Information
✉ Post Office
Railway Ave. **7 8**

ATTRACTIONS ●
Alaska SeaLife Center 8
Caines Head State Recreation Area 7

HOTELS ■
Breeze Inn 3
Hotel Seward 6
Van Gilder Hotel 5

RESTAURANTS ◆
Chinooks Waterfront 2
Resurrect Art Coffee House & Gallery 4
The Smoke Shack 1

The Alaska SeaLife Center ★★★   Alaska's only public aquarium and ocean wildlife rescue center offers up-close encounters with puffins, octopus, and other sea life, as well as the chance to observe ocean scientists at work. It should be on every visitor's must-see list, and if you have kids in tow, the center is pretty much a mandatory stop. Steller sea lions, porpoises, sea otters, harbor seals, fish, and other forms of marine life abound in the area, as well as umpteen species of seabirds. The ground-floor **fish lab** is a rehabilitation facility for sea otters. At the **Discovery Pool,** kids will enjoy a close encounter with sea creatures in open pools, while at the **Steller Sea Lion Habitat,** playful sea lions swim and sun themselves on the rocks in a 162,000-gallon habitat resembling sea-lion haul-outs in Resurrection Bay.

301 Railway Ave. (at milepost 0 of the Seward Hwy.). www.alaskasealife.org. ⓒ **800/224-2525** or 907/224-6300. Admission $25 adults and children 13 and over, $13 children 4–12, free for children 3 and under; special programs (including a Puffin Encounter, minimum age 12, and an Octopus Encounter; 1 hr., minimum age 6) $75 per person. Reservations suggested. Summer Mon–Thurs 9am–9pm; Fri–Sun 8am–9pm; winter daily 10am–5pm.

ATTRACTIONS BEYOND THE PORT AREA

Caines Head State Recreation Area ★★ Parts of this 7-mile coastal trail, south of town, are accessible only at low tide, so it's best done with someone picking you up and/or dropping you off by boat beyond the beach portion; **Miller's Landing water taxi** (www.millerslandingak.com; © 866/541-5739 or 907/224-5739) offers this service for $38 per person one-way, $48 round-trip. The trail has some gorgeous views, rocky shores, and the concrete remains of Fort McGilvray, a World War II defensive emplacement. Take flashlights and you can poke around in the spooky underground corridors and rooms. For an easy 2-mile hike to Fort McGilvray, start with a boat ride to North Beach. The main trailhead is on Lowell Point Road. Stop at the Kenai Fjords National Park Visitor Center at the boat harbor for tide conditions and advice. Check out **www.alaskastateparks.org** for more about these local trails.

BEST CRUISE-LINE SHORE EXCURSIONS

Kenai Fjords/Resurrections Bay Wildlife Cruise (8 hr.; $130 adults, $70 children): Board a day boat for a 5-hour cruise in Kenai Fjords National Park, narrated by a park ranger. Cruise past Bear Glacier and the hanging glaciers of Thumb Cove as you scan for wildlife, including puffins and bald eagles, whales, and Dall's porpoises. Lunch included. Some tours also visit the Alaska SeaLife Center (see above).

EXCURSIONS OFFERED BY LOCAL AGENCIES

Major Marine Tours (https://majormarine.com; © 907/274-7300) has one of the best tours in town, a **5-hour Kenai Fjords Wildlife Cruise** that explores the protected waters of Resurrection Bay. With a park ranger providing color commentary on the bay's wide world of creatures, which include whales, sea otters, Stellar sea lions, harbor seals, and birds galore, this is an outing that will have you oohing and aahing. Kids can participate in a Junior Ranger program and receive a badge, and they have binoculars on hand you can borrow. Oh, and they'll feed you all-you-can-eat salmon or prime rib for $19 per person. The trip costs $98 for adults, $49 for children under 12, free for children 2 and under; food is extra; advance reservations are suggested. Got time on your hands? The company also does 6- to 8½-hour cruises from Seward that do a more in-depth exploration of the Kenai Fjords National Park; its glaciers; and the ecology, history, and geology of the area.

   Kenai Fjords Tours (www.kenaifjords.com; © 877/777-4051) has a variety of land excursions and day cruises in Resurrection Bay and the Kenai Fjords National Park. A 6-hour cruise is priced at $162 for adults and $81 for children, while an 8½-hour, 150-mile cruise, including an all-you-can-eat wild Alaskan salmon and prime rib dinner, is priced at $172 for adults, $86 for children 12 and under. The company also offers full- or half-day cruises combined with kayaking packages at Fox Island for $199 or $149, respectively, for adults and children 12 and older.

   IdidaRide dog sled tours, 12820 Old Exit Glacier Rd., 3¾ miles off the Seward Hwy. (www.ididaride.com; © 800/478-3139 or 907/224-8607), gives dog lovers the chance to hang out with the ultra-athletic huskies at legendary Iditarod champion Mitch Seavey's racing kennel. The puppies (many on their way to Iditarod wins of their own) are there for the petting—and there are few things as cute as sled-dog puppies. Seriously. Feel the strength of the dogs by signing on for a 1½-hr. tour that includes dog-sled demonstrations and rides on a wheeled dog sled ($74 for adults, $37 for kids). IdidaRide also offers a **summer glacier dog-sledding adventure.** After your 15-minute scenic flight to the top of Punch Bowl Glacier, you'll meet your musher and an enthusiastic team of huskies ready to let you take the reins or simply sit back and enjoy the ride. Each 2-hour tour costs $529 for adults and $499 for children, with flights leaving from Girdwood Airport every 1 hour and 45 minutes between 8:30am and 5:15pm.

In addition to these tours, **fishing charters** are available from various operators in the harbor.

Where to Stay

The Breeze Inn ★   This large property, located right at the boat harbor, offers decent standard accommodations at reasonable rates—just don't expect anything fancy. The "classic rooms" are motel-like, with exterior entrances. Book one of the 22 executive-style rooms in the North Addition for mountain views and added amenities—including refrigerators and coffeemakers. Rooms in the Harbor View Annex indeed have Resurrection Bay views, plus interior corridors. Some rooms have a Jacuzzi and a king-size bed. The front desk offers up chocolate-chip cookies—and they're not half bad.

303 North Harbor Dr. www.breezeinn.com. ℭ **888/224-5237** or 907/224-5237. 100 units. $149–$279 double. Free parking. **Amenities:** Restaurant; bar; Wi-Fi (free).

Hotel Seward ★★   Alaskan-family-owned and right in the heart of downtown, the Seward Hotel is within walking distance of the Alaska SeaLife Center, restaurants, and shopping. Some rooms have large bay windows overlooking Resurrection Bay (request a bay-view room when you book). Amenities in the Alaskan Wing include pillowtop beds, flatscreen TVs, microwaves, and refrigerators. The **Historic Wing** has smaller rooms with similar amenities, but no elevator. Other facilities include an **espresso bar.**

221 5th Ave. www.hotelsewardalaska.com. ℭ **800/440-2444** or 907/224-8001. 62 units. $159–$289 double; $109 economy rooms. Extra person $10. Special packages available. Free parking. **Amenities:** Restaurant; lounge; Wi-Fi (free).

The Van Gilder Hotel ★   This 1916 hotel, listed on the National Register of Historic Places, is a charming place to stay, but be aware that authenticity means rooms tend to be small. Most rooms have antique-style brass beds, lace curtains, and pedestal sinks. Bathrooms are small and some are shared—one bathroom per two bedrooms.

308 Adams St. (P.O. Box 609). www.vangilderhotel.com. ℭ **800/478-0400** or 907/224-3079. 24 units. $79 double w/shared bathroom; $149–$199 double w/private bathroom. Extra person $10. **Amenities:** Wi-Fi (free).

1. Start the day in the rail-car restaurant, the **Smoke Shack,** where you can eat a meal so hearty you probably won't want to eat lunch.
2. Get the lowdown on all the creatures that live in the waters off Seward at the **Alaska SeaLife Center.** Leave plenty of time to watch the sea otters—these not-so-little guys are pretty darned entertaining.
3. Take an easy hike along Two Lakes Trail, at the base of **Mount Marathon,** and when you're not admiring the spruce and hemlock, look for salmon in **First Lake** (the other lake is called Second Lake, natch). The trail is an easy 1-mile loop.
4. Get a taste for the Iditarod with a 1½-hour **Ididaride** at champion Mitch Seavey's kennels. Pet the puppies. Puppies!
5. Finish out the day with a fresh-from-local-waters seafood meal at **Chinooks Waterfront,** where you can sip local brews, too.

Where to Dine

Chinooks Waterfront ★★ STEAK/SEAFOOD   Chinook's is a lively, noisy place, with big windows looking out across the small-boat harbor. It's a favorite with locals and visitors alike. Many of the menu items are pulled from local waters, so you can't go wrong by ordering up halibut, salmon, king crab, or scallops. Sip a local brew and enjoy the scene.

1404 4th Ave. www.chinookswaterfront.com. © **907/224-2207.** Main courses $15–$32. Daily 11am–11pm.

The Smoke Shack ★★★ AMERICAN   Smoked meats are the calling card at this tiny restaurant, with tables outside and inside an old rail car. For breakfast, go with the eggs Benedict, which come with house-smoked ham. At lunch, order the ribs or smoked green-chili burrito, or dive into a smoked burger such as the Black & Blue, which is topped with blue cheese. The Smoke Shack has a few chicken and veggie options as well.

411 Port Ave. (at the small-boat harbor). © **907/224-7427.** Main courses $9–$13; breakfast $6–$13. Daily 7am–3pm (breakfast all day on Sun).

VANCOUVER

Located in the extreme southwestern corner of British Columbia, Vancouver has the good fortune to be surrounded by both mountains and ocean. Like Seattle, the city is a top embarkation port for Alaska cruises; in fact, the two cities battle it out in terms of who's on first in any given year. Vancouver has grown in recent years (thanks in large part to foreign investment), with an expanding skyline. But the development boom has not diminished the quality of life in Vancouver, which has a rich cultural heritage that includes numerous First Nations tribes and a flourishing Asian community. As part of the push for the 2010 Winter Olympics and Paralympics Games, the city saw a host of developments, including a 12-mile rapid-transit line (known as the Canada

Downtown Vancouver

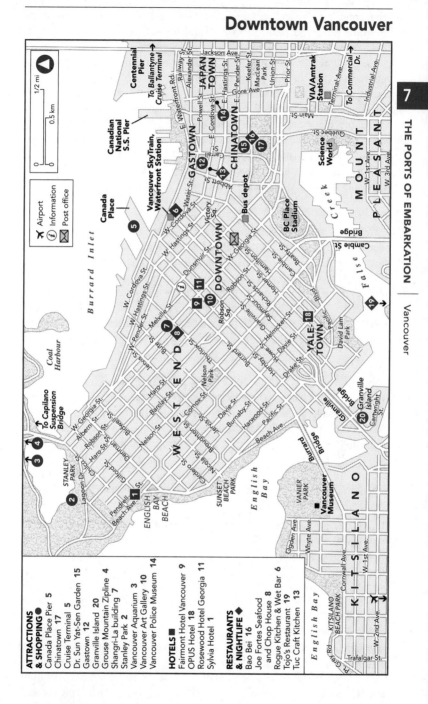

**ATTRACTIONS
& SHOPPING ●**
Canada Place Pier **5**
Chinatown **17**
Cruise Terminal **5**
Dr. Sun Yat-Sen Garden **15**
Gastown **12**
Granville Island **20**
Grouse Mountain Zipline **4**
Shangri-La building **7**
Stanley Park **2**
Vancouver Aquarium **3**
Vancouver Art Gallery **10**
Vancouver Police Museum **14**

HOTELS ■
Fairmont Hotel Vancouver **9**
OPUS Hotel **18**
Rosewood Hotel Georgia **11**
Sylvia Hotel **1**

**RESTAURANTS
& NIGHTLIFE ◆**
Bao Bei **16**
Joe Fortes Seafood
  and Chop House **8**
Rogue Kitchen & Wet Bar **6**
Tojo's Restaurant **19**
Tuc Craft Kitchen **13**

Line) connecting Vancouver International Airport to downtown and the opening of the luxury Shangri-La Hotel Vancouver, part of a 62-story mixed-use skyscraper, the tallest building in the city.

The city has a thriving **arts** scene, including numerous summertime festivals focusing on various forms of entertainment such as folk music, jazz, comedy, and fireworks displays. Residents and visitors alike relish the proximity to **outdoor activities:** You can ski on a world-class mountain, sailboard, rock-climb, mountain-bike, wilderness-hike, and kayak. For day-trippers, the city offers easily accessible attractions, including the historic **Gastown district** with its shops and cafes, and a bustling **Chinatown.**

Those traveling with teenagers will likely know Vancouver as the place where the movie *Twilight* and sequels were filmed. Vancouver is known as "Hollywood North" thanks to the abundance of movies and television shows shot here each year.

Shopping on Robson Street and Granville Island may not be the bargain it once was, but the stores, both local and international, are still enticing. You'll probably visit Vancouver at the beginning or end of your Alaskan cruise, since it's the major southern transit point. We recommend spending at least a day here before or after your cruise to have time to explore this gem of a city.

Note: Rates below are in Canadian dollars. At press time the conversion was C$1 = US $0.79 but may change based on the exchange rate at the time of your trip.

Getting to Vancouver

Cruise ships dock at the **Canada Place Cruise Terminal** at the north end of Burrard Street. A landmark in the city, the pier terminal is noted for its five-sail structure, which reaches into the harbor, and for its Heritage Horns, which play the first four notes of "O Canada" every day at noon. It's located at the edge of the downtown district and is just a quick stroll from the **Gastown** area (see below), filled with cafes, art galleries, and souvenir shops; and **Robson Street,** a mecca for trendy clothing stores. Right near the pier are hotels, restaurants, and shops, as well as the **Tourism Vancouver Infocentre.** The **Ballantyne Pier** cruise terminal farther to the east of the downtown core closed in 2014.

BY PLANE **Vancouver International Airport (YVR)** (www.yvr.ca/en/passengers), is 13km (8 miles) south of downtown Vancouver. Taxi rates are now fixed by destination from the airport; expect to pay $35 for a cab to Canada Place, and $31 to most of the rest of downtown. **Aerocar Service** (www.aerocar.ca; ⓒ **604/298-1000**) offers limousine service from YVR to Canada Place for a flat rate of $77, or sedan service for $64. **Trans Link** (www.translink.ca; ⓒ **604/953-3333**) offers service to Waterfront Station, adjacent to Canada Place, between 5am and 1am. Trains run from Airport Station across from the International Terminal, and tickets can be purchased at kiosks located at the station. If you're fine handling your own luggage, a one-way trip to Waterfront Station takes approximately 22 minutes and costs $9.10 per person, payable by cash (Canadian currency only), credit, or debit. For those with lengthy layovers or overnight stays, the **Fairmont Vancouver Airport** (www.fairmont.com/VancouverAirport; ℭ **604/207-5200**) is located right inside the pre-clearance area of the airport and offers soundproof rooms overlooking the Transborder Terminal and the runways, along with an exceptional spa and lounge.

BY CAR   From the airport, take Granville Street in and hope that the traffic's light. On a good day, the drive in from YVR to Canada Place should only take 30 to 40 minutes. In rush hour, allow yourself at least an hour to reach downtown. **Car-rental agencies** with local branches include Avis, Budget, Hertz Canada, and Thrifty, most of which have both airport and downtown pickup locations. If you plan to drive, note that the city's traffic is legendary and parking can be expensive.

Exploring Vancouver

INFORMATION   The **Tourism Vancouver Infocentre,** 200 Burrard St. (www.tourismvancouver.com; ℭ **604/683-2000**), is located next to Canada Place and is open daily from 9am to 5pm.

GETTING AROUND   Because of its shape and setting, Vancouver has lots of bridges—Burrard Bridge, Granville Bridge, Cambie Street Bridge, and, of course, the forest-green structure known as the Lions Gate Bridge. Cruise ships pass under the Lions Gate Bridge on their way to and from Canada Place. The bridges sometimes make driving in Vancouver a slow endeavor, particularly in rush hour, as people cross from the city over to North Vancouver. If you only have one day in Vancouver, you're going to have to be judicious about what you want to do. The **Aquabus ferries** shuttle visitors from Granville Island to False Creek, on downtown Vancouver's southern edge. Fares are $3.50 to $5.50 for adults (depending on destination) and $1.75 to $3.50 for seniors and children. Children under 3 ride free, and day passes are available (www.theaquabus.com; ℭ **604/689-5858**). A water taxi service called the **Bowen Island Express** runs between Granville Island and Bowen Island. It has six sailings per weekday from 6:30am to 6pm (9am–6pm on weekends), and the trip takes 35 minutes. Bowen Island makes for a perfect Vancouver day trip, with opportunities for hiking, kayaking, golf, dining, and shopping. One-way fares are $20 for adults ($40 round-trip) and $10 for children under 12; reservations are recommended (bowentaxi.com; ℭ **604/250-2894**).

You can easily walk the downtown area of Vancouver, but if you want transportation, you've got a few options. The city's public transit network, **Translink** (www.translink.ca; schedules and trip info ℭ **604/953-3333**; Mon–Fri 5:30am–12:30am, weekends 6:30am–11:30pm), includes electric buses, ferries, and the magnetic-rail SkyTrain that traverse Vancouver and Metro Vancouver. On the main routes, it runs from 5am to 1am daily. Schedules are available at many hotels and online. A new fare system introduced in 2016 requires riders to tap electronic cards, available at vending machines at most stations, in and out when using transit. Standard one-way trip fares are valid for 90 minutes; full-day-use cards are available for purchase from many SkyTrain station ticket machines, and take cash (Canadian currency only) and debit and

credit cards. **Taxis** are available through **Black Top & Checker Cabs** (www.
btccabs.ca; © 604/731-1111), **Yellow Cab** (www.yellowcabonline.com; © 604/
681-1111), and **MacLure's** (www.maclurescabs.ca; © 604/831-1111); call
them by phone or look for them around the major hotels.

The city has several great bicycle runs, including the Stanley Park seawall
that stretches from English Bay to Coal Harbour, and Pacific Spirit Park. You
can rent a bicycle from **Bayshore Bicycle Rentals** (which also rents Roller-
blades and tandem bicycles), 745 Denman St. (www.bayshorebikerentals.ca;
© 604/688-BIKE [2453]), or **Spokes Bicycle Rentals,** 1798 W. Georgia St.
(www.spokesbicyclerentals.com; © 604/688-5141); rates start at about $7.62
per hour, or $22.86 for a half-day, and $30.48 for a full day. Helmets (required
by law) and locks are included in the rate.

ATTRACTIONS WITHIN WALKING DISTANCE

Canada Place ★★★ Hands down, Vancouver's most distinctive landmark is Canada Place Cruise Terminal, with its five gleaming white Teflon
sails that recall a giant sailing vessel. The pier houses the **Vancouver Convention Centre** as well as the Alaska cruise-ship terminal. Check out **Canada's
Storyboard,** a 14×25-foot LED high-definition video screen featuring iconic
Canadian content. Walk along the waterfront behind the western building of
the Convention Centre, where there are markers showing Vancouver Island
history, such as the time an explosion caused a river to clog, trapping 30 million salmon. Don't miss **FlyOver Canada** (flyovercanada.com), a flight
simulation ride housed in the former IMAX theatre at Canada Place. Shows
run from 9:30am to 10pm, and tickets can be purchased online at a discounted
rate. The 32.8-foot-tall 2010 **Olympic Cauldron** also has a permanent home
on the west side of the Convention Centre.

At the foot of Howe and Burrard sts., next to the Waterfront SkyTrain Station. www.
canadaplace.ca.

Chinatown ★★★ Vancouver has one of the largest Chinatowns in North
America (though it doesn't hold a candle to those in New York and San Francisco), and, like Gastown (see below), it's a historic district. Chinese architecture and the **Dr. Sun Yat-Sen Garden,** 578 Carrall St. (www.vancouver
chinesegarden.com; © 604/662-3207; admission $14 adults, $11 seniors, $10
students, $28 for family with two adults, up to three children under 14; daily
May 1–June 14 10am–6pm; June 15–Aug 31 9:30am–7pm; Sept 1–30 10am–
6pm; Oct 1–Apr 30 10am–4:30pm; closed Mon Nov–April), are among the
attractions, along with great food and shops selling Chinese wares. Take the
45-minute tour (included with admission) to learn about the significance of
each element in the gardens. Along with the photogenic Chinese gates, bright
red buildings, and open-air markets, don't miss the amazing 6-foot-wide **Sam
Kee Building** at 8 W. Pender St., which holds the record for being the narrow-
est commercial building in the world.

In the area bordered by E. Pender and Keefer sts., from Carrall St. to Gore Ave.

Gastown ★★★   In 1867, "Gassy" Jack Deighton built a saloon in Maple Tree Square (at the intersection of Water, Alexander, and Carrall sts.) to serve the area's loggers and trappers. Today, the area named for him, Gastown, boasts cobblestone streets, historic buildings, gaslights, a steam-powered clock (near the corner of Water and Cambie sts.), street musicians, and a hipster vibe. It's so close to the ship pier that it's a must-see and an easy outing. Boutiques, including several home-design shops, antiques stores, and art galleries, stand beside touristy shops, restaurants, clubs, and cafes. Our coauthor, Fran Golden, can attest to the fine offerings at **Hill's Native Art,** 165 Water St. (http://hills nativeart.com/; ℂ **604/685-4249**); a raven totem pole in her living room is from the shop. Hill's has five outlets in British Columbia, but this was the first and features more than 1,200 Native artists, representing every tribe and nation of the Northwest Coast. For views of "Gassy" Jack's namesake statue, pop into **Chill Winston,** 3 Alexander St. (www.chillwinston.com; ℂ **604/288-9575**) and enjoy a cocktail and lunch on the fabulous outdoor patio.

In the area bordered by Water and Alexander sts., from Richard St. east to Columbia St.

Granville Island ★★★   A hearty walk from downtown (you may want to take a cab or water taxi), Granville is a delight for shoppers, with its vibrant daily market and streets lined with art studios and boutiques. Once an industrial center, where ironworks, sawmills, and slaughterhouses were the norm, today it's home to more than 300 businesses, including **Granville Island Brewing** (www.gib.ca; ℂ **604/687-BREW** [2739]; taproom open daily 11am–9pm); the **Granville Island Hotel** (www.granvilleislandhotel.com; ℂ **800/663-1840**); and the immensely popular **public market** (daily 9am–7pm), a foodie paradise. Take time to explore and chat with the local artists. If you do plan to walk from downtown, take the Burrard Bridge on the east side heading south, then turn left on W. 1st Ave. and follow it to the water. Although the island sits underneath the Granville Street Bridge, long on-ramps and heavy traffic make the walk complicated.

http://granvilleisland.com.

Stanley Park ★★★   Designated a national historic site of Canada, Stanley Park is the country's largest urban park and the green-space pride of the city. Best of all, it's just outside of downtown (about a 20-min. walk from Canada Place), attracting more than 8 million visitors a year. Its 1,000 acres contain rose gardens, totem poles, a yacht club, a kids' water park, beaches, miles of wooded hiking trails, a scenic 5-mile bike path along the waterfront, great views of Lions Gate Bridge, and the outstanding **Vancouver Aquarium** (www.vanaqua. org; ℂ **604/659-FISH** [3474]; admission $39 adults, $30 seniors/students/children 13–18, $22 children 4–12, free children 3 and under; daily summer 9:30am–6pm; guests with a valid Translink DayPass or CompassCard save $2 off admission). Check out the short movies in the 4D Theatre, which combine 3-D imagery with in-theater effects; catch one of up to four daily dolphin shows or four daily beluga shows; or try to be around when some of the penguins take a daily walk (or waddle) with a trainer for an up-close and hilarious experience. If you're around the park at 9pm, don't be surprised if you hear the **9 O'Clock Gun** go off. Located on the eastern extremity of the park's seawall, it has sounded nearly every night since 1898.

Downtown Vancouver, NW of the cruise-ship terminal. http://vancouver.ca/parks/parks/stanley. Park open daily sunrise–sunset.

Vancouver Art Gallery ★★★   With a permanent collection of more than 10,000 artworks, including an impressive number by British Columbia artist Emily Carr and the Canadian Group of Seven, the Vancouver Art Gallery is a must-do for those interested in the region's art. Only about 5% of the collection is on display at any given time in the impressive 1906 former courthouse, within easy walking distance of the cruise pier. International works including paintings, sculptures, graphics, photography, and video art are also on display. The **Annex Gallery** has rotating exhibits focused on art education.

750 Hornby St. www.vanartgallery.bc.ca. ✆ **604/662-4719.** Admission $24 adults, $20 seniors, $18 students (with valid ID), $6.50 children 5–12, free for children 4 and under. Wed–Mon 10am–5pm; Tues 10am–9pm. Tues evenings 5–9pm (admission by donation).

Vancouver Police Museum ★★★   Ensconced in a heritage building that once served as the city morgue and crime laboratory, over 20,000 artifacts, photos, and documents highlight Vancouver's colorful past and most notorious characters. Of particular interest is the old morgue itself, which has been preserved in its original state. The museum also offers some fantastic 90-minute, historically crime-themed walking tours of Gastown and Vancouver's Downtown East Side.

240 East Cordova St., http://sinsofthecity.ca. ✆ **604/665-3346.** Admission $12 adults, $10 seniors and students (with valid ID), $8 youth 6–18, free for children 5 and under. Tues–Sat 9am–5pm; closed Sun and Mon.

ATTRACTIONS BEYOND THE PORT AREA

Capilano Suspension Bridge ★★   It may be touristy, but it's still a treat to walk across this narrow, historic, 137m (449-ft.) bridge, located 70m (230 ft.) above the Capilano River in North Vancouver (about a 20-min. drive from downtown, assuming the city's legendary traffic doesn't rear its ugly head). It's been drawing travelers since 1889, and today sees more than 700,000 annual visitors. From its high vantage point, even the towering evergreens below look tiny (this attraction is not for those with a fear of heights). The adjacent park has hiking trails, history and forestry exhibits, a carving center, and First Nations dance performances during the summer months, as well as restaurants and a gift shop. The Treetops Adventure (included in admission price) lets you walk across 197m (646 ft.) of cable bridges high in the forest, while the Cliffwalk leads those brave enough to take it across a series of suspended and cantilevered walkways that jut out above the Capilano River.

3735 Capilano Rd. www.capbridge.com. ✆ **604/985-7474.** Admission $42.95 adults, $38.95 seniors, $33.95 students 17 and older with ID, $26.95 children 13–16, $14.95 children 6–12, free for children 5 and under. April 15–May 19 9am–7pm; May 20–Sept 4 8:30am–8pm; Sept 4–Oct 9 9am–6pm. The suspension bridge, Treetops Adventure, and Cliffwalk are not wheelchair-accessible. A free shuttle runs from downtown to the bridge, with pickups from Canada Place, the Hyatt Regency (Melville St. entrance), Blue Horizon (1225 Robson St.), and Westin Bayshore (1601 Bayshore Dr.). Or you can splurge on a $25 cab ride (each way).

Commercial Drive ★★★ No visit to Vancouver is complete without a visit to "The Drive," as it is affectionately known by Vancouverites. Spanning 22 blocks along Commercial Drive between Venables Street and N. Grandview Highway, The Drive is home to an eclectic selection of restaurants with cuisines that hail from around the world, including an eight-block Little Italy. Clustered in between: bars, cafes, shops, and taphouses boasting local and international brews. One of the city's most diverse and colorful communities, The Drive is a slice of authentic Vancouver.

In the area along Commercial Dr., from Venables St. to N. Grandview Hwy. From downtown, take the Skytrain to Commerical-Broadway, and start walking north on Commercial Dr.

Grouse Mountain Zipline ★★ Situated in the North Shore mountains of adjacent North Vancouver (actually its own municipality), Grouse Mountain is a ski and year-round mountain resort with a thrilling zipline high above the rainforest. On the five-line adventure circuit, you whip along at more than 40 mph, and if you can take a look, you'll see Blue Grouse Lake and other views whizzing by. Along the 2-hour ride, guides will tell you about the indigenous flora and fauna and its significance to the First Nations people (a three-line course is available late fall through spring). The **Grouse Mountain Alpine Experience Skyride** is a more restful way to view your surroundings, by way of North America's largest aerial tramway. More-adventurous visitors might want to do the **Ultimate Experience,** which includes the opportunity to stand inside a glass-enclosed pod at the top of a wind turbine. You can also check out shows at the **Theatre in the Sky,** attend a birds-of-prey demonstration at the **Birds in Motion** amphitheater, and take in a 45-minute live lumberjack show (included in ticket price). The mountain is only about 20 miles from downtown, but getting there can involve traffic, so build in extra time for the drive.

6400 Nancy Greene Way. www.grousemountain.com. ☎ **604/980-9311.** Three-line zipline $75, five-line $115, including aerial tramway up mountain. Daily 8:45am–10pm (time of last departure). Theatre in the Sky daily 9:30am–9:30pm. All Alpine Experience tickets, $44 adults, $40.95 seniors, $25.95 children 13–18, $15.95 children 5–12, $114.95 family (two adults, two children under 19). Free seasonal shuttle bus leaves from Canada Place every 20 min. (May–Oct 9am–1:30pm and 2:30pm–6pm); last bus back from the mountain is at 6:30pm.

BEST CRUISE-LINE SHORE EXCURSIONS

Capilano Canyon Walk & City Highlights (4 hr.; $114.95 adults, $49 children 12 and under): Walk alongside the canyon and through a rainforest with 500-year-old trees as guides describe the ecosystem and wildlife habitats. Then cross the Lions Gate Bridge, with its spectacular views of the skyline, and enjoy a snack and drink before returning to the airport or your downtown hotel.

City Tour (2½–3½ hr.; $49 adults, $29 children): This bus tour covers major sights such as Gastown, Chinatown, Stanley Park, and high-end residential areas. You'll also visit Queen Elizabeth Park, the city's highest southern vantage point and home of the Bloedell Conservatory, which commands a 360-degree city view and features an enclosed tropical rainforest complete with free-flying birds; the tour may also include Granville Island. *Note:* This tour is usually offered after the cruise and is available only to passengers with late-afternoon or evening flights. At the end of the tour, you are dropped off at the airport for your flight home.

EXCURSIONS OFFERED BY LOCAL AGENCIES

Stanley Park Horse-Drawn Tours (www.stanleypark.com; ✆ **604/681-5115**) has offered horse-drawn-trolley tours of the 405-hectare (1,000-acre) Stanley Park for more than a century. The narrated 1-hour tours depart from the Coal Harbour parking lot beside the Stanley Park information booth on Park Drive between 9am and 6pm during the summer months. Tickets are $42 for adults, $40 for seniors and students, $20 for children 3 to 12, and free for children 2 and under. Tours operate from February 25 through November 12.

The **Vancouver Trolley Company** (www.vancouvertrolley.com; ✆ **888/ 451-5581** or 604/801-5515) has old-fashioned (engine-powered) San Francisco–style trolleys with narrated tours on a circuit that includes Gastown, Chinatown, Granville Island, Stanley Park, English Bay and the West End, and other areas of interest. Two separate loops (red and green) are available, and you can get off and on as you like. Both routes conveniently begin at Canada Place. Day fare tickets are $47 for adults, $44 for seniors and youth ages 13 to 18, and $30 for children ages 4 to 12. Children under 4 ride free. Summer sunset tours to Grouse Mountain and the Capilano Suspension Bridge are also offered. The trolley operates year-round.

A Wok Around Chinatown (www.awokaround.com; ✆ **604/736-9508**) is a 4-hour walking tour that takes visitors around Vancouver's vibrant Chinatown. Departing daily at 10am from the Dr. Sun Yat-Sen Garden at 578 Carrall St. (see listing for "Chinatown" in "Attractions Within Walking Distance," above), the tour costs $70 per person and includes a dim sum lunch. A new walking tour, "A Wok Around Granville Island," departs daily at 10am from the intersection of 1505 W. 2nd Ave. and Anderson St., and costs $45 per person. Advance reservations are recommended.

An unusual way of seeing the city is **urban kayaking.** Paddle down False Creek (actually an inlet), which threads past upmarket Yaletown condos and the bustle of Granville Island, and float under the Granville and Burrard street bridges. If you have time, take a few hours to explore the rugged coastline of Stanley Park, Vancouver's 1,000-acre nature reserve. **Ecomarine Paddlesport Centres** (www.ecomarine.com; ✆ **604/689-7575**) is the place to go for kayak and standup-paddleboard rentals, sales, and guided tours from locations on Granville Island and Jericho Beach, with prices starting at $19 per hour for a standup paddleboard, $39 per 2 hours for a single kayak, and $52 per 2 hours for a double kayak. Rainforest and nighttime paddles are also available.

Where to Stay

Almost all of Vancouver's downtown hotels are within walking distance of shops, restaurants, and attractions, although you might want to avoid places around Hastings and Main after dark. While plenty of hotels are clustered around Canada Place, don't be afraid to stay farther afield: Most of Vancouver is served by an excellent transit network. Hotels closer to the pier will almost always be more expensive.

The Fairmont Hotel Vancouver ★★★   Extensively renovated in 2016, the grande dame of Vancouver's hotels is sometimes referred to as the "Castle in the City," its impressive copper roof a highly visible city landmark. Inside the marble interiors are public rooms of massive proportions—you know you are in a special place. Reflecting the same luxe sensibility, guest rooms feature marble bathrooms and mahogany furnishings and serve up stunning views of the city, harbor, and/or mountains. Afternoon tea comes with scones, tarts, and other bites; an accompanying "Children's Tea" has kid-pleasing snacks and sweets. It's one of four Fairmont hotels in Vancouver, three of which are downtown.

900 W. Georgia St. www.fairmont.com/hotelvancouver. © **866/540-4452** or 604/684-3131. 556 units. $279–$329 double; from $319 suite. Children 17 and under stay free in parent's room. Valet and self-parking $39 (plus tax). **Amenities:** 2 restaurants; lounge; babysitting; concierge; state-of-the-art health club & spa; high-speed Internet ($14/24 hr.; free for Fairmont President's Club members).

OPUS Hotel Vancouver ★★★   Travelocity named the OPUS Hotel Vancouver one of its "Top Five Trendiest Hotels in the World," and for good reason. Every room is stocked with an iPad for guest use and decorated in eye-catching colors, and stays include niceties like free Wi-Fi, a welcome beverage at check-in, and free luxury car service to any location in downtown. The funky OPUS also features lots of avant-garde artwork and a whimsical sensibility, the perfect complement to its location in the chic neighborhood of Yaletown. It's about a 20-minute walk from the cruise ship terminal, or 5 minutes by taking the Canada Line from the nearby Yaletown-Roundhouse station to Waterfront.

322 Davie St. http://vancouver.opushotel.com. © **866/642-6787** or 604/642-6780. 96 units. $299–$399 double; from $499 suite. Parking $39. **Amenities:** Restaurant; lounge; babysitting; concierge; fitness center; use of mountain bikes; Wi-Fi (free).

Rosewood Hotel Georgia ★★★   If the Fairmont Hotel Vancouver is the city's grande dame, the Rosewood Hotel Georgia is its thoroughly modern, yet classically styled counterpart. First opened in 1927, the hotel underwent a complete multi-year renovation that stripped it down to its bricks and mortar. Reopened in 2011, it features some of the city's most impressive design, replicating the Roaring Twenties in stylishly modern fashion. Even the most basic room starts at 325 square feet and features a massive bathroom with a walk-in rainforest shower. The per-night price can skyrocket in the summer months (welcome to Vancouver!), but it's worth it for a splurge. The clubby **1927 Lobby Lounge** is a local go-to for cocktails downtown (try the incredible Moscow Mule), while the fourth-floor **Reflections: The Garden**

Terrace is one of Vancouver's best-kept secrets. Just don't tell anyone we told you, okay?

801 W. Georgia St. www.rosewoodhotels.com/en/hotel-georgia-vancouver. ℂ **604/682-5566.** 156 units. Suites from $334, higher in-season. Parking $49, valet only with in-out privileges. **Amenities:** Restaurant; lounge; cafe; speakeasy (Thurs–Sun); garden terrace; babysitting & children's amenities; concierge; fitness center; spa; pool; Wi-Fi (free).

The Sylvia Hotel ★★ A local favorite, this 1912 building started out as an apartment building and was turned into a hotel in 1936. Several rooms and suites have kitchens, a nice touch if you're staying for more than a day or two. The location can't be beat: across the street from English Bay and just a short walk into Stanley Park. Locals come for the delicious Sunday brunch, and Vancouverites can always be found in the window-lined bar sipping cocktails with names like "The Vancouver." The staff is super-friendly, and the rates are quite reasonable, though it's worth noting that the rooms aren't air-conditioned and you'll have to leave the old-school room key at the front desk every time you leave. Still, you'll want to book pretty far in advance: The Sylvia has a loyal clientele that returns year after year.

1154 Gilford St. on English Bay. www.sylviahotel.com. ℂ **877/681-9321** or 604/681-9321. 120 units. Doubles $169–$229; suites $219–$450. Parking $15. **Amenities:** Restaurant; lounge; Wi-Fi (free).

Where to Dine

Vancouver's food scene is almost overwhelming, with authentic cuisines from almost every corner of the globe paired with plenty of Canadian and North American favorites. If you've always wondered what "fusion" cuisine is, it's on full display here thanks to the city's vibrant immigrant culture. Our only suggestion: Eschew the larger, internationally known chain restaurants for something local and unique. Each neighborhood has something different to offer.

Bao Bei ★★★ CHINESE It can be hard to choose a restaurant to dine at in Vancouver's vibrant Chinatown, but Bao Bei, a "Chinese Brasserie," stands out from the crowd. It's been a crowd-pleaser since it opened a few years ago, and its popularity has never waned. The menu is designed around small plates to share, but when you find one you like, such as the steamed pork dumplings or kick-ass house fried rice, you'll end up ordering one just for yourself. No reservations are accepted, so prepare to wait at the bar, which serves up creative cocktails like Cheung Po the Kid, a concoction of rum, Dubonnet, pomegranate molasses, and homemade Chinese plum bitters.

163 Keefer St. www.bao-bei.ca. ℂ **604/688-0876.** Walk-in only; no reservations. Main dishes $10–$22. Tues–Sat 5:30pm–midnight.

Joe Fortes Seafood and Chop House ★★★ SEAFOOD A landmark for locals and tourists alike, Joe Fortes has been garnering awards—for its food, its wine list, and its oysters—for over 3 decades. The bar here is hugely popular and attracts a young and prosperous local crowd, some of whom come to smoke cigars in the covered rooftop garden, high above Robson Street (an excellent spot for people-watching). Inside it's all about dark wood and seafood—including up to a dozen types of oysters on the menu daily (order them raw or cooked). Joe's Seafood Tower on Ice, with oysters, lobster, crab, clams, mussels, tuna, prawns, and scallops, is a thing of beauty.

777 Thurlow St. www.joefortes.ca. © **604/669-1940.** Reservations recommended. Most main courses $23–$50. Daily 11am–11pm.

Rogue Kitchen & Wetbar ★★ CONTEMPORARY   Sometimes, you just want a good meal and a cool atmosphere that doesn't come with a hefty bill. Rogue Kitchen & Wetbar at Waterfront Station (just a 2-minute walk from Canada Place) is just that: a trendy restaurant where locals go for good drinks and tasty, uncomplicated cuisine like beer-battered fish and chips, lobster mac & cheese, and a wild-salmon sandwich. Beer lovers, rejoice: A great menu offers beers from British Columbia, Canada, and all over the world. It's also a convenient stop for those exploring the city by SkyTrain or SeaBus, which connect at Waterfront Station.

601 West Cordova St., inside Waterfront Station. www.roguewetbar.com. © **604/678-8000.** Most main courses $15–$30. Sun–Mon 11:30am–11pm; Tues–Thurs 11:30am–midnight; Fri–Sat 11:30–1am.

Tojo's Restaurant ★★ JAPANESE/SUSHI   Hidekazu Tojo is a cult figure in Vancouver, and the accolades and awards his restaurant has received from around the globe are well-earned. A diner's best bet is to choose the *omakase* option (loosely translated as "Chef, I'm in your hands") and let the chefs show off their creativity using the day's fresh ingredients and your personal preferences. If you can't handle the price tag—unlike the occasional Hollywood celebrities, Japanese businesspeople, and well-heeled local crowd that frequent the place—you can still see what the fuss is about by going a la carte. Don't leave without checking out the menu of hot and cold sakes.

1133 W. Broadway. www.tojos.com. © **604/872-8050.** Reservations required for Omakase Bar. Omakase meals $80–$150 and up. A la carte menu of hot dishes $28–$55. Mon–Sat 5–9:30pm.

QUICK hits: 24 HOURS IN VANCOUVER

1. Head to Canada Place. You'll want to walk west to view the **2010 Olympic Cauldron,** located on the west side of the **Vancouver Convention Centre.**
2. Visit **Water Street.** Spend some time exploring the cool shops of **Gastown,** including its **Steam Clock** and statue of **"Gassy" Jack Deighton.**
3. Do lunch in **Chinatown.** While in the neighborhood, spend some time in quiet contemplation at the **Dr. Sun-Yat-Sen Garden.**

4. Take a walk in Stanley Park. You can get there via public transit, a taxi, or one of the **Vancouver Trolley Company's** hop-on, hop-off buses. If you're in the park around 5:30 or 6pm you can catch views of the cruise ships sailing past the **Brockton Point Lighthouse** at the western edge of the park.
5. Cocktails and views: Either cab or stroll the seawall over to **English Bay,** and end your evening with a cocktail at the **Sylvia Hotel.**

Tuc Craft Kitchen ★★★ INTERNATIONAL   Tucked away (pun intended) in an area of West Cordova Street that would have been considered sketchy a decade ago, Tuc Craft Kitchen epitomizes both the changing nature of Vancouver's much-maligned Downtown Eastside (Tuc sits on its western fringe) and the uniqueness of the city's vibrant food scene. Seasonally changing menus use locally sourced ingredients to create a unique take on international dishes, like the seafood tamarind bisque and the crispy pork curado. On weekends, be sure to stop by for brunch for a Tuc Mimosa (made with Summerhill Organic Cipes from BC's Okanagan Valley) and the sinfully delicious crispy chicken and waffles. You'll need reservations: This cool, funky restaurant usually fills up to capacity.

60 West Cordova St. www.tuccraftkitchen.com. ⓒ **604/559-8999.** Reservations recommended. Most main courses $18–$40. Daily from 5pm till late; Wed–Fri 11:30am–2:30pm; Sat–Sun 10am–2:30pm.

SEATTLE

Starting your journey to Alaska in the lower 48 is more popular than ever, with an estimated 218 vessel calls and 1 million passengers moving through Seattle in 2017. With seven cruise lines serving the city's two terminals, cruise options abound. And with a growing, vibrant city right at your fingertips, Seattle is a wonderful place to spend a few days before or after your trip.

Seattle's nickname, the Emerald City, is well deserved, where acres of parkland and plenty of evergreens keep the city green and lush year-round. Situated on Elliott Bay, with Lake Union dominating the center of the city and Lake Washington its eastern border, water activities are a must-do when visiting—even if there's only time to dine alfresco along the shores. In addition to outdoor activities, Seattle has museums and attractions for every interest, luxury and local shopping, historical sites, and fabulous dining and nightlife.

Seattle's **Bell Street Pier Cruise Terminal** is centrally located at Pier 66 along the waterfront, while the **Smith Cove Cruise Terminal** is about 10 minutes from the downtown core, though it isn't within walking distance. Either way, staying in the downtown core provides the easiest opportunities for exploring the city.

The **Seattle Waterfront,** in addition to the cruise terminal, is an almost 2-mile stretch of both touristy attractions and authentic gems. Seawall construction, which started in 2013, is ongoing, though waterfront businesses remain accessible. Start your waterfront stroll at Pier 54, home to **Ivar's Acres of Clams,** a long-time-favorite casual seafood spot that recently received a total remodel. Also on this pier, **Ye Olde Curiosity Shop** is a mix of touristy kitsch and oddball museum, with things like shrunken heads and a mummy. If you'd like to get out on local waters in a guided cruise, Pier 55 is home to **Argosy Cruises,** while Pier 57 holds the **Seattle Great Wheel** (buy tickets online to skip the ticket line) and new attraction **Wings Over Washington,** an indoor ride dubbed "Seattle's Flying Theater." The **Seattle Aquarium** on Pier 59 is a worthwhile trip (see "Attractions Within Walking Distance," below) as

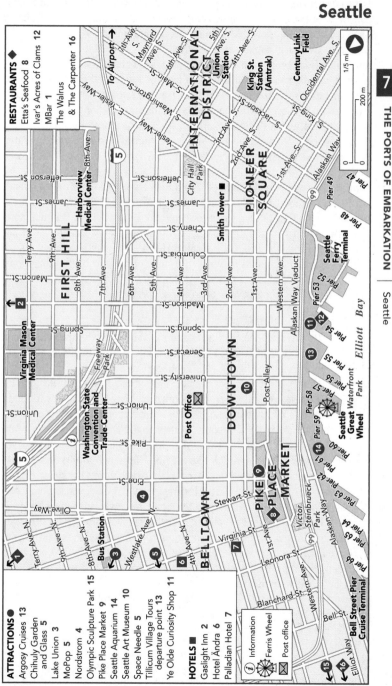

Seattle

RESTAURANTS ◆
Etta's Seafood **8**
Ivar's Acres of Clams **12**
MBar **1**
The Walrus
& The Carpenter **16**

ATTRACTIONS ●
Argosy Cruises **13**
Chihuly Garden
and Glass **5**
Lake Union **3**
MoPop **5**
Nordstrom **4**
Olympic Sculpture Park **15**
Pike Place Market **9**
Seattle Aquarium **14**
Seattle Art Museum **10**
Space Needle **5**
Tillicum Village Tours
departure point **13**
Ye Olde Curiosity Shop **11**

HOTELS ■
Gaslight Inn **2**
Hotel Ändra **6**
Palladian Hotel **7**

ⓘ Information
✸ Ferris Wheel
☒ Post office

is the northern end of the waterfront—here find the **Olympic Sculpture Park,** part of the Seattle Art Museum, with walking paths and sculptures from the likes of Louise Bourgeois, Alexander Calder, and Beverly Pepper.

Seattle Center is another spot worth visiting. Connected to downtown via the Seattle Center monorail, it's an easy trip (located about a mile from downtown, it's also a pleasant walk). If you haven't yet visited the **Space Needle,** a trip to the Observation Deck is fun to experience at least once. Another spot worth a visit is **Chihuly Garden and Glass,** home to the long-term exhibition of Dale Chihuly, renowned glass artist. (Save a little money by buying combo tickets for both attractions—and save even more if you visit before 10am.) Also here, check out **MoPOP** (formerly the EMP Museum)—see "Attractions Within Walking Distance," below.

Seattle is a city of neighborhoods, so if time allows, visit one or two outside the downtown core. Two excellent options are **Capitol Hill,** east of downtown (walk there via Pike or Pine streets or take Link Light Rail), or **Ballard,** north of downtown (if you don't have a car, King County Metro RapidRide D line runs from downtown to Ballard). Capitol Hill is a dense, urban neighborhood full of fantastic restaurants and bars and some of the best boutique shopping in the city, while Ballard has plenty of shopping and dining in historic buildings as well as an impressive lineup of small breweries.

Getting to Seattle

BY PLANE   **Seattle-Tacoma International Airport** (www.portseattle.org/seatac; ✆ 800/544-1965 or 206/787-5388), also known as **Sea-Tac,** is located about 14 miles south of Seattle. It's connected to the city by I-5. Generally, allow 30 minutes for the trip between the airport and downtown. Because the **Bell Street passenger ship pier,** also known as Pier 66, is superbly located a few minutes' walk from the heart of downtown, airport taxis will drop you at the terminal for about the same price as they would charge to go to any of the major Seattle hotels. A **taxi** between the airport and downtown will cost you between $40 and $50; to Smith Cove Cruise Terminal at Terminal 91, it's about $55. **Seattle Downtown Airporter** (www.downtownairporter.com; ✆ 425/981-7000), part of **Shuttle Express** (www.shuttleexpress.com), provides service between all the airport terminals and eight downtown hotels 24 hours a day. Vehicles leave the airport every 30 minutes during peak times; for service outside peak times or transportation from your hotel to the airport, call ahead to reserve a spot. Fares start at $18 one-way and children 17 and under are free, one with each paying adult. The company also offers shuttles to and from the cruise terminals (round-trip service from the airport to and from the pier is $44 per person). The cheapest option is **Link Light Rail** (www.soundtransit.org; ✆ 888/889-6368), with stops at the airport and downtown Seattle, plus destinations in between and beyond. Adult one-way fares are $3 between downtown and the airport.

BY CAR   The major freeway running through Seattle is **I-5.** Follow it south from downtown to Sea-Tac. I-5 runs north to the Canadian border, which leads, ultimately, to the road to Vancouver. Alaskan Way, a busy street, runs along the waterfront and past the newly expanded Bell Street Cruise Terminal. For Terminal 91, you'll head toward Magnolia Bridge. It's only a very short car or cab ride from any city hotel to the cruise terminals, which are no more than 10 minutes from even the most distant of the hotels listed here. If you're driving, parking is available at both terminals. Bell Street parking is $18.02 per day (plus tax), with a $1 discount per day if you book online (**www.cruise seattleparking.com**). Smith Cove is $21.31 per day (plus tax), with $1 off per day if you book online (**www.cruiseseattleparking.com**).

Exploring Seattle

INFORMATION   Seattle's visitors' bureau, **Visit Seattle,** operates a visitor information center in the Washington State Convention Center, 800 Convention Place, Galleria Level, at the corner of 7th Avenue and Pike Street (www. visitseattle.org; ✆ **206/461-5840** or 866/732-2695). It's open 9am to 5pm Monday through Friday and summer weekends.

GETTING AROUND   Nearly every major car-rental company has an outlet at Sea-Tac, and many companies also have offices in downtown hotels. Prices depend on the season and even on the day of the week (rentals on Fri, for example, when cruise passengers are likely to arrive in large numbers, will probably cost more than on, say, Wed). You can rent a car considerably cheaper if you look at locations beyond the airport. That said, if you're staying within the confines of downtown, a car is more of a liability than a plus because parking is very expensive. **Seattle Metro** (http://metro.kingcounty.gov; ✆ **800/542-7876** or 206/553-3000) operates buses in the downtown area and throughout King County. The standard fare is $2.50 to $3.25 for adults, $1 for seniors. Other options include **Like Light Rail,** with three stops downtown as well as service to Capitol Hill, the University of Washington, and points south of downtown including Pioneer Square, the International District, and the sports stadiums. Fares vary depending on distance traveled, with adult fares ranging from $2.25 to $3.25. The **Seattle Streetcar** (www.seattlestreetcar.org; ✆ **206/553-3000** has two separate lines, one running from downtown to South Lake Union and the other from Pioneer Square to Capitol Hill with stops in the International District and Central District. Fares are $2.25 adults and $1 seniors, with day passes available for $4.50 and $2, respectively.

ATTRACTIONS WITHIN WALKING DISTANCE
Chihuly Garden and Glass ★★★   The long-term exhibition space of world-renowned glass artist (and Tacoma native) Dale Chihuly is a visual feast of color. Find pieces both inside and outside in the landscaped garden, and take time to gaze up in the glass house, which features a 100-foot-long suspended sculpture. The space also features some of Chilhuly's private collections and an on-site restaurant, **Collections Café,** serving lunch and dinner.

305 Harrison St. www.chihulygardenandglass.com. ✆ **206/753-4940.** Admission $29 adults, $22 seniors, $18 kids 5–12, free children 4 and under. Early admission discount available. Mon–Thurs 8:30am–8:30pm; Fri–Sun 8:30am–9:30pm.

MoPOP ★★★ Find all things pop culture at this museum in Seattle Center. Originally known as the Experience Music Project, or EMP (the Frank Gehry–designed building was inspired by the rock-and-roll experience), the museum's new name now references the collection's focus on pop culture. Inside, exhibits range from a look at Jimi Hendrix's travels abroad and indie video games to horror movies and the Science Fiction Hall of Fame. Recent traveling exhibits have included "The Jim Henson Exhibition: Imagination Unlimited" and "What's Up, Doc? The Animation Art of Chuck Jones."

325 5th Ave. N. www.mopop.org. ℂ **206/770-2700.** $28 adults ($26 online), $25 seniors and students with ID ($23 online), $19 children 5–17 ($17 online), free for children 4 and under. Summer daily 10am–7pm; winter daily 10am–5pm.

Nordstrom ★★ Shoppers from around the world come to Seattle to pay homage to the original Nordstrom department store in the heart of downtown. It recently got a facelift, and now features **Habitant,** a casual bar and lounge on the third floor as well as two restaurants and a coffee bar. After shopping (including the ever-changing Pop-In@Nordstrom shop), go for a little relaxation at the Spa Nordstrom day spa. John W. Nordstrom founded the company in 1901 as a shoe store—and the women's shoe selection remains fabulous.

500 Pine St. http://shop.nordstrom.com. ℂ **206/628-2111.** Mon–Fri 9:30am–9pm; Sat 10am–9pm; Sun 10am–7pm.

Pike Place Market ★★★ Begun in 1907 by just eight farmers selling produce from their wagons, Pike Place Market is one of Seattle's most enduring institutions and a major tourist draw. In 2017, the brand-new **Market-Front** opened, adding even more room for restaurants, retail, and vendors. The market remains one the best places in the city to find fresh produce and seasonal specialties such as Rainier cherries, Washington asparagus, fresh king salmon, and Northwest hazelnuts. Make sure you go there hungry: You won't want to miss the multiple chances to snack. We highly suggest that you don't leave without trying a Dungeness crab cocktail, a fresh-baked cinnamon roll or *piroshki* (Russian meat pie), and, of course, coffee from any number of vendors, including the *original* Starbucks. Explore the shops underground, where you'll find wonderful specialty stores, including indie book publisher Chin Music Press and the flagship retail store of Eighth Generation, featuring work from Native American artists in a variety of forms (think wool blankets, jewelry, and fine art). At night the vendors clear out, but several excellent restaurants, bars, and theaters in the market keep it hopping.

Btw. Pike and Pine sts. at 1st Ave. ℂ **206/682-7453.** Daily 9am–6pm; individual businesses and restaurants may vary.

The Seattle Aquarium ★★ This fun spot on the waterfront features six major exhibits, with the interactive tide pool the perennial favorite, especially for kids. Other exhibits describe Puget Sound's underwater world, from otherworldly octopuses and jellyfish to adorable otters and seals. Each

September, visitors can watch salmon return up a fish ladder to spawn, an amazing sight.

1483 Alaskan Way, Pier 59, Waterfront Park. www.seattleaquarium.org. © **206/386-4300.** Admission $29.95 adults, $19.95 children 4–12, free for children 3 and under. Daily 9:30am–5pm.

Seattle Art Museum ★★★   Art fans will want to devote many hours to this top-flight museum, known as "SAM," where the collections include everything from African masks to Old Masters to Andy Warhol. The 40-foot-long sculpture "Middle Fork" from John Grade greets visitors, and the thought-provoking art continues throughout the building. Plan to devote at least some of your stay to the museum's impressive collection of Northwest Coast Native art.

1300 1st Ave. www.seattleartmuseum.org. © **206/654-3100.** Admission (suggested donation) $19.95 adults, $17.95 seniors, $12.95 students and children 13–19, free for children 12 and under; free to all 1st Thurs of month. Wed, Fri–Mon 10am–5pm (closed Tues); Thurs 10am–9pm.

Smith Tower ★★   Built in 1914, the Smith Tower was Seattle's first skyscraper and the tallest building west of the Mississippi. A recent renovation included the creation of a speakeasy-style bar in the observatory plus a small gift shop on the main level. The observatory's open-air viewing area gives visitors a 360-degree view of the city, while the bar features dishes like oysters, ceviche, and crab cakes as well as barrel-aged cocktails, beer, and wine.

506 Second Ave. www.smithtower.com. © **206/624-0414.** Admission $19 adults; $15 seniors, children, and military; save 10% when buying online. Sun–Wed 10am–11pm; Thurs–Sat 10am–12am.

The Space Needle ★★   Seattle's iconic landmark, the Space Needle, offers stunning views 518 feet above ground level from its observation deck, where high-powered telescopes let you focus in on distant sights. Be sure to check out the **SkyPad,** a 20-foot-by-8-foot touchscreen filled with Space Needle history and fun facts. The building is also home to **SkyCity,** a revolving restaurant. Renovations of both the restaurant and the observation deck began in fall 2017 and are scheduled for completion in summer 2018—check the website or call ahead for the latest information about any closures.

6th Ave. and Broad St. www.spaceneedle.com. © **206/905-2100.** Admission $29 adults, $22 seniors, $18 children 4–12, free for children 3 and under. Early and late admission discounts available. Mon–Sun 8am–midnight.

ATTRACTIONS BEYOND THE PORT AREA

Tillicum Village/Tillicum Excursion ★   Tillicum Village was built in conjunction with the 1962 Seattle World's Fair. The "village" is actually a large restaurant and performance hall fashioned after a traditional Northwest Coast Indian longhouse. Though it sounds cheesy, totem poles stand vigil out front, the forest encircles the longhouse, the waters of Puget Sound stretch out into the distance, and it's simply a beautiful spot. Since it's located at Blake Island State Marine Park across Puget Sound from Seattle, it's only accessible by tour boat or private boat. **Argosy Cruises** operates trips that include a scenic boat ride to and from the island, a lunch or dinner of alder-smoked salmon, and a performance by traditional masked dancers—members of 11 Northwest tribes. After the meal and dance performance, you can wander along forest trails to explore the island.

1101 Alaskan Way, Pier 55. www.argosycruises.com. ☎ **206/623-1445.** Admission/4-hr. tour $84 adults, $75 seniors, $32 children 4–12, free for children 3 and under (advance ticket discount available online).

BEST CRUISE-LINE SHORE EXCURSIONS

Seattle City Tour (4 hr.; $75–$100 adults, $45–$60 children): A basic spin around Pike Place Market, the World's Fair site, downtown Seattle, Lake Union, and more, offered by virtually all cruise lines. May include a stop at the Space Needle.

Seattle Underground Tour (4 hr.; $69 adults, $42 kids): A little history and a good share of tall tales are presented on this fun tour. It starts at a restored 1890s saloon, takes you literally under the streets of Pioneer Square, and includes a view of an original Crapper (toilet) imported from England. See what remained after the Great Seattle Fire of 1889; learn how mud on city streets was sometimes deep enough to consume dogs and small children; and hear about how the Yukon Gold Rush brought 100,000 adventurers to town. The tour ends at an underground gift shop.

Woodinville Wine Country (5 hr.; $100): Visit a couple of Woodinville's outstanding wineries, including the gorgeous Chateau Ste. Michelle. Sample red and white wines, and see if you find a new favorite. Minimum age: 21.

EXCURSIONS OFFERED BY LOCAL AGENCIES

Argosy Cruises (www.argosycruises.com; ☎ **206/623-1445**) has a variety of short cruises around the Seattle area, including a **Harbor Cruise** (for the best views, sit on the starboard side!), a cruise through the **Hiram Chittenden Locks to Lake Union,** and cruises around **Lake Washington** (which, among other things, take you past the fabled Xanadu, built by Bill Gates on the shore of Lake Washington). Cruises depart from Pier 55. Tickets for the 1-hour Harbor Cruise are $27 for adults, $22 for seniors, $13 for children 4 to 12, and free for children 3 and under; the 2½-hour Locks Cruise costs $44 for adults, $39 for seniors, $20 for children 4 to 12, and free for children 3 and under; and the 1½-hour Lake Washington cruise is $32 for adults, $27 for seniors, $13 for children 4 to 12, and free for children 3 and under.

Emerald City Trolley (www.emeraldcitytrolley.com; ☎ **855/313-3456**) is a hop-on, hop-off tour. Stay on the trolley for a 15-stop, 1½-hour narrated tour of some of Seattle's top landmarks or hop off at any stop to explore before catching another trolley to continue the tour. Stops include the Space Needle, Pike Place Market, and Pioneer Square. The popular Northwest Seattle tour includes stops at Gas Works Park, the Fremont Troll, the Ballard Locks, and the Kerry Park Overlook. Tickets for the downtown hop-on, hop-off tour are $34 for adults, $28 for seniors, and $20 for children 3 to 12; the Northwest Seattle tour is $28 for adults, $24 for seniors, and $17 for children 3 to 12.

Where to Stay

Gaslight Inn ★★★ This cozy eight-room Capitol Hill B&B, built in 1906, is a nice alternative to a big, bustling hotel and offers a chance to unwind before or after your cruise. Rooms are comfortably appointed (though two do share a bath), with lots of wood and eclectic artwork collected over the years by the innkeepers. Enjoy a continental breakfast before heading out for the day to Pike Place Market and other Seattle sites. Come evening, a dip in the heated pool (in season) or a glass of wine in the living room makes you feel as if you're staying at a good friend's house.

1247 15th Ave. www.gaslight-inn.com. ℂ **206/325-3654.** 8 units. $148–$208 (2 rooms have shared bath). **Amenities:** Seasonal heated pool; Wi-Fi throughout hotel (free).

Hotel Ändra ★★★ This Art Deco hotel is located in the trendy Belltown neighborhood, within minutes of Pike Place Market, the Seattle Art Museum, and downtown shopping. The 1926 classic brick and terra-cotta building has been updated to contemporary environs via a combination of traditional Northwest style (lots of wood and stone) and high-tech comforts. Frette towels and plump goose-down pillows and comforters are welcome luxuries. Not one but two amazing restaurants call the hotel home. **Lola,** run by top chef Tom Douglas, features the classic produce of the Pacific Northwest mixed with the cooking styles of Greece, while **Assaggio** offers bold, robust central and northern Italian cuisine.

2000 4th Ave. www.hotelandra.com. ℂ **877/448-8600** or 206/448-8600. 119 units. $189–$589 double. Valet parking $39. **Amenities:** 2 restaurants; concierge; exercise room; room service; Wi-Fi (free).

Palladian Hotel ★★★ This circa-1910 building was recently renovated to create this gorgeous boutique hotel. Moody decor inspired by old books is carried throughout the halls and into the rooms, with custom beds featuring a bookshelf headboard. Bath amenities from Atelier Bloem and celebrity pillows (think Brad Pitt in 19th-century military garb) mean luxury comes with a side of humor. **Shaker and Spear,** the on-site restaurant, serves comforting seafood, while the **Pennyroyal Bar** evokes a sophisticated speakeasy.

2000 2nd Ave. www.palladianhotel.com. ℂ **206/448-1111.** 97 units. $175–$295 double; $255–$495 suite. Valet parking $39. **Amenities:** Restaurant; cocktail bar; fitness center; evening social hour; PUBLIC bikes available for use (free); Wi-Fi (free for Kimpton Karma Reward members; $12.99/24 hr. for non-members).

Where to Dine

Etta's Seafood ★★★ SEAFOOD Fresh, fresh, fresh. With picture windows looking out at Pike Place Market, you'll probably be able to see some of the vendors from whom this seasonal menu is sourced. Chef/owner Tom Douglas serves what is arguably the best seafood in town—his signature crab cakes (crunchy on the outside, creamy on the inside) are worth the trip alone. The Etta's Salmon dish is so popular it has inspired its own line of spice rub

QUICK hits: 24 HOURS IN SEATTLE

1. Start your stay at the market. Get to the **Pike Place Market** early for coffee at the original Starbucks before perusing vendors and retail shops.

2. Do some beach time. Hop aboard the **King County Water Taxi** (www.kingcounty.gov/watertaxi; ✆ **206/684-1551**) to **Alki Beach** to check two things off your list: a ferry ride on Elliott Bay and an unbeatable view of the skyline from **West Seattle.** Wander the walking path along the beach for a late lunch—try the Hawaiian-Korean fusion cuisine at the casual **Marination Ma Kai** (www.marinationmobile.com; ✆ **206/328-8226**) or the first-rate seafood at **Salty's on Alki** (www.saltys.com; ✆ **206/937-1600**).

3. Head up the **Space Needle.** The observation deck at Seattle's iconic building has a 360-degree view of the city at 520 feet and is easily worth the cost of admission.

4. See breathtaking sculpture from Dale Chihuly both inside and out at the **Chihuly Garden and Glass. Tip:** Save on admission to the Space Needle and Chihuly Garden and Glass by purchasing a combo ticket from either attraction.

5. End the day with a show: The **Paramount** (www.stgpresents.org; ✆ **206/682-1414**) or **5th Avenue** (www.5thavenue.org; ✆ **206/625-1900**) theaters are home to musicals, including traveling Broadway shows, while the **Can Can** (www.thecancan.com; ✆ **206/652-0832**) in Pike Place Market has fun cabaret shows. Find a variety of musical acts at the **Triple Door** (www.thetripledoor.net; ✆ **206/838-4333**) or enjoy jazz at **Dimitriou's Jazz Alley** (www.jazzalley.com; ✆ **206/441-9729**). Both spots have dinner service, too.

and sauce now sold in markets. If you're not a seafood lover, other options include lamb T-bone, burgers, and salads.

2020 Western Ave. www.tomdouglas.com/restaurants/ettas. ✆ **206/443-6000.** Reservations recommended. Main courses $15–$36. Mon–Thurs 11:30am–9:30pm; Fri 11:30am–10pm; Sat 9am–3pm and 4–10pm; Sun 9am–3pm and 4–9pm.

Mbar ★★★ ECLECTIC   A relative newcomer, this South Lake Union rooftop spot is the ultimate in dining with a view. See downtown Seattle, the Space Needle, the Olympic Mountains, and more while enjoying dishes from executive chef Jason Stratton (whom you may remember as a contestant on season 13 of *Top Chef*). Pacific Northwest ingredients dominate the ever-changing menu, with dishes like Pacific octopus and spicy fried potatoes and tagliatelle with huckleberry marinara. Reservations for the main dining room are available, though the patio is first-come, first-served.

400 Fairview Ave. N. www.mbarseattle.com. ✆ **206/457-8287.** Main courses $26–$34. Mon–Tues 4–9pm; Wed–Thurs 4–10pm; Fri 4–11pm; Sat 5–11pm; Sun 5–9pm.

The Walrus and the Carpenter ★★★ SEAFOOD   If you're looking to enjoy fresh oysters while in Seattle, this restaurant from James Beard–award-winning chef Renee Erickson is one of the best places to go. Located in the historic Ballard neighborhood, the cozy spot always has a variety of fresh Pacific Northwest oysters on tap. The menu changes frequently to reflect what's in season, but expect salads, seafood dishes like steamed clams and smoked herring terrine, and a couple of meat dishes. This spot doesn't take reservations, so try to get here early to avoid a long wait.

4743 Ballard Ave. NW (about 4 mi. from the Port of Seattle). www.thewalrusbar.com. *©* **206/395-9227.** Main courses $13–$16, oysters market price. Daily 4–10pm.

JUNEAU

Because Juneau is also a major port of call, see the Juneau section in chapter 8 for a map and information on attractions and tours.

Getting to Juneau

BY PLANE   Juneau is served by **Alaska Airlines** (www.alaskaair.com; *©* **800/252-7522**) with daily nonstop flights from Seattle and Anchorage. Delta Airlines also has nonstop service from Seattle in summer. Because weather can wreak havoc with landing conditions, it's especially advisable, if you're flying to Juneau, to get there a day or two before your embarkation date.

BY BOAT   The vessels of the **Alaska Marine Highway,** commonly known as the **Alaska Ferry** (www.dot.state.ak.us/amhs), link Juneau with Alaska, British Columbia, and U.S. gateways as far south as Bellingham, Washington, but unless you have 2 or 3 days to spare, you probably won't use that service to get to your ship.

BY CAR   You can't drive to Juneau (there are no roads to the outside world) or get there by train. That leaves you with airplanes or long boat trips, period.

Exploring Juneau

INFORMATION   The **Travel Juneau Visitor Center** is right at the newly redone ship pier and boasts exterior tiles designed to resemble fish scales and an inside designed to look like a fishing ship (www.traveljuneau.com; *©* **888/586-2201** or 907/586-2201). It's open May through September daily 8am to 5pm. There is also a visitor kiosk at Marine Pier.

GETTING AROUND   A cab from the airport to downtown will cost about $25. The **Capital Transit city bus** (*©* **907/789-6901**) leaves the airport at 11 minutes and 27 minutes past the hour on weekdays only from 7:11am to 6:27pm (heading downtown) and costs $2 for adults and $1 for children; your luggage has to fit under your seat or at your feet. Ask the driver for the stop closest to your hotel; you may need a short cab ride from there. The passenger cruise-ship pier is right in town and an easy walk. However, with baggage it might be necessary to take a taxi, which shouldn't cost more than $8. Major car-rental companies have offices at the airport.

Where to Stay

Four Points by Sheraton ★★   This waterfront hotel has contemporary guest rooms with amenities that include 42-inch flatscreen TVs, free Wi-Fi, and Keurig coffee machines. Book a room in front for views of the Gastineau

Channel and cruise ships (less-expensive rooms have mountain or city views). Rooms are 100% smoke-free. The lively sports bar, **McGivney's Sports Bar & Grill,** is open for lunch and dinner (and breakfast, too).

51 Egan Dr. www.fourpointsjuneau.com. ⓒ **866/716-8133** or 907/586-6900. 106 units. $175–$269 double. Free parking and free airport transfers. **Amenities:** Restaurant/bar; business center; fitness center; room service; Wi-Fi (free).

The Jorgenson House ★★★

Staying in this luxury B&B in a historic home in a quiet Juneau neighborhood is worth the splurge not only for the gorgeous decor and surrounds but to chat with delightful owner Renda Heimbigner, a third-generation Juneauite. The house was built in 1915 by her uncle, Bill Jorgenson, at the height of the Klondike Gold Rush. He was president of the Alaska historical society, and his collection of vintage photos, artifacts, and artworks are on display throughout the home. A devoted foodie, Renda serves divine home-cooked breakfasts (included) in a glass solarium with views, and also recently started an on-site cooking school.

435 Alder St. (uphill, take a taxi). www.jorgensonhouse.com. ⓒ **907/723-4202.** 4 rooms. $399 double. Two-bedroom apartment $495. Rates include three-course breakfast. **Amenities:** Complimentary cookies and coffee/tea; Wi-Fi (free).

Prospector Hotel ★

It's nothing fancy, but this comfortable waterfront hotel is right next to the new Alaska State Museum. The hotel offers affordable rates on large standard rooms and suites, some with views of the water and small-ship pier, many with kitchenettes. It has a friendly staff and a fun pub called **T.K. Maguire's** serving steaks, seafood, and bottomless portions of fries.

375 Whittier St. www.prospectorhotel.com. ⓒ **800/331-2711** or 907/586-3737. 62 units. $129–$209 double. Free parking. **Amenities:** Restaurant; bar; Wi-Fi (free).

The Silverbow Inn ★★

The highlight of this boutique inn, run by a husband-and-wife team, is a hot tub on a deck overlooking downtown Juneau. The building dates to mid-1914, but it's gotten a very contemporary redo. Guests are treated to a complimentary full breakfast. Rooms are done up in a cheerful modern decor; bathrooms are oversize, and beds have 450-thread-count sheets. A special Family Room (queen bed, futon, and upper bunk) sleeps five.

120 Second St. (a hike uphill into downtown from the pier). www.silverbowinn.com. ⓒ **907/586-4146** or 800/586-4146. 11 rooms. $129–$289 double. Rates include full breakfast. Off-street parking (on a limited basis). **Amenities:** Hot tub; nightly Cookie & Cocoa Happy Hour; 24-hour coffee, tea, and snacks; Wi-Fi (free).

Where to Dine

See also **Tracy's King Crab Shack, Deckhand Dave's,** and **The Hangar on the Wharf** in chapter 8.

Red Dog Saloon ★ BREWPUB

Past the GENTS CHECK YOUR SIDE ARMS, LADIES WELCOME sign and the red swinging doors is a rowdy, fun atmosphere and decent pub grub (including Angus beer burgers and Alaskan clam chowder). The history of this place dates to the city's mining heyday. The Red Dog Saloon has sawdust on the floor and a frontier atmosphere complete with ragtime music and tall tales. Just don't expect a quiet meal. Around the corner (on Manila Square) is a huge Red Dog souvenir shop.

278 S. Franklin St. www.reddogsaloon.com. ✆ **907/463-3658.** Main courses $10–$15. Summer Mon 11am–11pm; Tues–Sun 9am–11pm.

The Rookery Café ★★ SEAFOOD/INTERNATIONAL   The pride of Juneau, Chef Beau Schooler is a James Beard Foundation award nominee. By day, the restaurant is an elevated coffee/sandwich shop, and at night locals and visiting foodies come for the small and large plates, such dishes as homemade ramen noodles, beef cheeks, crudo, salmon collars, and house-pickled beets and tomatoes, featuring locally sourced ingredients. The menus change regularly. Sitting at one of the long communal tables encourages conversation (but show up for dinner early—the place often sells out by 6pm).

Fun fact: Chef Schooler won the **Great American Seafood Cook-Off** in 2015, an honor bestowed 2 years later in 2017 on fellow Juneau chef Lionel Udippa, who works just a block away at fine-dining venue SALT. More attention for the Juneau foodie scene!

111 Seward St. http://therookerycafe.com. ✆ **907/463-3013.** Main courses $9–$17 (lunch), $15–$34 (dinner). Mon–Fri 7am–9pm; Sat 9am–9pm; closed Sun.

Twisted Fish Company ★★ SEAFOOD/GRILL/PIZZA   Cruise passengers flock to this lively, casual restaurant, probably because it's right at the cruise-ship pier. But it also does a great job with dishes such as salmon tacos and pizzas topped with salmon. If you want to get fancy, order the salmon on a silver plank or steak. Try to snag one of the tables with views of the Gastineau Channel. Beer selections from the Alaskan Brewing Company are on tap.

550 S. Franklin St. (behind Taku Smokeries). www.twistedfishcompany.com. ✆ **907/463-5033.** Main courses $14–$45 dinner. Daily 11am–9:30pm.

QUICK hits: 24 HOURS IN JUNEAU

1. Stroll the **sea walk** looking for jumping salmon and watch the ships come in. At the **Taku Fisheries,** commercial fishermen upload fish on a conveyer belt.
2. Take the MGT Blue Glacier Express bus from the ship pier to **Mendenhall Glacier** and hike one of the trails (the 3½-mile Eastern Glacier Loop if you have time).
3. Head back to town and do lunch at **Tracy's King Crab Shack** or **Deckhand Dave's,** both featuring local seafood (see chapter 8).
4. Do some **museum hopping:** We highly recommend a visit to the new **Alaska State Museum** in particular.

While you're there, check out the reasonably priced gift items at the nearby **Juneau Arts and Humanities Council** and the selection of authentic Alaska Native artwork, both traditional and contemporary, in the shop at the **Sealaska Heritage Cultural Center** in the Walter Soboleff Building.

5. Relax over a craft cocktail at **The Narrows,** or with views at **the Hangar on the Wharf.**
6. Head out on an evening whale-watch tour, or join a communal table for dinner at **The Rookery,** where the kitchen is overseen by James Beard award nominee Chef Beau Schooler.

WHITTIER

A bit of a peculiar place (which, here, is meant as a compliment—and could be said of many an Alaskan town), Whittier is cut off from the rest of Alaska by a 2½-mile tunnel cut into a mountain. The multipurpose one-lane tunnel is for both cars and trains. This marvel of engineering makes for some interesting challenges for those who live in town—as well as the thousands (and thousands) of people who explore Prince William Sound by kayak or boat. The last chance for cars to head into Whittier is at 10:30pm each night, and the last opening for cars heading back out to the Seward Highway is at 11pm. So, yeah, if you miss the chance to go through the tunnel, you have to make wherever you are your temporary home (a constant challenge for Whittier residents). But it's not just locals, day-trippers, and kayakers who pass through Whittier; it's also the go-to town for many cruise ships. Many ships disembark in Whittier and send passengers up to the big city by train or bus.

Now back to that bit about Whittier being a peculiar place: Most of the townspeople (218 at last count) live in a 14-story concrete building, **Begich Towers,** built by the U.S. Army. It has a grocery store on the first floor and a medical clinic on the third. The police department and post office are in the building, too. Begich Towers was built during the 1940s, when Whittier's strategic location on the Alaska Railroad and at the head of an ice-free deep fjord made it a key port in the defense of Alaska. The City of Whittier was incorporated in 1969. Today, with its barren gravel ground and ramshackle warehouses and boat sheds, the town maintains a stark military-industrial character. Consider the town's look as part of its charm. Kids don't even have to go outside to get to school—a tunnel leads from Begich to the classroom. It's so very Alaska—though many of the state's residents give the idea of living there some serious side-eye. Most Alaskans like their space—something Whittier residents don't really have.

Whittier doesn't have quite as many in-town to-dos as other Alaskan cities, but it's still a fun place to stop by for a bit. And if you're a fan of kayaking or fishing, get thee there, ASAP. You can take a water taxi out to Prince William Sound, one of Alaska's true treasures.

Getting to Whittier

BY PLANE   Fly to the **Ted Stevens International Airport** in Anchorage, then drive 60 miles south (app. 1½ hours). You're best off booking a transfer through the cruise line to get there.

BY BUS   The **Magic Bus** departs from the Anchorage Museum of History and Fine Art (at 7th and A sts.) at 3pm on most Whittier ship days (Saturdays and alternating Mondays and Wednesdays), and arrives in Whittier some 90 minutes later. Luggage is limited to two bags per passenger (extra luggage is allowed on a space-available basis, for an extra fee). The trip costs $65 adults, $33 kids, each way. For reservations, go to www.alaskatravel.com/bus-lines/anchorage-whittier.html or call ✆ **800/208-0200.**

BY CAR   It's possible to drive to Whittier from Anchorage by way of the Portage Glacier Highway through the Anton Anderson Memorial Tunnel at

Whittier

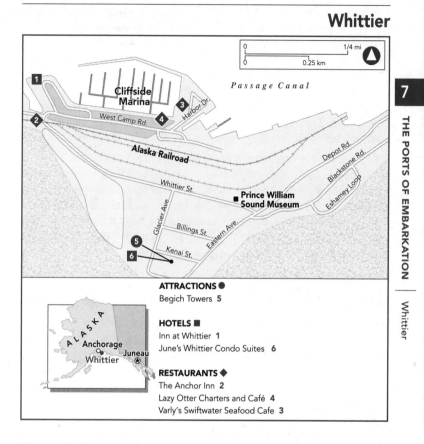

ATTRACTIONS ●
Begich Towers 5

HOTELS ■
Inn at Whittier 1
June's Whittier Condo Suites 6

RESTAURANTS ◆
The Anchor Inn 2
Lazy Otter Charters and Café 4
Varly's Swiftwater Seafood Cafe 3

Whittier. ***Be forewarned:*** Although, theoretically, Whittier is only a couple hours' drive or train ride from Anchorage, the journey can take much, much longer. That's because the tunnel on the outskirts of town is shared by both cars and trains, and while one is using it, the other can't. Get the schedule through the tunnel website (www.dot.state.ak.us/creg/whittiertunnel/schedule.shtml), through its phone recording (© **877/611-2586** or 907/566-2244), or by tuning in to 1610AM in Portage or 530AM in Whittier. The toll for cars is $13. Overnight parking in Whittier is $12 per day.

BY RAIL   You can get to Whittier from Anchorage on the Alaska Railroad (www.alaskarailroad.com; © **800/544-0552** or 907/265-2494). The one-way fare is $83 for adults and $42 for children ages 2 to 11. The dock is near the mouth of Whittier Creek. Nothing in Whittier is more than a 5-minute walk away. Don't look for taxi ranks or free shuttles—you won't need them.

Exploring Whittier

INFORMATION   For information about Whittier, there are three go-to resources: the **city government** © **907/472-2327,** ext. 101 (or by e-mail, info@whittieralaska.gov); the **Greater Whittier Chamber of Commerce** (www.whittieralaskachamber.org); and **Travel Alaska,** the state's tourism arm (www.travelalaska.com). The people at the harbormaster's office are also helpful and maintain public toilets and showers; it's the only two-story building at the harbor (© **907/472-2327,** ext. 110 or 115). Inside the cruise terminal, brochures promote area tour operators and the like.

GETTING AROUND   You can walk everywhere, but there's also a cab or two in town. Look for them when you get off the boat or train if you don't want to schlep your luggage around.

ATTRACTIONS WITHIN WALKING DISTANCE

Everything is easily accessible on foot. Visit the yacht harbor and the town's apartment building, and stop by the small, charming, and info-packed **Prince William Sound Museum** at the **Anchor Inn ★** (see listing under "Where to Dine," below), for a few exhibits highlighting the city's military and civilian history (suggested donation $3 for adults, $1.50 for children 12 and under).

ATTRACTIONS BEYOND THE PORT AREA

You can take the **Alaska Railroad** train (www.alaskarailroad.com; © **800/544-0552** or 907/265-2494) straight to Anchorage. It's a fun scenic ride (one-way $83 for adults, $42 for children 2–11, free for kids 1 and under).

BEST CRUISE-LINE SHORE EXCURSIONS

Shore excursions are only offered in Whittier in combination with transfers to Anchorage for pre- or post-cruise tours, or for those with evening or nighttime flights from Ted Stevens Anchorage International Airport (in which case you'll be dropped off at the airport after your tour).

Portage Glacier Scenic Cruise & Drive (4½ hr.; $115): Before you head home, there's an opportunity to see one more glacier, even if it's on the small side. This tour takes you to scenic Portage Lake and the Begich, Boggs Visitor Center in the Chugach National Forest, where you'll learn that the Portage Glacier is in retreat and no longer visible from the visitor center. No worries—your tour also includes a boat ride for a close-up view of the ice (from about 300 yards away). Don't nap on the motorcoach on the way to the airport or you'll miss some great mountain views.

EXCURSIONS OFFERED BY LOCAL AGENCIES

Several companies offer day trips to Prince William Sound's western glaciers. Besides the incredible scenery, the water is calm, making seasickness unlikely—for the queasy, this is a much better choice than Kenai Fjords National Park. Departures are timed with the daily Alaska Railroad train from Anchorage, described above, which means you'll have up to 6 hours for the trip. Some visitors see as much as possible, while others savor the scenery and wildlife sightings.

   Phillips Cruises and Tours (www.phillipscruises.com; © **800/544-0529** or 907/276-8023) has 2 day-cruise options out of Whittier on three-deck, high-speed catamarans. A 5-hour, 26-glacier cruise of the sound on the 338-passenger *Klondike Express* is $159 for adults, $99 for children 12 and under. A 3¾-hour cruise to the giant waterfalls of beautiful Blackstone Bay on the 149-passenger *Glacier Quest* costs $109 for adults, $69 for kids. Both cruises are narrated by rangers from the U.S. Forest Service and hot lunch is included.

Major Marine Tours (www.majormarine.com; ℂ **800/764-7300** or 907/274-7300) operates a 166-passenger vessel at a slower pace than Phillips' catamarans—it visits fewer glaciers, but spends more time waiting for them to calve. The route goes up Blackstone Bay, and the boat is comfortable, with reserved table seating. Food costs extra; the all-you-can-eat salmon and prime rib buffet is $19 ($9.50 for children). The trip lasts 4½ hours; the price is $119 for adults, $59.50 for children 12 and under.

Lazy Otter Charters (www.lazyottercharters.com; ℂ **800/587-6887**) offers kayak rentals (2-day minimum required; 2-day rentals $100 for a single kayak, $180 for a double kayak). The company also does escorted kayaking adventures on Prince William Sound, a full-day, 8- to 9-hour tour ($325 per person) including a water taxi ride to Blackstone Bay, lunch, and paddles past icebergs to two glaciers (Blackstone and Beloit).

Where to Stay

Inn at Whittier ★★★ This 25-room property is as good as it gets in Whittier; it's the fancy place in town, complete with an 150-seat restaurant. (But no need to pack your tux: Alaska fancy means you're still welcome to wander around in your casual kayaking gear or whatever makes you comfy.) The timber-framed structure has a lighthouse design in the center. Pick the view you want, whether the waters of Prince William Sound or a backdrop of mountains; both are impressive. You'll have the modern comforts: TV and free Internet access, and junior suites come with Jacuzzi tubs. If you splurge on one of the two-story townhouse suites, you get both a Jacuzzi and a fireplace (it is, after all, a pretty romantic spot—especially on a moody-weather night), perfect for those seeking a romantic interlude. The restaurant serves three meals a day, with lighter fare (including sandwiches) at lunch, and a seafood focus

QUICK hits: 24 HOURS IN WHITTIER

1. Grab some breakfast (and the town's best coffee drinks) at **Lazy Otter Charters and Café,** while you peruse the company's options for a day on the water. Don't miss the cinnamon rolls, which, if you're an early riser, should still be hot from the oven.

2. Take a guided kayak adventure. **Lazy Otter** (yes, the breakfast place) offers a full-day water taxi and kayaking trip. The escorted trip includes the water taxi and kayak rental, gear, guide, and lunch.

3. Relax over dinner at the **Inn at Whittier.** Take the edge off the soreness you built up while paddling (and, yes, it's totally worth it) with dinner and drinks at the inn.

(including Alaskan crab and salmon) at dinner. With fishing a popular visitor pastime, the chef is ready, willing, and able to prepare your catch on request.

5A Harbor Loop Rd. www.innatwhittier.com. © **907/472-3200**. 25 units. $149–$199 double; $180–$299 suite. Free parking. **Amenities:** Restaurant; tavern with fireplace; high-speed Internet (free).

June's Whittier Condo Suites ★   June's is the only B&B in Begich Towers, where everybody in town lives. Unless someone who lives in the town invites you to stay with them, it's the best way to get a taste of true Whittier life. The units come with views of the harbor, Billings Glacier, or the mountains, and all have full kitchens. Because you are staying in condos, features vary (check descriptions online). One unit comes with a desktop computer you can use; another has a sauna. Some have Wi-Fi. Most units sleep up to six people. It has a free shuttle to the harbor. Also in the building are a laundry, a grocery store, a nondenominational church, a video rental shop, and even a tanning bed.

100 Kenai St. www.juneswhittiercondosuites.com. © **888/472-6001** or 907/841-5102 (cellphone). 12 units. $165–$275 double. Free parking. **Amenities:** Wi-Fi (in some; free).

Where to Dine

Most dining spots in Whittier are for people who just want to grab a sandwich while passing through.

The Anchor Inn ★ AMERICAN   You will rub shoulders with fishermen and other colorful locals when you visit this casual spot, a combination restaurant, grocery store, laundromat, and bar (with live entertainment). The menu is simple: burgers, seafood, fried chicken, and steak. It has a few rooms available for overnight guests and also houses the small **Prince William Sound Museum ★**, highlighting the history of Whittier.

100 Whittier St. www.anchorinnwhittier.com. © **907/472-2354** or 877/870-8787. Main courses lunch $6–$12, dinner $12–$21. Open daily 7am–10pm.

Varly's Swiftwater Seafood Cafe ★★★ SEAFOOD   This small, friendly seafood shack on the water—across from the ferry dock in the area known as the Triangle—is a good enough reason on its own for a visit to Whittier. The menu features freshly caught halibut, cod, and shrimp straight from Prince William Sound, hand-battered, fried to perfection, and served with fries in plastic baskets. Ship and other maritime photos adorn practically every inch of the walls. Casual and kid-friendly, the place is run by the Varlamos family, operator as well of the town's pizza shop and ice cream parlor—you can even have a handmade pizza delivered here. Start your meal with homemade clam chowder or tomato-based seafood chowder and finish off with amazing rhubarb crisp. Choose from a selection of 30 imported and domestic beers or wine. Grab a seat outdoors on the deck to watch the goings-on in the harbor.

Across from the ferry dock, at the Triangle. www.swiftwaterseafoodcafe.com. © **907/472-2550**. Main courses $10–$18. Sun–Thurs 11:30am–9pm; Fri–Sat 11:30am–10pm.

THE PORTS & GLACIERS

Whether you are traveling on an Inside Passage or Gulf itinerary, you will likely call at two or more of the most popular Alaskan ports: Ketchikan, Juneau, and Skagway. You will also find yourself staring in awe at a glacier, either in Glacier Bay, Hubbard Glacier, or College Fjord. All are magnificent. Your itinerary may include the Russian-heritage town of Sitka, just outside the Inside Passage, and the lovely Canadian city of Victoria.

Some of the big-ship cruise lines offer longer cruises (for more details, see chapter 5) that allow additional exploration to less-visited areas, such as the classic Alaskan town of Haines. Small-ship lines can access certain regions more easily, thanks to their shallow drafts, and they also have the flexibility to visit smaller towns such as Wrangell and Petersburg and wilderness areas, including on shorter itineraries (for more details, see chapter 6).

See chapter 4 for details on shore excursions and tips on debarkation, what to bring along with you while you're ashore, and little matters such as not missing the boat. *Note:* Shore-excursion prices for children apply to ages 12 and under unless otherwise noted.

The "A Day in" feature in this chapter is a new addition to this book, and highlights favorite things to do in each port—both ours and local experts who were kind enough to share their favorites.

VICTORIA, BRITISH COLUMBIA

Although it's not in Alaska, the Canadian city of Victoria is a popular stop for cruises to Alaska departing from Seattle and San Francisco. The capital of British Columbia, Victoria is located on the southernmost tip of Vancouver Island, affording it some of the nicest weather on the coast, with one of the most charming inner harbors around. Framed by British Columbia's stately Parliament Buildings, Victoria has a healthy dose of all things British, from a spectacularly cozy pub scene to the grandeur of proper afternoon tea at the iconic **Fairmont Empress Hotel.** Farther afield, nearly a million visitors flock to **Butchart Gardens** each year to see its incredible floral displays.

Cruise ships don't dock directly in the Inner Harbour (see "Coming Ashore," below), but it's a pleasant if not downright enjoyable 30-minute walk, or a quick taxi ride, away. A stroll from the Ogden Point Cruise Terminal through the stately neighborhood of James Bay reveals the city's charmingly preserved heritage homes and immaculately kept streets, many of which are littered with local cafes, unique restaurants, and old-school corner stores. In fact, it's a good idea for any visitor to leave the more touristy downtown core in search of the real Victoria. Clean, safe, and filled with friendly locals, Victoria is a fantastic city to explore on foot by day and night.

Of course, there's plenty to see and do right by the picturesque Inner Harbour, too. Drinks in one of the Victorian-themed pubs, all of which offer locally produced beers on tap, is practically a requirement for any first-time visitor. You can zip around the harbor on the small green ferries that have been here for decades, or stop by one of the local arts-and-crafts markets in nearby **Bastion Square,** the entrance to which is marked by a commemorative arch (at View and Government sts.) that marks the location of the original Fort Victoria. Hardly a weekend in the summer goes by without local markets popping up. Take the time too to call on **Munro's Books** (1108 Government St.; www.munrobooks.com; ℂ **250/382-2464**), which was founded in 1963 by Jim Munro and his wife, award-winning Canadian author Alice Munro, and occupies an opulent space designed in 1909 for the Royal Bank of Canada.

For photographic opportunities—not to mention stalls selling tasty fish and chips—stop by **Fisherman's Wharf,** a neighborhood of colorful floating homes and buildings. Or head over to the historic Steamship Terminal, where the **Robert Bateman Centre** houses galleries devoted to the work of acclaimed Canadian wildlife artist Robert Bateman (http://batemancentre.org; ℂ **250/940-3630;** admission $10 adults, $8.50 seniors, $8.50 student 19+ with valid ID, free for youth 6–18 July/Aug, children 5 and under free; open daily 10am–5pm). You might even catch sight of Black Ball Line's **MV Coho,** which has been sailing from its dock adjacent to the Steamship Terminal to Port Angeles, WA, daily since 1959.

It's also nice to get out of Victoria for the day, especially if you've seen the main sights before. **Fort Rodd Hill** and **Fisgard National Historic Lighthouse** are situated in nearby Colwood and provide some amazing views of Washington State's Olympic Mountains across the strait. Or rent a car and take the 40-minute drive east to the pretty town of **Sidney,** which boasts an interesting collection of trails, local artisans, and bookstores.

COMING ASHORE   Spectacular as it would be to dock in Victoria's Inner Harbour, it's too small for major cruise ships, which tie up instead at the Ogden Point Cruise Terminal on the western edge of the city. It's about a mile into town, so if you don't mind a stretch of the legs, hang a right onto Dallas Road from the dock and then walk left on Oswego Street or Menzies Street, and you'll find yourself in the heart of the action—right on the Inner Harbour (both streets empty out near the British Columbia Parliament Buildings). If you have more time, take the Harbour Walk (well-marked from the ship

Victoria, British Columbia

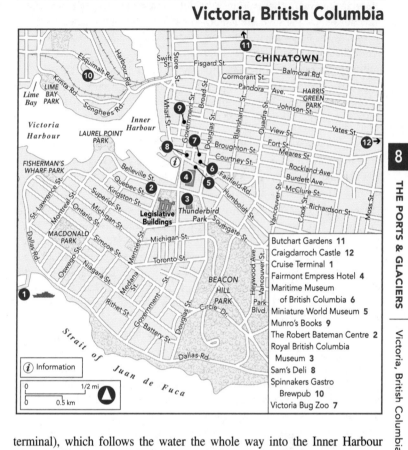

Butchart Gardens **11**
Craigdarroch Castle **12**
Cruise Terminal **1**
Fairmont Empress Hotel **4**
Maritime Museum
  of British Columbia **6**
Miniature World Museum **5**
Munro's Books **9**
The Robert Bateman Centre **2**
Royal British Columbia
  Museum **3**
Sam's Deli **8**
Spinnakers Gastro
  Brewpub **10**
Victoria Bug Zoo **7**

(i) Information

0 ———— 1/2 mi
0 ———— 0.5 km

terminal), which follows the water the whole way into the Inner Harbour (about a 40-min. walk). Shuttle buses from the cruise pier to the Fairmont Empress are $10 round-trip, half price for children 5 to 11, and free for children 4 and under. On the waterfront, flowers, milling crowds, and street performers—including, usually, a lone bagpiper—enliven the scene, and nearly all of Victoria's must-see gems are within easy walking distance.

Beautifully maintained, old wooden water taxis operated by **Victoria Harbour Ferry** ($6 each way; www.victoriaharbourferry.com; ✆ **250/708-0201**) ply the Inner Harbor. Catch one at Fisherman's Pier, about a 10-minute walk from the Ogden point terminal (with a stop near the Empress Hotel). It's worth taking a jaunt out on these fun little boats, even if you're going nowhere! Be sure you (and your camera) are prepared to take lots of pictures: Victoria's Inner Harbour is one of the most photogenic sights on the planet.

When planning your day in Victoria, it makes good sense to have a look at your cruise schedule. Some lines call here for an entire day, while others stop in Victoria for an evening only, typically from 6pm to midnight. Victoria is still enormously walkable (and safe) at night, but some attractions may be closed in the evening hours. Having said that, most of the big tourist-oriented attractions know the ships are in port, and will stay open for them.

Note: Rates below are in Canadian dollars. At press time, the conversion to U.S. dollars was C$1 = US$.79. Shore excursions are priced in U.S. dollars.

INFORMATION You'll typically see cruise-ship greeters handing out maps at the pier, but if not, pick up a city map at the **Tourism Victoria Visitor Information Centre** (www.tourismvictoria.com; *©* **250/953-2033**), on the waterfront at 812 Wharf St (open daily 8:30am–8:30pm May to Sept).

Best Cruise-Line Shore Excursions

Note that shore excursion prices quoted here are representative of what's available, but may differ slightly among cruise lines.

English Tea at Butchart Gardens (4 hr.; $119 adults, $79 children): The bus makes the 13-mile trip from the ship to one of Victoria's premier attractions, Butchart Gardens. Nestled in near Brentwood Bay, the 131-acre grounds showcase vibrant, amazing floral displays. Enjoy an elegant traditional afternoon tea with finger sandwiches, scones, and cream and all kinds of goodies, along with honest-to-goodness brewed English tea, served in the stately confines of the original Butchart family home. Note that tours of Butchart Gardens are typically also offered without the traditional afternoon tea option at a slightly reduced price.

Victoria by Horse-Drawn Trolley (1½ hr.; $60 adults, $30 children): It's the most touristy option, but there's no getting around the appeal of this romantic way to see the sights of Victoria. Expect a moderately paced tour of the Inner Harbour, Chinatown, the historic James Bay residential area, and Beacon Hill Park. Evening tours are particularly attractive—the Parliament Buildings switch their decorative lights on at dusk.

Victoria Pub Tour (3½ hr.; $99 adults only): Victoria is the craft-beer capital of British Columbia, and this tour, mostly on foot, takes visitors to several of the city's favorite watering holes to sample the local brews. *Note:* Minimum age is 19.

Excursions Offered by Local Agencies

Several local operators greet passengers right at the pier, offering rides into the city and longer tours using various modes of transportation. **Classic Car Tours** (www.classiccartours.com; *©* **250/383-2342**) gives tours in classic convertibles (perfect on a sunny day), with commentary that is both colorful and delightful. Tours start at $200 per car, for up to four passengers; prebooking is a good idea.

The bicycle rickshaws operated by **Victoria Pedicab Company** (www.victoriatours.net; *©* **250/884-0121**) are an unusual way to get around the city for about $60 per hour (for two people); from the ship pier to the downtown area, the standard charge is about $36 (for two people). A special 2½-hour package designed specifically for guests visiting by cruise ship is $90 and includes pickup from Ogden Point. Advance reservations are a must.

Gray Line Victoria (www.sightseeingvictoria.com; © 855/385-6553 or 250/385-6553) provides an express shuttle bus to Butchart Gardens (including admission), leaving from the Fairmont Empress Hotel 10 times a day from June to September beginning at 9am ($74 adults, $45.92 children 13–17, $26.09 children 5–12, free for kids 4 and under). The company also operates a 90-minute hop-on, hop-off double-decker bus tour that makes a number of stops in and around the city including Craigdarroch Castle ($40 adults, $28 youth, $15 kids 6–12; free for kids 5 and under). Tours depart daily at 9:30am from the Fairmont Empress Hotel; advance reservations aren't a bad idea.

Whale-watching cruises are another popular Victoria diversion; you can book one with **Prince of Whales** (www.princeofwhales.com; © 888/383-4884). A 3-hour tour in an open, Zodiac-style boat is $120 for adults, $95 students 13 to 17, and $85 children 8 to 12 (tour not available for kids 7 and under), with departures every half-hour in summer. If you don't want to get wet, or if you want to bring the kids, closed-boat whale-watching tours aboard the *Ocean Magic II* are available for the same price, and children under 7 are welcome. On closed-boat tours, kids up to 4 years of age sail free, and three departures (9am, 12:15pm, and 3:30pm) are offered July 1 to August 31.

On Your Own: Within Walking Distance

British Columbia Parliament Buildings ★ Built between 1893 and 1897 by the man who would go on to design the Empress Hotel (Francis Rattenbury), British Columbia's Parliament Buildings dominate Victoria's Inner Harbor. You can tour the attractive home of the Provincial Government's Legislative Assembly for free, either as part of a guided tour or a self-guided walk. Maps and guides are offered in several languages, and tours are conducted 7 days a week during the summer months.

501 Belleville St. www.leg.bc.ca/content-peo/Pages/Public-Tours.aspx. © **250/387-3046.** Free. Guided and self-guided tours Mon–Fri 9am–5pm year-round; weekend guided tours late May to early Sept only.

The Fairmont Empress Hotel ★★★ It's a splurge, but **afternoon tea** at this classic 1908 hotel has become a time-honored tradition that's been made all the better by the hotel's recent multimillion-dollar refit. Dress up a bit (the dress code bans torn jeans, short shorts, jogging pants, and tank tops) and head into the beautifully opulent (and wonderfully renovated) **Lobby Lounge,** overlooking the Inner Harbour, for a spread that includes—in proper British style—little tea sandwiches, raisin scones with heavy cream and strawberry preserves, and extravagant pastries (from the hotel's award-winning pastry chef). Choose from 21 different loose-leaf teas, including the exclusive Empress Blend. It's all served with pomp and circumstance, as befitting a price tag of $75 per person, or $108 per person accompanied by a glass of Veuve Cliquot champagne. You'll definitely need reservations.

721 Government St. www.fairmont.com/empress. © **250/384-8111,** or 250/389-2727 for tea reservations. Daily seatings 11am–6pm.

Maritime Museum of British Columbia ★   In its new digs on Humboldt Street (almost literally across from Miniature World, below), this maritime museum is fun for all ages. In addition to housing artifacts from ships of historic importance on the B.C. coast, interactive exhibits give visitors the chance to try their hand at tying marine knots or sending Morse code signal flag messages. The museum's permanent collection houses dozens of models of West Coast ships; featured exhibits include the search and discovery of the 19th-century Franklin Expedition's HMS *Erebus* on the Arctic seabed by Parks Canada in 2014. In 2018, a new exhibit will mark the centenary of the sinking of the Canadian Pacific steamship SS *Princess Sophia*, which foundered with great loss of life after being stranded on Vanderbilt Reef near Juneau as she made her way south to Vancouver in the fall of 1918.

634 Humboldt St. http://mmbc.bc.ca/. © **250/385-4222.** Admission $10 adults, $8 seniors and students, $5 youth 12–17, children under 12 free. May–Sept daily 10am–5pm.

Miniature World Museum ★   Marketed as "The Greatest Little Show on Earth," this quirky museum offers the world in miniature—as in dollhouse size. The collection has been continually updated over the museum's 40-plus years, and its quirky assortment of 80-plus displays include the building of the Canadian railway, the world's smallest sawmill, the world's largest dollhouses (purportedly), and the World of Dickens. It's located around the side of the Fairmont Hotel and is practically a Victoria icon.

649 Humboldt St. www.miniatureworld.com. © **250/385-9731.** Admission $15 adults, $11 seniors, $10 youths 12–18, $8 children 5–12 (under 5 free). Summer daily 9am–9pm (until 5pm in Sept).

Royal British Columbia Museum ★★★   The royal title of this major provincial museum was approved by Queen Elizabeth II and bestowed by Prince Philip in 1987. Far from boring, this spectacularly engaging museum covers everything from British Columbia's recent past to its First Nations cultures and the region's natural history, from prehistoric to present-day. Immersive backdrops and clever use of elaborate sets and sound effects re-create these unique periods well. Spend time checking out the extensive collection of artifacts, masks, and carvings in the **First People's Galleries.** The Old Town exhibit in the **Modern History Gallery** re-creates Victoria in its frontier days. The museum complex includes **Thunderbird Park,** with totem poles and a ceremonial house; **Helmcken House,** once the home of a pioneer doctor and one of the oldest houses in B.C.; and a **Native Plant Garden,** with more than 400 species. There's also an **IMAX theater** and an eclectic selection of featured exhibits that changes seasonally.

675 Belleville St. www.royalbcmuseum.bc.ca. © **888/447-7977** or 250/356-7226. Admission museum $22 adults, $16 seniors and youths 6–18, $16 students 19 and over with ID, free for children 5 and under. IMAX admission is extra. Museum open daily 10am–5pm.

Victoria Bug Zoo ★   If you are traveling with kids or just really into creepy-crawly things, this attraction takes you deep into the world of bugs.

You and your progeny will get to say eek while viewing hairy tarantulas and marvel at such creatures as giant walking sticks. It's all safe and fun. The zoo also features Canada's largest ant farm. Knowledgeable "bug guides" are on hand, and tours are conducted throughout the day. If you plan to visit with more than eight people, you'll need a reservation.

631 Courtney St. www.victoriabugzoo.ca. ℂ **250/384-2847.** Admission $12 adults, $8 seniors and students with ID, $8 youths 5–17, free for children 4 and under. Summer months Mon–Fri 10am–4pm; Sat–Sun 10am–5pm.

On Your Own: Beyond the Port Area

Butchart Gardens ★★★   A ride by cab, public bus, or other transportation (see "Excursions Offered by Local Agencies," above) and several free hours are required for a visit to this world-renowned attraction and National Historic Site of Canada. Started over a century ago by Jennie Butchart, the gardens lie 14 miles north of downtown Victoria on a 131-acre estate and feature English-, Italian-, and Japanese-style plantings as well as water gardens and rose beds. Restaurants and a gift shop are on-site. *Note:* You can catch a public bus (BC Transit Route 75) from downtown Victoria for C$2.50 (cash only) each way. The trip takes a little over an hour, and the #75 picks passengers up northbound on Douglas Street at Fort Street, next to the RBC Royal Bank kitty-corner to the Bay Centre in downtown Victoria. A cab ride costs you about $55 each way and is some 40 minutes from the cruise pier.

800 Benvenuto Ave., Brentwood Bay. www.butchartgardens.com. ℂ **250/652-5256.** Admission $32.60 adults and seniors, $16.30 children 13–17, $3 children 5–12, free for children 4 and under. Mid-June to Sept 2 daily 8:45am–10pm; hours vary rest of year.

Craigdarroch Castle ★★   Climb the 87 steps to the tower at this Victorian-era castle and you'll be rewarded with excellent views of Victoria. The elaborate Scottish Highlands–style castle was built in the 1880s by Scottish immigrant Robert Dunsmuir, who made his fortune in coal. The 39-room mansion is topped with stone turrets, has nice examples of stained glass, and is lavishly furnished with Victorian goods. The location is about a half-hour walk from the inner harbor (you may want to take a cab from the pier).

1050 Joan Crescent. www.thecastle.ca. ℂ **250/592-5323.** Admission $14.25 adults, $13.25 seniors, $9.25 students 13 and over with valid ID, $5 children 6–12, free for children 5 and under. Mid-June to Labor Day daily 9am–7pm; rest of year 10am–4:30pm.

Where to Lunch

Sam's Deli ★ DELI   A Victoria staple, Sam's Deli has been serving up monstrous hand-made sandwich creations since 1972. A successive series of owners has kept this small and almost-always packed deli bursting with customers eager to get their hands on one of nine made-to-order sandwiches, including shrimp & avocado or Montreal smoked meat. If it's crowded, take your sandwich to go for a great picnic lunch on the Inner Harbour.

805 Government St. www.samsdeli.com. ℂ **250/382-8424.** Weekdays 7am–5pm, Weekends 7:30am–5pm.

Spinnakers Gastro Brewpub ★★★ BREWPUB Canada's first inhouse brewpub, Spinnakers is a must for microbrew fans, but it's also a decent spot for nondrinkers—especially given its waterfront deck. In addition to brewing hand-crafted ales, the gastropub makes its own malt vinegar (delicious on the flaky halibut or salmon fish-and-chips) and soda creations. Victoria's beer history, which dates to the early 1840s, can be traced via a self-guided Ale Trail map (available around town) that also takes you to other stops including the **Canoe Brewpub & Restaurant,** 450 Swift St. (www.canoebrewpub.com; ☏ **250/361-1940**), an easy walk from the harborfront and featuring live music at night; and **Buckerfield's Brewery** at the Swans Suite Hotel, 506 Pandora Ave. (www.swanshotel.com; ☏ **250/361-3310**), especially for their summer Raspberry Ale, made with local berries.

308 Catherine St. www.spinnakers.com. ☏ **877/838-2739** or 250/386-2739. Restaurant daily 8am–11pm; taproom daily 11am–11pm.

A Day in Victoria

If you've got a full day to spend in Victoria, start with a leisurely walk from the Ogden Point Cruise Terminal through the neighborhood of **James Bay** to admire Victoria's quaint, well-kept residential areas before arriving at the spectacular **Inner Harbour.** If you haven't already made reservations in advance, drop into the **Fairmont Empress Hotel** to inquire about availability for its popular **afternoon tea;** later times may have walk-in spots available. Continue down Government Street to take in Victoria's primary shopping district. Finish your day off sipping tea at the Fairmont Empress or with a visit to the **Royal British Columbia Museum,** or take a journey farther afield to **Butchart Gardens** before returning to your ship.

If your ship only calls here for an evening (say, from 6pm to midnight), a night visit to **Butchart Gardens** should be at the top of your list. Although you can travel there independently, the safer option is to book this tour through your cruise line (so that in the event of traffic congestion on the return journey, your ship will wait for you).

If you've already been to the gardens, take a taxi to the Inner Harbour and enjoy cocktails at the trendy new **Q Bar at the Fairmont Empress,** which features cool drinks and a respectable list of local craft beers served up in a funky space overlooking the **Inner Harbour.** Live music is offered here 7 days a week from 6pm to 10pm. If you feel like stretching your legs, stroll past the **British Columbia Parliament Buildings,** illuminated at night, and enjoy a quiet walk through James Bay back to your ship.

CANADA'S INSIDE PASSAGE

Canada's Inside Passage is simply the part of an Inside Passage cruise that lies in British Columbia, south of the Alaskan border and running to Vancouver. On big ships, the first day out of Vancouver (or the last day going south) is usually a day at sea. Passengers get the chance to enjoy the coastal beauty of the British Columbia mainland to the east and Vancouver Island to the west, including some truly magnificent scenery in Princess Louisa Inlet and Desolation Sound.

In most cases, that's all the ships do, though: pass by the scenery—much of it at night. In their haste to get to Ketchikan, the first stop in Alaska, they invariably sail right past much of the Canadian Inside Passage.

One of the Canadian Inside Passage's loveliest stretches is **Seymour Narrows,** 5 or 6 hours north of Vancouver, just after the mouth of the Campbell River. It's so narrow that it can be passed through only at certain hours of the day, when the tide is right, often late in the day or in the wee hours of night. On the long days of summer, it's often possible to enjoy Seymour Narrows if you're prepared to stay up late.

The U.S./Canada border lies just off the tip of the Misty Fjords National Monument, 43 sailing miles from Ketchikan (and 403 miles from Glacier Bay, for those who are keeping count).

KETCHIKAN

Ketchikan is the southernmost port of call in Southeast Alaska, about 700 miles northwest of Seattle. Its 13,000 residents sometimes refer to it as "the first city." That's not because it's the most important city, or that it's the biggest, or even that it was literally the first built. The nickname comes from the fact that Ketchikan is usually the first city visited by any ship, boat, or barge traveling up the Inside Passage out of Vancouver or Seattle.

This is a fun port to visit. It's a historic fishing village with quaint architecture, salmon fishing, the great scenery found in just about every Inside Passage community, and **totem poles**—lots and lots of totem poles. But there are two things you'll have to contend with in Ketchikan: weather and crowds.

Upon arrival at the dock, look for the **Liquid Sunshine Gauge,** which the city put up to mark the cumulative rainfall for the year, day by day. We once checked and saw that the mark showed over 36 inches—and it was only June. The average annual rainfall is about 160 inches (more than 13 ft.!), and in the rainiest years has even topped 200 inches. Precipitation is so predictable here that the locals joke that if you can't see the top of nearby Deer Mountain, it's raining; if you can see it, it's going to rain! We've been here on joyously sunny days, too, so our advice is: Come prepared and don't let the rain dissuade you from activities. By the way, don't think that all that rain means this is a cold, snowy place in winter—it's often warmer here than in Cleveland in January.

> ### Running in Rain Boots
>
> Ketchikan for nearly a year beginning in May 2013 held the Guinness World Record for largest rain boot (Wellington boot) race in the world—nearly 2,000 locals and visitors participated in the event.

As for crowds, in the cruise season downtown Ketchikan sees the arrival of up to 10,000 cruisers some days. Visitors overflow from the sidewalks onto the streets—which has led former Ketchikan Borough Mayor Joe Williams (see "Excursions You Can Book Yourself," below) to suggest that maybe

Ketchikan should give in and just close some downtown streets to car traffic in summer. The city has a completely different character in winter.

The first block or so of buildings close to the pier have a high concentration of trinket shops, 32 of which sell jewelry, staffed by seasonal workers. Downtown attractions include the **Great Alaskan Lumberjack Show** (the performers are competitive "timber athletes," not loggers; Alaska's last pulp mill, the **Ketchikan Pulp Mill,** closed in 1997); and **Duck Tours,** which take you on land and into the water on amphibious vehicles.

If the crowds get to you, wander away from the hubbub and you'll find there's a lot to like about this place. From up close—say, on Stedman Street—historic **Creek Street,** the centerpiece of downtown, still presents a very photogenic side. It's often said (perhaps only by the Ketchikan Chamber of Commerce!) that it's the most photographed street in Alaska. Photographers will want to get a shot. Creek Street comprises a row of historic buildings on pilings over a stream up which salmon swim in their spawning season. Today the narrow wooden sidewalk is lined mostly with tourist shops, boutiques, and galleries specializing in offbeat pieces. In the early 1900s, this was Ketchikan's red-light district, with more than 30 brothels lining the waterway; a small sign at the head of the street notes that this was where "both the fishermen and the fish went up the stream to spawn." The most famous of the courtesans (or, at least, the most enduring) was Dolly Arthur (born Thelma Dolly Copeland). Not the most successful—nor, according to pictures we've seen, the prettiest—working girl, she nevertheless outlived the rest. **Dolly's House,** 24 Creek St. (www.dollyshouse.com; © 907/225-6329), is now a small museum with a hokey "Red Light" video tour. Just like the house's old clientele, you'll have to pay to get inside. We don't know what they used to pay, but today it'll cost you $10 for a (wink, wink) "quickie" tour.

Ketchikan is still a strong center of the Tlingit, Tsimshian, and Haida cultures (about 20% of Ketchikan residents trace some lineage to the tribes). These Southeast Alaska Native peoples have preserved their traditions and kept their icons intact over the centuries. They've also re-created **clan houses** and made replicas of totem poles that were irretrievably damaged by decades of exposure to the elements. The tall hand-carved poles are everywhere—in parks, in the lobbies of buildings, in the street. It should be no surprise to anyone that there are more totems in Ketchikan than in any city in the world. Exploring the totem poles with an interpreter who can tell you stories associated with the poles is highly recommended. One of our favorite things to do in Ketchikan, besides booking a shore excursion and getting into the gorgeous surrounding natural areas, is to walk the few blocks from the ship to Creek Street and take the **funicular railway** ($3) to the **Cape Fox Lodge,** for views of the city, Tongass Narrows, and Deer Mountain (if you want to linger you can get a decent lunch at the hotel restaurant). It's also an easy walk from here to **Totem Heritage Center** (see p.245). To stretch your legs on the way back, take the **Married Man's Trail** from Park Avenue to Creek Street (the trail was once a muddy secret pathway to get to the "working" ladies, but is now a staircase and boardwalk), with a stop at the **Salmon Ladder.**

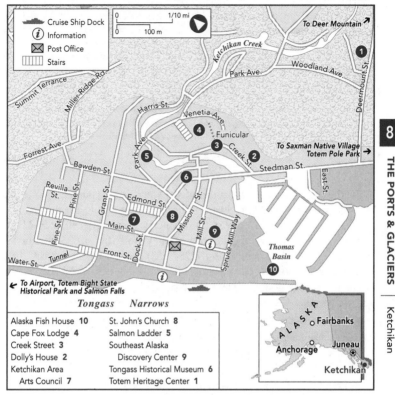

Legend	
Cruise Ship Dock	
(i) Information	
Post Office	
Stairs	

0 ─ 1/10 mi
0 ─ 100 m

To Deer Mountain ↗

Ketchikan Creek

Woodland Ave.

Park Ave.

Summit Terrance

Miller Ridge Rd.

Harris St.

Venetia Ave.

Forrest Ave.

Funicular

To Saxman Native Village
Totem Pole Park →

Park Ave.

Creek St.

Stedman St.

Bawden St.

Revilla St.

Pine St.

Grant St.

Edmond St.

Main St.

Mission St.

Mill St.

Spruce Mill Way

East St.

Thomas
Basin

Pine St.

Dock St.

Front St.

Water St.

Tunnel

← To Airport, Totem Bight State
Historical Park and Salmon Falls

Tongass   Narrows

Alaska Fish House **10**	St. John's Church **8**
Cape Fox Lodge **4**	Salmon Ladder **5**
Creek Street **3**	Southeast Alaska
Dolly's House **2**	Discovery Center **9**
Ketchikan Area	Tongass Historical Museum **6**
Arts Council **7**	Totem Heritage Center **1**

ALASKA

Fairbanks

Anchorage   Juneau

Ketchikan

8

THE PORTS & GLACIERS | Ketchikan

The city is enveloped in awe-inspiring wilderness. If nature is your thing, you will not be disappointed, whether you choose to get active kayaking or hiking or even snorkeling or sit back in a tour boat and let someone else do the heavy lifting. If you prefer to stay down by the pier, walk along the water-front to see the fishing boats. Ketchikan claims to be the "Salmon Capital of the World," and in fact, five species of wild Pacific salmon return from the ocean to creeks and streams near the town each year. The saltwater fishing is some of the best anywhere, and even if you don't try your own hand at reeling in the big one, it's fun to observe the fishing boats unload their catch.

While many of the shops downtown are operated by out-of-towners who only come here for the summer, there are some hidden gems, including the friendly hole-in-the-wall called **Salmon, Etc.** (www.salmonetc.com; ✆ **800/ 354-7256** or 907/225-6008), a few blocks from the ship pier at 322 Mission St., where you can buy cans of yummy smoked salmon. The locally owned shop has been in town since the early 1980s. Its smoked-fish products are so good, we always make a beeline here to buy a few cans to take home—at prices cheaper, by the way, than at the shops at Salmon Landing, a mini-mall closer

Ketchikan Story Project

Thanks to the Emmy Award–winning **Ketchikan Story Project,** visitors have an opportunity to dig deeper into the history and culture of this small city and its people. More than 300 residents were interviewed on or off-camera for the project, supported by the Ketchikan Visitor Bureau. Six short films focus on Native culture, fishing, aviation, logging, artists, and history. The free app (available at the App Store for iOS and Android) includes films, interviews, and an interactive town map to guide you to local attractions (it's worth downloading even if you're an armchair reader). Souvenir DVDs of the project are available for purchase at local retailers including **Parnassus Books,** 105 Stedman St. (✆ **907/225-7690;** $60 for a complete set of six). See the project online at **www.ketchikanstories.com.**

to the ship pier. Ketchikan has a decent arts scene, and a good place to check out what's new is the **Main Street Gallery** of the Ketchikan Area Arts and Humanities Council, 330 Main St. (www.ketchikanarts.org; ✆ **907/225-2211**). Among the town's excellent galleries are **Crazy Wolf Studio,** 633 Mission St. (www.crazywolfstudio.com; ✆ **907/225-9653**), owned by Tsimshian artist Ken Decker and his wife and featuring other artists as well; and **Arctic Spirit Gallery,** 318 Mission St. (www.arcticspiritgallery.com; ✆ **907/228-2277**), with a collection of handcrafted Native art from throughout Alaska.

COMING ASHORE   Ships dock right at the pier in Ketchikan's downtown area. Because half a dozen ships can be in port at one time, guardrails have been installed, and you'll need to cross to the town's main areas with a crossing guard.

INFORMATION   Our first stop in Ketchikan is usually the main office of the **Ketchikan Visitors Bureau,** located right on the dock, near Berth 2 (www.visit-ketchikan.com; ✆ **800-770-3300** or 907/225-6166). A summer satellite office is near Berth 3. At both you can pick up literature (including walking maps) and info on what's new in town (and get discount coupons for attractions). A city-operated **free shuttle bus** stops at all cruise berth areas and visits sights around downtown, including the Totem Heritage Center, which otherwise is about a 15-minute uphill walk.

Best Cruise-Line Shore Excursions

Bear Country & Wildlife Expedition (3½ hr.; $229): This extraordinary naturalist-led tour brings small groups at a time to the private Alaska Rainforest Sanctuary and the 1-mile trail that leads to a creek frequented by black bears in search of salmon. Viewing is from elevated areas that include a suspension bridge and tree platforms. You'll likely see bald eagles, too, with an opportunity to get up close with birds of prey at the Alaska Raptor Center. Minimum age is 12. (This tour operates only in the prime bear-watching period from late July through mid-Sept.) Pricier flightseeing tours to other bear-watching sites are also available (from $399 per person).

Lighthouse, Totems & Eagles (3 hr.; $119 adults, $65 children): On this award-winning tour you board either the *Totem Princess* or the *Lighthouse Endeavour* for a relaxing cruise to Totem Bight State Park (to view totem poles from the water), the Vallenar Rocks Wildlife Viewing Area (where you may spot deer and even bears), and past the historic Ward Cove cannery and Guard Island Lighthouse, with lots of opportunity for eagle-sighting along the way (binoculars provided). There's commentary about the region's maritime history, Tlingit culture, and timber and fishing industries, and they feed you too: A buffet aboard ship includes wild Alaskan salmon spread on crackers and other nibbles, plus really good hot chocolate.

Misty Fjords Flightseeing (2 hr.; $289 adults, $249 children): Everyone gets a window seat aboard the floatplanes that run these quick flightseeing jaunts over Misty Fjords National Monument. There are no ice fields and glaciers on this trip, but Misty Fjords has another kind of majesty: sparkling fjords, cascading waterfalls, thick forests, and rugged mountains dotted with wildlife. You'll come in for a landing on the fjord itself, or on a nearby wilderness lake. Once you've landed, you can get out and stand—carefully—on the pontoons to take pictures.

Mountain Point Snorkeling Adventure (3 hr.; $139): Believe it or not, you can snorkel around Ketchikan, where the climate is warm for Alaska. It's not the Caribbean, but the water isn't as cold as you think, and wetsuits are provided, as well as hot beverages for when you get out of the water. Undersea are amazing kelp with large fluttering leaves, fish, colorful starfish, sea urchins, sea cucumbers, and more.

Rain Forest Ropes & Zip Challenge (3½ hr.; $199): Traverse a zipline in harnesses between trees before rappelling to the ground. It's a new way to appreciate the Alaskan rainforest. This is real ziplining (unlike the offering in Icy Strait Point, which is more of a ride than ziplining). Instruction is given, and only minimal skill is required. A similar option is available in Juneau.

Tatoosh Islands Sea Kayak (4½ hr.; $179 adults, $105 children 8–12): There are typically two kayaking excursions offered in Ketchikan: this one (which requires you to take a van and motorized boat to the island before starting your 90-min. paddle) and a trip that starts from right beside the cruise-ship docks. Of the two, this one is far more enjoyable, getting you out into a wilder area rather than just sticking to the busy port waters. The scenery is incredible, and you have a good chance of spotting bald eagles, seals (whether swimming around your boat or basking on the rocks), and leaping salmon.

Totem Bight State Historical Park & Canoe Adventure (4 hr.; $139 adults, $99 children): This tour takes you by bus through the Tongass National Forest to see a historic Native fish camp, where a ceremonial clan house and totem poles sit amid the rainforest. You'll learn about the culture of the indigenous people and board a traditional 37-foot canoe for a paddle on nearby Lake Harriet Hunt.

Excursions You Can Book Yourself

A bevy of tour operators sell their excursions at the **Ketchikan Visitor Information and Tour Center** (✆ **800/770-3300** or 907/225-6166), right at the ship dock (near Berth 2). The best tour in town, if you can book it before it sells out, is by **Where the Eagle Walks** (www.wheretheeaglewalks.com; 3-hr. Ketchikan & Saxman tour $250 per person). Joe Williams, the 70-something former Ketchikan Borough Mayor, shares his insight into the community and especially the Native perspective as he takes you wandering around downtown and by van to the Native Village of Saxman, where he was born, raised, and lives and is the former Tribal President. You'll hear history, politics (ask him about Ketchikan's infamous "Bridge to Nowhere!"), folksy wisdom, and more on this enlightening jaunt. Williams also offers specialized tours in areas such as storytelling and the arts and will create custom tours on request; Princess Cruises taps him for downtown walking tours as well.

Allen Marine Tours (https://truealaskantours.com; ✆ **888/289-0081**) has cruises from Ketchikan to Misty Fjords National Monument on a high-speed catamaran built at the firm's own boatyard in Sitka. A 4½-hour tour is $199.95 for adults, $127 for children.

Alaska Travel Adventures (www.bestofalaskatravel.com; ✆ **800/323-5757** or 907/789-0052) operates several tours, including a Rain Forest Canoe & Nature Trail Adventure (3½ hr.; $99 adults, $74 children), where you board a 37-foot, 20-passenger canoe and paddle under the direction of an experienced guide on a secluded mountain lake, surrounded by Tongass National Forest. The tour includes a nature walk highlighting flora and fauna.

Southeast Sea Kayaks, (www.kayakketchikan.com; ✆ **800/287-1607** or 907/225-1258) offers guided paddle excursions (2½ hr.; $89 adults, $59 children 6–15) as well as rentals.

Baranof Fishing Excursions (https://exclusivealaska.com; ✆ **877/732-9453** or 907/225-4055), 3 Salmon Way (at the Alaska Fish House Marina), does fishing excursions from its own private marina; a 6-hour cruise in search of salmon and halibut, with all equipment provided, is $250 per person (plus the cost of a state fishing license); private charters are also available. Alaska Fish House will even cook your catch for you.

If you're looking to get totally zen with the wilderness, consider a 3½-hour hike with **Mindfulness Rainforest Treks** (http://www.teaguewhalen.com; ✆ **907/617-4854**). Local guide Teague Whalen takes up to seven visitors on a 2-mile walk through rainforest to the rural Coast Guard beach with views of Cleveland Peninsula, Prince of Wales Island, and sometimes whales. Tours are $100 adults, $70 for kids; for $20 you can add on a Tai-Chi or meditation focus.

On Your Own: Within Walking Distance

Creek Street ★★★ This former red-light district is now arguably Ketchikan's number-one tourist attraction. The view of Creek Street from the bridge over the stream on Stedman Street (the main thoroughfare) is striking, to say the least. Even allowing for a little Chamber of Commerce hyperbole, the "Most Photographed Street in the World" just might be!

Off Stedman St., along Ketchikan Creek.

St. John's Church ★ The oldest place of worship in town and its adjacent Seaman's Center—built in 1904 as a hospital and now a commercial building—are interesting examples of early-20th-century local architecture. As you stand at the church, look back toward the sea. Much of downtown is landfill; you used to be able to tie up your boat right near the church.

On Bawden St., at Mission St.

The Salmon Ladder ★★★ When the salmon are spawning (mid-July to mid-Sept), we could spend hours on the observation deck at the artificial salmon ladder (waterfall) just off Park Avenue, watching these determined fish make their way from the sea up to the spawning grounds at the top of Ketchikan Creek. How these creatures can keep throwing their exhausted bodies up the ladder at the end of their long journey from the ocean, never giving up though they fail in three out of four leaps, is one of those amazing mysteries of nature. Be prepared for the smell, though (not all the fish make it).

Off Park Ave., in Ketchikan Creek.

Southeast Alaska Discovery Center ★★★ Operated by the U.S. Forest Service, this museum is an easy walk from the ship pier and has impressive exhibits on the area's fishing, mining, and timber industries, ecosystems, and Tlingit, Haida, and Tsimshian culture—including some colorful totem poles at the entrance. A 20-minute film gives an introduction to the Tongass National Forest. Throughout the museum, videos amp up displays and feature rangers, Native storytellers, and other experts. It also serves as an information center for exploration of the Tongass.

50 Main St. www.alaskacenters.gov/ketchikan.cfm. © **907/228-6220.** Admission $5, free for children 15 and under. May–Oct daily 8am–4pm.

Tongass Historical Museum ★ This newly renovated museum opened with temporary exhibits in 2017 and is expected to be fully operational in 2018. Displays focus on the area's history, art, and culture. It has some Native artifacts in the permanent collection along with a bunch of oddball donated relics—including the skull of Old Groaner, a brown bear who was shot for attacking humans. Changing exhibits sometimes feature the personal collections of locals.

In the Centennial Building, 629 Dock St. www.ketchikanmuseums.org. © **907/225-5600.** Admission $3 for adults, free for children. Summer daily 8am–5pm.

On Your Own: Beyond the Port Area

Deer Mountain ★★ Experienced hikers may be tempted to do the 5½-mile trail up to the peak and back on a clear day, but be aware: It's a challenging up-and-down jaunt with steep switchbacks and plenty of uneven surfaces along the way, with only brief sections of boardwalk. You should also allow plenty of time for the hike—the Forest Service suggests 3½ hours for the upward hike alone. Plus, the higher you go (the trail ascends more than 2,600 feet), the better the chance you'll hit clouds. The trail continues on a bunch more miles after the peak, and it's not particularly well-marked when to stop (if you're up and over the summit, you've gone too far). A better bet is to aim for the clearing in the trees known as the "first overlook," just over a mile up from the trailhead (a hike that still involves plenty of increase in elevation). At this spot you'll be rewarded with spectacular views of the city, water, islands, and mountains that surround Ketchikan. Note that just getting to the trailhead itself is a sometimes steep 1½-mile trek from the cruise pier, so unless you're really looking for exercise, you may want to take a taxi. *Note:* The Ketchikan Visitors Bureau highly recommends that hikers borrow a free ELB (emergency location beacon) before heading out on any extended hike (available at the Ketchikan visitors center near Berth 2 or at the Discovery Center). In case of emergency, the ELB can be activated to assist rescue. Officials say that almost every summer there are hikers who try to cut time by going off-trail on the switchbacks and get lost.

The trailhead is where Ketchikan Lakes Rd. joins with Nordstrom Dr. (near the city dump). Before your hike, pick up a hiking map at the Southeast Alaska Discovery Center (see above) or a Ketchikan visitor center. www.fs.usda.gov/main/tongass. ☏ **907/225-2148.**

Saxman Native Village ★★   This vibrant community, with a world-class collection of two dozen standing totem poles, is about 2½ miles south of Ketchikan. DIY types will be tempted to hike or get here by taxi or Uber. But we highly recommend you consider doing a guided group tour—either booked through your cruise line or when you arrive. Here's why: The totem poles are best enjoyed with interpretation. You may not realize, for example, that a pole with William Seward at the top is not a tribute but actually pokes fun of the man who negotiated the Alaska purchase in 1867. A guide can also help visitors gain more insight into local efforts to preserve Native culture and arts—remember, this isn't just a tourist site, it's a community. Young people from Saxman, population 425, lead tours around town. As one local told us, it's a way to give the kids not only an appreciation for their culture but also confidence in public speaking. Another added benefit of guided tours: an invitation into the Beaver Clan House for a traditional dance and music performance by the Cape Fox Dancers—with visitors encouraged to participate in the final dance.

S. Tongass Hwy., Saxman. www.capefoxtours.com. ☏ **907-225-4421.** Purchase admission at the Village Store at 2711 Killer Whale Ave. Tours are about $40 per person (you join the next available tour, so you may want to check times in advance) and include commentary by a guide, opportunity to watch wood carvers, and a dance performance. If you just want to look at the poles, there is a $5 admission charge (download a map at www.experienceketchikan.com/support-files/saxman.pdf). A taxi or Uber to Saxman runs about $13. You can also get to Saxman on the city's Silver line bus for $2 (see schedules at www.borough.ketchikan.ak.us/145/Transit, or pick up a hard copy of the schedule at one of the Ketchikan visitor centers). **Note:** The Native-owned Cape Fox Corporation, which runs tours for the cruise lines, recommends you book your excursion through your cruise line. Guides selling tours at the pier may also include a quick visit to Saxman Totem Park.

Totem Heritage Center ★★★   Built by the city, this museum houses a collection of rare 19th-century totem poles, mostly unpainted, that were recovered from remote Tlingit and Haida villages. While they would traditionally have been left to rot on the ground where they fell, these poles—from a period that is considered carving's heyday—have been preserved with the permission of Native elders. Unfortunately, most of the stories associated with the poles have been lost. Newer works at the museum include an impressive Eagle Transformation dance rattle by Tlingit artist Norman Jackson. The museum is a National Register site.

Note: It's at least a 15-minute uphill walk from the pier to the museum, so you may want to take the free shuttle bus from the ship pier (which also stops at key sights around town).

601 Deermount St. www.city.ketchikan.ak.us/departments/museums/index.html. ℂ **907/225-5900.** Admission $5 adults, children free. May–Sept daily 8am–5pm.

Where to Lunch

Alaska Fish House ★★★ SEAFOOD   If being in a fishing village has you craving fresh fish or crab, grab a bench indoors or out at this casual fish shack on the harbor, run by the same folks who operate Baranof Fishing Expeditions. Go for the salmon burger or the silver salmon or halibut fish & chips, served with mesquite fries. The fish tacos are also tasty, and the smoked-salmon chowder is the perfect warm-up on a chilly day. Expect a line if several ships are in town.

3 Salmon Landing. https://exclusivealaska.com/our-restaurant. ℂ **907/225-4055.** Entrees $11–$24. Sun, Mon, Wed 10am–6pm; Tues 10am–8pm; Thurs–Sat 10am–9pm.

The Heen Kahidi at Cape Fox Lodge ★★ SEAFOOD/AMERICAN COMFORT   This restaurant in the Native Corporation–owned, hilltop Cape Fox Lodge is a favorite fine-dining spot among the locals. Come for the ambience, which includes contemporary and historic Alaska Native art (be sure not to miss the displays on the hotel's second-floor balcony) and views of the Tongass Narrows, the city, and marina. Lunchtime specialties include Alaskan halibut or codfish & chips and fish tacos, or try a smoky BBQ bison burger. You can get here via the funicular railway (see p. 238).

800 Venetia Way. http://capefoxlodge.com. ℂ **907/225-8001.** Lunch entrees $14–$19. Open for breakfast, lunch, and dinner, 7 days/week.

A Day in Ketchikan

The way we look at it, there are three ways to go in Ketchikan: city-, wilderness-, or totem-centric. You are unlikely to have time for all. So if you prefer to stay in the city, pick up a map and do a self-guided walking tour of historic Ketchikan that includes **Creek Street** and the **Totem Heritage Center.** To get out in the wild, take a kayak or skiff tour or a guided hike and watch eagles fly overhead (and possibly spot bears)—or grab a flight or fast boat to the natural wonders of the **Misty Fjords National Monument** (about 40 miles south of Ketchikan). If you like to fish, we recommend you head to sea with one of the local captains on a half- or full-day guided salmon fishing tour.

Have your catch prepared at the **Alaska Fish House** or get it flash-frozen and shipped home. Gain an understanding of Native culture and totem poles by visiting **Saxman Native Village** or **Totem Bight State Historical Park.**

MISTY FJORDS NATIONAL MONUMENT

The 2.3-million-acre, Connecticut-size area of Misty Fjords starts at the Canadian border in the south and runs along the eastern side of the Behm Canal. Revillagigedo Island, where Ketchikan is located, is on the western side of the canal. It is topography, not wildlife, that makes a visit to Misty Fjords worthwhile. Among the prime features of Misty Fjords are **New Eddystone Rock,** jutting 237 feet out of the canal, and the **Walker Cove/Rudyerd Bay** area, a prime viewing spot for marine life, eagles, and other wildlife. Volcanic cliffs (up to 3,150 ft. high), coves (some as deep as 900 ft.), and peace and serenity are the stock-in-trade of the place.

Only passengers on small ships will see Misty Fjords close up—its waterway is too narrow in most places for big ships. The bigger ships pass the southern tip of the Misty Fjords National Monument and then veer away northwest to dock at Ketchikan. Unfortunately, this means that large-ship passengers miss one of the least spoiled of all wilderness areas—unless, that is, you book a flightseeing trip to see it (see the sections on Ketchikan excursions, above).

Archaeologists believe local Indian tribes (Haida, Tlingit, and Tsimshian, primarily) lived here as far back as 10,000 years ago. The only way you're likely to see any trace of their existence now, though, is from a kayak or small boat that can get close enough to the rock face to let you see the few remaining pictographs etched into the stone along the shore.

Anglers in Misty Fjords are liable to think they've died and gone to heaven. The pristine waters yield a rich harvest of enormous Dolly Varden, grayling, and lake trout. It is possible to walk in the park, but only the hardy and the experienced are advised to do that. And it is necessary to follow some simple rules: Let somebody know where you are going and when you expect to return; keep to the trails (the wildlife—especially bears—don't always appreciate intruders); and carry out everything you carried in. That's the law.

By the way, the name Misty Fjords comes from the climatic conditions. Precipitation tends to leave the place looking as if it were under a steady mist much of the time. It also gives the waterway an almost spooky look. President Jimmy Carter named it a national treasure in 1978.

ADMIRALTY ISLAND NATIONAL MONUMENT

About 15 miles due west of Juneau, this monument comprises almost 1 million acres and covers about 90% of Admiralty Island. It's another of those Alaska areas that cruise passengers on the bigger ships will never see. The villages here, some of them Native, have recently begun to attract some small-ship operators. The Tlingit village of **Angoon,** for example, welcomes small groups of visitors off ships. Small ships may also ferry passengers ashore in a more remote area of the island for a hike.

Admiralty Island is said to have the highest concentration of **bears** on earth. Naturalists estimate that there may be as many as four of these creatures per square mile. Bears don't have a monopoly on the island, however. Also plentiful are **Sitka black-tailed deer** and **bald eagles,** and the waters around teem with **sea lions, harbor seals,** and **whales.** One of the largest concentrations of **bald eagles** in Southeast Alaska (second perhaps only to that in Haines in the fall) is found in the bays and inlets on the east side of the island. An estimated 4,000 eagles congregate there for the abundant and more easily accessible food supply.

TRACY ARM & ENDICOTT ARM

Located about 50 miles due south of Juneau, these long, deep, and almost claustrophobically narrow fjords are a striking feature of a pristine forest and mountain expanse with a sinister name: **Tracy Arm–Fords Terror Wilderness.** The place came by its name honestly after an 1889 incident in which a crewman from a U.S. naval vessel (name: Ford; rank: unknown) rowed into an inlet off Endicott Arm and found himself trapped for 6 hours in a heaving sea as huge ice floes bumped and ground against his flimsy craft. He survived, but the finger of water in which he endured his ordeal was forever after known as Fords Terror. The banks were so close on a recent Disney Cruise Line sailing that we spotted a bear through our binoculars. We also saw humpbacks as we entered the area, so keep your eyes peeled for wildlife.

The Tracy and Endicott arms, which reach back from Stephens Passage into the Coastal Mountain Range, are steep-sided waterways, each with an active glacier at its head: the **Sawyer Glacier** and **South Sawyer Glacier** in Tracy Arm and **Dawes Glacier** in Endicott. These calve constantly, sometimes discarding ice blocks of such impressive size that they clog the narrow fjord passages, making navigation difficult. When the passage is open, ships can get close enough for the incredible sight and the sound of calving glaciers (the crack of "white thunder" is amazing!). On a Regent Seven Seas cruise, we were thrilled when the captain ordered the tenders out at Sawyer Glacier for a great photo op.

A passage up either fjord allows eye-catching views of high cascading waterfalls, tree- and snow-covered mountain valleys, and wildlife that might include **Sitka black-tailed deer, bald eagles,** and possibly even the odd **black bear.** Around the ship, the animals you're most likely to see are **whales, sea lions,** and **harbor seals.**

BARANOF ISLAND

Named after the Russian trader Alexander Baranof, Russian America's first appointed honcho, the island's main claim to fame is **Sitka,** on the western coast, the center of Russian-era culture and the seat of the Russian Orthodox Church in Alaska. (The island name, by the way, is often spelled Baranov, which some people contend is the way Alexander himself spelled it.) **Peril Straits,** off the northern end of the island, separating Baranof from Chichagof Island, is a scenic passageway too narrow for big cruise ships, but some of the smaller ones can get through.

SITKA

Sitka differs from most ports of call on the Inside Passage cruises in that, geographically speaking, it's not on the Inside Passage at all. Rather, it stands on the outside (or western) coast of Baranof Island. Its name, in fact, comes from the Tlingit Indian *Shee Atika,* meaning "people on the outside." For the relatively short time it takes ships to get to Sitka, they must leave the protected waters of the passage and sail with nothing between them and Japan but the sometimes turbulent Pacific Ocean. If you're going to run into heavy seas at any point on an Inside Passage cruise, this is where you'll most likely find them. The town pier is one of the only places in Alaska where passengers on big ships may tender ashore in small boats rather than dock. But many big ships now use a dock near the town's ferry terminal, built by a private developer. So you may tender right into town or you may dock about 6 miles away, depending on what cruise line and ship you're on.

For us, this port is a must-do. Backing us up: The town was declared one of the 2010 Dozen Distinctive Destinations by the National Trust for Historic Preservation, in recognition of its historical architecture, cultural diversity, and commitment to historic preservation. In 2013 *Smithsonian* magazine even called Sitka one of the Top 20 Small Towns to Visit. You're going to love this place.

Step off your cruise ship here, and in some ways you step into the Russian Alaska of yesteryear. This is where, in 1799, trader Alexander Baranof established a fort in what became known as New Archangel. Today **St. Michael's Cathedral,** with its striking onion-shaped dome and ornate gilt interior, reflects that heritage, as does the all-female troupe the **New Archangel Dancers,** who perform during the cruise season in **Harrigan Centennial Hall.** The colorfully costumed, 30-strong troupe does a program of energetic Russian folk dances several times a day. The New Archangel Dancers also sometimes get together with a Tlingit dance troupe for a joint performance in the Sheet'ka Kwaan Naa Kahidi Community House on Katlian Street. The Tlingit heritage here goes back more than 10,000 years.

Most attractions in Sitka are within walking distance of the town pier (if you're at the private pier you'll catch a free shuttle to the town pier). The **Sitka National Historical Park,** a must-do attraction with its impressive (mostly reproduction) totem poles and excellent views, is about a half-mile walk along the pleasant seawalk (with interpretive signs and benches) from the town pier. One attraction that should not missed is a bit of a hike (about a mile from downtown): the **Alaska Raptor Rehabilitation Center.** A nonprofit venture, the center opened in 1980 to treat sick or injured birds of prey (primarily eagles)

Sitka

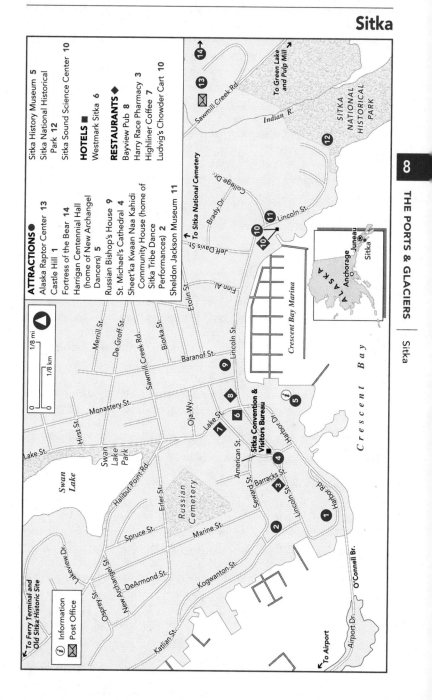

ATTRACTIONS ●

Alaska Raptor Center **13**
Castle Hill **1**
Fortress of the Bear **14**
Harrigan Centennial Hall (home of New Archangel Dancers) **5**
Russian Bishop's House **9**
St. Michael's Cathedral **4**
Sheet'ka Kwaan Naa Kahidi Community House (home of Sitka Tribe Dance Performances) **2**
Sheldon Jackson Museum **11**
Sitka History Museum **5**
Sitka National Historical Park **12**
Sitka Sound Science Center **10**

HOTELS ■

Westmark Sitka **6**

RESTAURANTS ◆

Bayview Pub **8**
Harry Race Pharmacy **3**
Highliner Coffee **7**
Ludvig's Chowder Cart **10**

and provide an educational experience for visitors. It's world-renowned. We admit that the sight of our majestic national bird close up, with its snowy white head and curved beak, gives us goosebumps. Go as part of a shore excursion or on the $10/day visitors' shuttle bus (See "Coming Ashore," below).

Sitka also has a WWII Naval history (including a Naval Operating Base that was on nearby Japonski Island), and the mountain- and ocean-view **Sitka National Cemetery** (803 Sawmill Creek Rd.). Laid out in the late–19th century, it was added to the National Register of Historic Places in 2012. Among those buried here is Captain Charles William Paddock, Olympic gold and silver medalist from the 1920, 1924, and 1928 Olympics.

In addition to its wealth of history and other attractions, Sitka is a year-round community that prides itself on its cultural offerings. Every year from early June to early July, this town of just under 9,000 year-round residents hosts a celebration of chamber music, performed by world-class practitioners of the art, in various halls throughout the town including the gorgeous, harbor-view theater at Harrigan Centennial Hall (the artistic director is Grammy Award–winning cellist Zuill Bailey). The **Sitka Summer Music Festival** has been held since 1972. Performances are day and evening; admission prices vary. We recommend it as a perfect complement to the sometimes frenzied and more modern entertainment found on cruise ships. Also in summer, the award-winning **Sitka Fine Arts Camp** (occupying the historic campus of the former Sheldon Jackson College) draws 1,000 talented kids from throughout Alaska and the U.S. (and they perform free shows). All this culture becomes particularly impressive when you consider that Sitka has as many boats as people—the main industry being fishing.

Like most places you'll visit, Sitka is also surrounded by wilderness—most of 100-mile-long Baranof Island is undeveloped. Head outside of town and you are surrounded by Tongass Forest. North of the city at the 9-hole Sea Mountain Golf Course, with its amazing views, challenging elevation, and tight fairways, locals wear waders (because of frequent rain) to hit buckets of balls, while keeping an eye out for bears. The tallest peaks surrounding Sitka may be snow-capped even in summer.

Despite visits by big cruise ships several times a week (the town also serves as an embarkation point for small ships such as those of Alaskan Dream Cruises), Sitka somehow manages to keep a quaint, small-town ambience. Walking along the harbor filled with fishing boats (and pleasure boats, too) you can catch snippets of conversations about the weekly fish count.

All the shops in Sitka are locally owned. One of Fran's favorite shops on the whole Southeast route is the locally owned **Sitka Rose Gallery** (www.sitkarosegallery.com; ✆ 888/236-1536 or 907/747-3030), in a pretty Victorian house at 419 Lincoln St. The gallery features the works of more than 100 Alaskan artists (no made-in-Taiwan merchandise here) at prices that are more reasonable than at bigger ports such as Ketchikan. At 202 Lincoln St., the **WinterSong Soap Company** (www.wintersongsoap.com; ✆ 888/819-8949 or 907/747-8949) sells locally made soaps in such fragrances as Alaskan Herbs

& Flowers (if you like what you buy here, you can replenish your supplies online). Renowned Tlingit master woodcarver Tommy Joseph (① **907/623-0705** or 907/738-3856) sells his and other artist's works at his studio, **Raindance Gallery,** at 205 Monastery St. (behind the Russian Bishop's House). New on the scene but very much worth a visit is **Alaska Pure Sea Salt Co.** (in the Bayview Trading Company building, across from the pier; www.alaskapureseasalt.com; ① **907/747-7258**), selling hand-crafted salt from the waters around Sitka, in a beautiful tasting room, where you can sample and purchase packets (an excellent souvenir!) of such original concoctions as Sitka Spruce Tip or Wild Blueberry salt (excellent on brownies!), or the Original Sitka Flake salt, hailed by foodies and featured in *Food & Wine* magazine.

Sitka Trivia: For those who need to know such things, although the Sandra Bullock/Ryan Reynolds movie *The Proposal* was set in Sitka, it was mostly filmed in Massachusetts.

COMING ASHORE   If you arrive by tender, you'll be dropped off within walking distance of the downtown area. Sitka is so small and the heart of town so close to the passenger pier that it's ideal for exploring on foot. Small buses (all-day pass $10) are also available to ferry you to local sights—such as the Raptor Center, for instance, which is 0.9 miles from downtown. If you arrived at the private pier (Old Sitka Dock) or the ferry dock, you're about 5 miles north of downtown. A complimentary shuttle bus or taxi will get you to the town tender pier. Right at the Old Sitka Dock are a crab shack and a few satellite shops selling fur and jewelry (the larger shops are downtown).

INFORMATION   Volunteers staff an info table at the recently remodeled **Harrigan Centennial Hall,** next to the Crescent Boat Harbor at 330 Harbor Dr. (① **907/747-3225**). Stop by its newly renovated small museum, operated by the **Sitka Historical Society** (http://sitkahistory.com), with exhibits on Tlingit and Russian history, the Alaska purchase, and the granting of civil rights to Alaska Natives. Outside Harrigan Hall operators sell various last-minute tours, based on availability. The hall is open Monday to Friday 8am to 10pm, Saturday 8am to 5pm (May–Oct), and sometimes Sunday.

For in-depth information, head to the new **Visit Sitka** visitor center just across the street at 104 Lake St. (www.sitka.org; ① **907/747-8604**).

Best Cruise-Line Shore Excursions

Artist Walk (2½ hr.; $70; minimum age 14): Go with a guide to several galleries for demonstrations in woodcarving, jewelry making, and ceramics. Includes time at Wild Arts Gallery & Studio, where glassblowers show you how to make a take-home souvenir.

Dry Suit Snorkel (2½ hr.; $140 adults, $89 children; minimum age 12): Keep your street clothes on, strap on a dry suit, and get in the water to view colorful starfish, crabs, and sea anemones. Time in the water is less than an hour (maximum weight 240 lbs.).

4×4 Wilderness Adventure (4½ hr.; $250): Board a boat for a ride through the islands of Sitka Sound, and then, on Kruzof Island, drive yourself off-road (following a guide) on a two-person Yamaha Rhino. You'll explore temperate rainforest and may spot brown bears.

Salmon or Halibut Fishing (4 hr.; $280): An experienced captain guides your fully equipped boat to a good spot for halibut and salmon; the rest is up to you. Your catch can be frozen or smoked and shipped to your home if you wish. *Note:* A $10 fishing license and a $10 king salmon tag are extra.

Sea Otter & Wildlife Quest (3 hr.; $130 adults, $100 children): A naturalist accompanies passengers on this jet-boat tour to discuss the various animals you'll encounter and explain the delicate balance of the region's marine ecosystem. They're so sure you'll see a whale, bear, or otter that they offer partial cash refunds if you don't. A 5 hr. version adds a visit to the Fortress of the Bear ($170 adults, $130 children).

Excursions Offered by Local Agencies

For kayakers, **Sitka Sound Ocean Adventures** (www.kayaksitka.com; ℂ 907/752-0660) has 2½-hour tours for beginners or advanced ($79 adults, $54 children 6–12; longer tours also available) and will pick you up at the pier.

Sitka Wildlife Tours (sitkawildlifetours.com; ℂ 907/738-1733) does 2-hr. whale-watching tours (and custom tours) in a six-passenger boat, from $135 per person (departure times vary by day; check online), and 2-hr. van tours that include the totem park and Fortress of the Bear, from $65 per person.

If your interest is fly-fishing, head off with **Fly Fish Sitka** (www.FlyFish Sitka.com; ℂ 907/738-2737), half-day excursions by boat from $250 per person. **Big Blue Charters** does 6-hour sport-fishing excursions, priced from $350 per person; four-person-minimum required (www.bigbluecharters.com; ℂ 907/747-5161).

Bike rentals are available at the **Yellow Jersey Cycle Shop,** 329 Harbor Dr. (www.yellowjerseycycles.com/rentals.html; ℂ 907/747-6317), from $20 for 2 hours; full-day rentals from $25. **Scooterbumz** rents scooters you can use to explore, from $35/hour (ℂ 907/738-4474; look for the van at the pier).

For a closer look at Sitka Sound, take off with **Four B Charters,** where transplanted South African Francois Bakkes takes you on a custom-crafted itinerary on his heated, six-passenger boat (facebook.com/fourbcharters; ℂ 907/351-7483). The Volcano Coast Ocean Raft Adventure, offered by **Sitka Alaska Outfitters** (www.sitkaalaskaoutfitters.com; ℂ 907/966-2301) is a 2½-hr. eco-adventure that gets you close to wildlife and coastal scenery in an inflatable raft ($300 for one person, from $175 for groups of 2 to 12).

On Your Own: Within Walking Distance

Castle Hill ★★★ At first we found the prospect of a climb up to the top of the hill—by way of a lengthy flight of stairs from the western end of Lincoln Street—a little daunting, but after climbing to the top, we have two words of advice: Do it. (Also, a graduated walkway up the back side is accessible through the alleyway from the main street.) The reward is panoramic views of downtown Sitka. This is where the first post–Alaska Purchase U.S. flag was raised in October 1867 (the 150th anniversary was celebrated in 2017). It was also on this site, in the 1830s, that the marauding Russians drove off the resident Kiksadi clan of Tlingit Indians and built a stronghold from which to conduct their fur-trading business. The last of the buildings within the walls of the stronghold was used by the first Russian American governor and was called Baranof's Castle (hence: Castle Hill). The structure burned some 60 years later, and its remains can still be seen, along with other reminders of those pre-Purchase days. This National Historic Landmark is managed by the Alaska State Parks Department.

Climb stairs near intersection of Lincoln and Katlian sts.

New Archangel Dancers ★★ Just watching the way these Russian folk dancers throw themselves around the stage makes us tired. Where do they get the energy? The dancers are all women—they even play the men's parts, complete with false beards if the dance requires it. When the troupe was organized in 1969, the men of the town pooh-poohed the idea. It'll never work, they said. Later, when the original handful of women proved that it could work, some of the men admitted they wouldn't mind joining in. Too late, guys: The founders decided to keep the show all-female. The 30-minute show is presented at least twice a day and sometimes as often as four times most days in the summer, largely determined by the number of cruise ships in town.

In Harrigan Centennial Hall, 330 Harbor Dr., near the tender docks. www.newarchangel dancers.com. ⓒ **907/747-5516.** Admission $10 adults, $5 for children 12 and under. Check online or call for performance times, which change daily. Tickets go on sale about a half-hour before each show.

Russian Bishop's House ★★ Owned and operated by the National Park Service, this is the house where Bishop Innocent Veniaminov, born in 1797, translated scriptures into Tlingit and trained deacons to carry Russian Orthodoxy back to their Native villages. Veniaminov and his followers allowed parishioners to use their own language, a key element to saving Native cultures. The house was built in 1842, and a lot of history is shared on ranger-led tours. Exhibits downstairs trace the development of New Archangel into Sitka.

Lincoln and Monastery sts. No phone; call Sitka National Historical Park Visitor Center. www.nps.gov/sitk. ⓒ **907/747-0110.** Admission free to first floor with also free ranger-led tours (offered every 30 min.). Mid-May to Sept daily 9am–5pm.

St. Michael's Cathedral ★ Even if you're not a fan of religious shrines, you'll be impressed by the architecture and finery of this rather small place of worship. One of the 49th State's most striking and photogenic structures, the current church is actually a replica; the original burned to the ground in 1966. So revered was the cathedral that Sitkans formed a human chain and carried many of the cathedral's precious icons, paintings, vestments, and jeweled crowns from the flames. Later, with contributions of cash and labor from throughout the land, St. Michael's was lovingly re-created on the same site and rededicated in 1976. A knowledgeable guide is on hand to answer

questions. Sunday services are sung in English, Slavonic, Tlingit, Aleut, and Yupik.

240 Lincoln St. (at Lincoln and Cathedral sts). www.stmichaelcathedral.org. ⓒ **907/747-8120.** Admission (suggested donation) $5. May–Sept open hours and days mostly when cruise ships are in port; Sun after services, although worshippers welcome to service.

The Sheldon Jackson Museum ★★★ On the former campus of Sheldon Jackson College, this state-operated museum houses one of the finest collections of Native Alaskan art and artifacts anywhere. It's named for Presbyterian missionary Sheldon Jackson, who helped fund construction of the museum building—Alaska's first concrete structure when it opened in 1897. Jackson also collected most of the artifacts, which date to between 1888 and 1900. The glass cases in the main gallery house such treasures as a helmet worn by local Tlingit battle leader Katlian, who fought off Russians in 1804— the helmet is covered in bearskin with a copper-eyed eagle on top. The museum also holds amazing examples of prized Aleut baskets (so tightly woven they can carry water); waterproof gut and fish skin clothing from Northwest Alaska; and, tucked into exhibit drawers, smaller items such as ivory carvings. If you have time, stroll over to the campus quadrangle, designed by the NYC firm Ludlow and Peabody and completed in 1911. Closed in 2007, the college was completely renovated by the **Sitka Arts Camp,** which now owns the property.

104 College Dr. (at Lincoln St.). www.museums.alaska.gov. ⓒ **907/747-8981.** Admission museum $7 adults, $6 seniors, free for youths 18 and under. Summer Tues–Sat 9am–4:30pm. Closed holidays.

Sitka National Historical Park ★★★ At just 107 acres, this is the smallest national park in Alaska, but don't let that discourage you—the place breathes history. This is where the Russians and the Tlingits fought a fierce battle in 1804. Inside the park is a beautiful **totem-pole trail,** which you can visit on your own or on a ranger-led tour. In the visitor center, exhibits explain the art of totem carving and a 12-minute film discusses Sitkans past and present. The park is about a 15-minute walk from the tender pier.

106 Metlakatla St. www.nps.gov/sitk. ⓒ **907/747-0110.** Free admission. Visitor center May–Sept daily 8am–5pm. Park trails May–Sept daily 6am–10pm.

Sitka Sound Science Center ★ In a rustic building across the street from the Sheldon Jackson Museum, this research and learning facility (which also used to be affiliated with the college) has an aquarium and touch tanks filled with local marine creatures, including brightly hued anemone and starfish. Outside is a salmon hatchery, and next door is an expansive gift shop and a stand selling **Ludvig's** signature clam chowder (see below) and sandwiches.

834 Lincoln St. www.sitkascience.org. ⓒ **907/747-8878.** Admission $5. Mon–Fri 9am–4pm, Sat 10am–2pm.

Sitka Tribe Dance Performances ★★ The Sheet'ka Kwaan Naa Kahidi, Sitka's Community House, stands on the north side of the downtown parade ground. It is a modern version of a Tlingit clan house, with an air-handling system that pulls smoke from the central firepit straight up to the chimney. The magnificent house screen at the front of the hall, installed in 2000, is the largest in the Pacific Northwest. Performances last 30 minutes and include three dances and a story. It's entirely traditional and put on by members of the tribe. Sign up for tours by calling ahead or visiting their website.

200 Katlian St. www.sitkatours.com. ✆ **888/270-8687** or 907/747-7137. Admission $10 adults, $5 children 3–12 (2 and under free). Performance times vary; check schedule on website.

On Your Own: Beyond the Port Area

Alaska Raptor Center ★★★ It's about a 20-minute walk from the waterfront, but this center is well worth seeing (and every cruise line offers it as a shore excursion). It's not a performing-animal show with stunts and flying action, but a place where injured raptors (birds of prey) are brought and, with luck, healed to the point whereby they can be returned to the wild. Some eventually can; those that cannot are housed permanently at the center or sent to zoos. Very few are euthanized. A flight-training center re-creates a little bit of rainforest in an aviary where recuperating birds learn to fly again. Visitors walk through in a tube with one-way glass so they can watch the birds without disturbing them. The tour through the center and along a wheelchair-accessible nature trail in the surrounding rainforest takes about an hour.

1000 Raptor Way (milepost 0.9), just across Indian River. www.alaskaraptor.org. ✆ **800/643-9425** or 907/747-8662. Admission $13 adults, $6 children 6–12, 5 and under free. May–Sept daily 8am–4pm; Oct–Apr call for hours of operation.

Fortress of the Bear ★★ This one-of-a-kind sanctuary opened in 2010 for orphaned Southeast Alaska Brown Bears—also known as grizzlies. It gives visitors a chance to view the creatures up close, in a ¾-acre re-created natural habitat. Black bears are now at the site, too, in a separate area. A raised viewing platform allows visitors to watch the bears. When we visited in 2017 there were three black bears and five brown bears in residence. All were cubs when rescued—one pair lost their mother when she ate too much plastic trash, another when she broke into the kitchen of a fishing lodge and was shot by the chef. Some of the black bears pose on cue. Research at the nonprofit facility, about 5 miles from the tender pier (take the $10 shuttle), is conducted by the Alaska Department of Fish and Game. The philosophy of project officials: Studying the bears in captivity can help wild bears. You may be visiting with a few hundred other people, but it's your best shot at seeing a grizzly in Alaska.

4639 Sawmill Creek Rd. www.fortressofthebear.org. ✆ **907/747-3032.** Admission $10 adults, $5 children 8–12, free for children 7 and under. Shuttle from the pier an additional $3. In the summer season daily from 9am–6pm.

Where to Lunch

In addition to the listings below, **Harry Race Pharmacy** (106 Lincoln St.) has a cool 1950s-style soda fountain (and also serves ice cream). The **Highliner Coffee** (http://stores.highlinercoffee.com), in the back side of Seward

Square Mall, serves lattes and other coffee drinks (coffee roasted on-site) and excellent baked goods (try the giant oatmeal cookies or a toasted bagel with delicious Alaskan salmon spread), and offers Wi-Fi for free with purchase.

Bayview Pub ★ PUB GRUB Overlooking the harbor, this sports bar (with 10 TV screens, darts, and foosball and pool tables) serves elevated pub grub—tasty salmon tacos, rockfish fish & chips, a rockfish burger—and has more than 25 beers on draft including several Alaska craft beers; the local brand is Baranof Island Brewing Company. The menu also offers traditional pub grub.

407 Lincoln St. (upstairs in the Bayview Trading Co. building). www.SitkaBayviewPub. com. ℂ **907/747-5300.** Open 11am–late (kitchen closes daily at 9pm). Main courses $14–$28.

Ludvig's Chowder Cart ★ STREET CART **Ludvig's Bistro** (256 Katlian St., www.ludvigsbistro.com; ℂ **907/966-3663**), serving rustic Mediterranean fare, is the best restaurant in town (with a nice wine bar upstairs), but it's only open for dinner. Fortunately for day-trippers, you can sample the cooking at **Ludvig's Chowder Cart,** a street cart serving fantastic spicy clam chowder (chorizo is the secret ingredient), salads, and salmon sandwiches.

The street cart is located in the Mill Building adjacent to the Sitka Sound Science Center. Main courses $9–$12. Tues–Sat 10:30am–2:30pm.

A Day in Sitka

Our favorite things in Sitka include walking the **seawalk** to the **Sitka National Historic Park** and spending time among the totem poles and trees, soaking in the rich and tragic history of the area. Download the new park app online to better understand what you are looking at. There are interpretive signs along the seawalk and benches where you can sit and admire the pleasure boats in the harbor. For sure, stop for the chowder at **Ludvig's Chowder Cart** (yum!). Heading back toward downtown, see if Tommy Joseph is in his studio (behind the **Russian Bishop's House**); you'll want to stop by and admire his work—he's one of the top Tlingit carvers in Alaska. The salt at **Alaska Pure Sea Salt Co.** is one of our favorite things, and we can't resist seeing what's in stock at **Sitka Rose Gallery** and the **WinterSong Soap Company.** Reenergize with a 'cuppa Joe at **Highliner Coffee** and if you still have energy, walk up to **Castle Hill** or head to the commercial fishing waterfront along Katlian Street to catch some fish tales—the **Murray Pacific** marine shop (475 Katlian St.) is a place where fishermen tend to hang out. You will also be well-rewarded if you head off on a **wildlife boat tour,** and doing a **snorkeling shore excursion** here gives you extreme bragging rights.

WRANGELL

Wrangell, located on the northern tip of 30-mile-long Wrangell Island, is increasing in popularity as a destination for small ships, including those operated by luxury lines—and for good reason. With a population of just 2,400, Wrangell has retained a wonderful small-town feel. Conversations are easy with

Wrangell

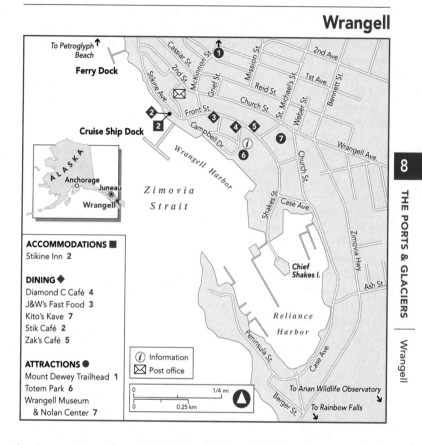

ACCOMMODATIONS ■
Stikine Inn **2**

DINING ◆
Diamond C Café **4**
J&W's Fast Food **3**
Kito's Kave **7**
Stik Café **2**
Zak's Café **5**

ATTRACTIONS ●
Mount Dewey Trailhead **1**
Totem Park **6**
Wrangell Museum
  & Nolan Center **7**

ⓘ Information
✉ Post office

locals, and you can follow their lead and picnic at the totem park (just past the City Market on Front St.), hike in a rainforest, and see ancient art on Petroglyph Beach. The main street, up from the waterfront and backed by mountains, is the Alaska you have come to see, with pristine wilderness right next door.

Valued for its position near the mouth of the Stikine River, which flows here from inland British Columbia, Wrangell began as a Tlingit stronghold and trading post (Tlingit people have lived on the island for 5,000 years) and became the site of a Russian fort built in 1834. The British Hudson Bay Company leased the fur lands from the Russians in 1840, and their flag flew until the U.S. purchase of Alaska in 1867. Wrangell is not only one of the oldest towns in Alaska but the only town in the state to have been ruled under three flags and by four nations: Tlingit, Russia, the United Kingdom, and the U.S.

Over the balance of the 19th century, Wrangell experienced three gold-rush periods, not to mention the lawlessness that went with the quest for riches, then settled into the role of a small, conservative, and somewhat isolated logging and fishing town. Two major fires destroyed much of downtown, the latest in 1952.

When the lumber mill closed in 1994, some feared that the town would disappear altogether. But local folk decided to make the most of Wrangell's location as a comfortable jumping-off point for wilderness adventures. Tourism became the town's mainstay.

The town has its own museum, eateries, and well-established tour operators offering kayaking and hiking trips; jet-boat excursions up the wild Stikine River; mainland tours to see black and brown bears fishing for pink salmon at the **Anan Wildlife Observatory** (in July and Aug); and salmon fishing charters. The U.S. Forest Service maintains gravel roads that lead to some stunning spots. The community even built a spectacular golf course with ocean and mountain views: **Muskeg Meadow** (www.wrangellalaskagolf.com; ℂ **907/874-4653;** $22–$44 per day; clubs and pull carts available for rent; free van pickup from the pier), where you might spot eagles overhead and the occasional bear and moose on the greens. Here, golfers abide by the "Raven Rule": If a raven steals your ball, you may replace it with no penalty—as long as you have a witness.

Wrangell galleries and stores sell local artworks. A shop in the new **Wrangell Cooperative Association Cultural Center,** 315 Front St.; ℂ **907/874-4304**), is part of a cultural revival plan by the local Tlingit tribe to encourage traditional arts, including totem carving. The shop sells reasonably priced jewelry, beadwork, sewn items such as aprons, and even carved paddles. Near the pier, check out the marine watercolors created on navigational charts by fourth-generation Alaskan Brenda Schwartz-Yeager at the **Pacific Northwest Gallery** (which shares space with Alaska Adventures and Charters at 5 Front St.).

Festivals help keep things lively. If you come here in late July, you may be able to help celebrate the annual, five-day **Wrangell BearFest** (www.alaska bearfest.org), with films, workshops, a symposium (that attracts renowned researchers), games, and other activities, all focused around bears.

COMING ASHORE   The cruise-ship dock is next to the Stikine Inn, right at the edge of downtown. Walk up Front Street to find most of the in-town attractions. The only road to the rest of Wrangell Island is the Zimovia Highway, which heads out of town for about 12 miles and then connects to more than 100 miles of gravel roads, maintained by the Forest Service.

Garnets for Kids

Be on the lookout for kids around town selling the semi-precious stones known as garnets, either loose or made into jewelry. The town's youth industry began when a 37-acre garnet ledge was bequeathed in 1962 to the Boy Scouts of America and the Presbyterian Church. The property was fully transferred to the church in Wrangell in 2002. Only children and adults accompanied by children can dig at the site, and only kids are allowed to collect the fruits of their labor (some local shops have displays helping them out). The proceeds often go toward college payments—we met a young local woman on our latest trip who was headed off to Dartmouth). For more about the Wrangell Garnet Ledge, go to **www.wrangellgarnet ledge.com**.

INFORMATION The **Wrangell Visitor Center,** 296 Campbell Dr., is in the Nolan Center in the heart of town (www.wrangellalaska.org; ✆ **800/367-9745**). If you're hiking or otherwise heading off-road, we recommend you stop by the center first to pick up a map. The Wrangell Museum is in the same building. The Forest Service's **Wrangell Ranger District Office,** 525 Bennett St., is on the hill behind town (www.fs.fed.us/r10/tongass; ✆ **907/874-2323**).

Best Cruise-Line Shore Excursions

Anan Wildlife Observatory (4 hr.; $399): A small boat takes you about 30 miles south of Wrangell to the mainland and this internationally known bear-observing site. You hike about a half-mile through forest to a viewing platform overlooking the small waterfall on Anan Creek, with views of the sea and breathtaking green oasis as far as the eye can see. When the pink salmon are running in July and August (the tour is only offered those months), bear spotting is easy. You may find yourself as close as 12 feet from a curious black bear (your guide carries both bear spray and a shotgun for protection). Brown bears fish in the stream as well. Sights on any given day may include a bear swatting away a pesky eagle or ripping into his salmon catch. On our latest visit, in early July, we spotted five black and two brown bears, but from mid-July to mid-August as many as 60 black bears and a dozen brown bears may be seen fishing here. The photo opportunities are astounding, but extreme caution is advised. The boat ride is about an hour each way; some tours get you there by floatplane. Independent tours are also available (see below). *Trivia:* Ask to see the rock where Ronald Reagan famously tripped when he stayed in Anan Creek.

Stikine River & Wilderness Glacier by Jet Boat (3½ hr.; $289): Stikine means "Great River" in Tlingit, and this glacier-fed waterway certainly lives up to its name. Naturalist John Muir called the river the "Yosemite 100 miles long." It's the fastest flowing navigable river in North America, running 330 miles through British Columbia and the mainland of Alaska before emptying into a rainforest delta about 5 miles north of Wrangell. Jet boats speed against the current, taking you to see incredible scenery: majestic mountains, waterfalls, glaciers, hot springs and salmon streams, plus eagles and snow geese, among a stunning number of birds, and sometimes even moose and bears. Tours usually stop at Shakes Glacier and Shakes Lake, where you can admire 3,000-foot cliffs and some 50 waterfalls. Some trips also stop for a dip at the Forest Service–owned Chief Shakes Hot Springs.

Excursions You Can Book Yourself

Several long-established operators have offices at the pier (advance reservations suggested). **Alaska Charters and Adventures** (www.alaskaupclose.com; ✆ **888/993-2750** or 907/874-4157) offers jet-boat trips on the Stikine River, naturalist-guided trips to Anan Wildlife Observatory, charter fishing (freshwater or saltwater), and hiking excursions, as well as private birding and photography tours. **Alaska Vistas** (www.alaskavistas.com; ✆ **907/874-3006**) offers kayaking (for beginners and advanced); jet-boat trips on the Stikine

River; day tours to the Anan Wildlife Observatory, and escorted hikes. Native-owned **Alaska Waters** (alaskawaters.com; ℂ **800/347-4462** or 907/874-2378) has Stikine and Anan options and fresh and saltwater fishing tours, as well as an in-town cultural tour. In addition to a full tour lineup, **Breakaway Adventures** (ℂ **888/385-2488** or 907/874-2488) has single and double kayak rentals ($40–$60 per day) and bike rentals. For flightseeing, check out **Sunrise Aviation** (www.sunriseaviation.com; ℂ **907/874-2319**).

If your ship stocks bikes, you might want to ride the paved, 4-mile **walking and biking path** that begins at the southern edge of downtown parallel to the Zimovia Highway and takes you along the water of the Zimovia Strait, ending near Shoemaker Bay Loop Road (and the Shoemaker Bay Recreation Area). Look for eagles in the trees, especially early in the season when they congregate here, as well as great blue herons. The Forest Service also has appealing mountain bike routes all over the island.

If you are planning on taking a taxi anywhere, be aware there may be only one operating in town.

On Your Own: Within Walking Distance

Chief Shakes Island ★★   This tiny inlet in the middle of Wrangell's small-boat harbor (about .7 miles from the main ship pier and across a wooden bridge) is the National Historic Register site of a replica 19th-century Tlingit community house and totem poles. The first Chief Shakes left a dynasty that lasted seven more generations—and the last of the line, Chief Shakes VII, passed away in 1944. The clan house opened in 1940, built under a Civilian Conservation Corps project. In 2013, a major restoration was completed with renowned Native carvers brought in to help train local carvers, and the house was rededicated. It's open for cruise groups, with a storytelling and dance presentation inside. Even if you don't go inside, come out and view the totems—such as the 44-foot Eagle—carved house posts, and harbor vistas.

Shakes St. The clan house is open for groups. ℂ **907/874-4304.**

Wrangell Museum ★★   This is an impressive museum for a small town, its galleries devoted to natural history, logging, fishing and Native culture. Among the important early Alaska Native pieces on display are mid-18th-century house posts painted with fish egg and minerals. The shop has attractively priced Native crafts and a wonderful selection of books on Alaska.

Nolan Center, 96 Campbell Dr. www.wrangell.com/museum. ℂ **907/874-3770.** Admission $5 adults, $3 seniors, $2 children, free under 6. May–Sept Mon–Sat 1–5pm.

On Your Own: Beyond the Port Area

Mount Dewey ★★★   Right behind downtown, you can stretch your feet while climbing this large, tree-covered hill for views of Wrangell and the Zimovia Strait. A popular half-mile trail winds up the 400-foot mountain from Third Street (behind the high school). You'll be following in the footsteps of John Muir, who wrote about a stormy night on the mountain in his 1879 book *Travels in Alaska.*

Petroglyph Beach State Historic Park ★ On this beach, just under a mile north of town, are 50 carvings in rocks believed to have been created over a long period of time (some say 1,000 years ago; others say longer) by indigenous people predating the Tlingits. There are depictions of animals and geometric shapes. Replicas have been carved to discourage visitors from doing rubbings of the originals. You will need to do some searching to find the ancient artwork. Viewing is best at low tide; in fact, it's not worth going within a hour of high tide because you won't be able to reach the petroglyphs. From the beach you may also may spot Stellar sea lions, harbor seals, and bald eagles.

The beach is off Evergreen Ave., but since that street doesn't have sidewalks, the best way to get there is a shortcut on Stikine, which starts near the pier, past the Stikine Inn. http://dnr.alaska.gov/parks/aspunits/southeast/wrangpetroshs.htm.

Rainbow Falls Trail ★★★ Across the road from the Shoemaker Bay Recreation Area (about 5 miles from town), this trail takes you through temperate rainforest on a manmade boardwalk of more than 200 steps (some a little tricky). You are rewarded with sights that include creeks, Sitka spruce and western hemlock, and a wonderful waterfall. The waterfall is a little less than a mile up, but continue another tenth of a mile where the trail ends above the waterfall for amazing views of the Zimovia Strait.

The trailhead is across from the Shoemaker Bay Marina; Shoemaker Bay is about 5 mi. south of town on the Zimovia Hwy.

Where to Lunch

For a quick bite, the **Pit Stop** food truck (www.facebook.com/thepitstop), 526 Case Ave., toward Chief Shakes Island, has great reindeer hot dogs.

Diamond C Café ★★★ AMERICAN/SEAFOOD Big breakfasts (including at lunchtime), with all the standards, plus such items as a halibut and cheese or shrimp and cheese omelet, are part of the attraction. The other is a chance to eavesdrop as locals discuss such topics as fishing and politics.

225 Front St. www.facebook.com/Diamond-C-Cafe-200703806648331. ✆ **907/874-3677.** Main courses $7–$17. Daily 6am–2pm.

J&W's Fast Food ★ FAST FOOD/BURGERS Grab a $7 burger or fish & chips and eat on the picnic tables, rubbing shoulders with local families.

120 Front St. www.facebook.com/thedropzoneburgers. ✆ **907/874-2120.** Lunch entrees $7–$13. Mon–Sat 8am–7pm; Sun 10am–7pm.

Stik Café ★★ SANDWICHES/BAKED GOODS The Stikine Inn has the fancy waterfront dinner place in town, the **Stikine Restaurant** (referred to by locals as "The Stik"), but if you're heading out on an independent tour or planning a picnic, the best place to pick up a sandwich, soups, breakfast burritos, or baked goods (and good coffee, too!) is here at the hotel's Stik Café.

107 Stikine Ave. www.stikineinn.com. ✆ **907/874-3388.** Paninis $7–$10. Daily 6am–6pm.

Zak's Café ★ AMERICAN This is the place for sit-down, home-style meals including seafood and steak, salads, and wraps. You can watch goings-on in the open kitchen, and while you're there, check out the transplanted owner's bizarre shrine to New England sports.

316 Front St. www.facebook.com/Zaks-Cafe-219081141437379. ✆ **907/874-3355.** Mon–Fri 11am–7pm; Sat 11am–2pm; Sun 10am–1pm.

A Day in Wrangell

The must-do attraction, in our opinion, is getting close to the bears at the **Anan Wildlife Observatory.** But doing a **jet-boat tour** (or even more adventurous **raft tour**) on the Stikine is both thrilling and fascinating—oh, if only there were time for both! This is also a town where you'll want to spend some time chatting with the friendly locals, some of whom have located here from elsewhere, attracted by the fact they are in the middle of nowhere, and maintaining a pioneering spirit. We highly recommend taking some time to wander and explore on your own before or after your tour.

PETERSBURG

Known for its Norwegian heritage and fishing fleet, Petersburg is a little fishing community of 3,200. It offers plenty of small-town atmosphere, but don't let that fool you: There are big-time fishermen here, some millionaires. Fish is what drew Norwegian immigrant Peter Buschmann, who came to open a cannery in 1898, near where Tlingit fishermen had a camp for at least 2,000 years. Buschmann killed himself 4 years after he arrived, but that inauspicious history should not hinder your impression. Many of his fellow countrymen followed, and today a number of town residents can claim Norwegian lineage. This is Alaska's "Little Norway," and it is a lovely, friendly place.

Set on Mitkof Island in Frederick Sound, the town has an appealing quirkiness. Docks, pilings, and wooden walkways make downtown feel as if it is floating on water. The quintessential Petersburg photo is of colorful, weathered buildings built on pilings over Hammer Slough, the tidal mouth of the creek that runs through town. It's a place that can boast of having a family of log-rolling champions—as exhibited in waterfront contests each year on the Fourth of July. Big cruise ships can't enter the narrow harbor, so cruise passengers who visit do so on small, laid-back ships and don't encounter big crowds—which is just fine with everyone concerned.

Nordic Drive has mostly businesses catering to local residents, including family-owned grocery and hardware stores. Neat white clapboard houses have colorful flower boxes, and storefronts are decorated with Norwegian floral motifs—you really might imagine you're in a fishing village in Scandinavia.

Surrounded by water, glacier-topped mountains, and rainforest, the town has wonderful trails for hiking and biking. Eagles perch in trees around town and on the beaches. You might spot a big sea lion or two hanging around the harbor, and sightings of frolicking humpback whales are frequent where Frederick Sound meets the Stephens Passage and Chatham Strait, north of Petersburg—one of the best humpback-whale-viewing spots in North America.

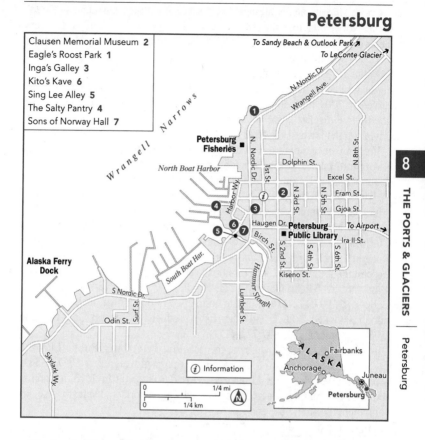

Petersburg

Clausen Memorial Museum **2**
Eagle's Roost Park **1**
Inga's Galley **3**
Kito's Kave **6**
Sing Lee Alley **5**
The Salty Pantry **4**
Sons of Norway Hall **7**

To Sandy Beach & Outlook Park
To LeConte Glacier

N. Nordic Dr.
Wrangell Ave.

Wrangell Narrows

Petersburg Fisheries

N. Nordic Dr.
North Boat Harbor

Dolphin St.
Excel St.
Fram St.
Gjoa St.

1st St.
N. 3rd St.
N. 5th St.
N. 8th St.

Haugen Dr. **Petersburg Public Library**
To Airport

Nordic Hbr.
Birch St.
Ira II St.

S. 2nd St.
S. 4th St.
S. 6th St.

Alaska Ferry Dock

South Boat Har.
Kiseno St.

Hammer Slough
Lumber St.

S Nordic Dr.
Surf St.
Odin St.
Skylark Wy.

(i) Information

0 ——— 1/4 mi
0 ——— 1/4 km

ALASKA
Fairbanks
Anchorage
Juneau
Petersburg

Nearby **LeConte Glacier,** the southernmost tidewater glacier in North America, is a prime place to visit for a half-day on small-boat tours. It's about 25 miles east of town.

It almost goes without saying: The fishing here is terrific. In fact, more seafood is landed here annually than in much better-known places such as Seattle, Gulfport, MS, and Key West. How much fish? In 2015, nearly 70 million pounds of seafood was landed and processed in town. The next year, local fishermen snagged a 396-pound halibut, and it didn't even break a record.

The town's economy is built primarily on salmon and halibut fishing. Four canneries—including **Petersburg Fisheries,** which celebrated its 50th anniversary in 2015—provide employment for some 800 migrant workers in summer. Take a stroll around the harbor for a fascinating first-hand look at a working waterfront. The processing companies are not typically open to visitors, but in the three harbors, north, south, and middle, nearly 700 vessels—from 12-foot rowboats to mega-tenders—work to haul hundreds of thousands of pounds of salmon back to the canneries. Big yachts are also a frequent sight in summer, despite the fact that in the warm months downtown smells, well, fishy.

Cruise ships typically arrange a performance for their passengers of traditional Norwegian folk dances performed by the local Leikarring Dancers, either shipboard or at the gorgeously renovated **Sons of Norway Hall,** built in 1912 and still the community's social hall and local source of pride.

About 10% of Petersburg's population is of Tlingit heritage. The dominating feature at the main downtown intersection is the **Eagle and Raven Poles,** carved in 2001 by well-known artists Tommy Joseph and Fred Beltran. An interpretive display at the totem park (at the corner of Haugen and Nordic drives, on the lawn of the federal building) provides details on the imagery.

Logging, once a mainstay in the community, returned in 2014 when nearby **Kupreanof Island** was the site for a major timber sale, scenes of which were featured on the TV show *Ax Men* on the History Channel.

Every one of the stores in town are locally owned—another source of pride—and shopping opportunities downtown include, naturally, the availability of Norwegian sweaters and other Scandinavian goods. Stop by **Lee's Clothing** for Norwegian hats, sweaters, and blankets along with gear from Patagonia, the North Face, and more (212 Nordic Dr.; www.facebook.com/leesclothing/; ℭ 907/772-4229). A dozen artists exhibit jewelry, paintings, and prints at the **Miele Gallery** (211 Nordic Dr.; www.facebook.com/Miele Gallery/; ℭ 907/772-2161), on the north edge of downtown. Pick up smoked salmon, smoked halibut, and other fishy products at **Coastal Cold Storage** (306 N. Nordic Dr.; ℭ 907/772-4172).

A few blocks from downtown, the beautiful **Petersburg Public Library,** 14 S. 2nd St. (corner of Haugen Dr.) (http://psglib.org; ℭ 907/772-3349; Mon–Fri 11am–8pm, Sat 11am–6pm, closed Sun), built in 2013, is another source of community pride. Stop by to see local artwork on display (it also has computers for public use and free Wi-Fi).

Those looking for today's colorful residents will want to stop for a drink at **Kito's Kave** (11 Sing Lee Alley; www.facebook.com/kitos.kave/; ℭ 907/772-3207; daily 10am–2am), the local dive bar, where you'll find music, pool tables, sports on TV, and historic photos on the walls—among them, John Wayne, who stopped by town on his boat in 1967, and Richard Burton and Jim Backus, who were here filming the 1960 movie *Ice Palace.*

COMING ASHORE The small cruise ships that visit here dock right near downtown or occasionally tender passengers ashore (the harbor is not deep enough for larger ships). The Alaska Marine Highway System uses the small, welcoming ferry terminal, about a half-mile from the town center.

INFORMATION For trail guides and natural-history publications, head to the **Petersburg Chamber of Commerce Visitor Information Center,** at 19 Fram St. (corner of 1st St.) (www.petersburg.org; ℭ 907/772-4636), about 6 blocks from the pier. It's open in summer Monday through Saturday 9am to 5pm and Sunday noon to 4pm. The **U.S. Forest Service–Tongass Ranger District office** is at 12 N. Nordic Dr. (ℭ 907/772-3871).

Best Cruise-Line Shore Excursions

Many of the small-ship lines that visit here include tour options in the cruise fare—usually a choice of a boat trip to the glacier, an escorted walk around town, a hike, or a bike ride—with more exclusive options such as fishing or flightseeing available for a fee. Some lines also offer jet-boat tours or trips to Anan Creek to spot bears (see our writeup in the Wrangell section, above).

LeConte Glacier by Boat (4½ hr.; $250): LeConte Glacier is the southernmost tidewater glacier in North America and is located at the end of a 7-mile-long fjord filled with blue icebergs, some quite huge. Don't be surprised if your boat bangs into smaller icebergs as your captain maneuvers closer to the glacier. You are likely to find the flattest of the icebergs inhabited by seals and their pups, especially early in the season. (For the more adventurous, some lines offer the opportunity to kayak around the icebergs. Bundle up, because it's likely to be cold!)

LeConte Glacier & Stikine River Flightseeing (1 hr.; $199): Fly over coastal mountains to the Stikine Ice Field and the mighty glacier, and experience the excitement of a takeoff and landing on the water.

Excursions Offered by Local Agencies

The full-service **Viking Travel** agency, on the corner of Nordic Drive and Sing Lee Alley (www.alaskaferry.com; ✆ **800/327-2571** or 907/772-3818), specializes in booking local guides for tours, kayaking, whale-watching, flights, fishing charters, and more (they are also experts in navigating the travel options of the Alaska Marine Highway). **Alaska Passage Adventures** (www.alaska passages.com; ✆ **907/772-3967**) is also locally owned and has full- and half-day LeConte Glacier Tours and kayaking among icebergs, as well as whale-watching excursions to Frederick Sound. **Tongass Kayak Adventures** (www.tongasskayak.com; ✆ **907/772-4600**) does whale-watching and LeConte Glacier tours, with or without sea kayaks.

Outstanding fishing is available for sport anglers, and charter boats can take you saltwater fishing for salmon and halibut. Mitkof Island has several salmon and trout streams; and you can fish right off the shore during the June and July king salmon run at road-accessible Blind River Rapids. If you want to set off on your own, car rental is available from $70 per day at the **Scandia House** hotel (www.scandiahousehotel.com; ✆ **907/772-4281**). **Pacific Wings** is among companies offering charter flights (www.pacwing.com; ✆ **907/772-4258**).

On Your Own: Within Walking Distance

Clausen Memorial Museum ★★ This is the place to discover the colorful history of Petersburg. Exhibits include a Tlingit dugout canoe, commercial fishing equipment, the lens from the Cape Decision Lighthouse, Nordic costumes, and the star attraction: a 126½-pound stuffed king salmon. The museum also shows a half-hour video called "The Town That Fish Built" and has a nice little gift shop. Outdoors is "The Fisk," a fish sculpture (*fisk* is Norwegian for fish), created by Pacific Northwest artist Karsten Boysen.

201 Fram St. (at 2nd St.). www.clausenmuseum.com. © **907/772-3598.** Admission $5, free for children. Mon–Sat 10am–5pm.

Eagle's Roost Park ★★ This municipal park is an excellent hilltop spot to picnic and admire the views. Be on the lookout for bald eagles, who like to perch and roost here.

N. Nordic Dr., just on the edge of downtown.

Sing Lee Alley ★★★ Sing Lee Alley was named for a local businessman who was killed on the street—yes, the town's history is colorful. Much of the street is built atop pilings over Hammer Slough. Along the wooden stretch you'll find the **Sons of Norway Hall,** a social hall built in 1912 and listed on the National Register of Historic Places. Next door is a bronze statue of fisherman and lifelong resident Bojer Wikan, commemorating mariners who have lost their lives at sea. There's also a giant model of a Viking ship used in the annual Little Norway Festival (third weekend in May). **Sing Lee Alley Books & Gifts,** 11 Sing Lee Alley (www.facebook.com/SingLeeAlleyBooks/; © **907/ 772-4440**), has a good collection of field guides and books on Alaska.

Sing Lee Alley.

Where to Lunch

Inga's Galley ★★★ SEAFOOD This seasonal restaurant creates daily specials based on the fresh catch of the day, such as seafood curry, halibut chowder, grilled shrimp, rockfish tacos with chipotle lime slaw, and divine fish jaws. You order at the counter and eat at outdoor tables under a tarp.

104 N. Nordic Dr. www.facebook.com/IngasGalley/. © **907/772-2090.** Mon–Sat 11am– 8pm from early May (breakfast beginning at 7am June–Sept). Main courses $10–$16.

The Salty Pantry ★★ BAKERY/ARTISAN FOODS This business started when the owner won a Path to Prosperity competition to encourage business development. The menu changes daily, but in addition to amazing baked goods, sandwiches (including bacon cheeseburgers) on house-made bread, and pizza, you might find crab quiche, chicken sausage cassoulet, crab mac & cheese, and rockfish enchiladas, as well as a variety of salads.

14 Harbor Way. www.facebook.com/thesaltypantry. © **907/772-2665.** Daily 6am–4pm. Main courses $8–$13.

On Your Own: Beyond the Port Area

The Big Loop Hike ★★ A favorite of locals, this 4.8-mile hike takes you around the perimeter of town and past the airport and muskeg meadows, with plenty of mountain and ocean views. Head up the hill by the totem poles at the corner of Haugen and Nordic drives to reach the Haugen Drive walking and biking path (a 5-foot shoulder that runs adjacent to the road to the airport) and follow the path all the way to Sandy Beach Park (which has some petroglyphs and ancient fish traps, hard to spot without a guide). Turn left and take Sandy

Beach Road to Nordic Drive and follow it along the Wrangell Narrows until you reach downtown. It's an easy loop, and a great way to stretch your legs.

Outlook Park ★★   On the beach side of Sandy Beach Road, about 1½ miles north of downtown, is a wooden shelter with fixed binoculars for viewing the surrounding Coastal Range, whales and other marine animals, birds, icebergs, and the boats in Frederick Sound. A local shipwright built the gazebo in the style of an overturned Viking ship in 2003.

A Day in Petersburg

If your passion is whales, go on a **whale-watching** tour. Otherwise, we recommend a trip to the **LeConte Glacier** to view icebergs and, if you're lucky, baby seals. The ride out includes a passage through 600-foot-deep water; the fun begins as your captain navigates around the massive ice (and bumps into smaller chunks). Anglers will have a blast on a **fishing charter outing,** and may just haul in the big one. Our other favorite thing in town is **walking the waterfront** and chatting with the commercial fishermen. Listen to local fish tales over a beer at **Kito's Kave** or while sharing a table at **Inga's.**

JUNEAU

Quick quiz: Can you name a state capital that cannot be reached by road from anywhere else in the state? Juneau, it is! Fronted by the bustling Gastineau Channel and backed by Mount Juneau (elevation 3,819 ft.) and Mount Roberts (elevation 3,576 ft.), the city is on the mainland of Alaska but is cut off by the Juneau Icefield to the east and wilderness to the north and south. To be sure, there are roads—150 miles of them, in fact—but all dead-end against an impenetrable forest or ice wall.

In 1900, Congress moved the territorial capital to Juneau from Sitka, which had fallen behind in the flurry of gold-rush development. Not all Alaskans believe Juneau is the right and logical place for a legislative center. Its inaccessibility, some argue, disenfranchises many voters, and every few years somebody puts a "move the capital" initiative on the ballot. So far, all the proposals have been defeated. Among Juneau's 33,000 residents, government is the city's biggest industry. However, tourism is not far behind: Besides the thousands of independent visitors who arrive by air and ferry, many more thousands come ashore during the 500 or so passenger-ship port calls made here each summer.

On any given day, four or five big cruise ships, as well as some small ships, may be in port (on a really busy day, those ships that can't get a place at the docks will have to tender their guests ashore). While the city is dependent on tourism, not everyone loves the crowds, and it's easier to grasp the residents' unhappiness when you think of the number of cruise passengers who pour into downtown—it's a different place when, say, 18,000 tourists arrive for the day.

To handle the crowds, the city recently completed work on a major $55-million overhaul of the ship staging area, including reconfiguring sidewalks and crosswalks and creating a pleasant sea walk. If you haven't been to Juneau for a few years, the changes might make your jaw drop. Included are two new concrete floating docks, capable of handling the largest ships visiting Southeast Alaska (the design quickly won awards). At the pier, check out the **Fisherman's Memorial,** a monument dedicated to those who lost their lives in the commercial fishing industry, and the **statue of Patsy Ann,** a famous deaf bull terrier born in 1929 and known for greeting steamships and visitors—rubbing her head is still considered good luck!

Juneau is a product of Alaska's golden past. It was no more than a fishing outpost for local Tlingit Indians when gold was discovered in a creek off the Gastineau Channel by two prospectors, Joe Juneau and Richard (Dick) Harris, in 1880. To be accurate, the gold was discovered first by Chief Kowee of the Auk Tlingit clan, who, in return for 100 warm blankets (more important to him than gold), passed on the information to a German engineer named George Pilz. Surveying sites around the Inside Passage for mineral deposits, Pilz gave the hitherto unsuccessful Juneau and Harris directions to the spot described by Chief Kowee—and they couldn't find it! Only when Kowee accompanied them on a second expedition did they succeed in pinpointing the source of the precious metal—and the rush was on. Mines sprang up on both sides of the channel. So rich was the area's gold yield that mines continued to be open for the next 3 decades, including the most successful of them all, the **Alaska-Juneau Mine** (aka the A-J), which produced a whopping 3.5 million ounces of gold before it closed in 1944. Head to the **Perseverance National Recreation Trail** (the trailhead is about 1½ miles from downtown) to see remaining mine buildings.

Today Juneau is arguably the most handsome of the 50 state capitals, despite a glut of souvenir shops near the pier (where you can buy anything from I LOVE ALASKA backscratchers to fur coats). The city runs with a mix of quiet business efficiency and easygoing informality. It has a good deal more sophistication to it than any city in Alaska outside of Anchorage (it's also known as a "blue" city in a "red" state).

Yet there is still the frontier-style **Red Dog Saloon,** 278 S. Franklin St. (© 907/463-3658), with its sawdust floor and swinging doors, a memorabilia-filled pub (serving food and drink including Alaskan Brewing Company selections) whose old-time raucousness may be tempered by its pursuit of the tourist buck (and a location adjacent to the Juneau Police headquarters). Another place to enjoy a not-so-quiet drink is the bar of the **Alaskan Hotel,** nearby at 167 S. Franklin St. (© 800/327-9347), built in 1913. On the National Register of Historic Places, the Alaskan is Juneau's oldest operating hotel. Recent additions to the imbibing scene include tastings at the **Amalga Distillery,** 134 N. Franklin St. (www.amalgadistillery.com; © 907/209-2015), producing gin, vodka, and single malt whiskey; and **The Narrows,** 148 S. Franklin St. (www.facebook.com/thenarrowsbaralaska/; © 415-205-3704), a fancy speak-easy serving craft cocktails and a choice of some 150 whiskeys.

Juneau's must-do attraction, the **Mendenhall Glacier,** is at the head of a valley a dozen miles away. The glacier is one of Alaska's most accessible and most photographed ice faces. On the way to and from the glacier, keep an eye

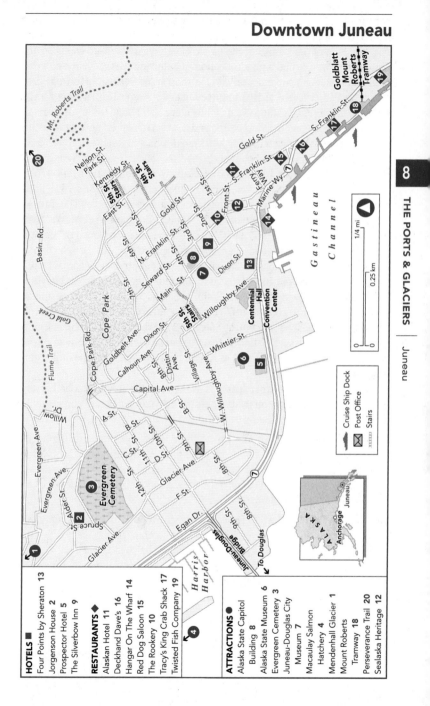

HOTELS ■

Four Points by Sheraton **13**
Jorgenson House **2**
Prospector Hotel **5**
The Silverbow Inn **9**

RESTAURANTS ◆

Alaskan Hotel **11**
Deckhand Dave's **16**
Hangar On The Wharf **14**
Red Dog Saloon **15**
The Rookery **10**
Tracy's King Crab Shack **17**
Twisted Fish Company **19**

ATTRACTIONS ●

Alaska State Capitol
  Building **8**
Alaska State Museum **6**
Evergreen Cemetery **3**
Juneau-Douglas City
  Museum **7**
Macaulay Salmon
  Hatchery **4**
Mendenhall Glacier **1**
Mount Roberts
  Tramway **18**
Perseverance Trail **20**
Sealaska Heritage **12**

out for eagles, who seem to like sitting atop light poles (we saw more than a half-dozen on one ride).

While a lot of the shops downtown are clearly geared toward capturing the tourist buck, you'll find a good selection of authentic Alaska Native artwork, both traditional and contemporary, in the shop at the **Sealaska Heritage** center in the Walter Soboleff Building (see below). **Annie Kaill's Fine Crafts Gallery,** 244 Front St. (http://anniekaills.com; © **907-586-2880**), has arts & crafts, including homemade pottery and jewelry. For cutting-edge creative gifts, check out **Aurora Projekt,** 171 Franklin St. (http://auroraprojekt.com; © **907/523-0405**), with its board-shop vibe for locally designed T-shirts and cards. The cooperative **Juneau Artist Gallery in the Senate Mall,** 175 S. Franklin St., Ste 111 (www.juneauartistsgallery.com; © **907/586-9891**), features the works of more than 25 local artists and craftspeople. The **Juneau Arts and Humanities Council,** 350 Whittier St. (near the Alaska State Museum) (www.jahc.org; © **907/586-2787**), has an excellent gift shop of reasonably priced local goods. For an edible gift, check out the selection of Barnacle brand salsa, pickles, seasonings, and other products made of kelp at the pop-up **At the Port** shop, located in a shipping container in the alley that runs between the waterfront and South Franklin Street, next to the library (www.barnaclefoods.com; © **907/957-4476**). **Hearthside Books,** 254 Front St. (www.hearthsidebooks.com; © **866/789-2750** or 907/789-2750), is locally owned and has a friendly staff that can help you pick a book to read on sea days. It also has a good selection of Alaska books, including those on the gold rush and Native culture.

Note: Free public Internet access is available at the Juneau Public Library, the big concrete building on the left past the ship pier but before you get to the Red Dog Saloon.

COMING ASHORE   If you arrive at one of the two new floating docks, you'll encounter a lively waterfront setting. The private South Frank Street dock, primarily used by Princess, is still close to the action, while the private AJ Dock is about a mile from town (it's not a bad walk, but shuttle buses are also available into downtown).

INFORMATION   Travel Juneau (www.traveljuneau.com; © **888/586-2201**) operates an impressively modern visitor center on the sea walk—with colorful tiles to mimic the scales of a salmon on the outside and a tall wooden ceiling resembling a fishing boat. Stop in to pick up a walking-tour map and visitor's guide before striking out to see the sights. There's also a smaller kiosk at Marine Park. Along the wharf are booths with vendors selling tours.

Best Cruise-Line Shore Excursions

Evening Whale-Watching Quest (3½ hr.; $169 adults, $129 children): Combine whale-watching from a jet-powered catamaran in Stephen's Passage with an evening buffet and a chance to enjoy Alaska's summer twilight. You are guaranteed to see whales or you get your money back. Humpbacks are likely—this is a known breeding area—and orcas possible.

Glacier Flightseeing by Floatplane (1¼ hr.; $229 adults, $205 children): Seeing the grand glaciers of Alaska is a thrill, and so is taking off and landing in the water in a floatplane. On this once-in-a-lifetime flight, you'll see five majestic glaciers of the Juneau Icefield, the fifth-largest ice field in the Western Hemisphere. From your window seat, you'll also catch views of waterfalls and lush green rainforests. Expanded floatplane tours visit the remote, log-cabin-style Taku Lodge for lunch (3½ hr.; $315 adult, $270 children) or take anglers to a remote creek for fly-fishing (5½ hr.; $499).

Glacier Helicopter (2¾ hr.; $419): This thrilling trip is definitely not for those who are faint of heart or out of shape. The excursion involves a flight to the Juneau Icefield and the glaciers found there. Some walking is involved (always in the company of a trained mountain guide). Accommodations may be made in advance for wheelchair-bound passengers, but generally a certain level of fitness is recommended—check with your cruise line for advice. Even more amazing versions include a dogsled ride on the ice field ($650) or a mountaineering trek to explore the glacier's deep crevasses ($549).

Gold-Mine History Tour (4 hr.; $69 adults, $45 children): Juneau's gold-rush history comes to life (especially for kids) as you visit the ruins of the AJ Gold Mine/Gastineau Mill. Don a hard hat for a walk along a 360-foot tunnel and a demonstration of early-20th-century mining equipment and methods.

Mendenhall Glacier & Whale Quest (5¼ hr.; $199 adults, $135 children): Twelve miles long and 1½ miles wide, Mendenhall is the most visited glacier in the world and the most popular sight in Juneau. This trip will take you by bus to the U.S. Forest Service Observatory, from which you can walk up a trail to within a half-mile of the glacier (which feels a lot closer) or take one of the nature trails if time allows. After this experience you hit the sea in search of whales in a water-jet-powered catamaran.

Mendenhall River Float Trip (3½ hr.; $149 adults, $99 children): Board a 10-person raft on the shore of Mendenhall Lake, and an experienced oarsman will guide you out past icebergs and into the Mendenhall River. You'll encounter moderate rapids and stunning views and be treated to a snack of smoked salmon and reindeer sausage along the way.

Excursions Offered by Local Agencies

At the pier, you'll find booths operated by various independent tour operators selling city and glacier tours starting at about $45 per person.

Ziplining in Juneau is provided through locally owned **Alaska Zipline Adventure** (www.alaskazip.com; ✆ **907/321-0947**), which will harness you up to fly above the treetops for $149 adults, $99 children 9 to 12 (minimum age 9), for a 3¾-hour excursion, including the ride. The company also offers combo zipline and Mendenhall Glacier tours for $199.

Juneau Food Tours (www.juneaufoodtours.com; ✆ **800/656-0713**) is an excellent small-group walking tour created by a local food writer Kelly "Midgi" Moore, where you eat and drink (including at Tracy's King Crab Shack; see below) while you learn the city's history (Juneau Bites food tour

$129; Bites & Booze tour $95). Juneau is also home to the award-winning **Alaskan Brewing Company** (https://alaskanbeer.com; ☎ **907/780-5866**), and a **Liquid Alaska Tours** (https://liquidalaskatours.com; ☎ **800/892-5504**) shuttle departs from the Alaskan Brewery Depot, 219 S. Franklin Street, 40 minutes past each hour, beginning at 10:40am. The cost ($20) includes transportation and a tasting at the brewery at 5429 Shaune Dr.

Liquid Alaska Tours also offers a Mendenhall Glacier Ice Adventure (from $289), where you paddle in a native-style canoe to an ice cave at the glacier. **Alaska Adventures Juneau** (http://alaskaadventuresjuneau.com; ☎ **907/789-3772**), has a bunch of custom packages including an Alaska Custom Hummer Excursion ($582 for 4 hours, for up to four people). For private flightseeing, check out **Juneau Adventure Tours** (http://www.juneauadventuretours.com; ☎ **907/723-8908**). Taking a creative approach to ecotourism is **Gastineau Guiding** (www.stepintoalaska.com; ☎ **907/586-2666**), which offers a naturalist-led photo safari that combines Mendenhall Glacier and a whale-spotting trip into the Stephens Passage by boat ($199 per person).

On Your Own: Within Walking Distance

Alaska State Capitol Building ★★★   We've often wondered how so lovely a capital city could come up with such an unprepossessing legislative home (ca. 1931). Still, the interior is worth a visit to see the old-fashioned woodwork and decorative details, especially in the lobby and legislative chambers (the governor's offices are on the third floor). The new bronze statue of William Seward out front was erected in 2017 to commemorate the 150th anniversary of the sale of Alaska to the U.S. (Like many things in Alaska, the sculpture was somewhat controversial, some noting that the Tlingit and Haida people were not asked to weigh in 150 years ago on the 1867 "Alaska Purchase.")

4th Ave. and Main St. ☎ **907/465-3853.** Free admission. Summer Mon–Fri 8am–5pm. Closed Sat and Sun.

Alaska State Museum (SLAM)★★★   Opened in 2016 on the site of a previous museum, the beautiful Andrew P. Kashevaroff State Library, Archives and Museum (SLAM) is an absolute must-do for those looking to explore Alaska's art, history, and culture. Pick up a map at the front desk and follow the suggested route for a great overview of the state and its people (you can see a lot in an hour). Exhibits include Alaska Native artifacts (such as masks, beadwork, canoes, and carvings). Touch screens and videos detail the Tribes of Alaska, the influence of foreigners, Russia America, the Gold Rush, political history, tourism (check out the exhibit on early steamships), and Alaska's role in the World Wars. There's also a gallery featuring temporary exhibits of the work of Alaskan artists, and a nifty museum shop.

395 Whittier St. (about a half-mile from the floating docks, along the sea walk). http://museums.alaska.gov. ☎ **888-913-MUSE** or 907/465-2901. Admission $12 adults, $11 seniors, free for youth 18 and under. Daily 9am–5pm (call about winter hours).

Evergreen Cemetery ★   This beautiful cemetery, which slopes toward the ocean, holds the gravesites of Joe Juneau, Richard Harris, and other pioneers. The old Alaska Native graves are located in the wooded area on the far side of the cemetery.

Seater St., just west of the downtown area.

Goldbelt Mount Roberts Tramway ★★★   The best place to take in Juneau's lovely position on the Gastineau Channel is an easy 6-minute ride in the comfortable 60-passenger cars of the Mount Roberts Tramway. Operated by Goldbelt, a Tlingit corporation, the tramway rises from a base alongside the cruise-ship docks and whisks sightseers 1,800 feet up to a center with a restaurant/bar, gift shop, museum, cultural film shows, a series of nature trails (bring mosquito repellent!), and a fabulous panorama. Don't miss it—but on the other hand, don't bother if the day is overcast: Some visitors have paid the fees for an all-day pass, reached the top, and been faced with a solid wall of white mist. You can also hike up the 4½-mile Mt. Roberts Trail to the peak.

At the cruise-ship docks. http://mountrobertstramway.com. ℰ **888/461-8726** or 907/463-3412. All-day pass $33 adults, $16 children 6–12, free for children 5 and under. May–Sept Mon noon–9pm; Tues–Fri 8am–9pm; Sat–Sun 9am–9pm.

Juneau-Douglas City Museum ★   The star attraction of this city museum is a Native basketry fish trap found in 1989 in the Montana Creek, about 13 miles from Juneau, believed to be the oldest fish trap in existence. Exactly how it works is subject to debate. Other exhibits focus on the city's beginnings and industries (including mining) and include a 30-minute video presentation. Hands-on exhibits are targeted to kids, and a gallery area highlights the works of Juneau artists.

Corner of 4th and Main sts. www.juneau.org/museum. ℰ **907/586-3572.** Admission $6 adults and ages 13 and up, $5 seniors, free for children. Summer hours Mon–Fri 9am–6pm; Sat–Sun 10am–4:30pm.

Sealaska Heritage and Walter Soboleff Building ★★   This impressive Alaska Native cultural center has three major public artworks including a walk-in clan house as well as changing exhibits—such as an extraordinary exhibit showcasing contemporary interpretations of traditional masks. The excellent gift shop has carvings and other Alaska Native artworks.

105 S. Seward St. www.sealaskaheritage.org/true-southeast. ℰ **907/463-4844.** Admission is $5 adults, $4 seniors, free for children under age 7. Daily 9am–8pm.

On Your Own: Beyond the Port Area

Glacier Gardens Rainforest Adventure ★★   Opened in 1998, this botanical garden was created in an area that had been decimated in a landslide. Privately owned, the garden has since expanded to 50 acres of landscaped gardens with alpine and other flowers and lush rainforest, including an eagle viewing area. A golf-cart shuttle takes you past the blooming flowers as you travel up Thunder Mountain, high above Gastineau Channel and past trees, waterfalls, and ponds. You can get to the gardens by city bus ($2) or cab (about $25 each way from downtown). There is also a greenhouse area with beautiful hanging plants, a gift shop, and a small cafe serving beverages and sandwiches (locals winter their plants here). Ships also sell prebooked tours to Glacier Gardens for those who prefer not to travel on their own.

7600 Glacier Hwy. www.glaciergardens.com. (?) **907/790-3377.** Admission $25 adults, $16 children 6–12, free for children 5 and under (includes guided 1½-hr. golf-cart tour). May–Sept daily 9am–6pm.

Macaulay Salmon Hatchery ★★★ About 2½ miles from downtown Juneau, the nonprofit **Douglas Island Pink and Chum (DIPAC)** hatchery operates this visitor center to educate the public about Alaska's wild salmon. Catch a bird's-eye view of outdoor hatchery operations, with brief commentary by local guides, and then head inside the facility to see impressive saltwater aquariums filled with more than 150 species of local marine life, including a 5,000-gallon tank and touch tanks for those who want to get up close and personal with sea creatures. An Extended Tour (mid-June to Aug only) takes visitors to an incubation room where salmon eggs are hatched and a "raceway room" where hundreds of thousands of tiny king salmon mature before they're ready for saltwater. The museum gift shop sells both local art and salmon products.

2697 Channel Dr. www.dipac.net. (?) **907/463-4810** or 877/463-2486. Admission $5 adults, $3 children, free under 2; Extended Tour $15 adults, $10 children. May–Sept Mon–Fri 10am–6pm; Sat–Sun 10am–5pm; winter by appointment only.

Mendenhall Glacier ★★★ Mendenhall is the easiest glacier to get to in Alaska and the most visited glacier in the world. Its U.S. Forest Service visitor center has glacier exhibits, a 12-minute movie called *Magnificent Mendenhall,* and rangers who can answer any questions. Check out the trail descriptions and choose from several that'll take you close to the glacier and Nugget Falls. The easiest ones are the .3-mile **photo trail** (which takes about 20 min. and provides an excellent glacial photo op) and the ½-mile **Trail of Time,** a self-guided nature path (which takes about 1 hr. to complete). The 3½-mile **Eastern Glacier Loop** follows the glacial trim line, with a lot of time in the forest. It takes about 2 hours and includes some moderate uphill climbing. If you hike, bring water, sunscreen, and bug spray. Bears occasionally are spotted in the forest; if you do encounter one, stand still but make a lot of noise.

Mendenhall is about 12 miles from downtown, and taxis and local bus services are readily available in town (bus $2 each way; taxis about $25) for those who want to visit independently of a tour. If you take a taxi out, make arrangements with the driver to also pick you up—and negotiate a round-trip price before you leave. Or take the **MGT (Mighty Great Trips) Blue Glacier Express,** a bus that offers round-trip service between the pier and the door of the glacier visitor center for $20 per person. No reservation is needed; just walk off the ship and get on one of the buses parked 50 yards away (just past the Mount Roberts Tramway). It's an old school bus painted bright blue—not necessarily the most comfortable way to go—but it has an advantage over city transportation in that it really takes you to Mendenhall Glacier, as opposed to dropping you off at the bus stop more than a mile away. Since it doesn't stop to pick up or drop off riders en route, the MGT Mendenhall Glacier Express gets you there in 25 minutes; although the city bus is cheaper, the ride takes closer to an hour. The MGT bus also comes with commentary, such wisdom as: "Why does the bald eagle have a white head? Because the raven flies above."

Off Mendenhall Loop Rd. www.fs.usda.gov/tongass/. ℰ **907/789-0097.** Admission to visitor center $5 adults, free for children 15 and under. May–Sept daily 8am–7:30pm.

Where to Lunch

See also chapter 7 for **The Rookery, Twisted Fish,** and **Red Dog Saloon.**

Deckhand Dave's ★★ FISH TACOS   A food cart/open-air dining scene takes place behind the Juneau Library (at least for now, at press time the property was for sale). This is where Tracy's (see below) got her start. The latest big hit is this open-air fish taco spot, started by a a 20-something local, Dave McCasland, who worked on commercial fishing boats and serves up amazing wild Alaskan fish tacos based on the local catch. Try the panko-crusted salmon tacos with housemade tartar sauce. McCasland said he lost sleep creating the recipe—but the results are yummy. Local beer and wine is served from a "boat" that was once part of a children's museum display.

356 S. Franklin St. www.deckhanddaves.com. ℰ **907/957-2212.** Main courses $12–$18. Daily 11am–8pm.

The Hangar on the Wharf ★ AMERICAN   A popular hangout with tourists and locals alike, this spot at the end of the docks (look for the blue building, a former aircraft hangar), serves up craft cocktails, seafood, and burgers and more than 125 beer selections (25 on tap), plus views of the Gastineau Channel, Douglas Island, and the takeoffs and landings of floatplanes heading out to the Taku Glacier Lodge.

2 Marine Way, #106. www.hangaronthewharf.com. ℰ **907/586-5018.** Main courses $11–$31. Daily 11am–10pm.

Tracy's King Crab Shack ★★★ SEAFOOD ˙ Right on the ship pier, this is the place to try giant boiled crab legs and Tracy's famous crab bisque (so popular that she now provides ship-home service). When *Top Chef* filmed Season 10 in Alaska, the hosts couldn't get enough of Tracy's delectable crab, even waiting in line with the rest of her fans (the place opens at 10:30am and there's a line even then). The open-air kitchen is on the pier so you can watch what's going into the boiling pots. Splurge on a large bucket and get a shareable 3 pounds of crab ($122) served with melted butter and garlic rolls. Or go with the Crab Shack Combo ($37)—giant king crab leg, crab bisque, and mini crab cakes—great with Juneau-made Alaskan Amber or a Denali Twister Creek IPA (among selections on tap).

406 S. Franklin St. www.kingcrabshack.com. ℰ **907/723-1811.** Daily 10:30am–8:30pm. Mains $11–$122.

A Day in Juneau

It's easy to get caught up in the tourist scene here, but make sure to also pause to appreciate the natural scenery. Juneau is simply a beautiful city, with mountains rising from the ocean. Our first goal is getting out to **Mendenhall Glacier,** not just to take in its magnificence, but also to see how far it's retreated since

THE LOWDOWN ON pot IN ALASKA

In 2015, marijuana was legalized in Alaska, and several fledgling businesses in popular cruise ports such as Skagway, Juneau, and Ketchikan offer locally grown products (and in some cases edibles, too). Cruise passengers can legally buy pot for consumption in Alaska, but there a rub: You cannot legally use it. That's because under state regulations, smoking marijuana is only allowed in private, and nowhere in public view except at licensed retail marijuana shops that have a designated spot for consumption. And at press time, no on-site consumption was allowed—though there was a move afoot to change that.

The State Marijuana Control Board approved a proposal in July 2017 to lay out guidelines for on-site consumption— eating or smoking in retail shops. Advocates are hoping that by spring 2018, Alaska could be the first state to allow cannabis café consumption (though they also may have to contend with towns and cities instituting their own bans).

Cruise passengers need to be aware that marijuana, including edibles, is **illegal on all cruise ships,** which operate under federal laws banning all consumption. Try to bring it on a ship, and you could get in big trouble.

Just like liquor, you must be over 21 to possess, consume, and purchase cannabis from a licensed store.

With that in mind, here are some of the new cannabis businesses: In Ketchikan, the **Stoney Moose** (127 Steadman St.; https://thestoneymoose.com; ℂ **907/220-0822**) is right in the Creek Street historic district, which 100 years ago was the city's red-light district. Juneau has two downtown dispensaries: **Rainforest Farms Café** (216 2nd St.; http://rainforestfarms.org; ℂ **907/209-2670**) and the **Fireweed Factory** (237 Front St.; ℂ **907/957-2670**). Close to the action in historic Skagway is the **Remedy Shoppe** (371 Third Ave.; www.remedyshoppe907.com; ℂ **907/983-3345**).

Juneau Cannabis Tours (http://juneaucannabistours.com; ℂ **907-500-8344**) is a fledgling business with plans to take participants on a walking tour to see two dispensaries, including part of a grow operation ($70 for a 2-hr. tour).

our last visit. Hiking trails for different views of the glacier is a worthwhile pursuit—just keep an eye out for bears! On the **waterfront,** it's fun to watch the commercial fishing boats download their catch, which go up conveyer belts at the **Taku Fisheries** (next to the Twisted Fish restaurant). Take a good look at the water while you're there—you may see some salmon jumping. Carl Uchytil, retired from the Coast Guard and now Juneau's port director (he oversaw the massive redo of the downtown waterfront), says his very favorite out-of-town excursion is a trip out to the **Taku Glacier Lodge,** combining the quintessential Alaskan experiences of a thrilling floatplane ride over a glacier (taking off and landing on water) and a salmon bake in a peaceful setting (you may even spot some bears). You'll also likely be pleasantly rewarded if you book a **boat tour to see whales,** either by day or in the summer evening sun. Another of Uchytil's favorites is a visit to the **AJ Gold Mine**—mining, after all, is what brought a lot people to this town in the first place. You can get there on a shore excursion or walk up about 1½ miles from the pier and hike the **Perseverance National Recreation Trail.** We're fans of the **Juneau Food Tours** offered by "Midgi" Moore and her team of "hosts" and concur with her philosophy that food memories can be as enduring as nature memories. Speaking of which, **Tracy's King Crab Shack** is simply awesome. If you have the time, don't miss a look at the Alaska Native artwork at the **Walter Soboleff Center** and in the new **Alaska State Museum.** Back at the waterfront, don't forget to say hi to the city's "official" greeter **Patsy Ann** (note that the dog hated her collar, which on her statue is depicted at her feet).

ICY STRAIT POINT, ICY STRAIT & HOONAH

Owned by Huna Totem Corporation, Icy Strait Point has been operating as a cruise ship destination since 2004 (the name didn't exist on maps before that time!). What you'll find here, thanks to a $40-million renovation in 2016, is a new dock, 24 shore excursions, 14 retail shops, three waterfront restaurants, walking trails, beaches, tribal and culinary theaters, and the world's largest zipline, which ends just steps from the new cruise ship dock—now upgraded to accommodate the largest ships in the world. The heart of Icy Strait Point is the historic **Hoonah Packing Company cannery.** The cannery was built in 1912 and is now a museum and retail center featuring historic machine displays dating back to its original opening.

If all that sounds awfully touristy, be aware Icy Strait Point is located on Chichagof Island, just 1.5 miles from the city of Hoonah, home of the largest Native Tlinglit settlement in Alaska with a year-round population of about 750, and a small number of seasonal residents adding to the summer population. The area is a prime location for authentic natural wildlife sightings. Chichagof Island hosts one of the highest densities of coastal brown (grizzly) bears anywhere in the world, with about 1.7 bears per square mile. The Northwest Trading Company arrived in town and opened a store in 1880; a mission and school were created shortly thereafter. The city got its first post office in 1901, and in 1944 fire destroyed much of the city, including Tlingit artifacts. The federal government led a rebuilding effort, and the city was incorporated in 1946. And while blue-collar Hoonah may have just been "discovered," the Huna Tlingit have resided here for thousands of years.

Icy Strait Point also provides access to one of the best whale-watching destinations in the world, Point Adolphus. For decades scientists have been studying whales at Point Adolphus, where a convergence of currents provides plentiful food for whales and other wildlife. According to local officials, Icy Strait Point visitors have seen whales on every single whale-watching excursion since 2004—tours guarantee sightings. Onshore, Hoonah is surrounded by new- and old-growth rainforest, where bald eagles are frequently spotted overhead. The waters around Icy Strait Point are teeming with halibut and five species of salmon, making it a paradise for anglers.

Alaska-size adventures abound in Icy Strait Point, with self-drive Zodiac raft tours, 4WD and ATV treks, and the aforementioned zipline, **ZipRider,** one of the top rides of its kind in the world. It is currently the only ride with

A local PERSPECTIVE

"When I think about growing up in Hoonah, I never would've imagined we would be sharing this beautiful and majestic haven we call home with guests from all over the world," said Russell Dick, President/CEO, Huna Totem Corporation. "We hope our visitors will take a piece of this beauty home with them through their experience." Among activities he recommends is wildlife excursions. "Icy Strait Point offers a front-row seat to Alaska's wildlife," Dick says. "There's nothing quite like seeing a humpback whale breech in the beautiful waters of Icy Strait, watching a bald eagle swooping down to snag a salmon, or witnessing a massive Alaska coastal brown bear teaching her cubs to fish in the Spasski River Valley."

six cables side by side, and does a vertical drop of more than 1,300 feet, at average speeds of 60 mph (though speeds of 82 mph have been clocked). The 45-minute bus ride up the mountain is worth the price alone, traveling through the town of Hoonah and offering breathtaking views.

COMING ASHORE The new cruise-ship dock is located in a beautiful natural setting with wildlife viewpoints built into the design. An electric shuttle is available to take passengers (and those with mobility challenges) to the Adventure Center or cannery and shopping areas.

INFORMATION Icy Strait Point guests arrive at the new Adventure Center, located where the dock meets shore. Visitor information is located here, and it's also the place to purchase independent tours, meet tour groups, or speak with port guides. The Adventure Center houses the **Mug Up Espresso Bar** and **Tip of the Iceberg gift shop.**

Best Cruise-Line Shore Excursions

ATV Expedition (2½ hr.; $174 adults and children; minimum age 8): Traverse the mountains of Chichagof Island in rugged fashion on a 4x4 expedition. You start high in the majestic mountains of Chichagof Island (after a drive by motorcoach through Hoonah). Your guide will provide a little area history and a brief orientation. Then you board a 4x4 Kawasaki Mule off-road vehicle and ride along a trail, taking in the Alaskan wilderness, rainforest, and tremendous views of Icy Strait.

Hoonah Sightseeing & Tribal Dance Combo (2½ hr.; $85 adults, $40 children): Tour the quaint Alaska village of Hoonah, the largest Tlingit settlement in the 49th State. Your guide will explain the village's history—including how the Huna Tlingits had to flee advancing glaciers—and describe modern Native life. Then see dancers perform in full regalia at the Native Theater, telling the story of the Tlingits. Learn about the ancient significance of the raven and the eagle.

Spasski River Valley Wildlife & Bear Search (2½ hr.; $119; minimum age 8): Explore the wilds of Chichagof Island in search of grizzlies. Your motorcoach travels through Hoonah en route to the bush country of the Spasski River Valley. Learn about the local flora and fauna on a short hike along gravel and boardwalk-lined paths through a rainforest to viewing platforms overlooking the Spasski River. Keep your eyes out for bears, salmon, bald eagles, and more, though sightings are not guaranteed.

Whales & Marine Mammals (2½ hr.; $179 adults, $109 children): Whale sightings are actually guaranteed on this boat cruise to St. Adolphus, about 12 miles from Icy Strait Point. The area is considered one of the best locations for humpback-whale-watching in Alaska, if not the world. The operators are so sure you'll see whales (and maybe even orcas), they offer a refund of $100 per guest if you don't (hasn't happened thus far). A naturalist is on board to point out other wildlife, including sea lions, eagles, and porpoises.

ZipRider Adventure (1½ hr.; $139 adults and children; weight restricted to between 90–275 lbs.): Ride on the world's longest zipline, 5,330 feet long with a 1,300-foot vertical drop, at speeds of up to 60 miles per hour. The highest point is 300 feet above the ground. If you dare to look down, you'll enjoy views of Port Fredrick, Icy Strait, and your cruise ship. You're harnessed in a seat for this ride; no skill is required.

Excursions Offered by Local Agencies

Icy Strait Point is operated by the Hoonah Totem Native Corporation. Tours can be booked at **www.icystraitpoint.com** or through your cruise line.

On Your Own: Within Walking Distance

The Beach ★★★   Icy Strait Point has a beach with a fantastic view of Port Frederick, where you can catch trout and salmon or just skip rocks for hours. The nature "loop" trail starts and ends next to the Adventure Center and is a .4-mile walk through a second-growth forest.

Icy Strait Point Cannery ★★★   Beautifully restored and reopened in 2004, this historic cannery complex is just a 5-minute stroll from the Adventure Center. It once was one of the most productive salmon canneries in the state. Its halls are filled with shops and a museum with a 1930s cannery display, as well as a cultural center. Tlingit carvers can be observed working on carvings. All the shops are owned by Alaskans, who sell local crafts and clever tourist items, like handmade soaps and candles. You even can have a message canned and shipped to friends back home. The original cookhouse is open for family-style dining, and a local Native craft market features several artisans.

108 Cannery Rd. www.icystraitpoint.com. ℰ **907/789-8600.** Open when ships are in.

On Your Own: Beyond the Port Area

Hoonah ★★★   A visit to this unspoiled little town provides a perfect chance to catch a glimpse of real Alaskan life. The largest Tlingit Indian village in Alaska is just a mile from the dock. The wilderness is so close that, as you walk along the bay, you'll likely see eagles flying overhead and may even spot whales from the pier. The town has grocery and hardware stores that cater to locals, who support themselves largely through fishing and logging. The atmosphere is much different than that of most ports used by cruise ships. Some visitors may like that; others may not.

Where to Lunch

All of the following are in the **Cannery complex** (108 Cannery Rd.; www. icystraitpoint.com; © **907/789-8600;** open when ships are in town).

The Cookhouse ★★ ALASKAN   The original Cannery cookhouse continues to keep seafood lovers happy with such dishes as fresh halibut and chips and Alaska Salmon BLTs. The Alaska Blue Burger is made with reindeer meat. Entrees $9–$20.

The Crab Station ★★ SEAFOOD   This eat-outside (under a tarp) restaurant is located on the dock over the water. Fresh local Dungeness crab is available for most of the season, as is king and snow crab. Don't miss the Alaska Crabby Bloody Mary ($18): In addition to shrimp, celery, olive, and local beach asparagus, this only-in-Alaska beverage features Dungeness crabmeat sprinkled on top, along with a snow crab leg! Entrees $15–$119 (when in season, Dungeness clusters from $17).

Duck Point Smokehouse ★ SEAFOOD/PIZZA   This restaurant features a spectacular waterfront view with firepit and such dishes as salmon that's freshly smoked inhouse and brick-oven pizza. Entrees $8–$18.

GLACIER BAY NATIONAL PARK & PRESERVE

Alaska has an estimated 100,000 glaciers, 616 officially named. So what's all the fuss about Glacier Bay? Theories on its popularity abound. Some think it's the wildlife, which includes humpback whales, bears, Dall sheep, seals, and more. Some think it's the history of the place: It was frozen behind a mile-wide wall of ice until about 1870; a mere 55 years later, it was designated as a national park, along with its 3.3-million surrounding acres. The glaciers are thought to be some of the fastest-moving in the world, some retreating and others advancing. Whatever the reason, Glacier Bay has taken on an allure not achieved by other glacier areas.

The first white man to enter the vast (60-plus-mile) Glacier Bay inlet was naturalist **John Muir** in 1879. Just 100 years earlier, when Capt. James Cook and, later, George Vancouver sailed there, the mouth was still a wall of ice. Today all that ice has ebbed back, leaving behind a series of inlets and glaciers whose calving activity entertains hundreds of cruisers lining the rails as their ships sit for several hours. It can take 200 years for ice to reach the point where it falls off the face of a glacier.

Each ship that enters the bay takes aboard a park ranger. The ranger provides commentary about glaciers, wildlife, and the bay's history over the

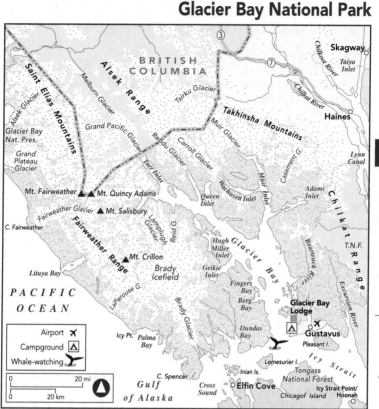

ship's PA system throughout the day. On large ships, the ranger may also give a presentation in the show lounge about conservation; on small ships, he or she will often be on deck throughout the day, available for questions.

Glacier Bay is the world's largest protected marine sanctuary. The bay is so vast that the water contained within its boundaries would cover the state of Connecticut. The bay is a source of concern for environmentalists, who would like to see cruise ships banned from entering or at least have their access severely curtailed. Ship operators, on the other hand, argue that no evidence shows that their vessels have any negative impact on the wildlife.

The park has numerous glaciers: 16 major tidewater glaciers (those that go all the way to the water) and 30 valley or alpine glaciers (those that compress between two hills but don't extend all the way to the water). In Tarr Inlet, at the Alaska/Canada border, two notable glaciers meet: **Margerie** and **Grand Pacific.** Margerie, on the Alaska side, is pristine white and very active, calving frequently; Grand Pacific, on the Canadian side of the line, is black, gritty, and not particularly active.

Visible from much of the bay (on a clear day) is massive **Mount Fair-weather** (elevation 15,320 ft.). Although Fairweather is taller than any mountain in the Lower 48, it ranks no higher than 19th among Alaska's peaks.

HAINES

This pretty, laid-back port is an example of Alaska the way you probably thought it would be. It's a small, scenic town with wilderness at its doorstep and only two stop signs. If you're not on one of the few ships that regularly visit Haines (pop. 2,400), you can easily reach the port on a day excursion from **Skagway.** The two communities lie at the northern end of the Lynn Canal, just 17 miles apart by water (350 miles by driving). The trip takes only about 45 minutes by **fast ferry** (www.hainesskagwayfastferry.com; ✆ **888/ 766-2103**) and is priced round-trip at $71 for adults, $36.50 for children. It's well worth taking, especially for those who have "done" Skagway before. But make sure to check return times so you get back to your ship on time.

The thing that's immediately striking about Haines is its setting, one of the prettiest in Alaska. The village lies in the shadow of the Fairweather Mountain Range, about 80 or so miles north of Juneau and on the same line of latitude as the lower reaches of Norway. Framed by high hills, it is more protected from the elements than many other Inside Passage ports.

Presbyterian missionary S. Hall Young and naturalist John Muir established Haines in 1879 as a base for converting the local Chilkoot and Chilkat Tlingit tribes to Christianity. They named the place for Mrs. F. E. Haines, secretary of the Presbyterian National Committee, who raised the funds for the exploration. The natives called it *Da-Shu,* the Tlingit word for "end of the trail." Traders knew the place as Chilkoot. The military, which came later and built a fort here in 1903, knew it as Fort Seward or Chilkoot Barracks. In 1897 and 1898, the town became one of the lesser-known access points (it was less popular than Skagway and Dyea) to a route to the Klondike; it was located at the head of what became known as the Jack Dalton Trail into Canada. At about the same time, gold was discovered much closer to home—in Porcupine, just 25 miles away—drawing even more prospectors to Haines. The gold quickly petered out, though, and Porcupine is no more.

 The **old fort** still stands. After World War II, and 42 years of service, it was decommissioned, but a group of veterans once stationed at Chilkoot Barracks would not let the fort die. In 1947, they bought the 85 buildings standing on 400 acres. They built a salmon smokehouse, a furniture-making plant, and the **Hotel Hälsingland,** among other business enterprises. They established art galleries and funded Indian arts training programs for local youngsters. The descendants of some of these modern-day pioneers still live in homes that their fathers and grandfathers built on the fort grounds. Designated a National Historic Site by the U.S. government in 1972, **Fort William Seward** should be a must-see on your list. The **Officers' Club Lounge** in the Hotel Hälsingland is a nice place to stop for a libation. It serves Alaskan and Yukon beers and a house special known as the Fort Seward Howitzer.

Haines

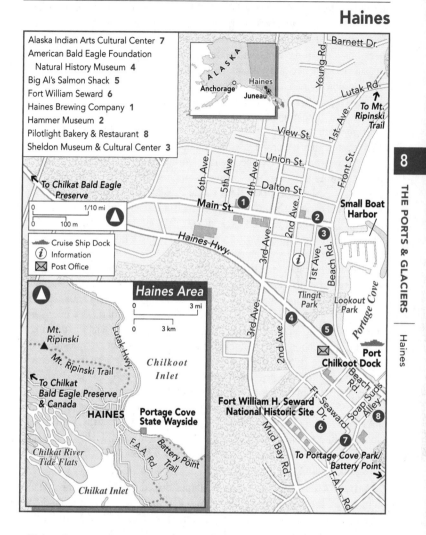

Alaska Indian Arts Cultural Center **7**

American Bald Eagle Foundation
   Natural History Museum **4**

Big Al's Salmon Shack **5**

Fort William Seward **6**

Haines Brewing Company **1**

Hammer Museum **2**

Pilotlight Bakery & Restaurant **8**

Sheldon Museum & Cultural Center **3**

ALASKA

Anchorage

Haines

Juneau

To Chilkat Bald Eagle
Preserve

0   1/10 mi

0   100 m

Cruise Ship Dock

Information

Post Office

Haines Area

0   3 mi

0   3 km

Mt.
Ripinski

Mt. Ripinski Trail

Lutak Hwy.

Chilkoot
Inlet

To Chilkat
Bald Eagle Preserve
& Canada

HAINES

Chilkat River
Tide Flats

**Portage Cove
State Wayside**

F.A.A. Rd.

Battery Point Trail

Chilkat Inlet

Barnett Dr.

Young Rd.

Lutak Rd.

To Mt.
Ripinski
Trail

1st Ave.

View St.

Union St.

Front St.

Dalton St.

6th Ave.

5th Ave.

4th Ave.

2nd Ave.

Main St.

Haines Hwy.

**Small Boat
Harbor**

3rd Ave.

1st Ave.

Beach Rd.

Tlingit
Park

Lookout
Park

Portage Cove

3rd Ave.

2nd Ave.

**Port
Chilkoot Dock**

Beach Rd.

Soap Suds Alley

**Fort William H. Seward
National Historic Site**

Ft. Seward Dr.

Mud Bay Rd.

To Portage Cove Park/
Battery Point

F.A.A. Rd.

8

THE PORTS & GLACIERS | Haines

Haines is so small that it can be covered on foot. You can see almost everything in 1 to 2 hours of reasonably flat walking. Shops worth a diversion include **Fun Guy Foraged Products,** 121 2nd Ave. (℗ **907/766-2992**), operated by a California transplant and featuring such gourmet items as dried Chilkat Valley mushrooms (including porcini and chanterelles) and local honey. Family-owned **Dejon Delights** sells fish smoked with local birch and alder (Portage St., just up from the ship dock; www.dejondelghts.com; ℗ **907/766-2505**). Stop by the tasting room at the award-winning **Port Chilkoot Distillery,** 34 Blacksmith St. (www.portchilkootdistillery.com; ℗ **907/766-3434**), to sample gin, bourbon, vodka, rye and absinthe made from pure lake water, organic grains, and local herbs. Or tap into the local microbrewery scene (root beer, too!) at **Haines Brewing Company,** 4th Ave. and Main St., http://haines brewing.com; ✆ **907/766-3823**). Haines has an art scene, too, and you can check out some of the works at the **Art on Main** gallery, 219 Main St. (www. alaskaartsconfluence.org/art-main-street; ✆ **907/303-0222**).

In addition to gold, military history, and Native heritage, the big attraction drawing visitors to Haines is eagles. The area is a magnet for these magnificent creatures—a couple hundred are year-round residents. Unfortunately, cruise passengers are unable to experience the annual **Gathering of the Eagles,** which occurs after the cruise season (usually Oct–Dec) and brings as many as 4,000 birds from all over the Pacific Northwest to the area in search of salmon. During this time, trees along a 5-mile stretch of the river (in an area known as the **Alaska Chilkat Bald Eagle Preserve**) are thick with these raptors—often a dozen or more sharing a limb. But even during the cruise season, you're likely to see at least an eagle or two. We once spotted eight in various swooping and tree-sitting poses on a bike ride out to Chilkoot Lake (about 10 miles from the cruise-ship pier).

The town also lays claim to the title "The Adventure Capital of Alaska," and many active travelers do visit here with the goal of catching salmon, photographing bears, doing multi-day rafting, kayaking or fishing trips, spotting whales, skiing, and seeing some of the most amazing wilderness scenery anywhere—including on the Haines Highway, which connects Haines to the Yukon. In 2009, the section from Haines to the Canadian border was designated a National Scenic Byway. If you want to view the scenery from the links, head to the **Valley of the Eagles Golf Links,** a par-36 nine-hole course with a PGA pro on staff (1½-mile Haines Hwy.; www.hainesgolf.com; ✆ **907/766-2401**).

Trivia: Tiny Haines has some Hollywood claim to fame. When the Disney movie *White Fang* filmed here in 1991, many locals were extras, with women even doubling for men in one fishing scene. More recently, Haines has been showcased on the Discovery Channel reality TV show *Gold Rush Alaska* (including filming at Porcupine Creek).

COMING ASHORE The Port of Haines dock is within walking distance of many of the town's main attractions—as long as you don't mind hills (where you dock is just down from the fort area). The walk to Main Street is about a half-mile, so the tourism folks provide a free shuttle.

INFORMATION Pick up walking-tour information at the **Haines Convention & Visitors Bureau visitor center,** at 122 2nd Avenue (www.visithaines. com; ✆ **800/458-3579** or 907/766-2234; Mon–Fri 8am–5pm, Sat–Sun 9am–noon and 1–4pm, closed weekends in winter). It's easy to explore the town on foot, or you can rent a bike at **Sockeye Cycle,** on Portage Street, right up the street from the cruise-ship dock (www.cyclealaska.com; ✆ **887/292-4154** or 907/766-2869); it's $65/day for a road bike rental and $45/day for a mountain bike or hybrid. The shop also offers escorted tours.

Best Cruise-Line Shore Excursions

Eagle Preserve Wildlife River Adventure (4 hr.; $160): A bus takes you on one of the most beautiful highways in the world, to the Chilkat Bald Eagle Preserve and a camp where you board flat-bottomed jet boats to traverse the narrows of the glacially fed Chilkat River. Along the riverbank you may spy eagles, bears, beavers, and moose, as sighted by your guide—take it from Fran, if anything can get your heart pumping on a chilly day on the river, it's the close-up sight of a bull moose! Also impressive is the untouched scenery, mountains as high as 6,000 feet, waterfalls, glaciers, forests, and flatlands.

Kroschel Wildlife Park (3½ hr.; $160 adults, $99 children): Steve Kroschel worked with wild animals for movies including *Never Cry Wolf* and the PBS *Wild America* series. At his private and interactive wildlife center, he now provides a home for orphaned and rescued critters including a Kodiak bear, moose, wolves (and wolverines), mink, reindeer, and more. Kids will love the fact that many of the animals can be touched (also a great photo op). The drive to Kroschel's property is through the Chilkat Bald Eagle Preserve.

Native Cultural Experience (2¾ hr.; $109 adults, $69 children): Travel by bus for 22 miles on the Haines Highway, a national scenic byway, through the Chilkat Bald Eagle Preserve on your way to Klukwan, a small Alaska Native village (the only remaining village of the Chilkat people). Here you'll visit a new, state-of-the-art **Jilkaat Kwaan Cultural Heritage Center,** designed in the style of a traditional tribal Whale House and containing art previously not available for view by the public. There are intricately carved panels and totems, some several hundred years old, and displays showcasing beadwork, carving, weaving, and even modern art. You'll also have the opportunity to watch carvers, learn about smokehouse techniques, and chat with Chilkat Tlingit people. The heritage center has a gift shop.

Wilderness Kayak Experience (4 hr.; $120 adults, $60 children 7–12): Located as it is at the top of the Inside Passage, Haines is an ideal place for kayaking. A short bus trip will take you to the launch site, and the goal as you glide in your kayak is to spot wildlife—depending on your luck, this might include humpback whales, porpoises, seals, sea lions, sea otters, moose, brown bears, and, of course, Haines' famous bald eagles.

Excursions Offered by Local Agencies

Chilkat Guides, 170 Sawmill Rd. (www.raftalaska.com; © **907/766-2491**), takes a rafting trip twice a day in summer down the Chilkat River to watch eagles. The rapids are pretty easy—there's a chance you may be asked to get out and push—and you'll see lots of eagles. The 4-hour trip includes a snack and costs $133 (minimum age 7). **Alaska Nature Tours** (www.alaskanature tours.net; © **907/766-2876**) has a variety of escorted tours, including a 4-hour walking tour of the Chilkat Bald Eagle Preserve ($95 adults, $75 children 12 and under; lunch included).

Sportfishing charters are available from local operators including **I Fish Haines** (www.ifishhainesalaska.com; © **907/314-0735**).

On Your Own: Within Walking Distance

Alaska Indian Arts ★   Located in the old fort hospital on the south side of the parade grounds, the center has a small gallery and a carvers' workshop where you may see totem-pole carving in progress.

13 Ft. Seward St., on the south side of the parade grounds. © **907/766-2160.** Mon–Fri 9am–5pm.

American Bald Eagle Foundation Natural History Museum ★★ Haines is proud of its location in prime eagle territory, and this natural-history museum celebrates the raptors. You can view live eagles (three bald eagles as of summer 2017) along with owls, hawks, and falcons in an enclosed aviary and up close during live bird presentations by staff. In the main building is an impressively large diorama of the Chilkat Bald Eagle Preserve—all 48,000 acres.

113 Haines Hwy. (at 2nd Ave.), 2 blocks from the town center. www.baldeagles.org. © **907/766-3094.** Admission $10 adults, $8 seniors, $5 children 8–12, free for children 7 and under. Mon–Fri 9am–5pm; Sat 11am–3pm; closed Sun.

Fort William Seward ★★★   The central feature of the town, rising right above the docks, Fort Seward was retired after World War II and redone by a group of returning veterans. It's not the kind of place you think of when envisioning a fort. It has no parapets, no walls, no nothing—just an open parade ground surrounded by large wood-frame former barracks and officers' quarters that today have been converted into private homes, the Hotel Hälsingland, a gallery and studio, and the Alaska Indian Arts center (see above). In the middle of the sloping parade ground is a replica of a Tlingit tribal house. Also added to the parade grounds—thanks to a local collector—is a harpoon gun that looks like a cannon and is fired on special town occasions. New in the fort is a **Sculpture Garden,** where local artists are being encouraged to create installations using recycled materials.

Just inland from the cruise-ship dock. Open all day.

Hammer Museum ★★   You'll learn more uses for hammers than you ever imagined at this quirky museum. The collection was started by Dave Pahl, a longshoreman and hammer nut (he even constructed the giant hammer in front of the building). On display are about 2,000 hammers from around the world, designed to do everything from bang nails to test the quality of cheese. Prized pieces in the collection include an 800-year-old Tlingit war hammer and an ancient Egyptian tool used around 2500 B.C. (donated to the museum by an archaeologist in 2008).

108 Main St. www.hammermuseum.org. © **907/766-2374.** Admission $5 adults, free children 12 and under when accompanied by adult. May–Sept Mon–Fri 10am–5pm; Sat 10am–2pm.

Sheldon Museum & Cultural Center ★★   Named for a man who moved to Haines in 1911 (and not affiliated with the better-known Sheldon Jackson Museum in Sitka; see p. 254), this small museum has a collection that includes Tlingit artifacts, gold-rush items, and assorted Haines memorabilia. Those interested in traditional crafts will want to see the Chilkat blankets and baskets; those interested in local history, the historical photos. Guided tours are available on request. A rotating exhibit (changing every 6 weeks) showcases the work of contemporary artists, giving insight into the local arts scene. A gift shop is on the first floor.

Corner of Main and Front sts. www.sheldonmuseum.org. © **907/766-2366.** Admission $7, free children 12 and under. Mid-May to mid-Sept Mon–Tues 10am–5pm; Wed 9am–5pm; Thurs–Fri 10am–5pm; Sat–Sun 1–4pm.

On Your Own: Beyond the Port Area

Chilkat Bald Eagle Preserve ★★★ Haines may be the best place in the world to see bald eagles. And this 48,000-acre park along the Chilkat River is ground zero for the species. From around mid-October to December, some 3,000 eagles reside here. But even during cruise season, you're likely to glimpse a few—between 200 and 400 eagles live here year-round. The best viewing is on the Haines Highway, between miles 18 and 21. The preserve is managed by the Alaska State Parks.

www.alaskastateparks.org. © **907/766-2292.**

Where to Lunch

Big Al's Salmon Shack ★ FOOD TRUCK/SEAFOOD   There's not much ambience (you sit at an outdoor picnic table), but this food truck serves tasty halibut or salmon fish & ships, smoked salmon, and other seafood treats. It operates seasonally only.

1 Haines Hwy. www.facebook.com/bigalssalmonshack/. © **541/231-0740.** Main courses $7–$15. May–Sept daily 11am–7pm.

The Pilotlight Bakery & Restaurant ★★★ AMERICAN/BAKERY This is a true gem with surprisingly good farm-to-table cuisine. Order up some house-baked sourdough bread and such delicious dishes as salmon burgers, rockfish tacos, elk burgers on brioche buns, bacon-wrapped Alaskan venison, and a wonderful Alaskan fishermen's stew filled with mussels, clams, halibut, calamari, tomatoes, and potatoes.

1 Soap Suds Alley (1 block from cruise-ship block). www.facebook.com/pilotlight bakery/posts_to_page/. © **907/766-2962.** Daily 7am–2pm and 5–9pm (call about off-season hours). Main courses (lunch) $10–$20.

A Day in Haines

Don "Duck" Hess and his wife, Karen, started **Chilkat River Adventures** in 1991, but he's lived in Haines more than 50 years, and he's exactly the kind of character you hope to meet in Alaska (you can book his Chilkat River tours through your cruise line (see the "Eagle Preserve Wildlife River Adventure" excursion above, or go to www.jetboatalaska.com). Duck Hess complains about people who "pay good money to go to Alaska and then spend time buying overpriced stuff at Diamonds International in Skagway, stuff not even made in Alaska." Don't let that be you! "Get out and see the wilderness," he advises. We're on the same page, and we very much recommend setting out with one of his guides in a jet boat on the **Chilkat River,** which puts you in the middle of nowhere but delivers everything, scenery-wise, that you've come to Alaska to see (plus if you're lucky, your guide will also educate you on remote, Alaskan-style subsistence living and such). If you want to stay in town, rent a bike and explore along the shore while checking the trees for eagles and soaking up the mountain scenery. Stop by the **Pilotlight Bakery** for an extraordinary taste of Alaska or at the **Haines Brewing Company** to wet your whistle. If you're on Main Street, stop to see the many hammers at the **Hammer Museum,** the kind of quirky place your friends will want to check out on Instagram.

SKAGWAY

No port in Alaska is more historically significant than this small town at the northern end of the picturesque Lynn Canal. In the late–19th century, a steady stream of prospectors began the long trek into Canada's Yukon Territory, seeking the vast quantities of Klondike gold that had been reported in Rabbit Creek (later renamed Bonanza Creek). Not many of them realized the unspeakable hardships they'd have to endure before they could get close to the stuff. They first had to negotiate either the **White Pass** or the **Chilkoot Pass** through the coastal mountain range to the Canadian border. To do so, they had to hike 20 miles, climbing nearly 3,000 feet in the process and, by order of Canada's North-West Mounted Police, had to have at least a year's supply of provisions before they could enter the country. Numbed by temperatures that fell at times into the -50s Fahrenheit (-40s Celsius) and often blinded by driving snow or stinging hail (they were, after all, hiking through mountain passes that gave Skagway its name—in Tlingit, *Skagua* means "home of the North Wind"), they plodded upward. They ferried some of their supplies partway up, stashed them, and then returned to Skagway before repeating the process with another load, always inching their way closer to the summit. The process took as many as 20 trips for some, and often their stashes were stolen by unscrupulous rivals or opportunistic locals. Prospectors who thought themselves lucky enough to be able to afford horses or mules found their pack animals to be less than sound of limb. One stretch of the trail through the White Pass (the more popular of the two routes through the mountains) is called **Dead Horse Gulch.**

Arduous as it was, that first leg was just the beginning. From the Canadian border, their golden goal lay a long and dangerous water journey away, part of it by lake (and, thus, relatively easy), but most of it down the mighty Yukon River and decidedly perilous.

The gold rush brought to Skagway a way of life as violent and lawless as any to be found in the frontier West. The Mounties (the law in Canada) had no jurisdiction in Skagway. In fact, there was no law whatsoever in Skagway. Peace depended entirely on the consciences of the inhabitants—saloonkeepers, gamblers, prostitutes, and desperadoes of every stripe.

Skagway

ATTRACTIONS ●

1898 Red Onion Saloon **9**
Case-Mulvihill House &
 Nye House **2**
Eagles Hall and
 Days of '98 Show **7**
Gault House **3**
Gold Rush Cemetery **1**
Historic Moore Homestead **6**
Lower Dewey Trailhead **13**
National Park
 Visitor Center **11**

Skagway City Hall **5**
Skagway Museum & Archives **4**
Skagway Visitor
 Information Center **9**
Soapy Smith's Museum **10**
White Pass and Yukon Route
 Railway **12**

Cruise Ship Dock
(i) Information
Post Office

DINING ◆

Red Onion Saloon **9**
Skagway Fish Company **14**
Woadies South East Seafood **8**

Pullen
Creek
Park

ALASKA
Anchorage ○ Skagway
Juneau ✦

The most notorious of the Skagway bad men was Jefferson Randolph "Soapy" Smith, an accomplished con man. He earned his nickname in Denver, Colorado, by persuading large numbers of gullible people to buy bars of cheap soap for $1 in the belief that some of the bars were wrapped in larger denomination bills. They weren't, of course, but the scam made Smith a lot of money. In Skagway he and his gang engaged in all kinds of nastiness, charging local businesses large fees for "protection," exacting exorbitant sums to "store" prospectors' gear (and then selling the equipment to others), and setting up a telegraph station and charging prospectors to send messages home—though the telegraph wire went no farther than the next room.

The gold-rush days of Skagway had their heroes as well. One of them, city surveyor Frank Reid, put an end to Soapy's reign; he shot Smith dead and was himself mortally wounded in the gunfight. In his honor, the local citizenry erected an impressive granite monument over his grave in the **Gold Rush Cemetery;** Smith's marker, on the other hand, is very simple, and his remains aren't even underneath it (they're 3 ft. to the left, outside consecrated ground). Perversely, though, it is the villain Smith whose life is commemorated annually on July 8, with songs and entertainment. The women of the gold-rush days are also given tribute—at least, those of ill repute—in a shore excursion called the "Ghosts & Goodtime Girls Walking Tour."

Unlike many other Alaskan frontier towns, Skagway has been spared the ravages of major fires and earthquakes. Some of the original buildings still stand, protected by the National Park Service. The **Klondike Gold Rush National Historical Park** contains some striking examples of these buildings. Other little touches of history are preserved around town (Skagway has an active historic district committee in place), such as the huge watch painted on the mountainside above town—an early billboard for the long-gone watch-repair shop of Herman Kirmse. Also remaining from the old days is the **White Pass and Yukon Route narrow-gauge railroad.** A golden spike was driven on July 29, 1900, connecting the railroad between Skagway and Whitehorse, to carry late stampeders in and gold out (the first engine ran on the first 4 miles of track in 1898). Today a ride on the train is a must for visitors. The round-trip to the summit of the pass, following a route carved out of the side of the mountain by an American/Canadian engineering team backed by British money, takes 3 hours from a departure site conveniently located a short walk (or an even shorter shuttle-bus ride) from the cruise-ship piers.

Having a sweet little historic town is nice for Skagway's 1,100 or so year-round residents, of course, but by itself, history doesn't pay the bills. So although Skagway is trying to hang on to its gold-rush heritage, it's also trying to make money off it. The White Pass & Yukon Route railway is the largest employer in town, and also owns the the Railroad Dock, and at press time had a lease on the other docks (which was up for renewal). Businesses, including souvenir shops and jewelry stores, have taken over much of the downtown during cruise season (they close the rest of the year), and many have gold-rush connotations only in the sense that they've opened to cash in on visitors' "gold." There's even a Harley-Davidson merchandise shop. (What's next? A Hard Rock Cafe?) A municipal ordinance prohibits clerks from standing outside fancy jewelry stores urging customers to come in, as they do in places such as the Caribbean. But step inside and you may be in for a hard sell—to make the sale, these seasonal workers may offer discounts, including a refund of sales tax.

You'll find high-end crafts, including Tlingit masks and silver jewelry, at **Inside Passage Arts,** 340 7th Ave. (www.insidepassagearts.com; © **907/983-2585**). **Inspired Artworks,** 555 Broadway (www.inspiredartworks.com; © **907/983-3443**), also sells regionally made art, jewelry, and crafts. The Skagway Development Corporation started a program in 2015 to promote and support locally crafted goods. Check shop windows for MADE IN SKAGWAY signs.

The town also has a burgeoning food scene. For local flavor, **Skagway Brewing Company,** at Broadway and 7th (www.skagwaybrewing.com; © 907/983-2739; Mon–Fri 10am–10pm, weekends from 11am), serves a signature Spruce Tip Blonde brewed with spruce tree tips (plus a decent pub grub menu). A cool new addition to the imbibing scene, the family-owned **Skagway Spirits,** a few blocks from downtown at 9th and Alaska (www.skagwayspirits.com; © **907/983-2040**; daily 1–8pm), makes its own vodka and gin. The tasting room is in a converted garage (take-home bottles are a wonderful souvenir!). If you've got kids or are just feeling nostalgic, stop by **Sweet Treats,** 6th and Broadway, behind Bites on Broadway, for candy in bins ($2.99 for a quarter-pound) and such favorites as candy cigarettes, NECCO wafers, and Razzles.

COMING ASHORE   Skagway has three docks: Railroad, Broadway, and Ore. Broadway is practically downtown, while the other docks are no more than a 10-minute walk (at press time there was also talk of an extension of the Ore Dock to handle larger ships). Frequent wheelchair-lift-equipped **municipal shuttles** ($2 one-way or $5 for a full-day pass; daily 7am–9pm) tote passengers who don't want to walk into town. Broadway is the street that runs through the center of town, but you do yourself a favor if you also explore shops, eateries, and other attractions on its branches.

Tip: After you've docked, take a few minutes to study the 400-foot-high cliffs alongside the pier. The paintings, names, and dates are not graffiti; they're a genuine history of the development of the cruise industry in Skagway over the past century (the tradition started in 1928). All of the paintings, mostly of ship-line logos, were done by crew members from visiting ships. Some are placed hundreds of feet up the cliffs, a practice authorities have tried to stop for safety reasons (and even with the threat of jail). Occasionally, some enterprising crew members attempt to revive the tradition, but they are quickly shepherded away from the cliff.

INFORMATION   Maps with routes for walking are available at the **Skagway Convention & Visitors Bureau visitor center** (http://skagway.com; ☏ **907/983-2854**), at the Arctic Brotherhood Hall, 245 Broadway, between 2nd and 3rd avenues (the building's driftwood-decorated, Victorian-rustic facade is itself an attraction). Located in the restored railroad depot, the **National Park Service Visitor Center,** 2nd Ave. and Broadway (www.nps.gov/klgo; ☏ **907/983-2921**), is the focal point for activities in Skagway. Rangers answer questions, give lectures, and show the fascinating 25-minute film "Gold Fever: Race to the Klondike." Several times a day they lead excellent walking tours of the 4-block Skagway Historic District. The park service's programs are free. The building houses a small museum that lays the groundwork for the rest of what you'll see. The visitor center is open May through September daily 8am to 6pm, and during the rest of the year Monday through Friday 8am to 5pm.

Best Cruise-Line Shore Excursions

Eagle Preserve Float Adventure (6½ hr.; $249 adults, $115 children 7–12): This outing combines a fjord cruise (45 min. to Haines) with a leisurely raft float (no whitewater rapids here) through the Chilkat Bald Eagle Preserve.

Gold Panning & Sled Dogs (3 hr.; $109 adults, $75 children): Gold mining never actually happened in Skagway—it was only a transit point—but the town now gets more gold-rush tourists than any other place. This kid-friendly excursion combines the popular activity of gold panning with a lesson from a professional Iditarod musher on how dogs played a part in the Klondike Gold

Rush—with a dog-sledding demonstration and an opportunity to interact with Iditarod sled dogs and their puppies. You also suit up in a parka and snow boots to step into a cold chamber to experience what 40 degrees below zero feels like, at least for a few minutes. All this takes place at the Alaska 360 dredge town, where costumed characters join the fun.

Golden Glass-Blowing Experience (3 hr.; $249 adults; $129 children; minimum age 7): Visit a working glass-blowing studio at the beautiful Jewel Gardens to learn how to blow or mold molten glass. You'll get to create your own ornament, compete with 24k gold. There are also non-hands-on tours of the organic show garden that include a Glassworks Theater demonstration by resident artists (3 hr.; $89 adults, $65 children).

Horseback Riding Adventure (3½ hr.; $199): Giddy-up on horseback to see the remnants of Dyea, once a booming gold-rush town, and explore the scenic Dyea Valley. Participants, of course, must be able to mount a horse and maintain balance in a saddle (minimum height: 4'10").

Ocean Raft Adventure (2 hr.; $150): Put on a special protective suit and goggles, sit back in shock-absorbing seats, and prepare to zoom. This excursion takes you racing down the Lynn Canal, the deepest and longest fjord in North America, on the same type of boat used by U.S. Navy SEALs and Coast Guard rescue teams. Stops along the way include checking an eagle's nest and seeing roaring waterfalls, and, weather permitting, Ferebee Glacier. It's all accompanied by plenty of colorful commentary (minimum age 10; minimum height 49").

Skagway Street Car (1½ hr.; $59 adults, $35 children): This is as much performance art as it is a historical tour. Guides in period costume relate tales of the boomtown days as you tour the sights both in and outside of town aboard vintage 1930s sightseeing limousines. Though theatrical, it's all done in a homey style, as if you're getting a tour from your cousin Martha.

White Pass Scenic Railway (3½ hr.; $159 adults, $65 children): The sturdy engines and vintage parlor cars of the famous White Pass & Yukon Route narrow-gauge railway take you from the dock past waterfalls and parts of the famous Trail of '98, including Dead Horse Gulch to the White Pass Summit, the boundary between Canada and the United States. Don't take this trip on an overcast day—you won't see anything. If you have a clear day, though, you can see all the way to the harbor; you might even spot a marmot fleeing the train's racket. All the trains are wheelchair-accessible. There are options for those who want to go one-way, for instance, and mountain bike back (mostly downhill) from Fraser, B.C. (4½ hr.; $225). Extreme options include a Heli-Hike & Rail Adventure (5 hr., $479), where you combine a helicopter tour and hike in the Tongass National Forest with a ride on the railway.

Excursions Offered by Local Agencies

M&M Tours is a municipal contracted tour brokerage that promises the best prices and has locations just off each of the docks and one location in town at 7th Avenue, off Broadway (www.skagwayalaskatours.com; ☏ **866/983-3900**).

Chilkat Cruises (www.hainesskagwayfastferry.com; © 888/766-2103) has a fast ferry that takes you to Haines in about 45 minutes. It runs several trips a day, costing $71 adults and $36.50 for children 12 and under, round-trip.

Ultimate Zipline Adventure, operated by Alaska Excursions (www.alaska excursions.com; © 907/983-4444), picks passengers up at the pier and travels 9 miles to Dyea, where a course with 12 ziplines (up to 750 ft. long) and four suspension bridges offers thrills plus views of waterfalls and forest. For 4 hours, it's $169 for adults, $149 for children. Alaska Excursions also has a thrilling Glacier Point Wilderness Safari where you boat, bike, and canoe to get close to the Davidson Glacier; depending on conditions, you may actually be able to touch the ice (6 hr.; $219).

For bike rentals, visit **Sockeye Cycle Co.** (http://cyclealaska.com; © 907/ 983-2851; road bikes $65/day, mountain bikes or hybrids $45/day).

On Your Own: Within Walking Distance

The Case-Mulvihill House, the Gault House & the Nye House ★★

All within a block of one another, these three buildings are striking examples of gold-rush-era Skagway architecture. You can view these three private residences from the street only, as part of a guided walking tour conducted by officers of the National Park Service.

The Case-Mulvihill House and the Nye House are on Alaska St., btw. 7th and 8th aves. The Gault House is on Alaska St., btw. 5th and 6th aves.

Eagles Hall and Days of '98 Show ★★

This is the venue for Skagway's long-running (since 1927) *Days of '98* show, a live melodrama of the Gay '90s featuring dancing girls and ragtime music. Follow the events leading up to the historic shootout that led to the end of Soapy Smith's crime reign. Daytime performances are at 10:30am, 12:30pm, and 2:30pm most days, timed so that cruise passengers can attend.

Southeast corner of 6th Ave. and Broadway. www.thedaysof98show.com. © 907/983-2545. Daytime performances $25 adults, $12.50 children.

Historic Moore Homestead ★★

The Moore Cabin was built in 1887 as the home of Capt. William Moore, the founder of Skagway. The cabin was restored recently by the National Park Service.

5th Ave. and Spring St. Free tours early May to mid-Sept daily 10am–5pm.

Skagway City Hall ★

This is not, strictly speaking, a tourist site, but as the town's only stone building, it's worth a peek.

Spring St. and 7th Ave.

Skagway Museum & Archives ★

This small, city-run museum collects things significant to Skagway history, everything from a Tlingit canoe to a 1931 Ford AA truck. It has items from the Klondike Gold Rush and Native baskets and carvings, as well as historic photographs. The building dates to 1900.

700 Spring St. (at 7th). © 907/983-2420. Admission $2 adults, $1 students, free for children. May–Sept Mon–Fri 9am–5pm; Sat 10am–5pm; Sun 10am–4pm.

Soapy Smith's Museum ★★   Also known as Jefferson Smith's Parlor or Soapy's Parlor, this was a saloon and gambling joint opened by the notorious bandit Jefferson Randolph "Soapy" Smith in 1897. Long in private hands, relocated a couple of times, and operated as a museum—complete with animatronic mannequins and gold-rush-era artifacts—this impressive building was falling into disrepair when it was purchased by the Rasmuson Foundation and gifted to the National Park Service in 2008. A rehab saved the artifacts inside, including the mannequin of "Soapy," who died in a gunfight in 1898.

2nd Ave., just off Broadway. www.nps.gov/klgo/learn/historyculture/jeffsmithsparlor.htm. *ℰ* **907/983-9200.** 30-min. guided tours on the quarter-hour Mon–Fri 9:15am–4:15pm (last tour 4:15pm). Weekends open 9am–5pm (no tours available). Admission $5 (purchase tickets at the Museum Store on Broadway and 2nd Ave.).

On Your Own: Beyond the Port Area

The Gold Rush Cemetery ★★   This small cemetery is the permanent resting place of Messrs. Smith and Reid. Aside from Reid's impressive monument, most of the headstones at the cemetery are whitewashed wood and are replaced by the park service when they get too worn. From here it's a short walk to scenic Reid Falls. (You can get a good look at the cemetery from the White Pass and Yukon Route carriages.)

About 1½ mi. from the center of downtown, up State St. (walkable if you have the time and inclination).

Lower Dewey Lake Loop Trail ★★★   You can get into the wilderness quickly from Skagway, and though this .9-mile trail may have you huffing and puffing as you climb upward 350 feet, the views of a glacial lake, the town, and the harbor are worth it. You can go straight up and straight down, or continue around the lake for a 3.6-mile hike. *Highly recommended:* Stop by the visitor center for a map before you set out.

To get to the trailhead, go east on 2nd Ave. past the railroad depot, turn left, carefully cross the tracks, and follow the creek about 400 ft. (to the north).

Yakutania Point Trail ★★   If a flat, easy hike is more your thing, this 1.6-mile jaunt takes you across the Skagway River and through the alders to a rock outcropping for views of the Lynn Canal and Chilkat Mountains. There's a covered picnic shelter if you want to linger.

Walk west on 1st Ave., and turn left (to head south) on Main St. The sidewalk takes you past the airport terminal. Cross the Skagway River on the footbridge and turn left for the trailhead.

Where to Lunch

We like the sandwiches, baked goods, and house-brewed Fireweed Zinger Tea at **Bites on Broadway bakery,** 648 Broadway (www.bitesonbroadway.com); and the breakfast burritos, wraps, coffee, and especially the smoothies at **Glacier Smoothies and Espresso,** 336 3rd Ave. (www.glacialsmoothies.com). Carts selling reindeer hot dogs are all around town.

The Red Onion Saloon ★ PIZZA/PUB GRUB   The town's honky-tonk since 1898 serves pizza, sandwiches, nachos, and such, which benefit from the fact they are served by Good Time Girls and Gents.

2nd Ave. and Broadway. http://redonion1898.com. ℰ **907/983-2222.** Daily 10am–10pm (and sometimes later). Main courses $7–$13.

Skagway Fish Company ★★★ SEAFOOD   Located near the Railroad pier, this spot specializes in fresh seafood (fish & chips, red king crab legs, Kake Alaskan oysters, and king crab bisque), but also has burgers and steaks.

201 Congress Way. www.facebook.com/SkagwayFishCo. ℰ **907-983-3474.** Daily 11am–9pm. Main courses $12–$42.

Woadies South East Seafood ★★ FOOD TRUCK/SEAFOOD   Away from the crowds, this outdoor spot (with tent-covered picnic tables) serves a tasty crab bisque, halibut, salmon, or rockfish fish & chips, and Dungeness crab you can have fun picking apart. It also offers corn dogs for the kids.

4th and State sts. www.facebook.com/WoadiesSE907/. ℰ **907/983-3133.** Daily 11:30am–7pm. Main courses $9–$39.

A Day in Skagway

Our favorite experiences are **hikes,** especially on the **Lower Dewey Lake Loop Trail,** maybe with a reward of a beer at **Skagway Brewing Company** or a G&T at **Skagway Spirits** (or carb-load pre-hike at **Bites on Broadway**). The city's **historic buildings** are a must-do for history buffs. If we had young kids in tow, we'd surely do the **Alaska 360** experience. For more adventuresome families, the **Dyea zipline** offers instant bonding (as does **horseback riding**). After you take the train ride up, it's also awesome to bike ride down from the White Pass—though your hands may hurt from squeezing the hand brakes.

HUBBARD GLACIER

Alaska's longest glacier accessible by cruise ships—it's about 76 miles long and 7 miles across—Hubbard lies at the northern end of **Yakutat Bay.** It also has a rather odd claim to fame: It is one of the fastest advancing glaciers in Alaska. So fast and far did it move about a dozen years ago that it quickly created a wall across the mouth of **Russell Fjord,** one of the inlets lining Yakutat Bay. That turned the fjord into a lake and trapped hundreds of migratory marine creatures inside. Scientists still can't tell us why Hubbard chose to act the way it did or why it receded to its original position several months later, reopening Russell Fjord.

Cruise ships in Yakutat Bay get spectacular views of the glacier, which, because of the riptides and currents, is always in motion, its visible 350-foot face (another 250 feet are below the waterline) calving into the ocean and producing lots of white thunder. It should be noted, however, that only one ship can get close to the glacier at a time, and if another ship is hogging the space, your ship may have to wait or may not get close at all.

COLLEGE FJORD

In the northern sector of Prince William Sound, roughly midway between Whittier and Valdez, College Fjord is not one of the more spectacular Alaskan glacier areas, being very much overshadowed by Glacier Bay, Yakutat Bay (for Hubbard Glacier), and others, but it's scenic enough to merit a place on a lot of cruise itineraries, mostly for **Harvard Glacier,** which sits at its head. On one visit, coauthor Fran got within a thousand feet of the glacier on a Carnival ship, and it was calving every few minutes. It was an unforgettable sight to behold.

The fjord was named by an 1898 expedition team that gave the glaciers lining College Fjord and their neighbor, Harriman Glacier, the names of prominent Eastern universities: hence, Harvard, Vassar, Williams, Yale, and so on.

CRUISETOUR DESTINATIONS

N o matter how powerful your binoculars, you can't see all of Alaska from a ship, and that's why the cruise lines invented the **cruisetour** (or what Holland America Line now calls Land + Sea Journeys): vacations that include a week on a ship and several days touring on land. In this chapter, we give you information on the most popular cruisetour destinations. See "Cruisetours: The Best of Land & Sea" in chapter 2 for a discussion of the various cruisetour packages offered.

DENALI NATIONAL PARK & PRESERVE

This is one of Alaska's most visited—environmentalists say overvisited—national park areas, with nearly 600,000 people a year coming to soak up the scenic splendor. There are lodges in the park: Camp Denali & North Face Lodge, Denali Backcountry Lodge, Kantishna Roadhouse, and Skyline Lodge. The Talkeetna Alaskan Lodge and the Mt. McKinley Princess Wilderness Lodge both have spectacular views of the Alaska Range and Denali (just be warned that both lodges are more than an hour's drive from the park's entrance). Other properties around the park include the Denali Princess Wilderness Lodge, the Grande Denali Lodge, Denali Bluffs, and the Denali Park Village, and the area now is home to more than 2,000 hotel rooms. Nearby Healy also has rooms. There are, however, times when demand for rooms in the area outstrips supply, so book early.

Wildlife is the thing in Denali: Somewhere in the realm of 169 bird species, 39 mammal species, and 758 vascular plant species are found there.

From May to September, the **Alaska Railroad** operates a service daily between Anchorage and Fairbanks that passes just within the eastern boundary of the park, offering passengers the choice between premium domed GoldStar Service railcars or the more basic (but less expensive and perfectly adequate) Adventure Class carriages. The train stops at a station inside the park near the Denali Visitor Center, and provides both northbound and southbound service. Alaska Railroad locomotives also tow the private railcars of Holland America Line and Princess, as well as those of Wilderness Express,

A mountain BY ANY OTHER NAME . . .

We've long been taught that the Athabascans of Interior Alaska called the mountain *Denali,* meaning "the high one." But at least one historian contends that the word *Denal'iy* actually referred to a mountain near Anchorage, now known as Pioneer Peak, and means "one that watches," and that the Native word for Denali, "the high one," is actually *Doleika.* In any event, Alaska Natives only used the area for seasonal hunting, as in no permanent settlements, and white men came only in search of gold. In 1896, a prospector named the mountain after William McKinley of Ohio, who was elected president of the United States that year.

All well and good, except that most Alaskans prefer the name Denali and since 1975 had petitioned to officially change it back. Ohio wouldn't allow it. Although congressmen from Alaska and Ohio compromised on the issue in 1980, changing the name of the national park to Denali and leaving the mountain named McKinley, Alaskans kept pushing for Denali. The name change finally came in 2015.

used by other major cruise lines (although Princess and Holland America now bus many of their passengers on the segment between Fairbanks and the park).

Besides the wildlife, the focal point of the park is North America's highest peak, Denali (the mountain's name was changed from Mount McKinley to Denali by President Obama in 2015). You could argue that Denali comprises the two highest peaks in North America: Its south peak towers over the Alaska Range at 20,310 feet, while its north peak rises to 19,470 feet. Permanently snow-covered mountains dominate the surrounding expanse: Mount Foraker, which stands a mere 17,400 feet; Mount Silverthrone, at 13,220 feet; Mount Crosson, at 12,800 feet; and many, many more giant heaps. It's an awesome sight, even from a distance. You just have to hope you can see it.

As with all enormous mountains, "the high one" creates its own weather system, and hidden-from-clouds seems to be its favorite flavor. Sadly, it's possible to be in the area for days and never catch a glimpse of the Alaska Range. Trust us, though: When you finally see it in all its splendor, you'll realize that it's worth the wait. It is one of our favorite Alaskan views.

Most visitors experience the park by bus. Private vehicles are tightly restricted for environmental reasons, and are allowed only to about mile 15 on the park road. That cuts down on your wildlife-viewing chances. However, you can get a ticket on a park shuttle bus or sign up for a **Tundra Wilderness Tour.** Both are run by the park concessionaire, which is allowed to operate much more deeply in the park. The tour buses have been upgraded in recent years to include drop-down video screens on which the driver shows live video of the animals you see along the road, giving all a better view. The drivers of these buses are knowledgeable about the flora and fauna of the area, and always seem to be able to spot Dall sheep on the mountainside or caribou in the vegetation—even bears. When the wildlife is close enough, the driver/guide will ask for quiet so as not to startle the animals. The tour or shuttle ride demands a long day—about 8 hours in not particularly luxurious vehicles—but if the weather holds and the viewing is good, it'll be the best $130 you ever spent ($60 children 15 and under). The cost for the shuttle bus varies by the destination—from $27 to Tolkat (6½ hr. round-trip) to $51 to the end of the road at Kantishna (13 hr. round-trip); children 15 and under free. For details about tours and shuttles, go to www.reservedenali.com or call ℂ **800/622-7275.**

FAIRBANKS

Alaska's second-largest city (after Anchorage) is friendly, unpretentious, and easygoing in the Alaskan tradition, although its downtown area is drab and a little depressing. Fairbanks' major attraction is the ***Riverboat Discovery,*** 1975 Discovery Dr. (www.riverboatdiscovery.com; ℂ **866/479-6673** or 907/479-6673), a four-deck stern-wheeler that operates 3-hour cruises twice a day throughout the summer on the Chena (*Chee*-nah) river. The boat visits a re-created Native village, the home and kennels of the late four-time Iditarod winner Susan Butcher, and an Athabascan Indian fish camp, and a flyby is performed by a bush pilot. The cruise costs $60 adults, $40 children 3 to 12, and is free for children 2 and under. Sailings are mid-May to mid-September.

The Binkleys, the family that owns the stern-wheeler, also own **Gold Dredge 8,** 1803 Old Steese Hwy N. (www.golddredge8.com; ℂ **866/479-6673** or 907/479-6673), a huge monster of a machine that dug gold out of the hills until 1959 and is now on display. Here visitors can pan for gold and, while riding on a replica of the open-sided Tanana Valley Railroad, study the workings of the dredge just as it operated a century ago. It's hokey, for sure, but good fun, especially for youngsters. Tours, which run daily (call for times), are $40 adults, $25 children 3 to 12, and free for children 2 and under. If you buy the Gold Dredge 8 tickets at the same time as you do the riverboat cruise, you can save $2 a head off the combined price.

Cruisetours and shore excursions almost always include the *Riverboat Discovery* and Gold Dredge 8.

PRUDHOE BAY

Prudhoe Bay is at the very end of the Dalton Highway, also known locally as the Haul Road, a 414-mile stretch built to service the Trans-Alaska Pipeline. The road connects the Arctic coast with Interior Alaska and passes through wilderness areas that include all sorts of scenic terrain: forested rounded hills, the rugged peaks of the Brooks Range, and the treeless plains of the North Slope. The route provides lots of wildlife-spotting opportunities, with strong chances of seeing caribou, Dall sheep, moose, and bear.

But the real reason to come way up here is to view the **Prudhoe Bay Oilfield.** (Indeed, Prudhoe Bay is, essentially, a company town run by oil giant BP, with a population of just 50 people or so.) Although touring an oil field may not be high on your vacation must-do list, the bay complex is no ordinary oil field. It's a historic site of great strategic importance and a technological feat. (And chances are, you'll be the only one on your block who's actually

FIRST TO THE top

It's the biggest. That's why climbers risk their lives on Denali. You can see the mountain from Anchorage, more than 100 miles away. On a flight across Alaska, Denali stands out grandly over waves of other mountains. It's more than a mile higher than the highest peak in the other 49 states. It's a great white triangle, always covered in snow, tall but also massive and strong.

The first group to try to climb Denali came in 1903, led by Judge James Wickersham, who also helped explore Washington's Olympic Peninsula before it became a national park. His group made it less than halfway up, but along the way they found gold in the Kantishna Hills, setting off a small gold rush that led to the first permanent human settlement in the park area. Wickersham later became the Alaska Territory's nonvoting delegate to Congress and introduced the bill that created the national park, but the government was never able to get back land in the Kantishna area from the gold miners. Today that land is the site of wilderness lodges, right in the middle of the park.

On Sept. 27, 1906, world explorer Dr. Frederick Cook announced to the world by telegraph that he had reached the summit of Denali after a lightning-fast climb, covering more than 85 miles and 19,000 vertical feet in 13 days with one other man, a blacksmith, at his side. On his return to New York, Cook was lionized as a conquering explorer and published a popular book of his summit diary and photographs.

In 1909, Cook again made history, announcing that he had beaten Robert Peary to the North Pole. Both returned to civilization from their competing treks at about the same time. Again, Cook was the toast of the town. His story began to fall apart, however, when his Eskimo companions mentioned that he'd never been out of sight of land. After being paid by Peary to come forward, Cook's Denali companion also recanted. A year later, Cook's famous summit photograph was re-created—on a peak 19 miles away and 15,000 feet lower than the real summit.

In 1910, disgusted with Cook, four prospectors from Fairbanks took a more Alaskan approach to the task. Without fanfare or special supplies—they carried doughnuts and hot chocolate on their incredible final ascent—they marched up the mountain with a large wooden flagpole they could plant on top to prove

been here!) The industry coexists here with migrating caribou and waterfowl on wet, fragile tundra that permanently shows any mark made by vehicles.

One of the few ways to catch a glimpse of the oil field is via the **Arctic Ocean Shuttle tour,** which operates between late May and early September from nearby Deadhorse Camp to the Arctic Ocean and passes through the oil field. It is operated by Deadhorse Camp, which works with the oil-field security company to allow access. Reservations for the shuttle are made online through a **reservation system** (www.arcticoceanshuttle.com) and must be made in advance. The tour emphasis is on the Arctic Ocean and not the oil fields. Shuttle trips are 1½ to 2 hours round-trip and depart from Deadhorse Camp at 8:30am and 3:30pm. Tickets are $69.

To get to the starting point, you usually drive the Dalton Highway one-way in buses and then fly back, with either **Fairbanks** or **Anchorage** being the other connecting point.

they'd made it. But on arriving at the summit, they realized that they'd climbed the slightly shorter north peak. Weather closed in, so they set up the pole there and descended without attempting the south peak. Then, when they got back to Fairbanks, no one could see the pole, and they were accused of trying to pull off yet another hoax.

In 1913, Episcopal archdeacon Hudson Stuck organized the first successful climb to reach the real summit—and reported that he saw the pole on the other peak. Harry Karstens led the climb (he would be the park's first superintendent, in 1917), and the first person to stand on the summit was an Alaska Native, Walter Harper.

Although Denali remains one of the world's most difficult climbs, about 21,000 people have made it to the top since Hudson Stuck's party. Since 1980 the number of climbers has boomed. Garbage and human waste disposal have become a resource-management challenge. In 1970, only 124 made the attempt all year; now more than 1,200 try to climb the peak annually, with about half making it to the summit. The cold, fast-changing weather is what usually stops people. From late April into early July, climbers fly from the town of Talkeetna to a base camp at 7,200 feet on the Kahiltna Glacier. From there, it takes an average of about 18 days to get to the top, through temperatures as cold as -40°F (-40°C).

Climbers lose fingers, toes, and other parts to frostbite, or suffer other, more severe injuries. During the season, the park service has a camp for rescue rangers and an emergency medical clinic at the 14,200-foot level of the mountain, and a high-altitude helicopter is kept ready to go for climbers in trouble. In 1995 the park service started charging climbers a $150-a-head fee (since raised to $365; climbers 24 years old or younger pay a $265 youth fee) to defray a portion of the rescue costs. The park and the military spend about a half-million dollars a year rescuing climbers, and sometimes much more. The cost in lives is high as well. As of the 2017 season, 126 climbers have died on the mountain, not counting plane crashes. Volunteer rangers and rescuers die as well as climbers. Monuments to those who never returned are in the cemetery near the Talkeetna airstrip.

—Charles Wohlforth

Two companies offer multi-night tours to Prudhoe Bay from Fairbanks. The **Northern Alaska Tour Company** offers a 3-day/2-night Arctic Ocean Adventure (fly/drive tour) from the city. Participants stay at Deadhorse Camp and take the Arctic Ocean Shuttle to the Arctic Ocean (www.northernalaska. com/arctic-ocean.htm). The **1st Alaska Outdoor School** also offers a 3-day/ 2-night Arctic Ocean/Prudhoe Bay trip from Fairbanks (driving both ways), also with a stop at the Arctic Ocean to let guests dip their toes into the (frigid) water (www.1stalaskaoutdoorschool.com).

Those wishing to drive to Prudhoe Bay/Deadhorse independently have two lodging options. The **Prudhoe Bay Hotel** (www.prudhoebayhotel.com), in Deadhorse, only makes reservations for independent travelers 7 to 10 days out. The hotel has 180 rooms, most of which are occupied by employees of the oil companies. Guests staying at the Prudhoe Bay Hotel who want to take the Arctic Ocean Shuttle have to make shuttle reservations in advance and drive 2½ miles south on the Dalton Highway to the Deadhorse Camp and

denali CHANGES

Visitor facilities in the park underwent a major upgrade over the past decade. Among the additions:

○ A complete rebuilding of the **Eielson Visitor Center**—the more remote of the two visitor centers in the park. What had been a small facility was completely demolished in 2005 and rebuilt bigger (and more environmentally friendly) over several years, reopening in 2008. Located 66 miles inside Denali's borders and reached by shuttle bus only (cars are not allowed), it has new exhibits and viewing areas. The shuttle bus from the park entrance to the center costs $34 for adults and is free for children 15 and under.

○ The **Murie Science and Learning Center,** near the entrance to the park, doubles as a visitor center in the winter months, when the regular visitor centers close.

○ The **Denali Visitor Center,** near the entrance to the park, includes exhibits and a theater housing the award-winning 20-minute film *Heartbeats of Denali.* The building has won kudos for its environmentally friendly design, including the use of integrated photovoltaic solar panels on its south-facing side and renewable and recycled materials. Many ranger-led activities either occur in the center (talks) or begin here (walks). It's open from mid-May to mid-September.

○ The **Morino Grill,** about 30 yards from the Denali Visitor Center, sells all-day coffee and boxed lunches, and serves made-to-order lunch and dinner. **Note:** This is the only restaurant in the park.

○ A revamped **Wilderness Access Center** is near the entrance to the park, where travelers board buses and get permits for campgrounds and backcountry tours. Snacks can be purchased here.

depart on the tour there. The Prudhoe Bay Hotel does not offer any tours for guests.

Deadhorse Camp (www.deadhorsecamp.com) is located at mile 412.8 of the Dalton Highway—just before you arrive into Deadhorse. It has 12 rooms (each with twin beds) available for independent travelers, which usually fill up a few weeks in advance. This is the starting point for the Arctic Ocean Shuttle.

Be aware: The drive to Prudhoe Bay is a long one over not particularly good roads, and it's not always terribly comfortable.

NOME & KOTZEBUE

There's no place like Nome. Well, we had to say it. But, really, this Arctic frontier town is special, combining a sense of history, a hospitable and silly attitude (we're talking about a place that holds an annual Labor Day bathtub race), and an exceptional location on the water before a tundra wilderness.

What it does not have is anything that remotely resembles a tourist destination. Anthropological, yes; touristy, no. It's little more than a collection of beat-up residences and low-rise commercial buildings. It looks like the popular conception of a century-old gold-rush town—which isn't really surprising, because that's what it is. But if it seems in need of a facelift, the inhabitants make up for that with the warmth of their welcome. They're probably glad to see a new face in the summer because they know they'll see precious few in the winter, when the the sun disappears for 3 or 4 months. Nome has local roads, but no highway link with the rest of the state.

The name Nome is believed to have been an error by a British naval officer in 1850, who wrote "? Name" on a diagram. The scrawl was misinterpreted by a mapmaker as "Nome." The population boom here in 1899 also happened by chance, when a prospector from the 1898 gold rush was left behind because of an injury. He panned the sand outside his tent and found it full of gold dust.

Be sure to find time to try gold panning. The city also has a still-sloppy gold-rush-era saloon scene, as well as bargains on **Iñupiat Eskimo** arts and crafts.

Your tour will also visit **Kotzebue** (pronounced *Kot*-say-bue) to the north, one of Alaska's largest and oldest Iñupiat Eskimo villages.

THE KENAI PENINSULA

The Kenai (*Kee*-nye) Peninsula, which divides Prince William Sound and Cook Inlet, has glaciers, whales, legendary sportfishing, spectacular hiking trails, bears, moose, and high mountains. Plus, it's easy to get to. It's not a long way from Alaska's tourist hub, Anchorage, and there's a good road to help you get there. The trouble is that there's an awful lot of traffic on it—not just tourists, but also Alaskan locals who drive down from Anchorage on weekends for outdoorsy pursuits. The traffic jams on Friday evenings and Saturday mornings, especially, can make the most jaded Los Angelenos forget the crush on the I-405 at rush hour, or New Yorkers the Lincoln Tunnel. Try to get to Anchorage a day or two before your cruise begins (or stay a day or two afterward) and make the trip in midweek. The scenery alone is well worth the effort.

People from Anchorage come here for the weekend to hike, dig clams, paddle kayaks, and, particularly, to fish. There's a special phrase for what happens when the red salmon are running in July on the Kenai and Russian rivers: **combat fishing.** Anglers stand elbow-to-elbow on a bank, each casting into his or her yard-wide slice of river, and they still catch plenty of fish (as well as, occasionally, each other!).

Cruisetours to the Kenai Peninsula include options for fishing, **river rafting,** and other soft-adventure activities.

You typically travel here by bus or rail from Seward or Whittier. Princess includes an overnight stay at its own Kenai Princess Lodge, a wilderness resort with a gorgeous setting on a bluff overlooking the river; other cruise lines provide overnight stays at other properties. Some tours combine a visit to Kenai Peninsula with an overnight in Anchorage.

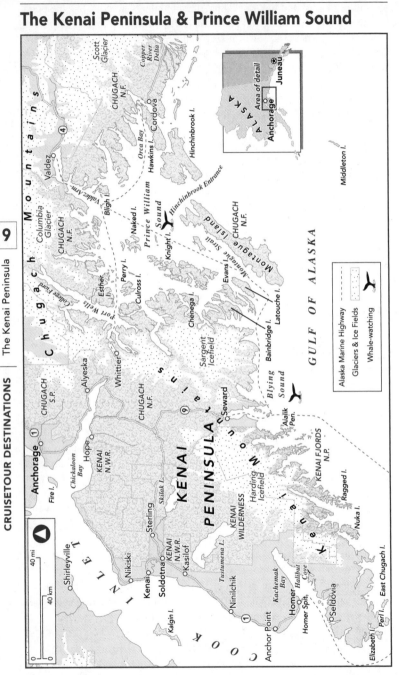

THE YUKON TERRITORY

You'll pass plenty of beautiful scenery along the way, but today the real reason to cross the Canadian border into this region is the same as it was 100 years ago: **gold** (or, rather, gold-rush history).

Gold was discovered in the Canadian Klondike's Rabbit Creek (later renamed Bonanza Creek—for obvious reasons) in 1896. In a matter of months, tens of thousands of people descended into the Yukon for the greatest gold rush in history, giving birth to Dawson City, Whitehorse, and a dozen other tent communities. By the turn of the century, the gold rush was on in earnest, and in 1900 the White Pass & Yukon rail route opened from Skagway to the Canadian border to carry prospectors and their goods.

Once part of the Northwest Territories, the Yukon is now a separate Canadian territory bordered by British Columbia and Alaska. The entire territory has a population of just over 37,000, two-thirds of them living in **Whitehorse,** the capital of the region since 1953. Located on the banks of the Yukon River, Whitehorse was established in 1900, 2 full years after the stampeders began swarming into Dawson City. Today the city serves as a frontier outpost, its tourism influx also giving it a cosmopolitan tinge complete with nightlife, good shopping opportunities (with some smart boutiques and great outdoor shops), fine restaurants, and comfortable hotels. The up-to-the-minute nature of the town—with the **Canada Games Centre,** a sports/convention center, and a modern **Visitor Information Center**—contrasts it with most of the Yukon (a historic **Waterfront Trolley** was not in service in 2017, but plans were to have it up and running again by summer 2018).

Dawson City was once the biggest Canadian city west of Winnipeg, with a population of 30,000, but it withered to practically a ghost town after the gold-rush stampeders stopped stampeding. Dawson today is the nearest thing in the world to an authentic gold-rush town, with old buildings, vintage watering holes, dirt streets flanked with raised boardwalks, shops (naturally), and some particularly good restaurants. You can get a decent meal at the restaurant at the **Aurora Inn** at the corner of 5th Avenue and Harper Street, with its European chefs (schnitzel is the featured dish every Sat). Enjoy a casual meal in truly fun surroundings at that Dawson staple, **Diamond Tooth Gertie's Gambling Hall** (full-service bar, poker, blackjack, roulette, slots, and three distinct floor shows nightly). There's a $12 admission charge for the shows—and don't bring the kids! But it's all good fun—plus the proceeds go to maintain visitor attractions. Another establishment worth a visit is **Bombay Peggy's Inn & Pub,** at 2nd Avenue and Princess Street. Along with a selection of locally brewed libations, the pub features works by Dawson-area artists. (And no, there is no plan to change the name to Mumbai Betty's!) Take a look also at the **Dawson City Museum,** in the Old Territorial Building on 5th Avenue, with one of the most comprehensive narrations found anywhere of the tumultuous years of the gold rush (www.dawsonmuseum.ca/; $9 adults, $7 seniors/students).

If you're on a Holland America Land+Sea Journey—highly likely, since that company operates nearly all the Yukon tours—you'll take a 1-hour flight between Fairbanks and Dawson City, a new option that eliminates the need for up to 2 days on a motorcoach and a hotel night.

Holland America also has another Yukon string in its bow—rights to enter **Tombstone Territorial Park,** about a 90-minute drive from Dawson City.

THE CANADIAN ROCKIES

Canadian Rockies cruisetours typically include travel by bus and/or train between Vancouver and either Seattle or Calgary.

Highlights of the tour include a visit to the parks at **Jasper** and **Banff,** which together comprise 17,518 square kilometers (6,832 sq. miles). The parks are teeming with wildlife, with some animals—such as bighorn sheep, mountain goats, deer, and moose—meandering along and across highways and hiking trails. There are also coyotes, lynx, and the occasional wolf (though they tend to give humans a wide berth), as well as grizzlies and black bears, both of which are unpredictable and best photographed with a telephoto lens.

The two "capitals," Banff and Jasper, are 287km (178 miles) apart and connected by scenic Highway 93 (a destination unto itself). Banff is in a stunningly beautiful setting, with the mighty Bow River, murky with glacial till, coursing through town.

The stylish **Fairmont Banff Springs** (www.fairmont.com/banff-springs; 𝒞 **866/540-4406** or 403/762-2211) was originally built in 1888 as a destination resort by the Canadian Pacific Railroad. Ever since then, tourists have been visiting this area for its scenery and hot springs, plus nearby fishing, hiking, and other outdoor activities. Today the streets of Banff are also an attraction, lined with trendy cafes and exclusive boutiques with international fashions.

Lake Louise is located 56km (35 miles) north of Banff and is a famed spot, deep green from the minerals it contains (ground by the glaciers above the lake) and surrounded by forest-clad, snowcapped mountains. The village near the lake is a resort destination in its own right. Nearly as spectacular as the lake is the **Fairmont Château Lake Louise,** 111 Lake Louise Dr., Lake Louise (www. fairmont.com/lake-louise; 𝒞 **866/540-4413** or 403/522-3511), built by the Canadian Pacific Railroad and one of the most celebrated hotels in Canada.

Between Lake Louise and Jasper is the **Icefields Parkway,** a spectacular mountain road that climbs through three deep-river valleys, beneath soaring, glacier-notched mountains, and past dozens of hornlike peaks. Capping the route is the **Columbia Icefields,** a massive dome of glacial ice and snow that is the largest nonpolar ice cap in the world.

Jasper isn't Banff. It was born as a railroad division point, and the town does not have the glitz of its southern neighbor. **Jasper National Park** is Canada's largest mountain park and provides an outdoor-oriented experience with opportunities to hike, ride horseback, fish, or even climb mountains.

ALASKA IN CONTEXT

Alaska is the largest state in the U.S. Just how big is it? If you put together Texas, California, and Montana—the next biggest states—Alaska would still be bigger. If Alaska were a country, it would be ranked at number 33, right before Venezuela—Alaska is twice as big as Sweden. We're talking 570,665 square miles. Yet in 2016, Alaska had a population estimated by the U.S. Census Bureau at just 741,894, making it the fourth least populous state in the Union. Theoretically, every resident could have nearly a mile to him or herself if they wanted it. There are remote parts of the 49th state that haven't even been visited by humans—but don't think temperatures that can reach minus 40 degrees are a deterrent. Alaskans are as hearty as they come.

A SHORT GOLD-RUSH HISTORY

The big Alaskan historic event that cruise passengers will hear a lot about is the 1898 **Klondike gold rush.**

The first prospectors actually came in search of gold even before Russia sold Alaska to the United States in 1867, and the American flag went up over Sitka. A few of them even struck it rich. In 1880 a major find on the Gastineau Channel led to the creation of the city of Juneau.

Other finds got some minor press attention, including one on the **Kenai Peninsula** in 1895. More people started to seek their fortune in Alaska.

In 1896, prosecutor George Washington Carmack and his Native partners, Dawson Charlie and Skookum Jim Mason, found gold in a tributary to the Klondike River in Canada's Yukon Territory. Word of the find traveled downriver fast. The three men set off one of the biggest gold rushes in history.

Prospectors flocked to the Klondike to stake claims and dig gravel from the water. Big chunks of gold were found, and some prospectors became instant millionaires.

"GOLD!" read newspaper headlines in 1897, as the men returned to Seattle with their riches.

At the time, the country was in the midst of a deep economic depression, with unemployment at 18%. Alaska was a place largely ruled and inhabited by indigenous people—and little changed for thousands of years. There were only 500 white residents in the 1880 census.

But an instant population was on its way. By 1898, some 100,000 gold-seekers had headed north, arriving in **Skagway** and **Dyea,** with plans to head on to the Canadian interior. Even the mayor of Seattle left for Alaska in hopes of striking it rich.

What the stampeders learned when they arrived was that most of the good claims had already been staked and getting to available gold fields would require a 600-mile wilderness trek. Most were unprepared for the arduous trek.

The **White Pass** above Skagway and the **Chilkoot Pass** above Dyea were the routes. To prevent famine, Canadian authorities required each miner to carry a year's worth of supplies—but this made for an exceptionally miserable journey. The White Pass was so difficult that some 3,000 horses died on the route—their bones still at the bottom of Dead Horse Gulch. The Chilkoot was so steep you couldn't even use animals to carry your supplies and instead had to carry them on your back.

The journey also required the miners to cross Lake Bennett to get down the Yukon through dangerous rapids. Many did not survive. Stampeders also died from everything from murder and suicide to malnutrition and hypothermia. But 30,000 gold-seekers did make it to Dawson City in the Yukon Territory.

While only a few of the Klondike gold-rush miners struck it rich, entrepreneurs saw opportunity and became prosperous building the towns and businesses that catered to the miners, saloons and brothels included.

The gold rush is credited with marking the beginning of contemporary Alaska. Within a few years Alaska had cities—albeit lawless ones. There were even telegraph lines, riverboats, and mail routes (via dog sled).

Some prospectors took their search for gold farther afield in Alaska and in the process founded dozens of towns. While some of the gold-inspired communities eventually became ghost towns, many survived. Created in the gold rush, for instance, were Nome (1899) and Fairbanks (1902).

The arrival of the railroad through White Pass in 1900 meant **Dyea** and the **Chilkoot Pass** were abandoned. The gold-rush town of **Skagway** has in modern times found riches from tourists as a popular cruise port (see chapter 8).

There are actually still people looking for gold in Alaska, and occasionally there is a strike of significance. In 1987, for instance, north of Fairbanks, one find produced as much as 1,000 ounces of gold per day for years. The TV show *Gold Rush* on Discovery Channel has highlighted more recent efforts to seek gold at Porcupine Creek, near Haines, Alaska, and Quartz Creek, in the Klondike region of Canada's Yukon Terriotry.

INTRODUCTION TO SOUTHEAST ALASKA'S NATIVE CULTURES

A memorable part of your cruise to Alaska will be the opportunity to experience Alaska Native culture. The presence of Alaska Native people can be traced back hundreds of thousands of years—to when the first descendants came across the Bering Land Bridge from Asia to North America.

Today, Alaska Native people make up less than 15% of the state's population. The majority are **Eskimo, Indian,** and **Aleut** and live in villages along the coastline and rivers of Alaska.

Many still practice traditional crafts and customs and lead traditional hunting and fishing lifestyles, though in cities including Anchorage, Fairbanks, and Juneau, Alaska Natives have very much embraced Western lifestyles, including tourism—blending language and social customs with modern life.

Alaska's Native people are divided into 11 distinct cultures with 11 languages and 22 dialects, from the **Inupiat** of the cold Arctic to the **Tlingit** (pronounced *Klink-get*) of the warmed Inside Passage. No other state holds such a range of Native cultures.

Cultural heritage is passed down from generation to generation, and while language and customs vary from region to region, many values and spiritual beliefs are shared.

Cruise passengers are most likely to encounter members of the Tlingit group. No one knows for sure when the Tlingit first settled on the Alaskan coastline and islands. The language is similar to the Athabascan of Interior Alaska and Canada, but also similar to the Navajo of the American Southwest.

It is known that in the 1700s, Tlingit paddlers steered cargo canoes as far as the Channel Islands off the coast of Los Angeles. In the 18th and 19th centuries, the Tlingit people were trade partners with the Russians, British, Americans, and interior tribes of Canada—and demanded tolls for use of the waterways of Southeast Alaska. In the 1800s, the Tlingits allowed gold miners to travel over the rugged Chilkoot Pass, between Skagway and the Klondike gold fields—for a fee.

Relative newcomers to Southeast Alaska include the **Haida** and **Tsimshian,** both entering Tlingit territory from British Columbia.

Today, many Alaska Natives live in small villages such as Hoonah (home to Icy Strait Point) on Chichagof Island and Metlakatla on Annette Island, as well as in major port cities including Juneau, Ketchikan, and Sitka. Here, in these villages, you may see such traditional practices as the drying of seaweed or salmon grilling on wooden planks. You may have a child peppering you with questions about what big cities like Anchorage were like. Just don't expect things to look as they did in the 1800s. While some traditions are upheld, you'll likely see more cars than canoes, people hauling bags from the Costco in Juneau, and satellite-TV dishes on many homes.

Index

See also Accommodations and
Restaurant indexes, below.

General Index

Map List

Photo Credits

Frommer's EasyGuide to Alaskan Cruises and Ports of Call, 2nd Edition

Published by
FROMMER MEDIA LLC

ISBN 978-1-62887-376-4 (paper), 978-1-62887-377-1 (e-book)

Editorial Director: Pauline Frommer
Editor: Alexis Lipsitz Flippin
Production Editor: Lynn Northrup
Cartographer: Roberta Stockwell
Photo Editor: Meghan Lamb
Indexer: Cheryl Lenser
Cover Designer: Howard Grossman

For information on our other products or services, see www.frommers.com.

Frommer Media LLC also publishes its books in a variety of electronic formats. Some content that appears in print may not be available in electronic formats.

Manufactured in the United States of America

5   4   3   2   1

ABOUT THE AUTHORS

Sherri Eisenberg has covered the cruise industry for almost 20 years, first as the Cruise Editor at *Travel Holiday* magazine and later as the Cruise Editor of *Travel and Leisure* magazine, Editorial Director for Cruiseline.com and later for ShermansCruise.com, and as a weekly cruise columnist for the *Los Angeles Times*. She has also written about cruising for numerous other magazines and newspapers, including *Condé Nast Traveler* and *Departures*. Eisenberg lives in Manhattan. She has no plants or pets and keeps a bag packed at all times so that she can hop a flight—or a ship—at a moment's notice.

Fran Golden is a well-known and award-winning travel writer. She is chief contributor for the cruise magazine *Porthole* and a contributing writer for *Virtuoso Life* magazine. Former travel editor of the *Boston Herald*, and creator of *USA Today*'s Experience Cruise website, she writes regularly for newspapers, magazines, and websites such as Bloomberg, the *Los Angeles Times*, *Condé Nast Traveler*, and the UK's *World of Cruising*. She is author or coauthor of several travel books including *Frommer's EasyGuide to River Cruising* and has written extensively about Alaska since 1998. Fran is married to fellow cruise writer David Molyneaux, and when they are not at sea they make their home in Cleveland.

ACKNOWLEDGEMENTS

The authors wish to thank contributing writers Jenna Schnuer, Aaron Saunders, Stacy Phillips Booth, and Lynn and Cele Seldon, and researcher Jessica Corso.

ABOUT THE FROMMER TRAVEL GUIDES

For most of the past 50 years, Frommer's has been the leading series of travel guides in North America, accounting for as many as 24% of all guidebooks sold. I think I know why.

Though we hope our books are entertaining, we nevertheless deal with travel in a serious fashion. Our guidebooks have never looked on such journeys as a mere recreation, but as a far more important human function, a time of learning and introspection, an essential part of a civilized life. We stress the culture, lifestyle, history, and beliefs of the destinations we cover, and urge our readers to seek out people and new ideas as the chief rewards of travel.

We have never shied from controversy. We have, from the beginning, encouraged our authors to be intensely judgmental, critical—both pro and con—in their comments, and wholly independent. Our only clients are our readers, and we have triggered the ire of countless prominent sorts, from a tourist newspaper we called "practically worthless" (it unsuccessfully sued us) to the many rip-offs we've condemned.

And because we believe that travel should be available to everyone regardless of their incomes, we have always been cost-conscious at every level of expenditure. Though we have broadened our recommendations beyond the budget category, we insist that every lodging we include be sensibly priced. We use every form of media to assist our readers, and are particularly proud of our feisty daily website, the award-winning Frommers.com.

I have high hopes for the future of Frommer's. May these guidebooks, in all the years ahead, continue to reflect the joy of travel and the freedom that travel represents. May they always pursue a cost-conscious path, so that people of all incomes can enjoy the rewards of travel. And may they create, for both the traveler and the persons among whom we travel, a community of friends, where all human beings live in harmony and peace.

Arthur Frommer

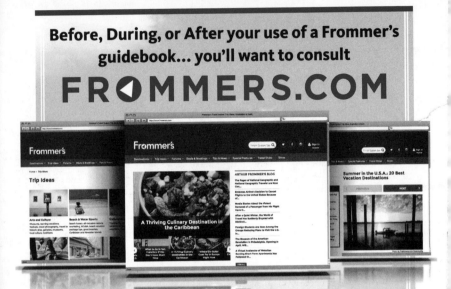